D0583815

Global Public Relations

This innovative text provides a structured and practical framework for understanding the complexities of contemporary public relations. It is an instructional book that guides the reader through the challenges of communication and problem-solving across a range of organizations and cross-cultural settings.

Written in a straightforward, lively style, the book covers:

- foundational theories, and factors that shape the discipline;
- communication across cultures;
- trends affecting the public relations profession throughout the world.

Incorporating case studies and commentary to illustrate key principles and stimulate discussion, the book also highlights the different approaches professionals must consider in different contexts, from communicating with employees to liaising with external bodies such as government agencies or the media.

Offering a truly global perspective on the subject, *Global Public Relations* is essential reading for any student or practitioner interested in public relations excellence in a global setting.

Alan R. Freitag is Associate Department Chair in the Department of Communication Studies at the University of North Carolina at Charlotte, USA.

Ashli Quesinberry Stokes is Assistant Professor in the Department of Communication Studies at the University of North Carolina at Charlotte, USA.

Global Public Relations

Spanning borders, spanning cultures

Alan R. Freitag and Ashli Quesinberry Stokes

Routledge
Taylor & Francis Group

LONDON AND NEW YORK

First published 2009
by Routledge
2 Park Square, Milton Park, Abingdon, Oxon OX14 4RN

Simultaneously published in the USA and Canada
by Routledge
711 Third Ave, New York, NY 10017

Routledge is an imprint of the Taylor & Francis Group, an informa business

Typeset in Berling and Futura by Graphicraft Limited, Hong Kong
Printed and bound by CPI Group (UK) Ltd, Croydon, CR0 4YY

British Library Cataloguing in Publication Data
A catalogue record for this book is available from the British Library

Library of Congress Cataloging in Publication Data
Global public relations : spanning borders, spanning cultures / edited by
Alan R. Freitag and Ashli Quesinberry Stokes.
    p. cm.
Includes bibliographical references and index.
ISBN 978-0-415-44814-7 (hardback) — ISBN 978-0-415-44815-4 (pbk.)
1. Public relations—Cross-cultural studies. 2. Intercultural communication.
3. Culture and globalization. I. Freitag, Alan. R. II. Stokes, Ashli Quesinberry.
HM1221.G56 2008
659.209—dc22

2008014022

ISBN10: 0-415-44814-X (hbk)
ISBN10: 0-415-44815-8 (pbk)
ISBN10: 0-203-89018-3 (ebk)

ISBN13: 978-0-415-44814-7 (hbk)
ISBN13: 978-0-415-44815-4 (pbk)
ISBN13: 978-0-203-89018-9 (ebk)

Contents

List of tables

List of figures

Foreword

Hugh M. Culbertson

The young discipline of public relations has given birth to an infant subdiscipline: international PR. This book bears witness to the fact that the infant, while still striving for maturity, has at least reached early adolescence.

The book is at least the fourth – all published since 1996 – that seeks to define and explain public relations worldwide. The first two were written by and for scholars and research-oriented graduate students. The authors and editors sought to describe the practice in varied nations and regions. Also, they tried to articulate the cultural, political, social and economic forces that have shaped it in ways that might later be disseminated more widely (Culbertson and Chen 1996; Srisamesh and Verčič 2003).

This volume defines public relations practice in a readable way for a larger audience – graduate and advanced undergraduate students, and practitioners gearing up to work in and with societies other than their own. The authors are experienced executive-level practitioners turned academics. They present a balanced, comprehensive look at the scholarly literature that helps shape international public relations in 2008, and they do so with a lively text.

Prior to the 1980s, the public relations discipline developed largely in North America and Europe. Early writings on international PR sought to help Western – especially US – practitioners survive abroad (Wouters 1991). However, it soon became apparent that public relations practiced in, say, Beijing or Manila differed greatly from that in New York, London, or Caracas. That realization came about partly as a by-product of three developments in Western scholarship. First was a focus on clients' *social, political and economic contexts* (SPE) in domestic PR. The author of this foreword noted two problems when he began teaching in the mid-1960s. Most research in the field then consisted of evaluation surveys conducted at or near the end of a program or a year's work. While useful in pleasing a client and recruiting new clients, such research often came too late to aid planning or execution. It seemed a bit like "crying over spilled milk". There was a need for *front-end research* done in time to help set policy and communicate about it. Such research could help the practitioner understand a client's *social, political, economic, and cultural contexts*.

Spurred by his brightest students, the author conducted a series of applied studies to clarify such contexts and the theoretical notions useful in articulating them. He and three former students eventually summarized their work in a book (Culbertson *et al.* 1993). They argued that such analysis was especially important in light of a second major development in the field: *issues management*. This concept came to the fore in the 1960s and 1970s, a time of great turmoil, change and challenge in the United States. Organizations found that they needed to be *proactive*, not reactive, in identifying emerging problems and issues before these reached crisis proportions. Only then could communicators prepare clients and publics for what might happen in the future. The saying "An ounce of prevention is worth a pound of cure" kept coming to mind as the author discovered an increasing number of practitioners writing not only for clients' publics but also to inform clients themselves. This trend, in turn, brought to the fore a third concept: *environmental scanning*. Identifying issues as they appeared on the distant horizon, in time to act and speak effectively, required careful study.

Among the concepts that seemed most important in defining SPE contexts were *cultural and subcultural beliefs*. These were stable assumptions held by all – or almost all – members of a society or other large group with shared identities and interests. Such ideas deal, at a basic level, with *what is, what is right, and what is important*. They help shape fundamental values and behavior (Culbertson *et al.* 1993, pp. 53–63).

As he began to study abroad, the author found that differences in such beliefs appeared to help account for many problems in cross-cultural communication. For example, gift-giving by a client to government officials or suppliers smacks of bribery to Americans, yet it is built into the cultures of the Philippines, Thailand, China and other Asian societies. How can one condemn as clearly unethical a practice that his or her host culture mandates?

The author learned more about the role of culture – as well as of political and economic development – as he advised a dissertation on Chinese public relations by Ni Chen, a contributor to this volume (Chen 1992). The two of them edited the first book that really sought to describe and define public relations in varied nations *as practiced and viewed by people in those nations* (Culbertson and Chen 1996).

In that book, two formulations turned out to be especially seminal. First, Dejan Verčič, Larissa Grunig and James Grunig defined nine generic principles that appeared to hold regardless of culture (Verčič *et al.* 1996). (See Chapter 1 of this book for a summary of these ideas.) Second, James Van Leuven focused on public relations evolution in developing countries, especially the rapidly developing "Little Tigers" of Asia: Singapore, Hong Kong, South Korea and Malaysia (Van Leuven 1996). He identified three stages that seemed to occur sequentially as nations go through the development process:

1. *Nation building.* As they escaped from colonial rule after World War II, many new countries had ethnic groups with major language and cultural differences as well as long-standing rivalries. If a country is to hang together, citizens must develop a sense of sharedness – a belief that they have important things in common. Only then will they be likely to pay taxes to a central government, salute a common flag and even die in battle to protect that flag.
2. *Marketing support.* Any nation needs a viable economy. And that requires marketing and public relations support to help attract investment, stimulate sales and enhance economic growth.
3. *Regional interdependence.* This requires a feeling that countries can profit from trade and foreign-policy alliances in an interdependent world that continually seems smaller. At the very least, they need to avoid blowing one another up – a real danger with modern weapons of mass destruction.

Analysis of these stages informed later writings in the field, including this book, as they sought to articulate issues relating to democratization, economic growth, and changing political structures (Tilson and Alozie 2004).

In their comprehensive volume, Sriramesh and Verčič (2003) focused heavily on two other seminal ideas. First, public relations practice is shaped in many ways by certain cultural dimensions proposed by Hofstede (1984, 2001). These include:

1. *Power distance*: the extent to which people in a society feel large differences in status, power and wealth are inevitable, natural and acceptable.
2. *Collectivism-individualism*: the degree to which one feels the group or collective is of primary importance – or that it exists largely to safeguard individuals and meet their needs.
3. *Masculinity–femininity*: whether people feel men and women occupy clearly different roles (the masculine view), or whether both can appropriately play the same roles (a feminist perspective). Obviously, as women have become more numerous and prominent in public relations, business and politics around the world, gender issues have come to the fore.
4. *Uncertainty avoidance*: tolerance for ambiguity. Some cultures emphasize a need to wait and see before acting, while others demand action "right now". If not appreciated, this difference can serve as an obstacle to cross-cultural communication.

A second key concept in the Sriramesh–Verčič volume was the character and reach of media within a society. In the United States, early public relations practitioners had focused heavily – often almost solely – on getting their clients' names and programs disseminated via print and over the airwaves. In recent years, this has changed among Americans for various reasons. And, in some nations, use of the media as a primary communication tool has encountered several obstacles. Thus, it seemed important to study:

1. *Media outreach* in a nation. Often illiteracy and lack of resources make print media and television unavailable to key publics.
2. *Media control* by government or business. Where media outlets are controlled by a narrow éite, they tend to slant and select news in ways that reduce credibility.
3. *Media access*. At times, because of government policy and media-management constraints, important sectors of society have little chance to disseminate ideas or information via the media. This may necessitate identification of alternative channels (Sriramesh and Verčič 2003, pp. 11–17).

Taken as a whole, this volume and other recent literature call attention to at least six continua that seem crucial for communicators and scholars around the world. Students need to study each chapter of this volume with an eye to discerning where any given nation stands on these continua. Included are:

1. Emphasis on *stability versus freedom*. Developing-nation governments tend to restrict freedom on the grounds that doing so is necessary to ensure stability as needed to bring economic and political development.
2. Freedom from *economic want* versus freedom of *expression*. Critics of US scholarship and practice tend to claim it emphasizes free expression while ignoring freedom from poverty and its many by-products.

3. *Freedom* to speak and write versus the *ability* to do so. Westerners and colonial administrators have sometimes ignored the idea that it does little good to be free to vote, speak and write when one lacks the resources, education and infrastructure to do so (Habermas 1989, pp. 118–38) or the felt power to do so (Friere 1997, pp. 25–51).
4. A focus on what benefits *society* – intranationally and worldwide – as well as partisan benefits for a *client or another narrow sector of society*. Some critics bemoan excessive fragmentation in today's world (Putnam 2000).
5. A focus on *public–public relations* as well as *client–public relations*. The latter seems to be central in writings about the so-called IABC Excellence study and the concept of symmetry (LA Grunig *et al.* 2002). Yet public–public relations becomes crucial as one deals with misunderstanding, a need for cooperation, and tolerance among ethnic, racial and religious groups (Daye 2004). This, in turn, suggests some convergence between public relations and peace studies.

We now note some quantitative evidence that international public relations is coming of age as a field of study. The four books noted here, including this one, offer chapters analyzing practice in at least thirty-eight nations (ten in Asia, four in Central and South America, two in Australia [Australia and New Zealand], nine in Africa, Latin America and Southeast Asia).

Obviously there are gaps. The literature discusses some 192 separate nations in today's world. However, regional books and growing emphasis on the international realm fill some of these gaps.

The field has "taken off" with amazing speed in just a little over a decade. And, as athletic coaches might say, the current volume, with its blend of academic and practitioner expertise, really does "take it to the next level".

References

Chen, N., 1992. Public relations in China: The introduction and development of an occupational field. Unpublished doctoral dissertation. Ohio University, Athens, Ohio.

Culbertson, H. M. and Chen N., 1996. *International Public Relations: A Comparative Analysis*. Mahwah, NJ: Lawrence Erlbaum Associates.

Culbertson, H. M., Jeffers, D. W., Stone, D. B. and Terrell, M., 1993. *Social, Political, and Economic Contexts in Public Relations: Theory and Cases*. Hilldale, NJ: Lawrence Erlbaum Associates.

Daye, R., 2004. *Political Forgiveness: Lessons from South Africa*. Maryknoll, NY: Orbis Books.

Friere, P., 1997. *Pedagogy of the Oppressed*. New York: Continuum.

Grunig, L. A., Grunig, J. E. and Dozier, D. M., 2002. *Excellent Public Relations and Effective Organizations: A Study of Communication Management in Three Countries*. Mahwah, NJ: Lawrence Erlbaum Associates.

Habermas, J., 1989. *The Structural Transformation of the Public Sphere*. Cambridge, Mass.: MIT Press.

Hofstede, G., 1984. *Cultural Consequences: International Differences in Work-related Values*. Beverly Hills, Calif.: Sage.

Hofstede, G., 2001. *Culture's Consequences: Comparing Values, Behaviors, Institutions, and Organizations across Nations*. Thousand Oaks, Calif.: Sage.

Putnam, R. D., 2000. *Bowling Alone: The Collapse and Revival of American Community*. New York: Simon & Schuster.

Sriramesh, K. and Verčič, D., 2003. *The Global Public Relations Handbook: Theory, Research, and Practice*. Mahwah, NJ: Lawrence Erlbaum Associates.

Tilson, D. J. and Alozie, E. C., 2004. *Toward the Common Good: Perspectives in International Public Relations*. Boston, Mass.: Pearson Education.

Van Leuven, J. K., 1996. Public relations campaigns in South East Asia from nation-building to regional inter-dependence. In H. M. Culbertson and N. Chen (eds), *International Public Relations: A Comparative Analysis* (pp. 207–22). Mahwah, NJ: Lawrence Erlbaum Associates.

Verčič, D., Grunig, L. A., and Grunig, J. D., 1996. Global and specific principles of public relations: Evidence from Slovenia. In H. M. Culbertson and N. Chen (eds), *International Public Relations: A Comparative Analysis* (pp. 31–65). Mahwah, NJ: Lawrence Erlbaum Associates.

Wouters, J., 1991. *International Public Relations*. New York: amacom.

Preface

In the mid-1990s, I attended the annual conference of the Public Relations Society of America while completing my doctoral work at Ohio University. An eager student of the emerging field of international public relations, and studying under the tutelage of international public relations pioneer Dr Hugh Culbertson, I was anxious to consume all the wisdom I could from this gathering of top professionals. There were disappointingly few workshop sessions addressing the international component of our profession, but I noted that one session on the topic was to be led by the head of one of the world's largest public relations firms. I knew I would have to get to the room early to get in, and even then expected that I might have to settle for standing room only. I arrived in plenty of time, delighted to capture a seat near the front. When the workshop starting time arrived, I was stunned to note that only a dozen professionals had drifted into this room, which could have accommodated seventy-five.

The noted speaker began his presentation, describing how his firm was increasingly establishing branch offices around the globe. He said that he populated these offices with top managers from the United States, professionals with deep professional experience. For subordinate levels, however, he tapped young and eager local nationals. These local nationals, he said, lacked the educational and experiential background to lead, but they were ambitious and quick studies. He went on to describe some of the clients and issues he and his teams were handling.

When question time came, a few of the original dozen audience members had already departed, so the session became more of a discussion among a core of interested members. I asked the speaker how long he predicted it might be before these young and eager local nationals he was hiring learned the ropes adequately and were able to step out on their own, and how long it might then be before their firms began opening branch offices in the United States to compete with the speaker's global firm on his own home territory. It was a serious question, but the response from the speaker and remaining audience members was, to my shock and annoyance, amused laughter. Comments revealed a conviction that such a notion was preposterous, that US public relations supremacy was enduring and unchallengeable. I suspect that there might have been a similar response had US automakers been asked in 1960 how soon the fledgling Japanese auto industry might be competing equally with Ford, General Motors and Chrysler, and we all know what has transpired in that arena. I recognized that our discipline was in peril. The overwhelming lack of interest suggested by the poor turnout for this conference session, coupled with the surprising attitude displayed by these practitioners, told me that a tocsin needed to be sounded.

I determined at that point to focus my career as an educator on helping to build better understanding of the complexities of international practice and to chip away at the US-centric view I feared would damage our profession's reputation and retard progress in this increasingly important field. I found in the University of North Carolina at Charlotte a willing partner in building an academic program crafted to generate a cohort of graduates, from the US and abroad, capable of excelling in a global setting. I was delighted to discover that there were like-minded professionals and scholars in the US and around the world, and you will find their names throughout the pages of this text as we cite their excellent work and showcase their considerable contributions. In the years since my disappointing experience at that PRSA workshop, our profession has made tremendous strides in building a body of knowledge for international practice and scholarship, and all gauges suggest that trajectory will continue. Witness, for example, the growing list of international public relations conferences such as one orchestrated by the Institute for Public Relations in Miami each March or the annual symposium in Bled, Slovenia. By the way, a fair number of public relations firms around the world now boast branch offices in the United States, and they are doing very well.

There are now a respectable number of texts available on various dimensions of international practice, and they range from rich theoretical treatises to lively case studies. Any practitioner facing an international assignment, or a student or scholar seeking supporting literature, enjoys a far richer trove than was available a decade earlier. So why add another book? We felt that there was a need for a textbook that would pull together the key principles, processes and frameworks of international public relations and present them in a fashion suitable for classroom use. Our hope is that this text will permit more colleges and universities to offer international public relations courses at the graduate and advanced undergraduate level. This text assumes that the student has acquired most or all the standard undergirding of public relations principles, writing, and campaigns, as well as an understanding of relevant law, ethics and theory. Of course, this text would be equally useful employed simultaneously with other advanced courses.

During my professional career, I was blessed with twelve years working in public relations or related fields "overseas". In that capacity I came to appreciate the challenges of building relationships and establishing shared meaning across cultures in professional settings. It would be entirely inaccurate to say that I experienced consistent success in that environment. On the contrary, one of the main reasons I returned to university following that career, concentrating on international public relations at the doctoral level, was to find out what it was I was supposed to have been doing all that time! Now it is my mission to ensure that new and early-career practitioners are better-prepared to turn those challenges into achievements. As I always tell my students, "All I ask is that you make the world a better place".

Alan R. Freitag

Acknowledgments

I, of course, thank my co-author, Dr Ashli Stokes, for her academic agility and superb writing. Her fresh ideas added a great deal of vitality to this work.

I thank the talented and brilliant contributors:

- Dr Ni Chen, Chapter 6 on China, Japan and South Korea
- Dr Isaac Blankson, Chapter 9 on sub-Saharan Africa
- Dr Ryszard Ławniczak and Prof. Gyorgy Szondi, Chapter 12 on Central and Eastern Europe

Thanks most sincerely to my department chair, Dr Richard Leeman, for his patience and consideration throughout this project.

A number of exceptional and promising undergraduate and graduate students aided immeasurably in the many tasks associated with attempting a work of this nature. My thanks to them: Lisa Mabe, Holli Frazier, Monica Unsworth, Jennifer Medeiros, Nicole Ramsey and Iryna Bugayova.

Above all, my deepest thanks and love to my wife, Robin, who was a "textbook widow" during the many months I dedicated to this project. I promise, dear, I'll take a break now.

Contributing authors

Dr Isaac Blankson is Associate Professor of International/Intercultural Communication and International Public Relations in the Department of Speech Communication at Southern Illinois University Edwardsville. In addition to teaching courses in public relations, electronic media, professional and technical communication, and intercultural/international communication, he serves as the Director of Technology for the department and advisor to the Public Relations Student Society of America chapter. His undergraduate education was in geography at the University of Ghana, Legon. He earned a master's degree in human geography from the University of Oslo, as well as a certificate in environmental geography. He earned a second master's in international affairs and a PhD from the School of Telecommunications at Ohio University. He also served as a media and public relations consultant in Ghana and worked in the Division of Student Affairs at Ohio University. His research focuses on communication technologies and media in new and emerging democracies, public relations practices in developing societies, and media criticism.

Dr Ni Chen is Associate Professor of Communication at the City University of Hong Kong. Before joining the faculty at HKBU, she was Assistant Professor of Mass Communication and Communication Studies at Towson University, USA. She also served as visiting professor at the Department of Speech Communication, University of Maryland, College Park, 1996–7. Having earned her PhD in mass communication-journalism at Ohio University in 1992, she has authored and co-authored a number of refereed journal articles, book chapters and conference papers, and is the co-editor of an internationally recognized book, *International Public Relations: A Comparative Analysis* (1996).

Hugh M. Culbertson is a professor emeritus in the E. W. Scripps School of Journalism at Ohio University. His major teaching interests encompass public relations, mass communication theory and research methodology. Culbertson has co-authored a widely used text, *Fundamentals of News Reporting*, published in its sixth edition by Kendall-Hunt in 1994. He is also co-author of *Research Methods in Mass Communication*, published by Prentice Hall and now in its second edition. He is senior author of *Studying the Political, Social and Economic Contexts of Public Relations: A Book* *of Theory and Cases*, published in 1993 by Lawrence Earlbaum Associates. And he is senior co-editor and co-author of *International Public Relations: A Comparative Analysis*, published in 1996 by Lawrence Earlbaum Associates. In all, he has authored or co-authored more than fifty articles in refereed journals along with ten published monographs and book chapters. Topics have ranged from public relations ethics to interpretation of artwork, professional beliefs in public relations and journalism, the implications of unnamed news sources within the press, agenda-setting, the role of media in creating a public sense of alienation from institutions, the implications of media use versus reliance, socio-psychological theory as applied to public relations, and critical theory of mass communication. In 1990 the Public Relations Society of America named Culbertson Educator of the Year. In 1985 he received the Pathfinder Award for excellence in research from the PRSA Research and Education Foundation.

Dr Ryszard Ławniczak is a professor at the University of Economics, Poznan (Poland), and Head of the Department of Economic Journalism and Public Relations. He was visiting professor at the University of Melbourne (1991) and at California State University, Fresno (1984, 1991). He also served as the economic advisor to the president of the Republic of Poland (1997–2005) and as consultant to the Polish premier (1994–7). His research interests include international public relations, foreign economic policies and comparative economics, and he coined the concept of *transitional public relations*. He has presented research papers and talks in Argentina, Australia, Austria, Belgium, China, the Czech Republic, Denmark, Dubai, Estonia, Germany, Hungary, Japan, Kenya, Lithuania, Mexico, Monaco, the Netherlands, Norway, Romania, Russia, Singapore, Slovenia, South Korea, Spain, Sweden, Switzerland, Ukraine, the United Kingdom, the United States and Vietnam.

Gyorgy Szondi is a senior lecturer in public relations at Leeds Business School, Leeds Metropolitan University, the biggest and most prestigious PR education center in Europe. Before joining the Business School, he was teaching in Estonia, where he set up and chaired the public relations program at Concordia International University. Prior to academia, Szondi worked for Hill & Knowlton, the international PR consultancy, in Budapest, and in its international headquarters in London. He has published several book chapters and journal articles on international public relations, public diplomacy, nation branding, PR evaluation, risk and crisis communication. He conducted several workshops training governmental and for-profit organizations in the UK as well as in Hungary, Poland, Estonia, Latvia and Lithuania. He holds a BA in Economics, an MSc in Physics and an MA in Public Relations from the University of Stirling, UK. He is currently engaged in a PhD at the University of Salzburg, researching the concepts of international public relations and public diplomacy for the European Union. Besides his native Hungarian, he is fluent in English and Italian, and has a good command of Estonian, Polish, German and French. Recently, Gyorgy has been mentioned among the fifty leading academic experts in the field of communication in Europe.

Part 1

Implied with the notion of studying public relations practice across borders and cultures is the notion that comparisons must be made among nations and among various paradigms within which public relations efforts are conducted. If we are to make those comparisons in a meaningful, productive way, we must first establish common ground in terms of definitions or descriptions of terms and concepts as well as the scope of what is to be addressed in this text. This we attempt in the first chapter. Next, we must make the case that what we now customarily call the public relations discipline, practiced in a variety of hybrid forms throughout most of the globe, was initially spawned in its fundamental contemporary iteration in the United States, shaped by a variety of converging dynamic forces and trends that coincidentally emerged there over the course of more than two centuries. As those forces and trends spread globally, so did public relations practice, though further refined by unique social, cultural and other influences. Finally in this first section of the text, we shall examine how scholars are applying theories, concepts and models to move forward our understanding of the complexities of professional communication across borders and cultures as well as the unique development of the discipline in national and regional settings. Equally importantly, we shall suggest directions for current and emerging scholars to continue building this critical body of knowledge.

Chapter 1

Common ground

Summary

Communication is a complex concept but a function critical to virtually all human interaction. Continued improvement of the human condition depends upon our effective conduct of communication interactions, but despite more than 10,000 years of recorded history we're still perplexed by our frequent inability to encode, transmit and decode even the simplest messages, either interpersonally or via the burgeoning spectra of mass-media channels. Communication between and among individuals, organizations and states has grown rapidly in volume and frequency but not necessarily in effectiveness. Current and future public relations professionals and scholars are uniquely positioned and prepared to lubricate and bolster communication effectiveness at micro and macro levels. This chapter aims to describe the common dimensions of the discipline upon which we can build a logical framework for understanding and pursuing global practice.

Chapter goals

- Understand the need for considering international public relations as a distinct facet of the discipline.
- Describe the public relations profession and establish basic standards of excellence.
- Distinguish public relations from related disciplines.
- Stress the importance of ongoing study of and preparation for international public relations practice.

The August 23, 2005, *Proceedings of the National Academy of Sciences* reports the results of a small study comparing how European-American and native Chinese students interpret a photograph. Not surprisingly, the students differed in their take on the photograph, but the underlying cultural differences that led to those distinctions are deep, profound, and represent the tremendous challenges facing today's public relations practitioners. The North American students looked at the photo and marked primarily the objects in the foreground of the scene. Chinese students, on the other hand, studied the background equally, assessing the entire scene collectively. Researchers Hannah-Faye Chua and Richard Nisbett of the University of Michigan see cultural differences manifested in the experiment. "They literally are seeing the world differently," Nisbett said. Asians, he said, see the world as socially more complex, while Westerners are individualistic, paying less attention to things beyond the individual object. He links this to our separate roots. Western culture sprang in part from ancient Greece, he says, with an emphasis on individual property ownership and individual businesses. Asian history was more defined by the need for integration and co-operation, such as the need for a system of irrigated agriculture that required farmers to get along, share, and ensure no one was cheated.

Interesting, but what has this to do with public relations practice? Quite a lot; and practitioners who understand and plan for these subtle and not-so-subtle differences among nations and cultures will enjoy the greatest success and satisfaction in the decades ahead. Additionally, they will contribute, as public relations practitioners ought, to making the world a better place.

What has occurred, and continues to occur, in the practice of public relations is the same sweeping trend that has affected virtually all dimensions of society: exponential progress in transportation and communication technology commingle with tectonic political changes to alter the fabric of global commerce and exchange. At the same time, unique cultural differences restrict the development and application of universal templates for public relations practice. The result is a vastly redesigned and dynamic playing field with a host of component forces reshaping the traditional public relations strategies and tactics that have characterized its practice. In Chapter 2 we shall discuss how those practices evolved, principally in the United States, and how US practitioners have tended, ethnocentrically, to export and superimpose those principles globally as universal absolutes. This is an approach not likely to meet with success given inherent cultural and societal differences that affect human communication, illustrated by the University of Michigan study described above.

You're probably an advanced public relations student at the graduate or undergraduate level, or a seasoned professional. You have likely heard the litany of blunders and disasters that have stemmed from failure to account for cultural differences: the attempt by General Motors to market the Chevrolet Nova in Latin America where "no va" means "It doesn't go"; a US campaign that employed the color white as a symbol of purity or freshness in Japan, where white is associated with death; the US vendor hawking T-shirts commemorating the Pope's visit to Cuba which, because of a misunderstanding of the importance of capitalization, said not "I saw the Pope" (*el Papa*) but "I saw the potato" (*el papa*); and there are many more. This, however, is not a text aimed at listing examples of PR goofs. Rather, it is a text designed to prepare the practitioner dedicated to professionalism for success in this 24/7, borderless, interconnected world and, in doing so, to advance the profession while perhaps, at least in some small way, improving the human condition.

Describing the discipline

A good way to begin is to establish common ground regarding the discipline of public relations. Just what do we mean by the term? Public relations scholar Rex Harlow once attempted to collect all published definitions of the term and found more than 500. They include the very simple, such as the Public Relations Society of America definition: "Public relations helps an organization and its publics adapt mutually to each other", or as some have quipped, not without basis,

"Doing good and letting people know it". Other definitions are more complex, but introduce greater precision. Here's a good one from an introductory text:

> Public relations is a leadership and management function that helps achieve organizational objectives, define philosophy, and facilitate organizational change. Public relations practitioners communicate with all relevant internal and external publics to develop positive relationships and to create consistency between organizational goals and societal expectation. Public relations practitioners develop, execute, and evaluate organizational programs that promote the exchange of influence and understanding among an organization's constituent parts and publics.
>
> (Lattimore *et al.* 2004, p. 5)

If we disassemble this definition, we shall find a number of components that make it a useful one even for international practice.

First, we should agree that public relations practice includes, as this definition does, the component of management and leadership. Some have said leadership is doing the right thing, and management is doing the thing right. That is simple, but accurate. We have come to understand that practitioners must not only have direct access to top organizational management, but must also possess and exhibit qualities of top management. The remainder of the definition's first sentence explains why: (1) practitioners must ensure their efforts support and contribute to overall organizational goals and objectives; (2) practitioners must participate actively and influentially in establishing and monitoring organizational values; and (3) practitioners must have the confidence of top management in order to recommend needed adjustments to organizational policies and procedures.

The second sentence of the definition describes the process by which practitioners create an environment in which these lofty responsibilities can be carried out: practitioners, more than any other organizational component, engage in an ongoing communication effort with all the constituencies that matter to the organization. Internally that could include employees, members, students, volunteers, and so on. Externally, as you probably know, that could include media (general and specialized), community members, government agencies at all levels, customers and clients, and so forth. Then there are hybrid publics that do not fit neatly into the external/internal categorization such as retirees, alumni, investors, and so on. Any good introductory public relations textbook will provide exhaustive lists and explanations of potential publics, so there's no need to delve deeply into that here. The point is that public relations practitioners build long-term relationships with these constituencies through ongoing dialogue. After all, these are the constituencies upon whom the success and prosperity of the organization depend. Implied in this process is the organizational core value that it is genuinely concerned about the values, motivations and welfare of these publics, and is willing to take reasonable measures to harmonize its own operations to address discord. Who better to facilitate this complex but mutually beneficial process than public relations professionals steeped in the highest forms of its practice?

The third and final sentence of this simple but comprehensive definition introduces the specific craft elements of the discipline that enable practitioners to carry out this challenging brief. While our intentions may be nobly elevated, we must still, on the one hand, recognize the art of the possible and, on the other hand, acknowledge limitations such as finite resources, legal and ethical constraints, and overarching issues. Doing so means that practitioners, whether engaged in local, regional, national or international projects and programs, must bring to the table fundamental skills including the ability to design, conduct and analyze qualitative and quantitative research; develop comprehensive, cohesive, purposeful plans and programs; supervise the preparation of collateral materials and events; and evaluate program effectiveness in order to make necessary adjustments. All this, and be a superb manager and leader as well! It is a tall order; but a dynamic global environment demands it, and our discipline has matured sufficiently to develop a reputation for meeting these responsibilities.

That, then, is what this text implies when it uses the simple term *public relations*. Actual practice may vary from nation to nation, from culture to culture, and this text will address those differences. However, it is this author's contention, and a position held by the discipline's leading scholars and practitioners, that any definition of the profession should include references to a planned, management-oriented, process-centered program, characterized by ongoing dialogue with internal and external publics, and contributing to and participating in responsible decision-making by top organizational leaders. Anything less diminishes the status of the term and should be labeled more accurately with terms such as *publicity, event planning, press agentry*, and so on.

The discipline in context

The reader may observe that this definition may apply to more fully developed nations such as the United States or nations of western Europe, but is unrealistic for developing and transitional nations such as in eastern Europe, Latin America, Africa and Asia. Perhaps that is partially true in practice, but the possibility is well established. Literature suggests that scholars and practitioners believe it is feasible to transcend cultural barriers and pursue public relations objectives effectively on a global scale, with the important caveats that goals be identified, pursued and gauged one public at a time, that standards of excellence be considered a desirable objective, and that, to do so, the practitioner must take into account variations in cultural contexts and syndromes (discussed in depth in Chapters 4 and 5). Most prominent among this body of literature is the landmark study by Verčič *et al.* (1993, pp. 17–30).

Verčič and his colleagues emphasized that public relations is influenced by its contextual cultures and political systems, and aimed for a "middle ground theory between cultural relativism and ethnocentrism". The researchers, in fact, developed a list of nine general principles of excellence they argued applied to the practice of public relations universally. A brief summary of those principles and a comment on their application to international public relations practice is in order.

Verčič and his colleagues consolidated a list of characteristics of excellent public relations compiled by the Grunigs (Grunig and Grunig 1992, pp. 285–325), and argue that these characteristics "will be generic, normative factors of excellent public relations applicable across cultures and political/economic systems" (Verčič *et al.* 1993, p. 36). Following is a summary of their conclusions:

1. *Involvement of public relations in strategic management:* The organization sets goals and missions relevant to the environment. Public relations units are involved in the planning process. Relationships are cultivated with relevant publics.
2. *Empowerment of public relations in the dominant coalition or a direct reporting relationship to senior management:* Strategic management of public relations is linked directly with strategic management of the organization.
3. *Integrated public relations function:* All public relations functions are integrated into a single department, or are very closely coordinated by other means.

4. *Public relations as a management function separate from other functions:* While public relations counselors provide advice and guidance to all other management functions on communication and relationship issues, it must remain separate and distinct from those other management functions.
5. *The role of the public relations practitioner:* At least one member of the organization's public relations unit must function as a communication manager (as opposed to a technician) who strategizes and directs communication programs.
6. *Two-way symmetrical model of public relations:* The organization's public relations function is dominated by two-way symmetrical modeling, though elements of the other three models may be evident.
7. *A symmetrical system of internal communication:* Internal organizational communication, central to effective management, must reflect symmetrical patterns. Organizational mission and goals must reflect employee input at all levels.
8. *Knowledge potential for managerial role and symmetrical public relations:* Among the organization's public relations unit must be managers who possess knowledge of public relations theory.
9. *Diversity embodied in all roles.* Organizations, and especially their public relations units, reflect diversity in order to communicate most effectively with varied internal and external publics.

As Verčič and his colleagues point out, the implementation of any or all of these characteristics may prove challenging in cross-cultural contexts. Consequently, the development of a cadre of public relations practitioners capable of accommodating those challenges is essential if an organization hopes to compete in such an environment. In fact, Verčič and his colleagues identify a number of specific variables with the potential to prevent effective implementation of these standards of excellence: the political-economic system; the culture; the extent of activism; the level of development; and the media system. In Chapters 4 and 5 we shall present approaches to constructing a framework to help practitioners incorporate consideration of these and other facets in their communication program and campaign planning.

What PR is not

The discipline of public relations is frequently blended with related disciplines, most often journalism, advertising and marketing. This is especially true in some international settings, and the global practitioner must be prepared to explain patiently the factors that distinguish public relations from these other important disciplines. Though there are similarities among the professions, and each borrows from the others to some extent, they vary on several planes. The manager who can distinguish among them will be able to apply them collectively and synergistically to the greater benefit of the organization.

Public relations shares a great deal with journalism, and public relations certainly evolved more from this dimension than from any other. Each heavily involves writing, and that writing must be characterized by economy, accuracy and precision. Practitioners of each must work to deadlines, and they must conduct extensive research as part of the writing process. For these reasons, many have successfully made the transition from journalism to public relations, at least at the technician level. Public relations, however, has a broader scope that incorporates management responsibilities for long-term planning, allocation of limited resources, and evaluation. Also, while journalists must strive for objectivity, public relations specialists function as advocates for the organizations they represent, and their writing may often pursue a persuasive purpose. In addition, while journalists write consistently for the same basic audience, public relations practitioners must address a wider spectrum of publics, both internal and external. Finally, a journalist communicates consistently through one channel – a daily newspaper, for example – but public relations practitioners employ numerous channels from employee bulletin boards, radio public service announcements, annual reports, direct mail, trade shows, the Internet, and news conferences, to speeches, advisory boards, interviews and more.

Advertising, like public relations, relies on mass media to communicate messages, and writing is certainly common to both. However, the major difference between the two is the degree of control over the message. Advertisers pay to place their material and, therefore, control the content and placement such as the time or date when the ad will appear; public relations practitioners seldom enjoy that luxury. Advertising is narrow in scope and purpose – generally to increase sales of a product in the short term – while public relations may aim to raise awareness of an issue, build organizational reputation, engender trust, shape opinion, and so on, and generally in the long term. Both advertising and public relations specialists need to evaluate the effectiveness of their efforts, but advertising can rely primarily on sales to gauge success, while public relations seeks to measure more subtle factors such as attitudes and opinions as well as behavior. Finally, advertising is principally a one-way communication effort, but public relations seeks two-way symmetrical communication through engagement in ongoing dialogue.

Marketing comes closer to mimicking public relations but remains distinct. One area of difference is target audience. Marketing focuses on consumers and customers or those with the potential to be consumers and customers. Public relations' publics include employees, government agencies, community opinion leaders, trade and technical media, and other publics whom marketers seldom target. Both marketing and public relations efforts are persuasive in nature; but, again, public relations seeks to foster dialogue – not a primary concern for marketers. Still, marketing and public relations can often support each other for greater effectiveness through ongoing programs of coordinated planning and communication.

Intercultural competence

A fundamental assumption of this text is the need to consider international public relations as a distinct subset of the discipline. It is appropriate to present the case for making that assumption. The premise is that public relations is practiced by means of communication at all its levels: symbolic; non-verbal; verbal; interpersonal; small group; mass; and so on. Communication, in turn, is a fundamental component of culture; indeed, the terms may, some scholars maintain, almost be used interchangeably. Consequently, a basic understanding of cross-cultural issues will permit an appreciation of the need to consider international public relations as presenting a unique set of challenges to the practitioner.

Put another way, differences exist among cultures, and those differences affect human communication patterns and processes. Public relations as a discipline dependent upon communication is impacted by those differences. One may predict, then, that an appreciation for and understanding of cultural differences would foster successful and satisfying performance in international public relations assignments and environments. The level of understanding one has of these issues may be referred to as intercultural or cross-cultural competence.

It is useful, too, to distinguish between the terms *cross-cultural* (or *intercultural*) and *international*. Certainly, international communication within the aegis of public relations will, in almost all cases, constitute cross-cultural communication. However, it is important to recognize that cross-cultural communication also occurs <u>*intranationally*</u>. For example, one would find unique cultural characteristics within the United States among the Amish, first-generation Asian-Americans, or Native Americans. Similarly, practitioners working in Turkey would need to be aware of cultural differences that affect communication patterns among traditional Turks in the western regions of the country and ethnic Kurdish populations in the east. Cross-cultural public relations implies, therefore, the attempt by practitioners from different cultures (perhaps different nations, but not necessarily) to create shared meanings within a context of pursuing specific communication goals and objectives.

In that regard, practitioners appear to be eager to expand their experience beyond national and cultural borders. A 1998 study of US practitioners revealed a pronounced desire for international assignments, but the study also found a marked lack of preparation for those assignments (Freitag 1999). The study assumed a practitioner would be better-prepared for professional international situations to the degree he or she had prepared academically for cross-cultural interchange and/or had previously experienced personal or professional foreign travel. The study suggested that is true, but also found US practitioners to lack those preparatory factors. For example, just 16 percent of these professional US practitioners had completed a university course in cross-cultural studies, and just 12.5 percent had completed a course in international business. Similar small percentages had studied international history, philosophy, political science, even literature. Competence in speaking a language other than English was also largely absent. Although two-thirds had studied another language at the university level, just one in six reported being fluent or even conversational in a language other than English. The survey additionally showed that just one in ten US public relations practitioners had studied a second foreign language beyond English. It is important to note, too, that this survey went only to members of the Public Relations Society of America, the foremost professional organization in the United States for the public relations profession. Just one in twenty people claiming the title of public relations professional holds PRSA membership, and these 5 percent surveyed on their international preparation are the practitioners most likely to pursue professional development. Figures for all practitioners in the United States, therefore, could be even more dismal.

Questions for discussion

1. Do you think US practitioners have made progress in this area since this study was published? Why or why not? What do you think are the reasons behind a lack of academic and experiential international background among US practitioners?
2. Do you agree with the assumption that academic course work and/or foreign travel can help prepare a practitioner for professional international assignments? Explain your position.
3. How do you think practitioners in nations other than the United States would compare to the US responses?

Is preparation useful in international public relations practice? Does preparation contribute to success and personal satisfaction with a job well done? Fred LaSor spent a 25-year career in the US Foreign Service, primarily in Francophone Africa. He served with the US Information Agency, essentially the public relations arm of the US State Department. Here's what he says:

> I took a great deal of satisfaction in the work I did, and I think that satisfaction was directly proportional to the amount of preparation I put into it. The more work I did before I went to a post, the better my success at the post and the more satisfaction I took out of my work when I was finished with it. This was so clear to me that without even really thinking about it, I found that every time I would be preparing for a new post, I would be putting more effort into learning about it and preparing myself for it. There is no question in my mind that I took more personal satisfaction out of doing a good job than not, and that doing a good job was directly proportional to the amount of effort I put into preparing myself before I went: logistically; culturally; and historically. Working, for me, in an overseas setting, I always found the historical setting to be very important. You had to be able, and were most successful, when you could sit down and talk to somebody from the country you were dealing in and be aware of where he was coming from in terms of the experience that he might have grown up under, his educational experience, in terms of what he considers to be his historical antecedents. Did he come through slavery? Did he come through being brutalized by a colonial régime? Does he consider his relationship to you one of inferior to a superior because of the experience that he had? All these things made sense only from the historical sense that I studied.

LaSor's comments seem coarse toward the end, but recall that he is speaking of his experiences in Africa, parts of which have been marked by difficult history. Nevertheless, he makes an important point powerfully: thorough preparation is essential to success in international assignments. Of course, the State Department provided official preparatory work before each of his assignments, but LaSor went well beyond that. He did a considerable amount of reading on the history and culture of the country to which he was being assigned, and before his first assignment to Africa he completed four graduate courses on French Colonial Africa, including courses in government and economics of the region. You can read more about Fred LaSor in the biographical profile at the conclusion of this chapter.

Additional wrinkles

In addition to cultural differences, the international practice of public relations is further complicated by the increasingly wide range of systemic differences in media upon which public relations campaigns often rely for a substantial portion of their effects. The proliferation of satellite broadcasting networks, digital transmission and multipoint production of publications, and the Worldwide Web have simplified information exchange, but cultural differences remain that affect the reception, retention and processing of that information. In a 24-hour, interconnected world, time zones and national borders are no longer significant barriers to information flow. Still, the international public relations practitioner must recognize and adjust accordingly for the factors that complicate communication campaigns and programs. Newsom and Carrell, for example, describe the "haphazard mass media delivery system of a global marketplace" and how this chaotic environment is affecting the practice of public relations (1995, pp. 89–102). McDermott compares international public relations under these conditions to three-dimensional chess (McDermott 1997). Although practitioners have been accustomed to "playing" on a two-dimensional board, the international dimension introduces additional complications that require practitioners to think and act along different vectors.

One of those vectors is the legal vector. Practitioners in recent years have increasingly been required to consider the legal implications of their plans and actions. A practitioner from Hungary or Argentina given an assignment in the United States, for example, would need to become at least somewhat familiar with a myriad of legal concerns that may affect his or her assignment there: for example, privacy law; copyright and trademark law; libel and slander law; and regulatory law from government agencies such as the Food and Drug Administration, the Federal Trade Commission, and the Securities and Exchange Commission. On the other hand, a US or Canadian practitioner sent to Poland in support of his or her organization's efforts there would need to become familiar with the law of *kryptoreklama*, which forbids the mention of a commercial product or service in news items – negating the effectiveness of news releases as part of a communication plan.

Another complex vector practitioners must wrestle with is that of ethics. This chapter has commented on the need for applying tools and techniques of public relations to the greater good of societies within which it is practiced, both to improve upon the profession's reputation and because it is the right thing to do – part of our leadership and responsible management obligations. If we accept Elfstrom's contention (1991), echoed by Kruckeberg (1996, pp. 81–92), that multinational corporations and other organizations possess the ability, even the obligation, to act as moral agents on a global basis, then application of standards of public relations excellence leads to the conclusion that the public relations unit of an organization plays a potentially significant role in that process. Doing so, however, presents a dilemma, which Kruckeberg describes as the risk of confusing cultural relativism with cultural tolerance.

Cultural relativism, he says, is akin to ethical relativism, and may prove a slippery slope; adopting cultural standards of behavior or ethics that violate organizational standards may risk violating public relations excellence. For example, bribing an editor to publish a news release because bribery is the norm in that particular culture will not serve well the organization's role as moral agent. Cultural tolerance, on the other hand, would accept the existence of that cultural practice without engaging in it, even if it meant the news release would not be published, at least by that editor.

Kruckeberg goes on to propose that a system of universal ethics be developed in which transnational organizations respect host-nation cultural principles, while insisting upon reciprocity in regard to their own standards. A decade has passed since Kruckeberg proposed this system of universal ethics, but the debate continues.

Further complicating public relations efforts globally is the spectrum of mass-media paradigms through which messages are likely to be conveyed. It would be a mistake of considerable proportions to assume that the mass-media context with which you're familiar in your native country is similar in all respects to the context you will find in another setting. Stark differences in such areas as media ownership, government control, purpose, licensing, access, credibility, and consumer uses and gratifications dictate the need to study comparative systems thoroughly and adjust communication strategies accordingly. In one setting, print media may dominate, but readership may correlate to affiliation with particular political parties. In another setting, low literacy rates and limited resources may require alternative approaches to mass media more prevalent in developed nations. Chapter 5 examines this issue in greater detail.

The case for competence

Why does this matter? Because public relations practitioners today are increasingly likely to find themselves in international and cross-cultural environments and must be prepared to lead their organizations and clients through these challenges. Freivalds, for example, cites international mergers as creating significant cultural problems for all concerned (1998, p. 19). He notes that, when Swedish telecommunications company Ericsson bought US facilities owned by GTE, language and cultural differences created problems. And when German lighting company OSRAM bought the US firm Sylvania the engineers from the two companies could not understand each other, despite using computer-based translation software. Freivalds further points out that Anglo-French mergers often experience frustration during management meetings, when lower-level British managers have decision-making authority, while their French counterparts must report higher up the chain. Additionally, he says, British managers are satisfied with a pragmatic, step-by-step approach to solving issues, but the French are more likely to wait for a comprehensive solution before moving forward. Similarly, US business managers are likely to express themselves with direct, straight-forward language, but their German partners in the same meeting may not express their thoughts at all. Such contrasts may come down to differences in emphasis on individual versus team efforts, Freivalds maintains. He describes similar difficulties encountered when British Telecom sought a partnership with US-based AT&T, and experienced by US-based General Motors when it finally resigned itself to moving its international headquarters back to Detroit from Zurich because of cultural challenges.

And practitioners need not leave their hometowns to experience an international environment in their professional careers. Charlotte, North Carolina, is roughly the twentieth most populous city in the US, but it can boast more than 650 foreign-owned firms operating in the city. Increasingly, those firms are run by US management teams because the overseas leadership recognizes the value of a "global-markets perspective" rather than a Japanese, British or German point of view (Suga 2005, p. D-1). This marks a change; Japanese companies, for example, formerly placed Japanese managers in charge of their overseas operations. Now those same companies see the merit of placing local managers in charge, with advisory roles for their own nationals. Public relations practitioners anywhere, consequently, may find themselves working in their home country but on behalf of foreign ownership. With international mergers and global operations, it is clear that the public relations profession will require practitioners adept at functioning in such a complex environment.

By undertaking this study of international public relations, you are implicitly agreeing to pursue the development of your cross-cultural competence, contributing to both the elevation of the public relations profession and the improvement of international communication and understanding. Freitag makes the case that such preparation will usher the practitioner into an ascending spiral of increasing and cumulative competence, as well as a pattern of professional and personal satisfaction (1999). The argument is that practitioners with appropriate cultural preparation will be more likely to seek and accept international assignment opportunities, to perceive their experiences to have been successful and satisfying, to gain additional cultural competence with each assignment, and to reinforce their international assignment seeking behavior. The spiral might be depicted graphically as in Figure 1.1.

The point in Figure 1.1 is that initial preparation for international public relations assignments – such as completing a course in international public relations, studying the language, understanding the social, political, cultural and other differences that distinguish the environment you will be working in – suggests an eagerness to embark on such assignments. Note that initial preparation is termed "cultural general", while assignment preparation is termed "cultural specific". "Cultural general" refers to the approach taken by the first two sections of this text – understanding the factors that complicate public relations efforts in cross-cultural settings in general. "Cultural specific" refers to the approach taken in the third section of this text – understanding the particular environment in which the assignment will occur. In both cases, preparation also portends personal and professional satisfaction as well as success in the assignment. With each successful assignment, you gain valuable experience and add to your cumulative understanding of cultural barriers to communication and how to address them. That, in turn, contributes to your reputation as a practitioner skilled in international settings, making it more likely you will be called upon to exercise those skills. Thus, by embarking on this fascinating and challenging journey, you are preparing to advance the discipline, contribute to your organization's success, and build a career marked by responsible leadership at the vanguard of the profession.

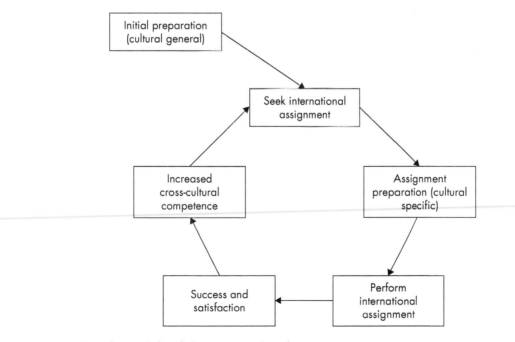

FIGURE 1.1 Cumulative Cultural Competence Spiral

Questions for discussion

1. Which nations or world regions do you think are best-prepared to prosper in a global economy? Why?
2. Is it an overstatement to claim that the discipline of public relations can play a central role in facilitating global commerce and exchange? Explain your answer.
3. What steps might a public relations practitioner take to distinguish himself or herself as an international PR specialist?

Featured biography: Fred LaSor

Fred LaSor served with the US Information Agency – essentially the public relations arm of the US State Department – for more than twenty-five years, mostly in Francophone Africa, but also in Asia and South America. His international experience began, though, with a Peace Corps assignment in India following college.

LaSor recalls his exposure to US businesses' public relations efforts in Africa during the 1960s. The private-sector public relations representative he occasionally encountered in his official capacity was typically "an American businessman who happened to be there doing something else and would be hired by a contractor coming in to handle public relations". These people were generally well steeped in the local culture, though they lacked public relations skills. More often, however, US business representatives made no effort to bridge the cultural divide. US businesses often provided electrical equipment wired to the US standard of 110 volts instead of the local standard of 220 volts, neglected to have sales brochures and even instruction manuals available in languages other than English, and insisted upon working in inches and feet, pounds and ounces, instead of metric measurements. He says most US business-related public relations practitioners were in the information-disseminating mode, not interested in public discourse.

Two-way symmetrical communication, along with sensitivity to cultural nuances, is an important element of effective public relations, LaSor maintains. An example he provides is the importance of cultivating and nurturing personal relationships through which messages may be more effectively exchanged and without which communication may be largely ineffective. "In much of what we used to call the Third World, the personal relationship is of absolute, utmost importance," he observes. "I always devoted a great deal of time to actually getting to know people. And the people who are most successful at our business not only knew their counterparts (in the diplomatic corps), but knew their families. Absolutely, critically important." He said in the United States business and personal relationships are separate, compartmentalized. "But in Asia, in Latin America, in Africa, those things are all part of the context."

LaSor points to the changes he witnessed in marketing US goods overseas during the time he served with USIA. He says US goods used to enjoy considerable popularity and success, so long-range, relationship-building communication efforts were not undertaken or perceived as needed. Now, though, the competition for those markets has accelerated, and the absence of those relationships is a limiting factor for the United States. Now, he notes, there are ample competing products from France, Japan and elsewhere, so long-term, relationship-building approaches to public relations in support of international market development are increasingly important and evident.

He said message-crafting was much more complex in his international assignments. "The message that I carried was mandated from Washington, DC," he explains. "I had to learn the cultural milieu and cast it (the message) in terms that made sense in that culture."

He says, too, that language skill is essential, but it is just a beginning. "If you have gone through the effort of learning another language and learning it well, you pick up a new appreciation for the fact that people, even though they may be speaking in English, may not be communicating to the same cultural world that you are." He remembers a typical occasion when a local citizen of an African nation was speaking with him and his wife in English. LaSor had learned the native language, but his wife had not, and each ascribed different meanings to the citizen's message. LaSor was able, because of his language ability, to understand the translation process through which the English message had come, and was therefore more closely attuned to the originally intended meaning.

LaSor agrees that there is a cumulative value in international experiences. "I think, because I had worked in Asia and then went to Africa, it was easier for me to work in Africa."

He was not optimistic about US public relations practitioners' ability to function in international settings. His experience is that practitioners from other nations are making considerable progress, however. Within the diplomatic corps, for example, he cited the Chinese and the Russians as possessing highly polished skills in the area of relationship-building on a personal level. The Chinese, he said, have exceptionally well developed language skills. He relates an episode concerning a conversation with his Russian counterpart in Kenya. The gentleman spoke in "beautiful English" and was thoroughly at ease discussing nineteenth-century American literature, about which, LaSor admits, the Russian knew more than he.

Recommended websites

"Dipnote", US State Department blog site for diplomats   www.blogs.state.gov

"All about" international public relations   http://aboutpublicrelations.net/international.htm

Proceedings, 2006 International Public Relations Conference   http://ipr.wieck.com/files/uploads/9th_IPRRC_Proceedings.pdf

Proceedings, 2007 International Public Relations Conference   http://www.instituteforpr.org/files/uploads/IPRRC10_Proceedings.pdf

International Public Relations Association   http://www.iprasummit.org/index.php

References

Elfstrom, G., 1991. *Moral Issues and Multinational Corporations*. New York: St Martin's Press.

Freitag, A. R., 1999. Cultural competence correlates of public relations functions and models: a profile and assessment of US practitioners' preparation for international assignments. PhD, UMI.

Freitag, A. R., 2002. Ascending cultural competence potential: an assessment and profile of US public relations practitioners' preparation for international assignments. *Journal of Public Relations Research*, 14 (3), pp. 207–27.

Freivalds, J., 1998. When cultures clash. *Communication World*, 15, October–November, p. 19.

Grunig, J. and Grunig, L., 1992. Models of public relations and communications. In J. Grunig, ed. *Excellence in Public Relations and Communication Management*. Mahwah, NJ: Lawrence Erlbaum. Ch. 11.

Kruckeberg, D., 1996. Transnational corporate ethical responsibilities. In H. M. Culbertson and N. Chen, eds. *International Public Relations: A Comparative Analysis*. Mahwah, NJ: Lawrence Erlbaum. Ch. 4.

Lattimore, D., Baskin, O., Heiman, S. T. and Toth, E. L., 2004. *Public Relations: The Profession and the Practice*. New York: McGraw-Hill.

McDermott, P. M., 1997. [Workshop on international public relations] Annual convention of the Public Relations Society of America. Nashville, Tenn., November 8.

Newsom, D. A. and Carrell, B. J., 1995. Global advertising and public relations. In J. C. Merrill, ed. *Global Journalism: Survey of International Communication*. 3rd edn. White Plains, NY: Longman.

Suga, M., 2005. Leading in a global economy. *The Charlotte Observer*, August 28. p. D-1.

Verčič, D., Grunig, L. and Grunig, J., 1993. Global and specific principles of public relations: evidence from Slovenia, [conference paper] Association for the Advancement of Policy, Research, and Development in the Third World. Cairo, Egypt. Also in Culbertson, H. and Chen N., eds. *International Public Relations: A Comparative Analysis*, Mahwah, NJ: Lawrence Erlbaum, 1996. Ch. 2.

Chapter 2

Evolution of the profession

Summary

Before embarking on a survey of public relations around the globe and exploring approaches to practice across borders and cultures, it is useful to examine the development of modern public relations within the context of the forces that spawned it. Using the US as our benchmark for comparative purposes, we shall look at the dynamic conditions that fostered the need for the profession we now call public relations, and we shall consider global trends influencing its continued maturation.

Chapter goals

- Briefly consider the roots of contemporary public relations.
- Identify and describe the social, political and economic conditions that gave rise to the need for an effective system of managing communication and nurturing relationships between organizations and their publics.
- See how and to what extent those conditions have spread beyond the United States and anticipate how unique circumstances would create equally unique styles of public relations practice.

Nearly every public relations textbook includes among its early chapters one describing the history of the profession, and there's merit in doing so – for several reasons. Understanding the cultural roots of public relations will help the practitioner and the scholar to appreciate the dynamic forces that have shaped the discipline and continue to influence its development. Second, a grasp of how those forces affect the profession will allow the practitioner and the scholar to predict, anticipate and be prepared for directions the profession is likely to take in the coming years. Additionally, the international practitioner who understands the correlation between public relations history and practice will be able to analyze environments critically in regions and countries he or she is not familiar with, especially where public relations is experiencing its early stages, then plan strategies compatible with current dynamic trends. Finally, the responsible practitioner and scholar will be able to incorporate that understanding into best practices and meaningful research and teaching that benefit the profession by building its capacity to improve the human condition.

In the history chapter of those public relations textbooks, authors sometimes speculate on the most distant past, pointing out instances of ancient employment of what could be construed as public relations techniques. Cutlip *et al.* (2000, p. 102) cite the archeological discovery of a clay tablet in Iraq dating from 1800 BC; the tablet describes recommended agricultural techniques to help farmers maximize their yield and thus, the authors argue, the tablet constitutes early use of persuasive communication techniques designed to achieve a goal – national productivity and well-being. Others maintain that the Rosetta Stone, a relic among the collection of the British Museum in London, is fundamentally a news release because, though it unlocked the key to deciphering Egyptian hieroglyphics, it basically touted the pharaoh's achievements. Some describe Jesus' apostles, and especially Paul and Peter, as highly effective public relations leaders given the profound results of their communication campaigns. Of course, one could argue that the God of the Bible recognized from the beginning that public relations would be critical to human progress by appointing a "spokesman" for Moses (his brother, Aaron) when Moses was commissioned to lead the Israelites from slavery, through the wilderness, to the promised land (see Exodus 4:10–16).

Even during the Middle Ages, and especially within the Roman Catholic Church that so influenced not just theology but also politics and even economic matters, embryonic evidence of nascent public relations can be seen emerging, some argue. For example, the establishment by Pope Gregory XV in 1622 of the Congregation for the Propagation of the Faith (Sacra Congregatio de Propaganda Fide), an institution for directing foreign missions and training priests to spread the faith, is also seen as a milestone in the emergence of public relations. The institution was renamed the Congregation for the Evangelization of Peoples (Congregatio pro Gentium Evangelisatione) by Pope John Paul II in 1982 because of the negative connotation of the word *propaganda*, but that negative taint did not emerge until the word was linked with nefarious activities associated with World War I in the second decade of the twentieth century.

Typically, public relations textbooks, especially those written from a US American viewpoint, continue by extracting evidence of public relations tactics employed during that nation's colonial and revolutionary experience in the eighteenth century, then describe activities of prominent figures in the development of modern practice – figures including Amos Kendall, P. T. Barnum, Ivy Ledbetter Lee, Edward Bernays, Doris Fleischman, Arthur Page and others. We shall assume that the advanced public relations student or practitioner reading this either is familiar with those elements of the discipline's history or is capable of pursuing further secondary research to learn more about them. Clearly, efforts to communicate effectively and especially persuasively have occurred since the dawn of human communication. The purpose of this chapter, though, is not to review specific milestones in public relations history, but rather to examine the societal forces that precipitated those milestones, thus shaping the way in which public relations practice would develop in response to those forces and in anticipation of the impact of those forces on the rest of society. To do that, we shall use the US experience because that is where societal forces and conditions conspired to mold what we would consider to be contemporary public relations practice. In recent years, as the profession has increasingly taken root in many other developed and developing countries, it is absorbing new facets and nuances as a result of variations in those forces, and there is no reason to believe that the process will cease. Wilcox and Cameron (2007, pp. 46–7) offer a summary of the historical underpinnings of public relations in Germany, Great Britain, Australia, Taiwan, the Philippines, Spain, Russia and Thailand to illustrate the unique vectors the profession has taken in those nations as a result of their individual circumstances, and Part 3 of this text examines some of those cases and others in more depth. Further, this chapter concludes with a look at some of those emerging forces that are taking the profession in new directions, directions that would not have occurred if the United States had retained exclusive ownership of the profession. The key point is that public relations did not spontaneously appear, fully formed, then look about for things to do. The ideas behind the American colonies' Declaration of Independence in 1776, outlining an unprecedented concept of citizen self-governance, set in motion an extraordinary sequence of events and trends that precipitated the appearance of the public relations profession. Those ideas spread to Western Europe, Latin America, Asia, Africa, and to Central and Eastern Europe, and with each iteration the function of public relations has developed with unique characteristics, influenced by the peculiar social, historical, political, economic and cultural dynamics that define each region.

Although US public relations textbooks almost invariably follow this episodic approach to the discipline's history and development, relying on historical events alone has its limitations. These names, dates and circumstances make for interesting reading and straightforward exam questions, but more important are the forces that converge to create those circumstances and events. German scholars Hoy *et al.* (2006), for example, are critical of this traditional approach that uses a chain of events to reveal an evolutionary development of the public relations profession, and they suggest that alternative histories based on a social and cultural analytical approach may be more useful. We suggest here that a hybrid model suits our purposes: that historical facts and events are manifestations of underlying social and cultural currents, and are, therefore, useful in so far as they help us understand those trends. Litanies of events describe the past, but they do not help us forecast the future unless we understand the component forces that shaped them and that are likely to continue influencing events.

Let us begin by identifying and examining the underlying social trends that, at least in the United States, drove the need for an organizational function that we have come to define as public relations. Seitel (2004, pp. 25–6) lists a number of those trends, beginning with the *growth of large institutions*. The United States was dominated in its first hundred years by individual agriculture – family farms – plus limited, localized small businesses and "cottage" industries. Relationships between and among citizens, producers, merchants and consumers were direct, personal, face-to-face. Communication was largely unmediated. However, there were seeds of change.

Growth of large institutions

On a personal level, in the 1950s when I (author Alan Freitag) was a youngster in a large Midwest US city, going to the grocery store for Mom meant hopping on my bicycle and pedaling a few blocks to a house that looked pretty much like mine, except that it was a small store with an apartment upstairs where the owners lived. The husband would be in the back of the store at a small meat counter, chopping and wrapping meat orders when they were requested, and the wife was at the tiny checkout counter at the front of the store, marking in a spiral notebook the few items on the list I had brought from home and that I had found easily in the two or three short store aisles. No cash was exchanged. The owners knew me and my family. They asked about my family members by name – how one sibling was doing in college, how another was recovering from the flu. They knew sometime in the coming days one of my parents would stop in and make good on the bill. It was our neighborhood store, and no one thought of going elsewhere. I seriously doubt whether the store owners ever contemplated retaining the advice and counsel of a public relations firm to help them with "branding" or relationship-building. Now, fifty years later and living in the southeast United States in a comparably sized city, I can drive within ten minutes to five massive, competing supermarkets. Each has a breakfast cereal department far larger than the entire neighborhood grocery store of my youth. There are as many as thirty long aisles, plus separate departments for cheese, produce, baked goods, prepared salads, flowers, seafood. There's usually a pharmacy. One even has a bank. There are at least a dozen high-tech checkout lanes and four more where I can check out all my items by scanning them at a computer – I never even have to interact with a human. The only way the store knows I have been there is because I scanned an individually bar-coded card, a process that records all my purchases for future marketing purposes; the grocery store chain's central computer will now automatically e-mail me coupons for the types and brands of items I habitually purchase. Each store is part of a vast chain. The owners of these chains are not family; they are countless faceless shareholders. Somewhere there's a headquarters where executive officers manage operations under the guidance of a board of directors. In at least one case, the headquarters for my neighborhood supermarket in the southeastern United States is in Brussels, Belgium. Establishing and nurturing the relationships upon which the success of the larger organizations depend – relationships with customers, employees, unions, suppliers, subcontractors, government agencies, community leaders, investors, media representatives and others – requires extensive knowledge, research, analysis, planning and strategizing, plus the application of a complex mix of specialized skills and the ongoing evaluation of effectiveness of those efforts. That is a big challenge that must be undertaken by appropriately educated and experienced professional communicators.

That same evolution that has affected the familiar arena of grocery stores occurred in the United States in other sectors: manufacturing, distribution, transportation, banking, dry goods, pharmaceuticals, energy, media, forest products, and just about any sector you might name. From the latter half of the nineteenth century, throughout the twentieth century and continuing in this century, the United States has experienced this dynamic development, and similar changes subsequently occurred in other global regions, often with substantially increased velocity. With this change has come the shaping of the public relations discipline needed to address the many challenges associated with the change as well as the spread of the discipline along with the spread of the phenomenon.

An example of those challenges is clearly manifest in the so-called "robber baron" era in the United States. Around the turn of the nineteenth to the twentieth centuries, a group of men including William Vanderbilt (railroads), J. P. Morgan (banking), John D. Rockefeller (oil), John Jacob Astor (real estate), Andrew Carnegie (steel), James Duke (tobacco), Jay Gould (finance) and others earned membership in a group of businessmen dubbed the robber barons. The sobriquet is a pejorative one ascribed because they accumulated their vast wealth through anti-competitive and unfair business practices. They have even been accused of employing deception, violence and certainly dishonesty to obtain their huge economic power. On the other hand, some have defended their activities, highlighting their humanitarian and charitable activities, and arguing that these industrialists contributed considerably to establishing US business leadership and the phenomenon of a vast middle class, substantially raising the average standard of living. Regardless of the view taken, the robber barons were buffeted by societal ire, concentrated in the efforts of a group of journalists who came to be known as the "muckrakers". The implication is obvious. These muckrakers, such as Upton Sinclair and Ida Tarbell, published books, magazine and newspaper articles decrying the scandalous activities of the robber barons. As the wave of negative publicity fomented an increasingly agitated public, the robber barons tried bribing newspapers and magazines with advertising in return for the cessation of negative articles, which, of course, did not work. They tried hiring publicity agents to gloss over their organizational blemishes and present a rosier picture; but that, too, was unsuccessful. Eventually, elected officials, sensitive to the sentiments of their constituencies, began to pass legislation to break up monopolies, govern labor policies, and otherwise influence and even control business activities. Unions emerged to address collective grievances and demand better working conditions. It was apparent that these captains of industry were no longer able to defend their activities in the face of a groundswell of negative public opinion.

An excellent example of the marriage of institutional growth and the development of communication campaign techniques is provided by the link between US expansion to its western territories in the nineteenth century and the maturation of the railroad industry. Railroad companies had acquired vast lands in the west and needed to persuade a growing population that opportunities awaited them in these distant parts. Making aggressive use of advertising, guidebooks, excursions, pamphlets and media relations tactics, the railroads enticed settlers westward, leading to rising freight and passenger revenues. Of course, promotional material often seriously overstated claims and were in many cases blatantly fraudulent, but they do mark the continuing march toward contemporary public relations practice (see Cutlip 1995).

John D. Rockefeller, prominent among the robber barons, hired Wall Street reporter Ivy Ledbetter Lee in 1914 to take a new approach to the difficulties Rockefeller and his company, Standard Oil, were facing. Lee believed strongly that honesty and accuracy would earn the public's trust; he had demonstrated that when hired by the coal industry in 1906, setting out his Declaration of Principles to newspaper editors – principles that stressed frankness, openness, promptness and accuracy. Lee's values applied to the robber barons' dilemma marked one of those salient milestones that, precipitated by circumstances, ushered in the era of contemporary public relations practice.

Sidebar: Ivy Lee

Ivy Lee's 1906 Declaration of Principles is worth presenting here. Clearly an important milestone in the development of contemporary public relations, the Declaration succinctly articulates many of the tenets that underlie current practice. Here is the statement Lee distributed to newspaper editors, describing what his approach would be on behalf of the coal industry:

This is not a secret press bureau. All our work is done in the open. We aim to supply news. This is not an advertising agency; if you think any of our matter ought properly to go to your business office, do not use it. Our matter is accurate. Further details on any subject treated will be supplied promptly, and any editor will be assisted most cheerfully in verifying directly any statement of fact. Upon inquiry, full information will be given to any editor concerning those on whose behalf an article is sent out. In brief, our plan is, frankly and openly, on behalf of business concerns and public institutions, to supply to the press and public of the United States prompt and accurate information concerning subjects which it is of value and interest to the public to know about. Corporations and public institutions give out much information in which the news point is lost to view. Nevertheless, it is quite as important to the public to have this news as it is to the establishments themselves to give it currency. I send out only matter every detail of which I am willing to assist any editor in verifying for himself. I am always at your service for the purpose of enabling you to obtain more complete information concerning any of the subjects brought forward in my copy.

Organizations continued to grow and consolidate throughout the twentieth century, though increasingly under the influence of government-imposed restrictions and public expectations of honesty and fairness. However, organizational growth by itself would not have been sufficient to drive the need for professional public relations. In the former Soviet Union, for example, no one would dispute that organizations were large or, more accurately, that there was basically one institution – the state. Still, you would have been hard pressed to discover a rigorous public relations community in the Soviet system. There were communication programs, of course, but they were entirely one-way and confined largely to propaganda in the pejorative sense of the word. Also, there was no segmenting of publics; the public was simply viewed as an amorphous mass. So other factors beyond the growth of large institutions must have been involved in creating the need for professional public relations, and they were.

Growth of democracy

Another sweeping trend contributing to the emergence of the public relations discipline has been the *growth of democracy*. With victory in its Revolutionary War in the late eighteenth century, the nascent United States of America began a journey of enormous challenge and complexity, not always with pronounced success – witness legalized slavery, the Civil War, the nation's regrettable treatment of Native American Indians, several economic depressions, the Civil Rights struggle, and prolonged maltreatment of women as citizens. Nevertheless, despite its scars and blemishes, the United States has managed to hone a society reasonably adept at governance under consent of the governed. A load-bearing support beam of that concept is that public opinion matters. At first, the opinion of only a select few mattered – generally white men with wealth, land, or other bases for influence. Gradually, painfully slowly, legal rights such as voting and social entitlements including respect and opportunity extended to blacks, women and other groups.

The power of that public opinion is evident throughout the fabric of US society. Government officials are elected, and elections are, to a high level of confidence, fair and free from manipulation and corruption. And US citizens elect their officials at all levels and to exhaustive lengths:

president, members of Congress, governors, lieutenant governors, mayors, attorneys general, treasurers, auditors, sheriffs, city and county council members, state legislators, registers of deeds, judges, district attorneys, even coroners. They vote on bond issues and policy referenda. They vote on school and road construction projects. They vote on whether to build sports stadiums. US citizens have an extraordinary level of direct influence through the ballot box over how they are governed. Consequently, elected officials interested in retaining their positions, and those supporting or opposed to referenda, bond issues and other election ballot items, are obligated to monitor public opinion and pursue communication efforts accordingly. Clearly they must be responsive to public sentiment and pursue policies that reflect that sentiment or they will lose their positions. It was public sentiment, for example, that compelled elected officials to enact legislation reining in the excesses of the robber barons; in that case, public opinion trumped even the enormous economic influence wielded by the barons. President Franklin Roosevelt banked on supportive public opinion when he undertook drastic measures, often in contravention of constitutional checks and balances, to address the crisis of the depression in the 1930s. Public opinion strongly influenced public policy in the late 1960s and early 1970s in regard to the war in Vietnam. More recently, trends in public opinion are compelling the US government to address the issues of the environment and immigration.

As US citizens slowly discovered the power of their own opinion, and especially how that power could be coalesced and forcefully expressed, the need for systematic approaches to understanding, harnessing and employing that power precipitated the further development of public relations. During the twentieth century and beyond, public relations counselors were increasingly called upon by politicians and candidates for public office and by special-interest citizen groups. For example, examine the important contributions of public relations pioneers Ed Bernays and Doris Fleischman when they were retained by the nascent National Association for the Advancement of Colored People in the early 1920s (see Tye 1998; see also the PR Museum website listed at the conclusion of this chapter). Corporations and non-profit organizations increasingly recognized the need to understand, influence and be responsive to public opinion. Government agencies at all levels added public relations specialists (often called public information or public affairs specialists) to their staff. British scholar J. A. R. Pimlott, serving a British Home Civil Service Fellowship in the United States more than sixty years ago, observed and wrote about the interplay between US American democracy and the rapidly emerging public relations profession. "It became more necessary to communicate with the public," he noted. "It proved to be more efficient to be open than to be secretive" (1951, p. 236). He added that there was already a need for and an effort to provide professional and technical schools to prepare communication professionals to carry out public relations activities on behalf of large institutions including government agencies. He predicted presciently: "[T]here is every sign that the trend in that direction will gather speed" (p. 257). Initially, of course, there were few guidelines to direct public relations activities. As the four evolutionary models described in the first chapter suggest, early efforts ranged primarily from the press agentry to the public information models. Eventually, as professional public relations societies emerged, textbooks were published, college curricula were developed, and the discipline was increasingly recognized as a valued, vital function within any organization, the profession came into sharper focus, and that process is ongoing.

This idea of democratic government migrated around the globe, slowly at first, but with increasing velocity in the twentieth century. Western Europe, Latin America, Africa and Asia eventually eschewed absolute monarchies and dictatorships or shed the control of colonial powers to adopt democratic structures. In all cases, social, economic and cultural traditions continued to influence those structures, but a common thread underlying each newly democratic nation was the increasing importance of public opinion. With that realization have come the spread and growth of public relations, abetted by hard lessons learned and tenets forged in the United States. As with variations on democratic structures, cultural influences have shaped public relations in unique ways wherever it has established roots, fueling the need to pursue deeper understanding of those differences. Davis (2002), for example, exhaustively describes the development of public relations practice in Great Britain, suggesting it began several decades behind US emergence of the discipline but with considerably greater speed and with characteristics unique to Britain's democratic structures. Hand in hand with the growth of large institutions and the growth of democracy is another dynamic force behind the emergence of public relations, though – *increasing sophistication of the publics*.

Questions for discussion

1. What evidence have you seen in your environment and/or your experience that supports or refutes the contention that the growth of large institutions and the growth and spread of democracy are influencing the development of public relations practice?
2. In what ways would the growth of democratic structures and policies affect media relations? Community relations?
3. How would the growth of large institutions affect internal communication?

Sophisticated publics

As institutions grew and democracy became increasingly entrenched in the United States, these two trends drove another – the increasing sophistication of the publics. When society was defined by family-owned farms and small cottage industries, there was little need for education, and even literacy was limited to a select few. Of course, literacy is a complex concept, and there's no need to analyze it deeply here, but despite the obvious limitations of literacy data and the questionable validity of historical data it is a useful way to illustrate a broad trend and deduce its impact. As late as 1860, according to some resources, as much as 95 percent of the US population could be described as illiterate, and the rate for blacks was twice that of whites. Similarly, women were far more likely than men to be illiterate. By 1900, however, just about 10 percent of the population remained illiterate, though distinctions between male and female, white and black remained. Probably sparked by the Reformation in the sixteenth and seventeenth centuries, and the concurrent development and spread of the printing press, there grew a gradually increasing thirst for knowledge through reading. When combined with the growth of democracy in the fledgling United States, that mixture spawned increased interest in public debate and a desire to monitor and influence the trajectory of public affairs. Sales of books during the eighteenth and nineteenth centuries exploded, and the popularity of newspapers accelerated. Larger and larger audiences began to consume political and clerical speeches as they were published in newspapers, bulletins and books. Public libraries and public schools proliferated, and town halls in the United States became common gathering places for public debates. Perhaps the trend goes back to the fact that many early settlers in the American colonies shared a Calvinist Puritanical background that demanded literacy for the study of scriptures. So even this trend of an increasingly sophisticated public is the confluence of several related subtrends. Nevertheless, as we made the transition into the twentieth century, public opinion increasingly mattered. It mattered to governments at all levels, and it mattered to business – especially to those businesses reflecting the parallel trend of growth of large institutions. The public were voters, citizens and consumers; and, as they became more aware and engaged in democratic processes and social issues, those large institutions recognized the need for increasingly formalized communication infrastructures and processes.

As publics became increasingly interested and involved in the functions of business, government and even non-profit institutions, they themselves recognized both the growing distance between ordinary citizens and the leadership of those organizations as well as the limited effectiveness of single, disparate voices in public discourse. Consequently, with their increasing sophistication they were increasingly able to organize themselves into more well-defined social movements, adopting persuasive communication techniques to accomplish their goals. Most notable in the United States have been the civil rights movement, the women's movement and the environmental movement, but countless smaller movements and citizen organizations have been spawned as people acquired the communication tools to effect change. Like the growth of large institutions and the growth of democratic structures, increasing sophistication of the public has gained purchase around the globe. Figure 2.1 depicts the continuing fall in world illiteracy rates (based on UNESCO data), a trend

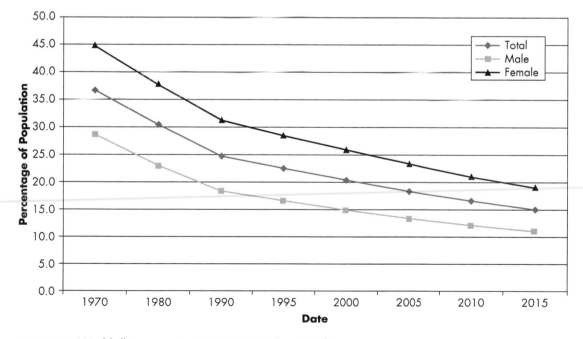

FIGURE 2.1 World illiteracy rate 1970 to 2015 (projected)

that portends increasing citizen activism and the continued need for communication frameworks that accommodate productive two-way communication between organizations and their constituencies. In the United States and in other developed nations, those frameworks have historically been crafted and lubricated by public relations professionals, though the discipline was necessarily shaped and developed by that same process. Again, it is a case of social, political, economic and other changing contexts commingling with the maturation of the public relations discipline, resulting in the current state of the practice in the United States. As you will read about in later chapters, those forces and others, such as emergence from colonialism, postwar recovery, or the integration of multiple ethnic groups into a cohesive national identity comprise additional needs and component forces necessitating the development of unique strains of public relations in other countries. However, as Figure 2.1 shows, if imperfectly, the literacy and public sophistication trend that led enormous changes in the fabric of the US and other developed nations continues to advance and should alert organizational leadership everywhere to the challenges and opportunities that follow.

Communication technology

The final trend addressed here that strongly influenced the development of public relations practice in the United States is an obvious one: technology. For thousands of years of recorded history, and until the middle of the nineteenth century, the fastest a complex message could be transmitted from one human to another was dictated by the speed of a horse. Then Samuel Morse invented the telegraph, and messages could be conveyed at basically the speed of light. What a leap forward! Of course, message diffusion was still limited because encoding and decoding messages required peculiar skills and equipment, and the coded messages had to be transmitted via a hard wire, requiring an elaborate and fragile infrastructure. Then, in the 1870s, Alexander Bell's invention eliminated the need for encoding and decoding, and his telephone was quite simple to use, so it vastly improved the human capacity to diffuse messages and share information across great distances. In the early twentieth century, Guglielmo Marconi's radio permitted the transmission of messages without the need for the extensive wire network. Soon after, a number of technologies merged to permit the addition of visual images to messages transmitted without wires – television. Then, in the late twentieth century, the Internet and the Worldwide Web propelled us into an entirely new era. To say that these developments have had a profound impact on the shaping of public relations practice would be a great understatement. The fact that this enormous leap from horses to the Internet has taken place in the blink of an eye in terms of the full spectrum of human history suggests that we had better fasten our seatbelts for whatever comes next; the velocity of technology change and advancement appears to be accelerating rather than diminishing.

   Hiebert (2005) says: "[T]he new communication technologies may well be the most conducive to democracy of all the mass media" (p. 1), and suggests that, historically, each communication technology advancement has nudged the world increasingly toward democracy. As each advancement permitted more segments of society to enter the sphere of public discourse, the competition escalated between those seeking dialogue and those seeking control. As Hiebert points out, though, as one level of communication technology becomes entrenched, there is a tendency for centralization of power in terms of control of that level. He cites the increasing monopolization of newspapers in the United States in the late nineteenth century, but adds that the advent of radio in the early twentieth century mitigated newspapers' influence. More recently, economic and legislative developments have permitted the concentration of broadcast media ownership within fewer and fewer corporate centers in the United States and elsewhere, limiting, some say, the free flow of ideas and information; but the simultaneous emergence and diffusion of the Internet is serving the same function broadcasting served earlier: providing equal access to the marketplace of ideas. With the Internet, a multitude of competing interests have the power to seek and share information and messages. Of course, the multiplicity of channels permitted by the Internet adds to clutter and confusion, and public relations professionals are adjusting to the challenge of making sense and use of this new communication technology.

Aside from the traditional advantages communication technology has given to public relations, such as word processing, desktop publishing, budgeting, and database management, there is an arena less discussed in the literature – commercial services now available to practitioners. The confluence of public relations' increasing value with the advent of sophisticated software and other digital technologies has resulted in a proliferation of services designed to expand practitioner capabilities, streamline and organize research and planning, vastly amplify communication efforts, and permit increasingly precise evaluative analysis. Here are examples of commercial organizations designed to assist public relations practitioners:

- *PR Newswire (www.prnewswire.com)* and *Business Wire (www.businesswire.com):* These are news and information distribution networks. They can distribute material electronically directly to the desks of journalists and editors all over the world, and they can target geographically, topically, or in a variety of other categories. They can also produce and distribute audio and video news releases.
- *Cision (formerly Bacon's) (http://us.cision.com/), Burrelle'sLuce (www.burrelles.com):* These companies provide a spectrum of services but specialize in media monitoring. They're often referred to as "clip services", but that is an oversimplification. They can monitor nearly all print and broadcast media as well as the Internet for information pertaining to your organization. Additionally, they can provide statistical-analysis reports and broadcast transcripts. Clips and reports can be provided in hard copy or electronically, and all services can be tailored to specific requirements. These companies also publish, in hard copy and electronically, extensive media directories listing and describing in detail print and broadcast media outlets along with background information on individual journalists to help target news distribution.
- *Vocus (www.vocus.com):* This company can provide some of the services offered by other companies listed above, but also provides software for managing public relations functions such as organizing and cataloging collateral materials, managing contacts, monitoring legislative issues, and coordinating compliance reporting.
- *VNR-1 (www.vnr1.com):* This company produces and distributes video and audio news releases for broadcast and online applications. It also produces public service announcements and business videos, coordinates satellite media tours, and conducts media training.

It is clear that technology is changing the scale of public relations activities; and, though these companies are US-based, they and others like them have global capability, and there are certain to emerge similar support organizations throughout the developed and developing world of public relations.

Before concluding, we should make the important point that historically public relations in the US traces much of its practice back to journalism (Botan 1992). As a result, public relations there makes use frequently of the mass media as a primary communication channel for public relations messages. In highly developed countries such as the US, competitive mass media, high literacy rates, broad access to the media, and competing businesses and causes mean students must master excellent writing skills to engage the important media channels effectively (Botan 1992). In addition, because public relations in the US developed under constitutionally protected freedom of the press, governmental bodies had little authority over the profession. Unlike some regions examined in this textbook, public relations in the US developed largely after national unity was achieved and did not serve as a major unity-building tool of government. Indeed, the Gillett Amendment of 1913 attempted to prohibit the government from directly practicing public relations. Today, many US citizens view governmental use of public relations, especially on behalf of a particular party, with skepticism. Nevertheless, the government is often cited as being the largest single employer of US public relations professionals (Botan 1992).

Although some may still be skeptical of governmental applications, public relations in the United States is thriving. A survey conducted by the PRSA and Bacon's Information – the 2006 State of the Profession Opinion Survey – gives students a glimpse into the status of the profession there. Nearly 15,000 practitioners believe public relations has earned a seat at the management table by demonstrating skills in media relations, community relations, marketing, and brand management, to name just a few (Public Relations News 2007). Practitioners believe their work is helping to move client organizations forward in terms of reputation, market share, and financial success/sales (PRSA 2006). The survey revealed that the median salary in public relations is $71,480 overall, with entry-level practitioners earning $26,000 and seasoned executives earning a median salary of $94,800.

Conclusion

Why does this matter? Why concern ourselves with the past? Isn't it more important to focus on the future? Of course, the future is key, especially in the study of international public relations, but we can better prepare for emerging developments if we study and understand the trajectory that brought us to where we are today. Public relations practitioners, at least in the United States, wield enormous influence; Cutlip (1995) maintains that practitioners are "providing nearly half of the mainstream media's daily content" (p. 283). That is power. That is agenda-setting potential. Above all, that is responsibility. Our discipline's history is fascinating, but it is also a mix of noble advances and embarrassing abuses. As the public relations profession continues to spread globally, and as organizations increasingly recognize its power to move and shape public opinion, our need for thoughtful consideration increases commensurately. Students pursuing public relations in reputable programs and practitioners committed to ethical professional development need to step to the fore and steer the course. A valuable lesson of history is that we can make a significant difference; we can make the world a better place. By understanding our past we can better move ahead in ways that serve our society's good. Your reading this text marks you as a contributor to that effort.

Questions for discussion

1. Consider another trend – increasing expectations for corporations to behave as responsible citizens – and suggest how that trend will affect and be affected by public relations.
2. Think about some of the important milestone events in the history of your country and speculate on the role of communication in those events. How might your country's history have been different if ethical public relations had been exercised more prominently and from a much earlier date?
3. What measures do you recommend for maintaining and even elevating the status of responsible, ethical public relations practice?

Featured biography: Edith Wilson

Sometimes our job isn't to make things look better than they are, or to spin for individual agendas at the expense of the larger institution. Sometimes our job is to make sure that the facts are out in public view, in a straightforward and truthful way with sufficient detail so that corrections can be made.

(Wilson 2007)

Since 1975, Edith Wilson has built a prestigious career in communication, public affairs and public policy. Early in her career, she served as the director and founder of a small advocacy organization called the Food Action Center in Washington, DC. She later worked for the New Transcentury Foundation and as communications director for CARE International. For a decade, she worked at Burson-Marsteller with a wide range of corporate and government clients, rising from client service manager to Senior Vice-President for International Affairs in 1993. She also served as chief of staff to United States Senator Carol Moseley Braun, worked in several political campaigns, and spent two years as a fellow at the Democratic Leadership Council's think-tank. For the past ten years, she has served in various capacities with World Bank Group, currently as a senior advisor in External Affairs.

Wilson has worked widely in public relations and public affairs, and her multicultural knowledge is extensive – though she notes that many of her colleagues at the World Bank have even more. She specializes in designing communication and public affairs programs for governments, improving governance issues such as transparency and economic reform programs, and using public diplomacy and communications to build support for development policy. She has worked with Canada, Japan, Australia, New Zealand, Kuwait, Bahrain, Indonesia, Mexico, Kenya, Cambodia, Bolivia, Morocco, and a number of European nations.

Her recent anti-corruption work with World Bank Group stands out. Wilson led an effort to raise the visibility of anti-corruption issues and position the World Bank as a leading actor against fraud. She conducted an audit of the role of communications and outreach in deterring and preventing fraud and corruption. The audit included interviews with more than seventy people, including board members, staff, regulators, and counterparts in other international financial institutions. It resulted in a detailed policy report with recommendations for communication strategy and policy that was approved by the World Bank Board of Executive Directors.

Wilson made the World Bank's media strategy for its anti-corruption work proactive and affirmative; and, to improve transparency, designed its first annual integrity report. The report included detailed investigation and sanction data, and was distributed via news conferences, news releases, presentations, and the Web in three languages. The report provided concerned publics such as shareholder governments, developing world partners, donors, beneficiaries, and companies working with World Bank Group with information they had never had before.

Wilson also believes in the importance of internal communication, an area in which she worked with private-sector clients while at Burson-Marsteller and more recently at the World Bank. During a recent corporate governance crisis at the World Bank, new internal communication tools such as comment boards allowed free expression of staff views and proved vital to resolution of the crisis. Although ignored at first, communication exploded during the controversy, with management *and* staff updating each other with realtime information in external websites as well as on the Intranet.

Wilson analyzed the impact of the events from a communication perspective. "Everything [was] being reported by everyone. The combination produced an unprecedented explosion of information, data, issue monitoring and citizen opinion the likes of which our staid, formal, top-down, sheltered, bureaucratic institution had never imagined. . . . This is just one manifestation of the changing world of communication and of the new social media to which we must help our clients and colleagues adapt, and that we as professionals must learn to ride as a surfer rides a wave, or be crushed by the wave as it bears down on us."

Wilson has been a frequent speaker and presenter during her career, and sometimes a teacher. She has also been an adjunct professor at the Elliot School for International Studies of George Washington University. More recently, she gave the keynote speech at the 4th Annual World Public Relations Festival in South Africa in June 2007. Her speech there focused on the role of communication in making development sustainable. She discussed six areas: understanding stakeholder and two-way communication; the importance of explaining problems before introducing solutions; organizing and coordinating government communications efforts adequately and professionally; the need for countries seeking to establish an international identity to focus all outward communication on a core message; the unfortunate disconnect between public-sector communication needs and private-sector communication and public relations capacity; and the role of communication in good governance, including the need for humility, courage and integrity in practice.

Throughout her career, Wilson has stressed the importance of research, strategy and creativity. She has broad experience with developing communication programs. Most importantly, she embodies a commitment to the public relations profession. As she said to the communications professionals gathered in Cape Town: "I believe, passionately, that communication is a vital part of making development work more sustainable, that it contributes to good governance and can be a force against bad governance – and I also believe passionately that what you do every day matters so much to making this a better world."

Recommended websites

The Arthur Page Society   http://www.awpagesociety.com/

History of propaganda   http://www.historians.org/projects/GIRoundtable/Propaganda/Propaganda4.htm

Ivy Ledbetter Lee's papers   http://infoshare1.princeton.edu/libraries/firestone/rbsc/finding_aids/lee.html

Museum of Public Relations   http://www.prmuseum.com/

References

Botan, C., 1992. International public relations: critique and reformulation. *Public Relations Review*, 18 (2), pp. 149–59.

Cutlip, S. M., 1995. *Public Relations History: From the 17th to the 20th Century*. Hillsdale, NJ: Lawrence Erlbaum.

Cutlip, S. M., Center, A. H. and Broom, G. M., 2000. *Effective Public Relations*, 8th edn. Upper Saddle River, NJ: Prentice Hall.

Davis, A., 2002. *Public Relations Democracy: Public Relations, Politics and the Mass Media in Britain*. Manchester/Hillsdale, NJ: Manchester University Press/Lawrence Erlbaum.

Hiebert, R. E., 2005. Commentary: new technologies, public relations, and democracy. *Public Relations Review*, 31, pp. 1–9.

Hoy, P., Raaz, O. and Wehmeier, S., 2006. From facts to stories or from stories to facts? Analyzing public relations history in public relations textbooks. *Public Relations Review*, 33, pp. 191–200.

Pimlott, J. A. R., 1951. *Public Relations and American Democracy*. Princeton, NJ: Princeton University Press.

Seitel, F. P., 2004. *The Practice of Public Relations*, 9th edn. Upper Saddle River, NJ: Prentice Hall.

Tye, L., 1998. *The Father of Spin: The Birth of Public Relations*. New York: Crown Publishers.

Wilcox, D. L. and Cameron, G. T., 2007. *Public Relations Strategies and Tactics*, 8th edn. New York: Pearson.

Wilson, E. R., 2007. How communications helps make development sustainable and why it matters to good governance, [keynote speech] 4th Annual World Public Relations Festival. Cape Town, South Africa, 14 May.

Chapter 3

Theories and methods

Summary

At the outset, the reader is cautioned that this chapter does not attempt to present some sort of unifying theory to explain or describe international public relations practice, nor does it prescribe a regimen of appropriate research methods suitable for expanding the body of knowledge in the discipline. Rather, the chapter will profile existing research, identifying, categorizing and organizing the rather eclectic library of properties available to the scholar or practitioner trying to explore one or another sub-category of this arena. We begin with a survey of theories that have informed research into various aspects of international public relations practice, then identify principal research methods that scholars have employed to move the discipline forward. We conclude with recommendations for additional vectors of research that should be considered in our profession's continuing quest to expand our understanding of the discipline.

Chapter goals

- Have a clear understanding of the theories involved in international public relations.
- Have a working knowledge of the primary research methods involved in the field.
- Apply the theories and research methods to their unique international assignments.
- Utilize what was learned in this chapter to contribute to future progression of the discipline.

Theory

The term "theory" in a public relations context evokes a variety of emotional responses. To the consummate scholar it generates visions of deep, penetrating truths about the underpinning explanations for human and mass-communication behaviors, purposes and consequences, along with opportunities for groundbreaking research. To the practitioner and to many students it conjures up feelings ranging from trembling fear, through head-spinning bewilderment, to judgments of absolutely pointless academic exercises. Perhaps for this text a middle ground is most appropriate. Theory, while extremely useful in describing, explaining and predicting the cause–effect relationships that matter in public relations, must be tempered by the recognition that communication is not physics. We can develop and apply general concepts and central tendencies to the academic and applied dimensions of public relations, but absolutes will prove elusive. That is evident in the generally accepted practice of using $p < .05$ (probability that result could have been produced by chance; in this case, less than a 5 percent likelihood) as the standard level of significance in quantitative communication research; such a loose standard would be vastly unacceptable in the hard sciences such as medical research. If it were not so, our practice would be far simpler – we could *guarantee* results because we would be able to predict with certainty the outcomes resulting from our communication efforts. Similarly, absolutes in international public relations practice may prove even more elusive, given the additional complexities that have an impact on our efforts. Still, the use of theory in international public relations research provides a cohesive and purposeful infrastructure that permits meaningful comparisons as well as construction of multifaceted models to aid in the conduct of our practice.

Hill and Dixon (2006) describe a model of communication perspectives that comprises a series of concentric circles of widening communication contexts. The center circle relates to intrapersonal communication, the next circle interpersonal communication, then small group, followed successively by organizational, intercultural, public, mass, and finally international communication. "To communicate effectively in any context," the authors maintain, "one must understand all of the communication events occurring in the smaller circles subsumed by that context's circle" (Hill and Dixon 2006, p. 67). In that respect, an understanding of international public relations, either theoretical or practical, requires a broad base of knowledge in each of those communication components, and the opportunities for research are rich, unfettered by artificially imposed parameters. Existing literature does not disappoint us; scholars have taken a wide array of approaches to "peeling the onion" of international public relations.

For this chapter, a review was made of articles appearing in several (but not all) leading English-language refereed journals in our discipline, as well as of chapters in key texts dedicated exclusively to international public relations. Analysis of these properties suggests that each can be described as belonging to at least one of four basic categories: (1) theoretically based research; (2) case studies (with or without theoretical underpinnings); (3) country studies (again, with or without theoretical underpinnings); and (4) "think" pieces. Each category is useful in its own right. The categories are not necessarily mutually exclusive because a number of articles and chapters can arguably be listed in more than one category. However, for expedience and structure, the four categories serve their purpose as a useful way to think about the body of literature.

The first category, theoretically based reports, forms the important foundation for any study of international public relations. As in other facets of public relations, researchers in this field often borrow theories from other disciplines, generally the social sciences, but occasionally from business and even from other fields within communication. Often, too, researchers combine more than one theory to test or demonstrate a multifaceted concept. Case studies can incorporate theoretical underpinnings or merely provide a detailed description of an episode or issue in order to derive important lessons learned; both approaches are useful for expanding our understanding of international practice. Moss and DeSanto (2002), for example, assembled a collection of international public relations cases, each one explained within the context of at least one theoretical concept.

Parkinson and Ekachai (2006), on the other hand, dedicate nearly three-quarters of their international public relations text to case studies that focus on describing, analyzing and critiquing the campaign process, emphasizing principles of practice rather than abstract theory. Both case-study approaches are extremely useful, either for researchers exploring new avenues for investigation or for practitioners trying to understand more fully the emerging environment facing us.

The library of country studies continues to grow; and, because culture, national infrastructure and other factors are constantly changing, even existing country studies must regularly be refreshed, so there will be an ongoing need to generate these valuable additions to the international public relations body of knowledge. The challenge will be to develop appropriate and consistent approaches to country-study research and reporting, which we shall address later in this chapter.

The fourth category, "think" pieces, is unique and often defies classification. Essentially essays based on extensive observation, analysis and rumination, unspoken permission to publish in this category is and ought to remain a limited privilege extended to only the most erudite of scholars.

The most common theory employed in international public relations research – at least in the books and journals reviewed – is the one concerning the well-recognized *four evolutionary models* of public relations development and practice: press agentry, public information, two-way asymmetric and two-way symmetric. This model, initially proposed by Grunig and Hunt (1984), has been a mainstay of public relations research since proposed and continues to serve as a guiding principle in the international realm. The list of researchers who have incorporated the Grunig–Hunt model into their international research is substantial: B. Lee (2004), Bardhan (2003), Huang (2001), Kim and Hong (1998), Grunig *et al.* (1995), Culbertson (1996), Chen (1996), Ekachai and Komolsevin (1996), Sriramesh (1996), Alanazi (1996), González and Akel (1996), Freitag (2004), and Ogbondah and Amiso (2004), to name several prominent examples, have tested international public relations waters using the Grunig–Hunt model.

Results are varied and illustrate a central challenge to international research: the fact that the overwhelming bulk of public relations research originated in the United States. That means, in most cases, that the theories we have come to rely upon in our understanding of the practice are based on research involving US populations, US media, and so on. In fact, populations involved in surveys, focus groups and other human-subject research are frequently selected from extremely narrow segments hardly representative of a global or even regional population. That is not to fault those pioneering researchers, but does suggest the need for caution in making assumptions upon which research efforts are built; those assumptions may prove invalid, diminishing the accuracy of research findings. To their credit, researchers in international public relations appear to be using US-developed theories in ways that test and refine those theories in international settings.

An excellent example is the work done by Van Leuven in his effort to characterize the evolution of public relations practice in Singapore and Malaysia. Rather than the Grunig–Hunt four-phase model, Van Leuven (1996) observed and described a three-phase development of the practice beginning with nation-building, then market development, and finally regional interdependence. As with the four-phase model, though, he found elements of all three phases to be operative as he conducted his research, and further suggested that the three phases he described may eventually blend into something resembling the Grunig–Hunt model: "Many attributes of public relations management as defined by US theory are barely discernible in newly industrializing economies until the regional interdependence phase" (Van Leuven 1996, p. 220). Van Leuven and Pratt (1996) expanded these findings to include Africa, noting that "[F]ormulations of public relations concepts, even normative and idealized ones, cannot be transferred automatically across cultures without first accounting for levels of societal development, whether public relations is regarded as a relationship-building process or a communication campaign or program, and assumptions about the nature of the relationships being established" (Van Leuven and Pratt 1996, p. 104). Venkateswaran (2004) reinforced Van Leuven's findings in Malaysia, confirming the risks of simply overlaying US-based theories across other cultures. She concluded: "Public relations theories within the United States are molded within a framework of Western ideals of democracy and a free-market economy," adding, "Just as products (goods, services, and ideas) cannot be marketed in a standardized fashion throughout the world, there is no such thing as standardized international public relations" (Venkateswaran 2004, p. 405). Like Van Leuven, Holtzhausen *et al.* (2003) tested the applicability of the symmetric/asymmetric models among South African public relations practitioners and found that the models fell short of describing the nature of practice there; rather, economic, social and political realities informed the state of the practice.

This does not mean that early theoretical public relations efforts in the United States must be abandoned, but it does suggest that those findings need to be tested and refined in international contexts. The same could be said for communication research in general at both the human and mass-media levels. And it could be said of any theories, principles or constructs developed, for practical reasons, within narrowly segmented populations. The watchword is caution.

Like the Grunig–Hunt evolutionary model, Broom and Smith's (1979) description of four *roles* typically carried out by public relations practitioners – expert prescriber, communication facilitator, problem-solving process facilitator, and communication technician – has provided grist for international public relations research. Dozier (1983) and many others have proposed collapsing the first three roles into simply a management role. Though, again, based on research solely on US subjects, role theory offers a valuable starting point for comparison in other cultures, and researchers have taken that approach. Coombs and his colleagues (1994) employed role theory to compare practice in Austria, Norway and the United States, finding a greater emphasis on professionalism (management orientation) in Austria than in the other two countries – reflective, the authors maintain, of a higher cultural regard for training and education. Piekos and Einsiedel (1990) followed a similar approach to examine public relations practice in Canada, finding substantial similarities to US practice. In both projects, though, the researchers began by assuming the accuracy and efficacy of the descriptive roles Broom and Smith initially described.

Excellence theory (Dozier *et al.* 1995) has spawned several research projects and is likely to prove fruitful in continuing studies, given its broad base of principles, each of which could constitute a vector for research. Developed initially as a "global theory" describing generic principles – normative principles, according to the authors – that would constitute the way public relations practice *should* reflect the highest order of values, researchers have subsequently tested the theory in specific settings to help describe and define practice in those settings. Properties addressing excellence theory provide a model for the maturation of public relations theory in international contexts. As originally conceived, and based on an examination of public relations practice only in the United States, Canada and the United Kingdom, there were fourteen fundamental principles in three general areas: (1) empowerment of the public relations function; (2) communicator roles; and (3) organization of the communication function and its relationship to other management functions. Verčič *et al.* (1996) subsequently tested excellence theory in Slovenia, consolidating the original fourteen principles to nine, and finding the nature of practice there to have been evolving rapidly, with inconclusive results for several of the principles.

Borrowing theories from other realms of communication has been employed in international research, and the approach is likely to yield worthwhile results. Chay-Nemeth (2001) borrowed *theories regarding publics* and their formation from the rhetorical component to study the issue of HIV/AIDS in Thailand, and Dutta-Bergman (2005) invoked *Habermas's theory addressing communicative action*, applying it to a critical analysis of the rhetoric of civil society. He specifically examines narratives from the Philippines, Chile and Nicaragua, concluding, remarkably, that a dialogic approach to relationship-building in those cases "serves the élite and silences the poor" (Dutta-Bergman 2005, p. 287). Furthermore Wan and Pfau (2004) and their colleagues tested *inoculation theory* to determine if an inoculation strategy is appropriate for communication campaigns in Taiwan. The classic *co-orientation model* of communication was applied by Park (2003) to test attitudes and opinions about professional standards in South Korea, comparing views of government and corporate practitioners. Taylor (2000) chose a "Neighborliness" communication campaign in Malaysia to explore the efficacy of a *relational communication* approach to persuasive public relations efforts.

An important area of public relations research has been *crisis communication*; it appears that the field has attracted researchers in the international public relations area, too. Ihlen (2002) seized upon an unfortunate episode faced by Mercedes-Benz when a journalist test-driving one of their automobiles experienced a rollover. The researcher combined *rhetorical, crisis-response* and *coherence* theories to profile the auto company's unfolding approach to restoring their venerable reputation. The work cited earlier by Wan and Pfau (2004) involving inoculation theory was conducted within a context of crisis communication. B. K. Lee (2005) tested Hong Kong participants' reactions to an imaginary aircraft crash to test and refine a path-analysis model designed to predict the effect of an organization's acceptance of responsibility for a crisis. And the work cited previously by Ogbondah and Amiso (2004) involving Shell Petroleum's role in and response to civil unrest in the Niger Delta region of Nigeria helps us understand the suitability of traditional Western crisis-response approaches in this unique setting.

Perennial communication theory favorites *agenda-setting* and *propaganda* have also surfaced in international public relations research. Henderson (2005) studied a New Zealand communication campaign concerning genetic engineering using a complex combination of theories that collectively provide an agenda-setting paradigm. L'Etang and Muruli (2004) used the qualities of propaganda to profile British government communication efforts in colonial Kenya.

Van Leuven and Pratt (1996) offer several propositions that could easily be developed into theories, basing these propositions on their study of public relations practice in Malaysia and Singapore. They propose four hypotheses, though their research did not directly test them:

1. The more urban the society and the more developed its communication infrastructure, the greater the use of mass media for public communication campaigns. The converse, they say, holds as well, adding that rural, dispersed societies will employ campaigns incorporating interpersonal communication strategies along with field agents.
2. The greater the level of market development, the more likely it is that government ministries will use private-sector advertising and public relations specialists as campaign advisors. Further, advanced market development will predict campaigns conceptualized as persuasion programs.
3. The more stable the government, the more tolerant it is of dissent, and the more attentive government officials are to public opinion. Government officials in more stable governments will

be more responsive to pressure groups and citizen involvement pertinent to nation-building campaigns.

4. As literacy increases and the number of commonly spoken languages/dialects decreases, public communication campaigns will make greater use of media channels rather than field agents.

Moving outside communication, theories from other disciplines are migrating into public relations and offer a deep pool of possibilities. Discussed in greater depth in Chapter 4, the arena of *cultural syndromes* has informed several important research efforts in international public relations. Verčič *et al.* (1996), cited earlier for their work in excellence theory, also incorporated the cultural syndromes of individualism/collectivism, power distance, interpersonal trust, uncertainty avoidance, and masculinity/femininity into their research in Slovenia. Likewise, Sriramesh and Yungwook (1999) employed those syndromes in their meta-analysis of research into public relations practice in India, Japan and South Korea. The researchers identified, among other findings, pronounced evidence that a strong collectivist nature present in these cultures influenced public relations practice in a variety of ways. Similarly, Rhee (2005), marrying excellence theory with cultural syndromes, opined that public relations practice in South Korea has been favorably influenced not only by a bent for collectivism but also by an embrace of elements of Confucianism.

Symbolic politics was the theoretical paradigm chosen by Saxer (1993), taking a page from political science research. He makes the case that in German-speaking countries public relations scholars take a macro-level or sociological view toward the discipline as opposed to the meso-level or management view espoused in the United States. Curtin and Gaither (2006) borrowed the *Circuit of Culture Model*, developed by Britain's Open University, to describe the complex process of creating meaning within various cultural contexts. The scholars deeply analyzed the long-term effort led by the World Health Organization to eradicate smallpox as a case study to link the model to international public relations, especially to the challenge of segmenting and describing publics in the fluid dynamics affecting and affected by cultural processes.

A theoretical construct likely to have far-reaching application in international public relations is the concept of *public diplomacy*, a theory Freitag (2004) used in examining the evolving state of public relations practice in Peru. He applies earlier research linking the propaganda model of public diplomacy to the press agentry model of public relations, the public information model of public relations to the self-portrayal approach, the two-way asymmetric model of public relations to the information approach to public diplomacy, and the two-way symmetric model of public relations to the dialogue model of public diplomacy.

Having sampled theoretical directions scholars have taken in exploring international public relations, perhaps we can summarize principles to help guide continued research. Here are recommended guidelines:

1. Accumulate as broad an understanding as possible regarding existing international public relations literature. Whether you're preparing to write a paper for a graduate or advanced undergraduate course, or developing a proposal for a graduate thesis or dissertation, explore what is out there.
2. Once you have identified the basic issue or problem you plan to research, and have tentatively identified theories and concepts that might help illuminate the issue or problem, spread the net wider and review literature in other disciplines that might address those theories and concepts. Start with basic public relations, then try other areas within communication, then

explore linked fields such as marketing and advertising. Finally, look into related issues in the social and behavioral sciences. The ease of mining electronic databases makes this task far less onerous than it once was.

3. Do not be married to a theory from the start, unwilling to recognize the greater applicability of another theory you uncover during the investigative process. At the same time, avoid discarding theories haphazardly when you discover another interesting theory. That is a difficult balance to strike; but, if you move forward deliberately and thoughtfully, your instincts will serve you well. Also, look for opportunities to let two or more intersecting theories help focus your ensuing research efforts. Doing so can help build on existing research but explore new and exciting prospects.

4. Avoid making unwarranted assumptions when applying, testing or refining an existing theory in a new cultural setting. Trace your chosen theory or theories back to their origins. Determine what assumptions guided theory development and the setting in which those theories were developed. Are those assumptions culture-specific? Were initial findings affected by unique cultural factors? If so, that does not negate the usefulness of the theory in your new cultural setting, but it does dictate the need for you to avoid the mistake of presuming that assumptions can be applied universally. Instead, make testing those assumptions part of your research.

Methods

Conducting public relations research is challenging enough without the added burden of adjusting for cultural peculiarities. Still, scholars have continued to follow both traditional and innovative paths to discovery, with their efforts pointing the way toward ever improving efficiency and effectiveness. The student or practitioner can consult the spectrum of published research to identify many methodical approaches that have guided research to date. In this section, we shall examine those methods, discussing advantages, disadvantages and challenges for each in so far as they can be part of international public research. For student scholars, this will help them consider and choose appropriate methods to pursue research questions and test hypotheses. For practitioners, this will aid in weighing and analyzing their research preparatory to international and/or cross-cultural encounters.

Some of the barriers facing international public relations researchers apply across the spectrum of methods and need to be part of the calculus in designing research projects for academic or applied purposes. Here are the basics:

1. *Language:* This is an obvious one, but it goes well beyond simply being able to communicate. Language is a barrier to potential collaboration. It presents challenges in the preparation of research materials such as survey instruments. Direct, literal translations may not adequately convey the essential, accurate meaning of a message.

2. *Culture:* Beyond language, differences in communication styles, outlined in the next chapter, can often be a barrier to shared meaning. Direct questioning through in-depth interviews may be appropriate in some cultures but cause discomfort in others. Focus groups, interviews and surveys might be affected by the perceived relationship between participants.

3. *Fit:* Methods the researcher is accustomed to in her culture may not be relevant in another culture. For example, content analysis procedures appropriate for analyzing major media in

highly developed nations could prove useless when folk media in developing cultures need to be analyzed.

4. *Expense and time:* Conducting research by "remote control" – remaining in one's home country while trying to conduct an online survey or analyze media in other countries is far from ideal. Yet the cost of spending extended periods in or making frequent trips to another country may be prohibitive for most researchers. Scholars in industrialized nations clearly have an advantage here, and that presents a problem: scholars in less developed nations are marginalized in their efforts to contribute to the body of knowledge in international public relations, so their voices are less likely to be part of the fabric of understanding, rendering it less comprehensive.

Now let us take a look at individual research methods, explore how they have been used in international public relations research, and consider issues affecting those methods beginning with quantitative methods and progressing through qualitative approaches. The student or practitioner needs to become familiar with the proper application of each method, not only to conduct meaningful and valid research, but also to evaluate intelligently the validity and rigor of existing research. Of course, this is not a "how-to" text; you will need to take separate courses and study other texts such as that by Stacks (2002) (which guides much of the following commentary) to acquire those research skills.

Surveys

This is the most common quantitative method, and probably the most common method overall used for public relations research, and its popularity carries over into the realm of international public relations research. Stacks explains the distinction between polls and surveys, pointing out that polls are shallow, quick-look assessments at a very limited number of items or variables, while surveys are typically longer and more complex and attempt to get deeper into attitudes and opinions. In either case, researchers generally employ *sampling* to permit surveying a small but representative group, then use statistical analysis to gauge profiles of the larger census the sample represents. This is probably the first place international researchers encounter difficulties. Especially in less developed nations, obtaining full census listings, from which samples can be drawn, may be a challenge. Phone listings, addresses, census data, and so on, may be unavailable or unreliable, rendering samples less than ideal. Some international researchers have often resorted to convenience and snowball sampling, exasperated at attempts to apply the more reliable and valid techniques they had become accustomed to using. Acknowledging limitations associated with these less than desirable sampling techniques is important; but, regrettably, not all published research recognizes its own limitations. For example, some studies use convenience sampling, then apply inferential statistical analysis to the results. As Stacks points out: "Your goal is to establish within a certain degree of confidence that your results represent true differences as found in the population under study and were not the result of other things nor were they randomly found in the population from which you sampled" (Stacks 2002, p. 240). The researcher applying inferential statistical analysis to a convenience sample, then claiming 95 percent confidence that the findings are significant and applicable to the population from which the sample was drawn is being disingenuous. Be on guard when reviewing literature for your campaign or research project. If you cannot legitimately project your sample survey results to the greater population, you are conducting informal, not formal research. That may be necessary because of limitations, but you owe it to your readers to acknowledge it.

Language, naturally, may be an issue for researchers working in nations other than their own. Translations of materials such as survey instruments should be done – or at least reviewed – by native speakers to capture nuances and idioms correctly. Be prepared to adjust your survey items to fit more comfortably into the language of your survey participants. Consider cultural differences as well. For example, in a male-dominated culture, you may encounter difficulties in getting women to participate in a survey. Fit is a consideration here as well. The online survey you design for your US or Canadian research is likely to be inappropriate in Bolivia or Ghana where computer access is limited. And expense may be an obstacle in nations where postal costs render a mail survey prohibitive.

Still, researchers have successfully overcome these obstacles and have accumulated valuable survey data in international public relations. One can also conduct important research within one's own culture and/or nation. For example, identifying your own culture's central tendencies along the spectra of the various cultural syndromes described in the next chapter would be extremely useful. Similarly, gauging your own culture's stereotypical views of other cultures would be illuminating. In either case, no translation or undue expense would be required.

Questions for discussion

1. Consult a good text on research methods, such as the Stacks text cited. Follow the steps required for conducting a valid survey. For each step, consider the challenges that might come into play in a culture other than your own regarding that step. For example, if the step requires conducting a door-to-door survey in a particular community, think of that community as being in a region very different from your own and suggest conditions that might make carrying out the survey difficult.
2. Suggest and outline two or three basic research ideas for survey projects you could conduct within your own culture and nation that would still contribute to the international public relations body of knowledge.
3. Pick a country other than your own in which you would like to conduct international public relations research. Do you think an online survey would be more or less successful in that country compared to your own? Why?

Content analysis

Quantitative content analysis is a method absent from international public relations research, though qualitative content analysis appears in several instances. Chay-Nemeth (2001) used qualitative content analysis to help describe the various publics relevant to the AIDS situation in Thailand, and Freitag (2002) examined media coverage of the 2000–1 Ford–Firestone crisis as it appeared in media and other reports in seventeen nations. Certainly, the combination of language and access conspires to hamper efforts to conduct meaningful quantitative content analysis in which, for example, various nations' coverage of a single issue is compared. Further, cultural differences manifested in unique styles of journalism may render statistical comparisons difficult. For example, would it be appropriate or useful to compare source use between major newspapers in Saudi Arabia with those in Turkey and Venezuela? Newspapers in Turkey are fairly independent, those in Saudi Arabia are under government guidance, and some of those in Venezuela are likely to be associated with special interests. Still, doing so may help us understand more deeply what those differing journalistic styles look like, and would provide benchmark data to monitor change.

As with surveys, researchers need to exercise caution through every step of the content analysis process. If a quantitative approach is chosen, researchers need to think through issues such as defining manifest or latent content to be examined, identifying a unit of analysis that applies logically to all media to be coded, defining category systems that work across the spectrum of media, and, as with surveys, executing a sampling procedure that permits inferential statistical analysis across all cultures and nations from which coded media are drawn. Then, actual coding must stand up to scrutiny. Can individual coders reliably code material from multiple cultures, languages and/or nations? How did you train coders to deal with those differences? How did you test coder reliability? Even if the analysis is being done in only one country, but the research intent is to illuminate some dimension of international public relations practice, the research report must make the case that the content analysis was conducted in a manner suitable for the unique style of journalism in that setting. For example, recall in the first chapter the comparison of how people from different cultures interpreted the same photograph; similarly, if graphic content is to be analyzed, describe how you take into account those differing interpretive styles.

Experiments

Many have called the experiment the "queen" of research methods because of the high degree of control exercised in its conduct. The unique structure of the experiment permits the researcher to establish the critical element of causality – not merely correlation. Stacks laments that public relations researchers seldom employ experiments, probably because they lack time or expertise, or because public relations research has tended toward the descriptive and qualitative. At its most rudimentary, an experiment involves a carefully controlled independent variable acting on an equally carefully measured dependent variable; the dependent variable must, of course, undergo that careful measurement before *and* after treatment by the independent variable. The purpose is to predict the effect of the independent variable on the dependent variable. Although experiments are ordinarily associated with highly controlled laboratory conditions, a *field* experiment may be conducted in a natural setting – such as the offices of a public relations firm or a public relations classroom.

Several international public relations researchers have employed the experiment to plumb one or another theory. Kaman Lee (2005) did so to develop her crisis-response path analysis for publics in Hong Kong, and Taylor (2000) used a quasi-experimental design in evaluating the effectiveness of Malaysia's neighborliness campaign; but, as Stacks says, few public relations scholars or practitioners have ventured into this territory. It is time for that shortcoming to be addressed.

The experimental method has clear applications to international public relations research. In an applied setting, consider testing messages, collateral material design, website navigability, strategic and tactical plans, and so on. In the theoretical realm, consider comparing the effect of various fear-appeal levels among different cultures, third-person effect in a nation previously untested for this phenomenon, or media richness theory among employees of a multinational firm. As in surveying, random selection of participants remains essential to permit generalization of results to the greater population represented by the sample. In addition, strict control is required to ensure that any effect on the dependent variable can be attributed only to the independent variable and not to extraneous factors. Because comparison of results is central to experimental design, a control group – one that receives a different treatment or no treatment at all – is equally essential.

Qualitative

Qualitative methods for international public relations research could typically include focus groups, depth interviews, and participant-observation. Historical research and case studies would also fall into this category. Just because these are generally considered "informal" research methods does not imply that they require any less rigor. In fact, the demand for rigor is intensified by the risk of permitting personal bias, preconceptions and unwarranted assumptions to taint the research process with these methods. Although results from these methods cannot be projected to the greater population, and no generalizations may be legitimately drawn, the value in these methods lies in their ability to add richness and context to the body of knowledge. For this reason, the scholar or practitioner who combines formal, quantitative methods with qualitative approaches to understand a public relations issue – called *triangulating* – is truly adding depth and texture to our body of knowledge.

Focus groups are essentially group interviews conducted by a single moderator. Focus groups are generally five or six people to as many as fifteen – fewer or more than that creates challenges. Participants should be carefully selected and screened, and should be somewhat homogenous for each individual session. The moderator should be well experienced and familiar with the issue to be discussed. The moderator should be skilled at facilitating free flow of thoughts and ideas, but should also be adept at staying on point. The researcher should learn everything there is to learn about preparing for, conducting and analyzing focus groups – there are abundant sources. Transcripts of focus groups are analyzed for thematic content, and can be enormously valuable in preparing subsequent survey instruments to gauge quantitatively strengths of attitudes and opinions narratively expressed during the focus groups. It is generally wise to conduct more than one focus group to research a principle or issue within a given population, stratifying each focus group appropriately, such as by demographic categories.

Individual depth interviews, like focus groups, must be carefully planned. The researcher must consider the key questions to be addressed and the best order in which to ask them. Of course, selecting whom to interview must be carefully considered as well. The interviewer must maintain control of the interview, but not in an obtrusive way that prevents the interviewee from offering thoughtful introspection and thorough responses. The researcher must begin with a thorough knowledge of the topic to be discussed; this facilitates following any useful path the interviewee chooses within the parameters of the research project's aim. The researcher will likely need to interview anywhere from ten to several dozen subjects using this method, and should follow a well-structured procedure for each interview and for each project. Van Leuven (1996), for example, conducted twenty depth interviews in Malaysia and Singapore to develop his three-phase nation-building model of public relations. Obviously, the time demand for this method of research is considerable, and conducting face-to-face interviews in one or more countries other than your own presents special challenges. Hocking *et al.* (2003) recommend a five-step process:

1. Develop the research question.
2. Select interviewees (consider *snowball* sampling in which one interviewee recommends other appropriate interviewees, who do likewise).

3. Schedule the interviews.
4. Conduct carefully formatted interviews.
5. Analyze data gathered.

Analyzing the data means mining data using historical, rhetorical-critical, or content-analysis techniques. There is computer software available that can assist with this sort of qualitative analysis of transcribed data.

Participant-observer research is appropriate and useful for describing and analyzing people's behavior, routines and strategies for adapting to new situations. You could also ascertain and identify roles people play in given settings, deducing unwritten rules of behavior. All these areas would be beneficial to understanding the dynamics of international public relations encounters. In participant-observer research, the researcher still needs to follow a highly structured procedure including a literature review, theory explication, articulation of research questions, and so on. The researcher must also determine appropriate ways to record information as objectively as possible while participating in the group (formal or informal) being studied. Collected data may then be organized for analysis and reporting, perhaps as empirical models for comparison with theoretical models. If observation is being made of a culture other than your own, there is high risk that behaviors may be misinterpreted, so you will need to be armed with a thorough understanding of that culture, especially its communication patterns.

Historical research, of course, could include depth interviews with figures who participated in or closely observed the events being studied, but it would also certainly include exhaustive examination of secondary artifacts such as documents, archives, testimony, and so on. The challenge with historical research is to locate and analyze all relevant primary and secondary resources, with emphasis on the former, then distill and assemble all the data in a coherent narrative that conveys clearly the key principles and points that emerge from the data. Historical context is useful in international public relations because understanding how the practice is conducted in any culture is aided by an understanding of the historical context that spawned the practice. For example, we discussed in Chapter 2 how historical forces conspired to shape public relations as it emerged in the United States, and in Chapter 11 you will read about the influence of Latin America's colonial experience on practice there today.

A special type of historical research is called the case study. A case study may entail direct observation of an event, institution or person by the researcher, even as a participant observer, or it can involve depth interviews with participants before, during and/or after the event or about the person/institution. In either situation, observations and interviews would be bolstered by examination of artifacts associated with the subject of study – artifacts such as news releases and other public relations products, media coverage, memos, reports, meeting minutes or transcripts, and so on. International public relations case studies do not always include theoretical underpinnings, but resting the study on a theoretical foundation certainly enhances the value of the report – theoretical conclusions can be projected into other situations to aid practitioners in successfully navigating similar situations and permit scholars to expand our theoretical understanding of the discipline.

Country studies

A final research method we shall cover here that is, perhaps, unique to the study of international public relations is the country study. In this context, the purpose of a country study is to reveal to the scholar or practitioner all aspects of the country that are likely to have an impact on public relations. This might inform planning for a communication campaign, development of a practical or academic seminar, or preparing for a short- or long-term assignment to the country. What should a country study address? Think of all those aspects of a country or culture that could affect communication from the interpersonal to the mass level, including international communication. That would certainly include relevant legal and ethical issues, infrastructure such as telecommunications and transportation, literacy, communication patterns, and a host of other factors. But how do you organize such a huge undertaking? Fortunately, Zaharna (2001) has created a purposeful and manageable framework for just such a project. Here are the areas she recommends covering in a country study for public relations purposes:

Political
- What is the basic political structure? Democratic, authoritarian, or totalitarian?
- Who holds the decision-making power?
- How strong are the political institutions?
- What role do formal institutions play in the decision-making process?
- Are political divisions apparent? What are their relationships to each other?
- What role does the public play in decision-making?
- Where does your client fit in the political power structure?

Economic
- What is the basic economic structure?
- What is the level of economic development?
- How centralized is the economic decision-making power?
- What economic power does the government hold? The private sector?
- What is the relationship between private and public sector?
- Where does your client fit in the economic structure?

Mass media
- What is the level of mass-media development?
- What different media outlets exist?
- What is the relationship between the mass media and the political power base?
- What is the relationship between the mass media and the economic power base?
- What medium appears to be most frequently used or prevalent?
- What credibility do the media hold with the public?
- How frequently does your client rely on the mass media? For what purposes?

Infrastructure
- What is the level of development?
- What is the level of communication? Is it reliable?
- Is transportation involved in the project? Are the roads or public transportation reliable?
- What technological capabilities exist? Are they reliable?
- Is steady, reliable electricity a factor?
- What precautions or contingency plans does your client have if infrastructure is a factor?

Legal structure
- Is the "rule of law" written?

- What is the relationship between the legal system and the political power base?
- Are there specific legal codes dealing with communication activities?
- Do you need a legal advisor? Do you have a legal advisor?

Social structure
- What is the dominant religion?
- What is the general level of education? Literacy rate?
- Is race or ethnicity a factor? How homogeneous or heterogeneous is the population?
- How do the people tend to "divide" themselves? Race? Religion? Ethnicity?
- How geographically dispersed is the population? Rural? Urban?

To these items we should add cultural syndromes described in detail in Chapter 4, and throughout the outline the writer should focus on each item's potential impact on public relations practice. Obviously, nearly every item is likely to change over time, some more rapidly than others. Consequently, even though a country study has already been published, any report more than five years old is liable to require updating, so scholars are encouraged to monitor the inventory of these public relations country studies to ensure shelf lives remain current.

We have looked at theoretical approaches to international public relations research and at some of the primary methods in evidence and appropriate to that research. There are certainly more theories and additional research methods suitable for this area of study; but, for the advanced student, this survey provides a launch point for your own research projects or for purposeful and productive research in anticipation of international assignments. Despite the many challenges that face international public relations researchers, important work is being completed and published, and scholars are improving steadily in both focused theoretical frameworks and methods that stand up to scrutiny. Perhaps most importantly, rapidly growing interest around the globe is leading to fruitful partnerships across countries and cultures, permitting innovative collaborative efforts to be brought to bear on this difficult area of public relations. This is a promising trend. Thanks to the continuing expansion of Worldwide Web access, such collaboration is feasible even at student level, and that augurs well for the future of the profession.

Questions for discussion

1. Using Zaharna's framework for country studies, which of the items do you anticipate would likely experience rapid change? Which would change more slowly? Explain why.
2. What might be some of the cultural pitfalls that could affect a researcher's conduct of a case study in a culture other than his/her own? How might those pitfalls be overcome?
3. As a student, describe a participant-observer research project you could engage in that would pertain to international public relations. Describe the group you would study. Describe the patterns, routines or other phenomena you would investigate. How would you ensure that your participation would not affect your findings?

Featured biography: Lisa Bottle

Lisa Bottle is Vice-President of Corporate Communications with Goodrich Corporation, a leading global supplier of aerospace and defense systems equipment, based in Charlotte, North Carolina, USA. As the company's global corporate communications professional, Bottle is responsible for all internal and external communications for Goodrich.

Throughout her career, Bottle has often encountered cultural differences while working across international borders. For example, while working in France, Bottle, along with other British and North American employees, had a difficult time adjusting to the way meetings were conducted with their French colleagues. Bottle describes instances where the French would have "sidebar" conversations in meetings, which she found distracting and somewhat offensive. She said it was only when she went through business culture awareness training that she learned that in "Anglo-Saxon" business cultures there is typically a much more linear approach to doing business. She reflects about this lesson: "We learned that in the French business culture it was quite normal for several activity 'bubbles' to be going on simultaneously, so having sidebar conversations at meetings was totally acceptable." The training enlightened Bottle, along with her British and North American counterparts, and as a result they were able to work together more effectively with their French colleagues.

Language and the flattening effect of the Internet are two challenges Bottle has encountered when conducting public relations in an international setting. Bottle maintains that cultural differences and sensitivities must always be considered when planning and conducting public relations campaigns. No matter how small or local the communications issue may be, the Internet enables messages to be immediately available to anyone around the world. Consequently, the translation of Goodrich's communications into multiple languages is a significant aspect of Bottle's work because it aids in ensuring an appropriate sense and tone of the communications for the company's international audiences.

Bottle notes that Goodrich's publics are not typical consumers, but rather other large corporations, governments and international partnerships, which creates unique cross-cultural challenges. According to Bottle: "Other corporations and governments have their own unique cultures, which frankly can be more difficult to navigate than when dealing with different countries!" She further explains that taking the time to understand different influences and cultural sensitivities is essential when crafting international communications.

Having spent the majority of her career in the aerospace industry, Bottle has worked primarily with media in Europe and North America. Based on her experience, she has found public relations practice in the UK and the US to be very similar. However, she has noticed differences between the two countries in the area of general business practice. "When I moved to the US in 2002, I found the working environment to be faster-paced than in the UK, with higher expectations of levels of responsiveness. However, as the 'Blackberry' culture has pervaded the business world, I see less and less difference between the two countries."

Bottle has experienced a number of personal benefits from her international public relations practice. She highlights the opportunity to travel and experience new cultures, as well as the exhilaration she feels as a result of the challenging nature of international work. She also says her internationalism has provided her with "a realization that, although there are many differences between countries and cultures around the world, we're ultimately all part of the same human family".

Recommended websites

International Communication Association   http://www.icahdq.org/

Association for Education in Journalism and Mass Communication   http://www.aejmc.org/

Council of Communication Associations   http://www.councilcomm.org/

International Association for Media and Communication Research   http://iamcr.org/

The Pew Research Center for the People and for the Press   http://people-press.org/

The Web Journal of Mass Communication Research http://www.scripps.ohiou.edu/wjmcr/

MIT Communications Forum http://web.mit.edu/comm-forum/index.html

The Public Relations Resource Centre http://praxis.massey.ac.nz/home.html

Global Alliance for Public Relations and Communication Management http://www.globalpr.org/

Institute of Public Relations – PR Research and Education http://www.instituteforpr.org/

References

Alanazi, A., 1996. PR in the Middle East: the case of Saudi Arabia. In H. Culbertson and N. Chen, eds. *International Public Relations: A Comparative Analysis*. Mahwah, NJ: Lawrence Erlbaum, pp. 239–56.

Bardhan, N., 2003. Rupturing PR metanarratives: the example of India. *Journal of Public Relations Research*, 15 (3), pp. 225–48.

Broom, G. M. and Smith, G. D., 1979. Testing the practitioner's impact on clients. *Public Relations Review*, 5 (3), pp. 47–59.

Chay-Nemeth, C., 2001. Revisiting publics: a critical archaeology of publics in the Thai HIV/AIDS issue. *Journal of Public Relations Research*, 13 (2), pp. 127–61.

Chen, N., 1996. PR in China: the introduction and development of an occupational field. In H. Culbertson and N. Chen, eds. *International Public Relations: A Comparative Analysis*. Mahwah, NJ: Erlbaum, pp. 121–53.

Coombs, W. T., Holladay, S., Hasenauer, G. and Signitzer, B., 1994. A comparative analysis of international public relations: identification and interpretation of similarities and differences between professionalization in Austria, Norway, and the United States. *Journal of Public Relations Research*, 6 (1), pp. 23–39.

Culbertson, H., 1996. Introduction. *International Public Relations: A Comparative Analysis*. Mahwah, NJ: Erlbaum, pp. 1–13.

Curtin, P. A. and Gaither, T. K., 2006. Contested notions of issue identity in international public relations: a case study. *Journal of Public Relations Research*, 18 (1), pp. 67–89.

Dozier, D. M., 1983. Toward a reconciliation of "role conflict" in public relations research. Western Communication Educators Conference. Fullerton, Calif.

Dozier, D. M., Grunig, L. A. and Grunig, J. E., 1995. *Manager's Guide to Excellence in Public Relations and Communication Management*. Mahwah, NJ: Lawrence Erlbaum.

Dutta-Bergman, M. J., 2005. Civil society and public relations: not so civil after all. *Journal of Public Relations Research*, 17 (3), pp. 267–89.

Ekachai, D. and Komolsevin, R., 1996. PR in Thailand: its functions and practitioners' roles. In H. Culbertson and N. Chen, eds. *International Public Relations: A Comparative Analysis*. Mahwah, NJ: Erlbaum, pp. 155–70.

Freitag, A. R., 2002. International media coverage of the Firestone tire recall. *Journal of Communication Management*, 6 (3), pp. 239–56.

Freitag, A. R., 2004. Peru's Fujimori: the campaign to sell the administration's neoliberal policies. In D. J. Tilson and E. C. Alozie, eds. *Toward the Common Good: Perspectives in International Public Relations*. New York: Allyn & Bacon, pp. 83–101, 215–38.

González, H. and Akel, D., 1996. Elections and earth matters: PR in Costa Rica. In H. Culbertson and N. Chen, eds. *International Public Relations: A Comparative Analysis*. Mahwah, NJ: Erlbaum, pp. 257–72.

Grunig, J. and Hunt, T., 1984. *Managing Public Relations*. New York: Holt, Rinehart & Winston.

Grunig, J. *et al.*, 1995. Models of PR in an international setting. *Journal of Public Relations Research*, 7 (3), pp. 163–86.

Henderson, A., 2005. Activism in "paradise": identity management in a public relations campaign against genetic engineering. *Journal of Public Relations Research*, 17 (2), pp. 117–37.

Hill, L. and Dixon, L., 2006. The intercultural communication context: preparation for international public relations. In M. Parkinson and D. Ekachai, eds. *International and Intercultural Public Relations: A Campaign Case Approach.* New York: Allyn & Bacon.

Hocking, J. E., Stacks, D. W. and McDermott, S. D., 2003. *Communication Research*, 3rd edn, New York: Pearson Education.

Holtzhausen, D. R., Petersen, B. K. and Tindall, N. T. J., 2003. Exploding the myth of the symmetrical/asymmetrical dichotomy: public relations models in the new South Africa. *Journal of Public Relations Research*, 15 (4), pp. 305–41.

Huang, Y. H., 2001. Values of PR: effects on organization–public relationships mediating conflict resolution. *Journal of Public Relations Research*, 13 (4), pp. 265–301.

Ihlen, Ø., 2002. Defending the Mercedes A-Class: combining and changing crisis-response strategies. *Journal of Public Relations Research*, 14 (3), pp. 185–206.

Kim, Y. and Hong, L. C., 1998. Craft and professional models of PR and their relation to job satisfaction among Korean PR practitioners. *Journal of Public Relations Research*, 10 (3), pp. 155–75.

Lee, B., 2004. Corporate image examined in a Chinese-based context: a study of a young educated public in Hong Kong. *Journal of Public Relations Research*, 16 (1), pp. 1–34.

Lee, B. K., 2005. Hong Kong consumers' evaluation in an airline crash: a path model analysis. *Journal of Public Relations Research*, 17 (4), pp. 363–91.

L'Etang, J. and Muruli, G., 2004. Public relations, decolonization, and democracy: the case of Kenya. In D. J. Tilson and E. C. Alozie, eds. *Toward the Common Good: Perspectives in International Public Relations*. New York: Allyn & Bacon, pp. 215–38.

Moss, D. and DeSanto, B., 2002. *Public Relations Cases: International Perspectives*. New York: Routledge.

Ogbondah, C. W. and Amiso, G., 2004. Fire at Nigeria's treasure base: an analysis of Shell Petroleum's public relations strategies in the wake of the Niger Delta crisis. In D. J. Tilson and E. C. Alozie, eds. *Toward the Common Good: Perspectives in International Public Relations*. New York: Allyn & Bacon, pp. 255–78.

Park, J., 2003. Discrepancy between Korean government and corporate practitioners regarding professional standards in public relations: a co-orientation approach. *Journal of Public Relations Research*, 15 (3), pp. 249–75.

Parkinson, M. and Ekachai, D., 2006. *International and Intercultural Public Relations: A Campaign Case Approach*. New York: Allyn & Bacon.

Piekos, J. M. and Einsiedel, E. F., 1990. Roles and program evaluation techniques among Canadian public relations practitioners. *Public Relations Research Annual*, 2, pp. 95–113.

Rhee, Y., 2005. Global public relations: a cross-cultural study of the excellence theory in South Korea. *Journal of Public Relations Research*, 14 (3), pp. 159–84.

Saxer, U., 1993. Public relations and symbolic politics. *Journal of Public Relations Research*, 5 (2), pp. 127–51.

Sriramesh, K., 1996. Power distance and PR: an ethnographic study of southern Indian organizations. In H. Culbertson and N. Chen, eds. *International Public Relations: A Comparative Analysis*. Mahwah, NJ: Lawrence Erlbaum, pp. 171–90.

Sriramesh, K. and Yungwook, K., 1999. Public relations in three Asian cultures: an analysis. *Journal of Public Relations Research*, 11 (4), pp. 271–92.

Stacks, D. W., 2002. *Primer of Public Relations Research*. New York: The Guilford Press.

Taylor, M., 2000. Toward a public relations approach to nation building. *Journal of Public Relations Research*, 12 (2), pp. 179–219.

Van Leuven, J. K., 1996. Public relations in South East Asia from nation-building campaigns to regional interdependence. In H. Culbertson and N. Chen, eds. *International Public Relations: A Comparative Analysis*. Mahwah, NJ: Lawrence Erlbaum, pp. 207–22.

Van Leuven, J. K. and Pratt, C. B., 1996. Public relations' role: realities in Asia and in Africa south of the Sahara. In H. Culbertson and N. Chen, eds. *International Public Relations: A Comparative Analysis*. Mahwah, NJ: Lawrence Erlbaum, pp. 93–105.

Venkateswaran, A., 2004. The evolving face of public relations in Malaysia. In D. J. Tilson and E. C. Alozie, eds. *Toward the Common Good: Perspectives in International Public Relations*. New York: Allyn & Bacon, pp. 405–25.

Verčič, D., Grunig, L. A. and Grunig, J. E., 1996. Global and specific principles of public relations: evidence from Slovenia. In H. Culbertson and N. Chen, eds. *International Public Relations: A Comparative Analysis*. Mahwah, NJ: Lawrence Erlbaum, pp. 31–65.

Wan, H. H. and Pfau, M., 2004. The relative effectiveness of inoculation, bolstering, and combined approaches in crisis communication. *Journal of Public Relations Research*, 16 (3), pp. 301–28.

Zaharna, R. S., 2001. "Inawareness" approach to international public relations. *Public Relations Review*, 27, pp. 135–48.

Part 2

Now that we have explored the foundations of public relations and, we hope, presented fundamental principles that undergird its history and current practice, a second task before we begin a survey of regional practice is to seek guidelines that permit meaningful comparisons and examinations of those regions. As we have seen in the first three chapters, public relations influences and is influenced by its environment including especially the social, political, economic and cultural contexts in which it has and continues to develop. The next three chapters, therefore, aim to address that challenge from several directions.

First, we shall look at the important cultural dynamics that affect human communication, particularly at the individual and small-group levels. As public relations evolves from its roots in mass media and publicity to a much more relationship-based discipline, understanding the nuances of human communication and behavior in various cultural settings will aid our ability to anticipate and navigate differences. Second, we shall examine some of the overarching structural characteristics that may vary from one nation or culture to another, and that can and should affect public relations planning and activity. We shall focus on media systems, legal systems and ethics. For both cultural and structural issues we shall provide examples of how differences in these areas might affect public relations practice.

This section of the text concludes with a sweeping survey of global practice that illustrates the manifestation of unique cultural, social, political and economic contexts. Within that broad milieu we shall take a look at public relations education and professional associations. We shall also discuss variances in public views of our profession. By the end of the next three chapters, you will be primed and ready to begin a purposeful and illuminating trek around the world to discover and gauge similarities and differences in practice in the world's major regions.

Chapter 4

Comparative cultural metrics

Summary

The chapter examines comparative cultural metrics essential in comparing one culture to another. Major and secondary metrics are discussed. Major comparative metrics such as high-context versus low-context, individualism versus collectivism, power distance, uncertainty avoidance, masculinity–femininity, and relationship versus task orientation are presented in detail. Secondary cultural metrics such as chronemics, proxemics, haptics, occulesics and kenisics are discussed. The point is that understanding how to gauge their differences from one culture to another will aid the practitioner in adjusting communication activities to account for those differences.

Chapter goals

- Stress the importance of understanding cultural differences in the international public relations profession.
- Examine major comparative cultural metrics.
- Describe secondary cultural metrics.
- Show the application of cultural metrics in comparing different cultures.

Shortly before noon on a pleasant sunny day, a young man is standing on the university campus near the central cafeteria. Casually but neatly dressed, he holds several textbooks from his college classes under one arm. As a young lady, an attractive co-ed, is about to pass by, he hesitantly asks her, "Do you know what time it is?" "A few minutes before noon," she casually replies after glancing at her watch, then she continues her purposeful steps toward a meeting with a few friends. "Glad that's all he wanted," she thinks as she moves on. "How could she be so rude and inconsiderate," the young man is thinking. "Guess I really must have blown it."

What happened in this brief encounter was a catastrophic communication failure precipitated by the two parties' inability to overcome a major cultural barrier. You see, the young man was an exchange student from Jordan now on a campus in the southeastern United States. The young lady was a US American, probably from the southeast. The cultural barrier was one concerning high-context versus low-context communication. We shall talk about it in detail later, but basically it is a phenomenon pertaining to the degree to which context matters in communication. In the United States, a low-context communication culture, people say what they mean and mean what they say; communication context matters little, and pure content is paramount. As Carolina Panthers football coach John Fox is noted for saying: "It is what it is". The young Jordanian, on the other hand, comes from a culture where messages are typically more subtle, less direct. He's accustomed to framing meaning using many more cues than simply the words he utters or writes. The circumstances in which the communication is conveyed, the relationship between the interlocutors, even history all play a part in adding meaning to the message. In the case of our exchange student, he was taking the following into consideration:

- It was around noon – lunchtime.
- He was standing near the entrance to the cafeteria. The young lady was in one of his large lecture classes that morning.
- On arriving for the past several meetings of that class, he had said "good morning" to her, and she had smiled back.
- He was aware that she passed by this spot each day around this time.
- He had a wristwatch.
- He carefully phrased his question, asking not "What time is it?" but rather "Do you know what time it is?" He, of course, knew exactly what time it was.

The young man, without thinking much about it, had taken all this into account and, because he was fairly new to the United States and had not yet acquired a fuller understanding of US communication patterns, assumed incorrectly that the young lady would just as quickly process all these cues to deduce his true message: he was asking her to join him for lunch. He would never be so bold as to pose the question so directly, however. Further, he mistook her smile and eye contact in response to his friendly morning greetings to mean that she was inviting his interest, though she considered it merely a polite but perfunctory response. As a result, he is slightly offended and perhaps has his ego bruised a bit, he is prepared to tell his Jordanian family and friends about the rudeness of US Americans, and the young lady may have missed an opportunity to share a pleasant meal with a new friend while broadening her awareness of other cultures. All these unfortunate results from a simple but failed exchange.

Now transpose this minor breakdown to any number of exchanges across cultures but among corporate executives, non-profit administrators, government officials, and the consequences quickly escalate. Yet alarmingly few people in these important positions truly understand the depth and extent of cultural differences as they affect human communication. In this chapter we shall discuss a host of major and secondary metrics scholars use to compare one culture to another. Applying these techniques to public relations, which after all is applied communication, can aid the practitioner in becoming the organization's expert on the delicate art of encoding and decoding messages accurately when they cross cultural boundaries, whether *inter*nationally or *intra*nationally. A word of caution, however. It would be profoundly naïve to consider that every individual in every culture acts and reacts in accordance with a standard descriptive profile for that culture. On the contrary, wide variances are likely. Still, there is obvious merit in gaining an appreciation of the central tendencies in regard to communication patterns for a culture to aid in anticipating and planning for barriers that might limit shared meaning, whether in professional or personal exchanges. In addition, it has been said that the last thing a fish notices is water. That describes our inability to recognize and analyze our own culture; we're so immersed in it, usually from birth, that we fail to think of our own communication patterns as part of a cultural framework. By exploring a series of metrics useful in discerning one set of cultural patterns from another, we can also conduct an introspective analysis of our own patterns; and that, in turn, will aid us in preparing for cross-cultural encounters.

Major cultural metrics

Let us begin by describing the major comparative metrics scholars have identified and refined, and that aid us in discerning challenges to communicating between and among cultures. These major metrics are tremendously important in public relations contexts because they address both communication patterns and relationship-building. Although they concern interpersonal communication and relationships, organizational efforts in those areas are really a sum of the many individual exchanges involved. Consequently, public relations practitioners who understand and apply these metrics are more likely to enjoy success in their public relations efforts on behalf of their organizations or clients.

High-context versus low-context

To some extent, all communication takes part of its meaning from the context in which it occurs. The phrase "I don't like that idea" has one meaning when uttered by the CEO in the boardroom to a mid-level manager who has just presented her approach to a major issue, but has a different level of meaning if it is a husband and wife discussing where to go out for dinner. Yet, as the story of the Jordanian exchange student illustrates at the beginning of this chapter, there are clearly degrees to which various cultures place importance on contextual elements. Edward Hall distinguished between cultures on the high-versus-low-context scale this way:

> A high-context (HC) communication or message is one in which most of the information is either in the physical context or is internalized in the person, while very little is in the coded, explicit, transmitted part of the message. A low-context (LC) communication is just the opposite; i.e., the mass of information is vested in the explicit code.

> (Hall 1976, p. 79)

As Neuliep points out, "No culture exists exclusively on one end of the continuum," and the concept is best-understood as a spectrum along which various cultures will exhibit central tendencies among their populations (2000, p. 41).

Low context   High context

The context within which a communication occurs, and that can contribute to the richness of the communication's meaning, can be made up of a variety of factors. Those might include the setting and circumstances, the relationship between interlocutors (such as subordinate–superior), and the attitudes and opinions that might color how a message is encoded and decoded. It follows logically that the greater the accumulation of shared experiences between communicators, the greater the clarity that can be achieved with very economical exchanges. Hall even says communication in a high-context situation can be quite efficient and effective. The challenge for the public relations practitioner is to build relationships, even across cultures, that permit that level of exchange. Often, of course, public relations planners are developing campaigns and programs aimed toward audiences with whom no or only a limited relationship has been established. In those cases, the practitioner must explore contextual patterns within that audience's culture and incorporate those patterns into campaign and program materials and components.

On an interpersonal basis, one characteristic of high-context cultures that may make low-context communicators uncomfortable is the acceptability of silence. Braithwaite says silence in a high-context culture conveys understanding or even deference, particularly in communication between two participants of unequal status (1990, pp. 321–8). In contrast, silence in a low-context culture might indicate disagreement, apathy, or even ignorance.

Further, people in high-context cultures tend to link the communication with the person, while people in a low-context culture are often at pains to separate the communication from the individual. A low-context culture, such as the United States, tends to focus on the action or behavior in isolation. "This isn't about you," a boss may say. "It's about the mistake you made. Don't take it personally." A person from a high-context culture, such as Japan, could not help but take such an admonition extremely personally. A boss more sensitive to the high-context syndrome would have taken a far more indirect approach, infused with courtesy, respect and discretion, knowing that the effect of subtlety would be adequate to convey the meaning accurately.

Sidebar: Mixed messages

Here is a scenario between a low-context public relations manager and a high-context subordinate. Ms Jones is from the Chicago headquarters of the PR firm. She has a meeting in Japan with a Japanese account representative, Mr Hydeki, managing a campaign for the US-based firm. Also participating in the meeting are several Japanese members of the program team:

Ms Jones: We have reviewed the plan you submitted and we like your overall approaches to the issue. However, we are not clear on the timeline for many of the plan's elements. Can you clarify for me when you expect to implement each of the elements?

Mr Hydeki: We shall certainly consider that carefully.

Ms Jones: Yes, I'm certain you will. However, our client will expect a more definitive timeline for the project. Can you at least provide start dates and end dates for the major parts of the plan?

Mr Hydeki: Perhaps it would be best if I discussed that with you in the coming weeks.

Ms Jones: We shall, of course, be communicating a lot in the coming weeks and months, but I return to the United States tomorrow and I really need to have some solid dates to give to the client.

Mr Hydeki: Yes, I can see where that would be useful.

Ms Jones (becoming exasperated): Look, I see Ms Fujama is heading the trade show effort. Ms Fujama, what is the status on preparations for that?

Ms Fujama smiles, looks to Mr Hydeki, then looks down at the table, but remains silent.

Ms Jones: Look, I have to provide some dates to the client. How about if I tell the client that we expect to launch the program in early March, and that the entire plan will unfold over the following six months?

Mr Hydeki: If that seems good to you.

In this exchange, Ms Jones failed to pick up on Mr Hydeki's reluctance to provide specific dates. That could have stemmed from a number of causes: perhaps circumstances are not yet clear on that issue; perhaps there is some disagreement among team members on date – in this culture, such a disagreement would never have surfaced in the presence of the manager from headquarters. On the other hand, Mr Hydeki failed to realize that Ms Jones's low-context culture would require a more definitive response. Ms Jones also violated a cultural syndrome ("power distance" – described later in this chapter) that prevented Ms Fujama from speaking out in a meeting at which her supervisor was, in her cultural view, the only person who could appropriately speak.

Table 4.1 shows how Lustig and Koester (1999, p. 111) distinguish characteristics that might differ (again, in terms of central tendencies – not necessarily for all members of a culture). By "ingroups" the authors refer to members of a group who are familiar with embedded rules and rituals and who, therefore, are able to communicate more efficiently using non-verbal cues and contexts. Pilots, for example, can communicate with air traffic controllers with an incredibly efficient set of codes necessary to coordinate a very complex function; "outgroups" would have great difficulty interpreting the full meaning of the succinct radio messages that transpire within such a group. In high-context cultures, members of ingroups and outgroups are quickly exposed. Similarly, commitments and loyalty among ingroup members in a high-context culture are strong and enduring. Public relations practitioners from a low-context culture will encounter considerable difficulty in

TABLE 4.1 Characteristics of high- and low-context cultures

High-context cultures	Low-context cultures
Covert and implicit	Overt and explicit
Messages internalized	Messages plainly coded
Much nonverbal coding	Details verbalized
Reactions reserved	Reactions on the surface
Distinct ingroups and outgroups	Flexible ingroups and outgroups
Strong interpersonal bonds	Fragile interpersonal bonds
Commitment high	Commitment low
Time open and flexible	Time highly organized

penetrating those loyalties. Loyalties and commitments in low-context cultures, in contrast, are quickly made and easily broken.

Individualism versus collectivism

A cultural syndrome related to high-context versus low-context communication, but going beyond the communication dimension, is *individualism versus collectivism*. This dimension can be viewed as the degree to which individualism is valued in a society and bears directly on the nature of business relationships and encounters public relations practitioners are likely to experience. In any society, people must interact with each other, depend upon each other and support each other if the society is to flourish. At the same time, individuals have responsibilities in seeing to their own needs. The challenge is to find a balance between individual responsibilities and rights on the one hand, and collective well-being on the other. Some societies stress the collective responsibilities over individual identity, while others revere and encourage individual achievement. Societal norms will dictate the degree to which allegiance belongs to one's group or to one's self. This is one of four extremely useful indicators identified and described by cultural scholar Geert Hofstede as the result of a massive survey of more than 100,000 IBM employees in more than seventy countries. The other indicators are power distance, uncertainty avoidance, and masculinity–femininity. We shall explore each of Hofstede's metrics, but let us first take a closer look at individualism–collectivism (Hofstede 1980; Hofstede 1991).

As with high-versus-low-context communication patterns, individualism can be assessed along a spectrum. In fact, Hofstede created what he called an individualism index, or IDV, to gauge cultures along the spectrum. His survey results suggest that Australia, Belgium, the Netherlands and the United States can be placed at the extreme individualism end of the spectrum, while Indonesia, Venezuela and Guatemala can be found at the extreme collectivism end. In the middle of Hofstede's IDV one would find countries such as Finland, Austria, Spain and Israel. Keep two things in mind: first, this survey was conducted more than twenty-five years ago and, second, Hofstede used all completed surveys from each country to derive a single mean index for the entire country. Societies are constantly changing, and the velocity of change, even at the cultural level, has been rapid indeed during the past twenty-five years. Additionally, it would be a mistake to assume that each citizen of any country would predictably adhere to the mean on this or any of Hofstede's indices. Rather, these metrics are useful only in so far as they suggest central tendencies.

People in individualistic societies are generally expected to take care of themselves, perhaps of their immediate families, but little personal responsibility extends to the broader society, except that which is required by law or by other provisions. In collectivist societies, on the other hand, individual comfort and achievement are subjugated to a greater good – perhaps that of the extended family, the community, or the society as a whole. Someone from a collectivist society, such as Ghana in Western Africa, might be confused by what he or she might regard as callous disregard for societal welfare upon observing some behaviors in an individualistic culture. That Ghanaian, seeing the plight of the homeless in the United States, would wonder why other members of the community do not take the homeless in and see to their needs until they can fend for themselves; the Ghanaian would not understand why members of the society would permit such a shameful blot to persist. US citizens, in contrast, would argue that homelessness is generally the consequence of individual choices for which only the individual bears responsibility; providing support from their own bounty would only reinforce and encourage further poor individual choices, individual-istically oriented persons might say.

Not surprisingly, economic development appears to be a predictor of this metric. Those nations more economically developed tend to be more individualistic, and poorer nations tend to be more collectivist. What cannot be determined from Hofstede's data is whether individualism results from economic prosperity or contributes to it.

Based on Hofstede's IDV metric, an Australian practitioner, steeped in his or her own culture, would feel very comfortable speaking out, even disagreeing with other members of the group, but someone from a collectivist culture such as Pakistan would be quite taken aback by such public disloyalty to the group. The practitioner steeped in individualism will be more likely to take risks, be assertive, be direct. The practitioner from a collectivist paradigm will favor harmony and will avoid personal recognition in favor of collective credit. The individualist practitioner was prob-ably taught from childhood to be independent, to speak his or her mind, to ask questions boldly. As Reynolds and Valentine (2004) point out, major life decisions are on the shoulders of the indi-vidual: career choice, selection of marriage partner, child-raising style. They point out that those in individualist cultures accept the premise that relationships (or contracts) can be broken when-ever one party chooses to do so. Such arrangements, including friendships, can be severed when they interfere with personal needs or goals. Individualist people prize privacy and avoid crowding, but collectivist people are not fazed by crowded situations such as on subway trains or in elevators. Individualist practitioners focus on the outcome; collectivist practitioners focus on the process. Individualist practitioners separate business relationships from personal relationships; collectivist practitioners see the two areas of relationships as seamless. Do you see where conducting public relations activities, even at the research and planning stages, would be a challenge when these cul-tural barriers are crossed?

Not only are the two viewpoints different, but also each views the other in a negative light. In collectivist cultures, focusing on personal needs and gratification is considered self-centered and short-sighted because such an approach fails to take advantage of the group's broader perspective. A collectivist executive from Japan might look with disfavor on a US-style office setting where each worker has his or her own office space; the executive would see more wisdom in a setting where office workers sit around large tables to permit collaboration. Similarly, that executive would wonder why US office workers, at the end of the day, would simply head home individually rather than socialize for a time with colleagues – often the time when new ideas are spawned.

Table 4.2 shows Reynolds and Valentine's summary of differences between individualist and collectivist cultures (2004, p. 11). The authors offer recommendations for bridging these differences. They say that those from individualist societies, working with collectivist counterparts, need to allow time for relationship-building, focus on the context of the relationship, and aim to arrive at decisions consensually. They should also be prepared for indirect communication patterns (accepting, for example, brief periods of silence). They should avoid asking direct questions and must exercise more patience than they may be accustomed to. Those from a collectivist background working with individualist counterparts, on the other hand, should make an effort to focus on the transaction, introducing facts, data and logic into the process. They should concentrate on more direct communication and respect their counterparts' time constraints. Perhaps if both camps are able to make these concessions, the effort will be successful.

Power distance

Simply put, *power distance* is the degree to which the culture believes power should be distributed among its members. Low power-distance cultures, such as those in Austria, Israel and Denmark, according to Hofstede's data, minimize social and class inequalities, while high power-distance cultures, such as Malaysia, Guatemala, Panama and the Philippines, would be more acutely aware of those differences. Consequently, a Danish public relations manager might become frustrated when attempts to engage subordinates from Malaysia in a participatory problem-solving process fail to elicit their involvement; the Malaysians' cultural profile would not ordinarily permit them to participate on an equal plane with their boss.

TABLE 4.2 Characteristics of individualistic and collectivist cultures

Individualist cultures	Collectivist cultures
Transaction oriented (focus on results)	Relationship oriented (focus on process)
Short-term gains	Long-term growth
Emphasis on content (facts, numbers, ratios, statistics)	Emphasis on context (experience, intuition, the relationship)
Reliance on linear reasoning	Reliance on circular reasoning
Independent	Interdependent
Competitive, decision-driven	Collaborative, consensual
Direct, explicit communication	Indirect, circuitous communication
Personal accountability	Protection of "face"
Private offices	Open office plan
Linear time, impatient	Flexible time, patient

Different cultures ascribe status and social power to some people for varying reasons. In one culture, age and education might create wider chasms between social power strata. In another culture, gender and physical strength might be the measures of merit. In still others, wealth, birth order, family pedigree, occupation or a number of other attributes might matter in determining the status factor in a relationship between people. Hofstede says power distance is not an assessment of the appropriateness of social stratification – cultures with high power distance, high stratification, do not consider that stratification right or wrong, just the way it is. In fact, high power distance cultures often simply view distinct stratification as a source of order and predictability. Low power-distance cultures, however, see the lack of stratification as diminishing class inequalities. Low power-distance cultures are more comfortable questioning or even challenging authority and circumventing hierarchical organizational structures. Not surprisingly, population size appears to be a predictor of power distance. Greater population complicates social order and leads to complexity in rules and formalities in social and professional settings. The other two predictors of power distance are latitude and wealth.

As with individualism/collectivism, Hofstede created a metric on which to gauge cultures in terms of power distance, calling it the PDI. The scale, though dated, is helpful in creating a descriptive profile for nations that Hofstede's research plumbed. Children in high-PDI cultures are expected to be obedient to their parents and other elders, and students are to be respectful of their instructors. In the professional setting, high-PDI cultures, predictably, would exhibit more autocratic and directive decision-making processes, and subordinates would be uncomfortable without close supervision and guidance. Low-PDI employees, on the other hand, would value their independence and would expect to be part of the decision-making process. Low power-distance cultures avoid, for the most part, privileges and status symbols, while in high power-distance cultures those same privileges and status symbols are expected. In low power-distance cultures, public relations practitioners can expect less formal professional and social encounters, but should be prepared, in high power-distance cultures, to experience highly formalized, even ritualized expectations in the same settings.

Uncertainty avoidance

Uncertainty avoidance, the third of Hofstede's cultural syndromes, is a little more abstract and challenging to understand. It refers to the ability of members of a culture to adapt to change and cope with uncertainty. Put another way, it is the degree to which members can accept ambiguity. Once again, Hofstede has given us an index – the UAI – on which to gauge cultures. According to Hofstede, high UAI nations – Greece, Portugal, Belgium and others – prefer homeostasis and order, expecting societal compliance with extensive rules and regulations. Dissent and deviation are frowned upon, and members are resistant to change. Neither do they take risks. People in high UAI cultures often will appear busy, and can even behave aggressively when facing down threatened uncertainty and change. Gudykunst and Kim (1997) would say a high UAI, already indicating discomfort in the face of change, would further complicate cross-cultural encounters because the encounter itself would constitute change; the high UAI individual would prefer to avoid such encounters. The process of overcoming that reluctance to seek cross-cultural encounters would lend itself to the spiral of cross-cultural competence described in Chapter 1 – the frequency and accumulation of cross-cultural experiences would commensurately reduce the uncertainty associated with those experiences, leading to diminishing discomfort with each experience.

To some extent, Hofstede says, everyone shares a degree of uncertainty and preference for the familiar. However, he says, a culture's laws, religion and other factors contribute to socialization of its members in a collective context. Those in a culture characterized by a low UAI accept life's events as they come and do not require extensive systems of rules governing behavior or processes; they accept what is different and tolerate ideas that veer even radically from the norm. High UAI cultures prefer rules and do not care much for ideas that deviate from the norm; they're averse to risk. High UAI cultures are more apt to be ruled by the clock, while low UAI cultures are less concerned with time and deadlines. A practitioner from a low UAI culture might observe a high UAI practitioner and judge that person to be unnecessarily emotional, even aggressive, but the high UAI practitioner might judge the low UAI counterpart to be not just easygoing but lazy. The low UAI practitioner might seem unconventional and unpredictable to the high UAI practitioner, and the latter might appear rigid and strictly controlled to the former.

Though, again, the data set is old, Hofstede found Anglo and Nordic cultures, along with Singapore, to reflect low UAI tendencies. That is, they have relatively little anxiety in unfamiliar situations. Latin Europe, Latin America, Korea and Japan, on the other hand, score high – they would be less comfortable in unfamiliar situations. Predictors of UAI are less pronounced than for individualism/collectivism and power distance. Cultures advanced in modernization seem to tolerate change more readily, to be comfortable with less rigid rule systems and to prefer to resolve conflict through negotiation.

Masculinity–femininity

The last of Hofstede's four metrics is *masculinity–femininity*, and it refers simply to the degree to which a culture values achievement and assertiveness (masculinity) or nurturing and social support (femininity). Does the culture revere accumulation of wealth (masculinity) or compassion and care for others (femininity)? Hofstede's data permitted him to create a masculinity index (MAS) and suggested Japan, Austria, Venezuela, Italy, Switzerland and Mexico led the high MAS list, while Sweden, Norway, the Netherlands, Denmark and (then) Yugoslavia scored lowest, indicating strong tendencies toward traits associated with femininity.

It would be easy to become confused by what seems to be sexist language associated with this metric, so perhaps an *achievement-nurturance* scale would be more appropriate these days, but the body of literature is well established using Hofstede's nomenclature, so scholars and practitioners generally accept the original designation. Additionally, those in low MAS cultures (high femininity) are more likely to value gender equality and less socially prescriptive gender roles. Preference for nurturance in those cultures extends to both men and women.

As with individualism and power distance, the principal predictor for this metric is climate – warmer climates predict more masculine cultures, while colder climates, farther from the equator, are prone to feminine (nurturing) characteristics. Hofstede suspects colder climates demand more technology for survival, bringing with it a need for education and, ultimately, equality.

Questions for discussion

1. Most texts addressing intercultural competence (and there are many) provide summary lists of national scores for Hofstede's cultural dimensions of power distance, uncertainty avoidance, individualism/collectivism, and masculinity/femininity. Retrieve a table of those scores. Knowing that the research resulting in these values is decades old, suggest how at least some of those scores may have changed.
2. What are factors that might influence changes in the central tendencies suggested by national scores on those indices?
3. Select two countries with significant differences in their index ratings. Talk about the challenges public relations practitioners from one of the cultures might experience in planning a communication campaign within the other culture.
4. The research project that led to these findings was enormous and would be difficult to replicate. Suggest practical ways of updating these data through solid research and especially in ways that would benefit the public relations profession.

Relationship versus task orientation

The essence of this cultural syndrome is apparent from its title: some cultures place more value on relationships, including in professional settings, than on immediate task completion and dedicate greater effort to cultivating those relationships than to completing the task. That is not to say those cultures fail to complete the task, but rather that they view developing the relationship as a necessary precedent. As Gardenswartz and colleagues (2003) point out, the task-oriented Swiss or Germans would prefer to avoid countless meetings and after-hours socializing, seeing such activities as barriers to completing the work at hand. For Mexicans or Arabs, however, failing to precede task-related efforts with time spent on becoming familiar and comfortable with other participants would be seen as the barrier. In Chapter 8 we shall discuss the Chinese concept of *guanxi*, the complex matrix of relationships that must be considered carefully in any professional or personal activities. A task-oriented manager working in a relationship-oriented culture will remain frustrated and will likely not achieve goals without accommodating the development and nurturing of relationships essential to team cohesion in that setting.

Fallon (1997) suggests the following measures, among others, for task-oriented managers working in relationship-oriented settings, and the measures would certainly apply to public relations practitioners:

■ Have yourself introduced by someone respected and trusted by the relationship-oriented participants.
■ Demonstrate genuine interest in your relationship-oriented colleagues.
■ Do more listening than leading, especially at the start.

- Look for ways to give others opportunities for training, visibility and even additional connections that might contribute to their professional career development. Similarly, seek ways to help your colleagues achieve respect and esteem.
- Learn about and extend courtesies to their family members.
- Socialize with your relationship-oriented colleagues.

Other cultural metrics

In addition to these preceding major comparative metrics, cross-cultural scholars have identified a host of less overarching, but no less meaningful measures that help us compare one culture to another. In many cases, these metrics are more easily recognized because they are more directly linked with specific human behavior. In a tactical sense, they present more immediate challenges to cross-cultural encounters because they manifest themselves even in the most casual and seemingly inconsequential aspects of business or personal relationships.

Chronemics

This metric has several dimensions. Most fundamentally, cultures can be categorized on a spectrum ranging from polychronic to monochronic. Monochronic societies view time as something linear that can be divided into neat, precise packages or blocks. Merit is attributed to those who can manage and control their time efficiently. For most, Germany and Switzerland might come to mind as cultures in which high value is placed on this trait. Carté and Fox (2004, p. 157) recommend that in working with colleagues from highly monochronic cultures you take the following measures:

- Fix appointments well in advance to convey the importance of the issue.
- Provide meeting agendas in advance and stick to them.
- Arrive on time.
- Start and end meetings at the agreed time.

Further, the authors recommend interrupting as soon as you do not understand some point – waiting until the end of the meeting can be perceived as wasting time. And reveal bad news quickly rather than holding it for an opportune moment in monochronic cultures – that could be perceived as an attempt to conceal it and could damage your reputation and trustworthiness.

On the other hand, polychronic cultures are far less servants to the clock, and managing relationships is viewed as more important than managing time. Cultures in Latin America, India, Italy and the Arab world are often associated with this approach. When working with these cultures, Carté and Fox suggest taking the following precautions:

- Set appointments with short notice and be prepared for last-minute changes.
- Allow ample time between appointments.
- Expect to wait and to use that time productively.
- Try to establish a basic agenda at the beginning of a meeting, but do not stick to it rigidly.
- Do not rush through a meeting; there will likely be interruptions, sidebars and discussions of marginally related issues.

■ Do not establish or hold others to rigid deadlines.
■ Soften bad news, delaying it as necessary to prepare colleagues for receiving it.

A complexity of chronemics is the somewhat confusing paradox in some cultures between the decision-making process and the implementation of those decisions. Germans in general, for example, value highly structured meetings but can still take their time making final decisions. The Spanish, conversely, are likely to be polychronic and may prefer less structured meetings, but they often take decisions quickly. Similarly, the Japanese may take a long time to arrive at a decision, but expect prompt implementation of the decision once taken.

Another dimension of the time issue is focus on long-term versus short-term results. Polychronic cultures are apt to take a long-term view of issues; but, again, the profiles are not always consistent. The Swiss, for example, tend toward the monochronic, but are like the polychronic Japanese in taking a long-term view.

Finally, another time-related metric useful in cross-cultural comparisons is that of future versus past. The United States tends to be future-oriented, often viewing the past as a barrier to progress, an esteemed value. Other cultures, especially China, Japan, India and much of the Middle East, place high value on history and tradition, embracing lessons of the past. Future-oriented practitioners could mistakenly view past-oriented counterparts as unmotivated, while the past-oriented practitioner may see in a future orientation a superficial understanding and a lack of context. Future-oriented practitioners should be sure to include pertinent background in proposals and other materials to counter this gap, and past-oriented practitioners should strive to include a future cast in their packages.

Proxemics

This term refers to the preferred structure of our personal space in various settings. Each of us creates a "bubble" around us, and we may be uncomfortable when that bubble is penetrated inappropriately. Distance can also contribute to the total meaning of a message – an angry person who is very near to us is more threatening than one who is far away. In terms of distance, cultures such as those of Latin America are much more comfortable maintaining little space during conversations, personal or professional. Northern European cultures, on the other hand, prefer more distance between interlocutors. Such a person, preferring more space, might be perceived as evasive and elusive. The person comfortable in close quarters might be viewed as intrusive by someone from another culture.

The concept of proxemics is further complicated by categorization of circumstances. Scholars have identified four levels of spatial territory, each of which can differ from one culture to another. Intimate distance defines the bubble appropriate for conversations of the closest nature, and this can range from 15 to 45 centimeters. The next level, for friendly conversations among good friends, can range from roughly half a meter to 1.5 meters. The distance for conversations among casual acquaintances can range from one to three meters, and public distance for formal speaking settings or with strangers is generally three meters or more. Violation of the appropriate social distance for a given culture can interfere with clear message exchange, so awareness can be critical. The simple action of pulling an office chair closer to a counterpart in another culture may risk damaging a professional relationship even before significant conversation begins. The practitioner from a culture that traditionally maintains greater distance in all situations should be prepared, in other cultures, for lengthy handshakes and uncomfortable nearness; the practitioner must not reveal that discomfort, though, or he/she may appear discourteous and cold.

Haptics

This term refers to touching and is closely related to proxemics. Most cultures accept a degree of touching, such as a handshake, at the beginning and termination of professional and personal encounters. Some cultures, though, place emphasis on physical contact during conversations, and this can cause confusion in less tactile cultures where a touch meant to be polite, social or professional may be interpreted as inappropriately friendly, even intimate or suggestive. Also, in highly haptic cultures, men may touch each other more frequently, sometimes walking arm in arm as they talk – this could certainly be misinterpreted by someone from a less haptic culture. Remland and Jones (1995) found southern Europeans to be more tactile/haptic than northern Europeans. Middle Eastern and Latin cultures also tend toward highly haptic behavior during conversations, while Asian cultures are considerably less haptic.

Cultures differ also in where it is appropriate to touch someone and who can touch whom. In Thailand, the head is considered the center of one's spirit and power, so must never be touched. In Japan, it would be extremely uncomfortable to be touched by a stranger. In China, it might be acceptable for persons of the opposite sex to shake hands, but not in Malaysia. Likewise, touch between the sexes in Muslim settings would be inappropriate – an act requiring ritualistic cleansing before prayer.

Occulesics

Though you probably do not think about it much, you will likely agree that eye movement can contribute significantly to message meaning. This is certainly true in international settings, and ignorance of cultural differences can lead to misunderstandings and even strained relationships. Ling (1997) notes that some cultures use a lowered gaze to show respect, but this may wrongly be gauged as evasiveness, a lack of interest or even insulting by someone from a culture that values direct eye contact. On the other hand, the former culture may view direct eye contact as insulting, while the latter culture uses direct eye contact to convey attention and interest.

Kenisics

Kenisics refers to a non-verbal component of communication involving body movement and positioning, either as a whole or via any part or parts of the body. Many of you have probably studied this aspect of non-verbal communication, but probably only in the context of your own culture. It would be quite easy to convey or shade a message unintentionally in another culture, or to misinterpret, consciously or subconsciously, a message from someone in a business or social setting if you do not consider cultural differences in kinesic symbols. Common kinesic movements in one culture may make no sense in another culture or, worse, may have a very different meaning, perhaps an unfortunate one. Groundbreaking research in this area was reported by Ekman and Friesen (1969, pp. 49–98) in which they identified five categories of kinesic body movements or postures: emblems; illustrators; affect displays; regulators and adaptors.

Emblems have direct verbal counterparts, though meanings may differ from one culture to another. The classic example is the well-known British "V" made with the index and middle finger held erect (palm outward), symbolizing victory; the same gesture simply refers to the number two in the United States but may be taken offensively in Australia. Similarly, the sign for "OK" in some cultures is a circle made with the thumb and index finger, but the same symbol can be an insult or even a vulgar reference in other cultures – imagine the discomfort if such a gesture is made, however well intended, in an intercultural business setting. Illustrators are gestures, usually with the hands, meant to add to or emphasize points being made verbally in a conversation, presentation, and so on. Meanings differ less across cultures than do emblems, but the extent to which illustrators are incorporated differs from culture to culture, with Latin cultures making more extensive use, Anglo-Saxon cultures using them moderately, and Asian cultures using them least. A problem lies in one culture's assessment of what use or non-use of illustrators indicates: an Asian practitioner, unfamiliar with Latin cultural non-verbal communication patterns, may interpret extensive use of illustrators as a lack of intelligence, while the Latin practitioner may interpret Asian non-use of illustrators as a lack of interest.

Affective kinesic movements or postures refer to body and facial movements that convey or reveal emotional states. Again, meaning differs little across cultures, but the degree to which affective kinesics are incorporated in speech patterns differs significantly and can be misinterpreted by the participant unschooled in these cultural differences. The Japanese practitioner, socially trained to restrain outward manifestations of his emotions, might appear less agitated than his Italian colleague, but that does not necessarily suggest that he is less perturbed. Regulators also refer to body movements and facial expressions, sometime subtle, but that help regulate and even control a conversation. These can include simple nods or eye movement to indicate engagement and understanding. Though subtle, there can be differences between cultures in the degree to which individuals exhibit these regulators, so confusion or misinterpretation is a risk. Vargas (1986) reports confusion in the United States because white educators misread black students' more subtle use of regulators, conveying, in the mind of white educators, lack of understanding.

Finally, adapters are supposedly the subconscious but deeply revealing postural changes some scholars in the 1970s claimed held the secrets to understanding the real thoughts of your conversation partner. It seems that those claims were overstated and that how one crosses his or her legs or positions a chair likely relates less to subconscious thoughts than to comfort or convenience. Still, the practitioner needs to exercise care in such movements because even unintentionally he or she may convey meaning in another culture; taking a more comfortable position in a chair, for example, that reveals the bottom of one's shoe may be taken as offensive in Arab cultures and in Thailand.

Taken together, this array of syndromes – chronemics, proxemics, haptics, occulesics and kinesics – might present a confusing array of possibilities and permutations across the many cultures you're likely to encounter in your public relations career. It would be difficult to assemble a comprehensive table of appropriate and inappropriate behavior across all those cultures, matching each culture's preferences, habits and traditions in comparison to other cultures, and doing so might be more confusing than useful. Nevertheless, fundamental awareness that these differences exist and should be considered before, during and following professional cross-cultural encounters will reduce the astute practitioner's likelihood of either committing unintentional blunders or misinterpreting messages from others.

Sidebar: How are your chronemics?

Carté and Fox (2004, p. 156) provide a practical guide to gauging one's own culture and other cultures through a series of simple questionnaires. Table 4.3 is an example of one such instrument they recommend to assess one's position on the chronemic spectrum. The authors suggest that you use the scales first to identify your own cultural tendencies in your work setting. Compare your profile to the setting for which you might be preparing, and these scales may help you develop appropriate communication strategies. For example, if you anticipate finding yourself in a monochromic society,

be prepared to arrange appointments well in advance, provide advance meeting agendas, arrive on time, and start and end on time. On the other hand, in polychromic settings you may expect to receive short-notice meetings, to be kept waiting, to experience a flexible agenda, and to have meetings run over time.

The authors recommend using this and other similar indices in conducting self-assessments, but practitioners and researchers may find value in administering them to representatives of various cultures.

TABLE 4.3 Chronemic Assessment Instrument

Monochronic						Polychronic				
I prefer to deal with one task at a time in a structured fashion.						I prefer to have several tasks running at the same time.				
50	40	30	20	10	0	10	20	30	40	50
Speed						Patience				
Too much analysis leads to paralysis.						Taking my time helps me make the right decision.				
50	40	30	20	10	0	10	20	30	40	50
Short-term						Long-term				
I prefer to focus on the here and now.						I need to see beyond the horizon and plan accordingly.				
50	40	30	20	10	0	10	20	30	40	50
Future						Past				
Tradition gets in the way of progress.						Change needs to respect tradition.				
50	40	30	20	10	0	10	20	30	40	50

Conclusion

There are other measures that help us contrast one culture with another, and the serious student or practitioner can find exhaustive material on the subject. There are a number of cultural characteristics, too, that help us define and understand particular cultures. For example, in Chapter 8, in addition to a discussion of *guanxi*, the reader will also become acquainted with the importance of Confucianism in Chinese and other Asian cultures. You should now be developing an increasing appreciation for the complexities of conducting public relations activities in cross-cultural settings. Now that you have acquired an understanding of some of the major barriers to interpersonal communication in such settings, we can introduce additional challenges at the macro-communication level, also critical to successful communication campaigns.

Featured biography: Thomas G. Mattia

Thomas G. Mattia is director of World Public Affairs and Communications and Senior Vice-President of the Coca-Cola Company headquartered in Atlanta, Georgia, USA. A 35-year veteran of public affairs, Mattia is responsible for leading the Coca-Cola Company's global affairs and communications. His role also includes leadership of the company's Public Policy and Corporate Reputation Council. Mattia's career includes a variety of executive positions with IBM, Hill & Knowlton, and GCI Jennings. He spent about five years with Ford Motor Company as head of International Public Affairs. Prior to joining the Coca-Cola Company, he served as Vice-President of Global Communications at technology services leader EDS. Mattia now serves on the board of the Metro Atlanta Chamber of Commerce and the Board of the High Museum of Art. He is a member of the Arthur W. Page Society, the International Association of Business Communicators (IABC) and the Public Relations Society of America (PRSA).

Mattia admits that only after becoming a part of the company did he fully understand the universal power of the Coca-Cola brand. Mattia describes the Coca-Cola brand as appealing universally because "it is approachable and affordable, it is the easiest way of relaxation, escape, joy, or congratulations you can give to yourself. The strength of the Coca-Cola brand is its simplicity. This is what allows it to cross the borders". Mattia points out another reason for the brand's success – its local connection. He explains that local communities have always played an important role in the success of the Coca-Cola business because "the water is local, the ingredients are sourced locally, it is produced locally, and it is distributed and sold locally".

The health and sustainability of local communities are central to the Coca-Cola Company's business. "Sustainable community is our corporate social responsibility (CSR)," Mattia says, "because if the community that surrounds our facilities is not strong and sustainable, then our business won't be sustainable, either." Mattia believes CSR does not work when it exists separately from business. CSR is most powerful for the community and business when corporations view business through the lens of social responsibility. Mattia says that in the old days the head of public relations would be expected to focus on profits more than on CSR or anything else; however, today the Coca-Cola Company focuses its attention on environmental responsibility as much as possible. Protection of the environment, including recycling and water use, has become one of the most significant goals of Coca-Cola's business. This focus "changes the dynamic of the discussion and the way the company runs the business and puts communication in the center of all its activities". As a result, public relations is "the greatest leverage point that exists within any enterprise – business, NGO or government, and communication is central to creating, sustaining, and maintaining the reputation of that enterprise". Mattia points out that public relations practitioners have the responsibility to be socially conscious and help the company act responsibly because "good communicators inside the enterprise are not only the voice out, but also the ears in".

Mattia firmly believes that the business environment is becoming far more global. Successful public relations people will be those who can "skim across the surface, travel through a variety of societies, and be able to engage in various cultures and love that engagement". Mattia remembers his relatively sheltered childhood in New Jersey when he did not go overseas until he started his professional career. However, he has always had a great passion and appetite for knowledge, and has read voraciously. He loves history and spends a lot of time studying other countries, trying to understand their cultures. Mattia advises students and future specialists to prepare themselves for the profession through reading and learning as much as possible about different cultures. Getting along with other nationalities and being sensitive to their values is a very important component of effective communication. Mattia also advises to expect to make mistakes; he suggests admitting them in order to learn from them. Mattia says public relations is often not just about understanding the language, but about taking time to understand the culture. It is significant to "listen to local people, get to know what they have to say, what is important to them, and what different things mean to them".

Recommended websites

Communication Tools for Understanding Cultural Differences   http://www.beyondintractability.org/essay/communication_tools/

High- and low-context cultures   http://www.culture-at-work.com/highlow.html

Power distance index   http://www.clearlycultural.com/geert-hofstede-cultural-dimensions/power-distance-index/

Geert Hofstede Cultural Dimensions   http://www.geert-hofstede.com

Hofstede's personal website   http://www.info.wau.nl/people/gertjan/gj-uk.htm

A portal site with a large number of links to worldwide resources   http://www.worldjump.com/

The CIA Factbook   https://www.cia.gov/library/publications/the-world-factbook/index.html

Geographia – world travel destination, culture and history guide   http://www.geographia.com

Kwintessential Cross Cultural Solutions   http://www.kwintessential.co.uk

References

Braithwaite, C. E., 1990. Communicative silence: a cross-cultural study of Basso's hypothesis. In Carbaugh, D., ed. *Cultural Communication and Intercultural Contact*. Hillsdale, NJ: Lawrence Erlbaum. pp. 321–8.

Carté, P. and Fox, C., 2004. *Bridging the Culture Gap: A Practical Guide to International Business Communication*. Sterling, Va: Canning.

Ekman, P. and Friesen, W. V., 1969. The repertoire of non-verbal behavior: categories, origins, usage and codings. *Semiotics*, 1, pp. 49–98.

Fallon, M., 1997. Human resources operations in China. In T. Fron, ed., *China Practical Staff Employment Manual*. Hong Kong: Pearson.

Gardenswartz, L., Rowe, A., Digh, P. and Bennet, M. F., 2003. *The Global Diversity Desk Reference: Managing an International Workforce*. San Francisco, Calif.: Pfeiffer.

Gudykunst, W. B. and Kim, Y. Y., 1997. *Communicating with Strangers: An Approach to Intercultural Communication*. New York: McGraw-Hill.

Hall, E. T., 1976. *Beyond Culture*. Garden City, NY: Anchor/Doubleday.

Hofstede, G., 1980. *Cultural Consequences: International Differences in Work-related Values*. Beverly Hills, Calif.: Sage.

Hofstede, G., 1991. *Cultures and Organizations: Software of the Mind*. London: McGraw-Hill.

Ling, C. W., 1997. Crossing cultural boundaries. *Nursing*, 72 (3), pp. 32–4.

Lustig, M. W. and Koester, J., 1999. *Intercultural Competence: Interpersonal Communication across Cultures*. 3rd edn. New York: Longman.

Neuliep, J. W., 2000. *Intercultural Communication: A Contextual Approach*. New York: Houghton Mifflin.

Remland, M. S. and Jones, T. S., 1995. Interpersonal distance, body orientation, and touch: effects of culture, gender, and age. *Journal of Social Psychology*, 135 (3), pp. 281–97.

Reynolds, S. and Valentine, D., 2004. *Guide to Cross-cultural Communication*. Upper Saddle River, NJ: Pearson Education.

Vargas, M. F., 1986. *Louder than Words: An Introduction to Non-verbal Communication*. Ames, Iowa: Iowa State University Press.

Chapter 5

Structural comparisons

Summary

In the last chapter, we considered various aspects of human culture that affect public relations practice, especially those aspects that influence human communication. In this chapter, we shall examine several other factors that vary from one nation and/or culture to another that also potentially affect planning and carrying out effective communication programs and campaigns. We shall begin by looking at media systems, then consider legal structures, and finally ethical structures. Doing so will more thoroughly address the elements of Zaharna's (2001) "In-Awareness" model designed to aid in avoiding false assumptions and misguided expectations that threaten to derail otherwise sound public relations efforts. In doing so, we shall not yet provide specific, country-by-country analyses of these structures, but we shall outline an approach to recognizing, understanding, and allowing for these differences. The important thing here is not in memorizing the nature of these structures in scores of countries, but rather in knowing what questions to ask, what research to conduct, and how best to identify and explain in meaningful ways the nature of the differences. Having a framework by which to draw those meaningful comparisons will aid, too, in monitoring evolving changes in these structures.

Chapter goals

- Recognize differences in media systems among countries and consider the effects of those differences on public relations practice.
- Suggest a framework for discerning international variations in legal issues that affect public relations practice.
- Explore the difficulties of accommodating differing ethical frameworks in the context of public relations activities.

Media

The media are a public particularly important for international public relations practitioners. To be successful in media relations on an international stage, George (2003) points out that relationships with the media should be developed before they are needed. It would be a mistake, however – and one commonly made – to assume that media throughout the world operate on much the same common principles. Because public relations efforts often rely heavily on mass media, planning those efforts based on misperceptions about how media function could do worse than simply render your plan ineffective – it could result in severe damage to reputation and credibility. Media structures develop in a country as the result of several forces, primarily the social, economic and political environments within which media operate. Consequently, it is difficult to isolate media from those environmental factors, so understanding those dynamics will be useful, and our discussion will blend those elements. A term sometimes used to describe the study of communication and mass media systems is *metacommunication*.

In creating a list of questions to ask about national media structures, a good place to start is with an approach published nearly fifty years ago. In *Four Theories of the Press*, Siebert, Peterson and Schramm (1963) proposed a scheme of four basic categories into which they allocated the various media systems around the world. It is a bit dated now (for example, one of the categories was labeled "Soviet-totalitarian") but no less useful. With that framework as an initial guide, we shall begin our list of questions to ask with an adaptation of their approach.

1. *From what political paradigm did the media develop, and what is the purpose of the media?* If the political history is characterized by *authoritarian* rule, absolute monarchy, or dictatorship, the media are likely to serve the purpose only of that power; any public relations strategies involving media will need to reflect and reinforce that power, or more likely are simply not going to be accepted for distribution. It is conceivable that communication campaigns supporting development efforts under these circumstances may achieve some success, but it is more likely practitioners will encounter serious ethical dilemmas. In these societies there are highly restrictive official or unofficial rules about what media may convey, and supporting your public relations efforts is not likely to meet the leadership's criteria. Interestingly, in the broad tapestry of world history since the birth of mass media, usually associated with the development of movable type in the sixteenth century, the authoritarian paradigm is the most frequently observed approach to mass media.

What Siebert, Peterson and Schramm called the Soviet-totalitarian model could be relabeled the *radical ideology* model and might be reflected by Islamic monarchies and other states in which the government and dominant religious ideology are so entwined as to be indistinguishable. This category differs from authoritarian environments in that the aim of the government and the media is not merely the enforcement of power but also of a very narrowly defined religious ideology. Because the government wields authority over the media, the aim of the media is to ensure the success and the maintenance of the ideological principles upon which the government is based and that guide stringently all aspects of citizens' lives. Public relations media strategies in these instances would have to be compliant not just with the government policies but also with religious law and custom. Siebert, Peterson and Schramm were originally referring to communist régimes in which the media served only to support the ideology of the party, and were thinking primarily of the former Soviet Union and its satellite nations; that style of régime remains only in North Korea, Cuba and, to a lesser extent, Vietnam. China, of course, remains a communist nation, but reforms have somewhat altered the media landscape there. Again, public relations practitioners coming from other paradigms, certainly from a contemporary Western paradigm, may encounter ethical barriers in either the radical ideological or traditional communist dimensions of this category.

It is most likely public relations practitioners and students reading this find themselves in the *libertarian* paradigm. This would be an environment that embraces democratic principles emerging in Britain and the United States beginning in the late seventeenth century and subsequently taking root in Europe, South America, Asia, Africa and the Middle East, if tentatively in some cases. As we discussed in Chapter 2, this is the paradigm that created opportunities for the public relations profession to emerge and flourish. It is the approach that stresses individual (including corporate) rights and a free-market economy and sees ensuring citizens' protection and well-being as the government's central purpose. In this environment, media owners and operators are assumed to be capable of distinguishing right from wrong and will, by nature, exercise their right to disseminate information in a responsible way without the need for restrictive rules. In practice, libertarian societies have found it necessary to invoke restrictions in regard to disseminating material that constitutes sedition or that could cause personal harm, but the censorship and control typical of authoritarian or radical/ideological systems are absent. In fact, an essential characteristic of the libertarian structure is that the media actually serve as a check on the government. Public practitioners have learned to work successfully in this environment, representing the interest of their organizations or clients by adapting their messages to the interests of the media owners and operators – generally to build their audiences by providing them with information and entertainment they prefer. In fact, the system is so well suited to contemporary practice that media relations generally dominates practitioner activities.

A fourth category, spawned from the libertarian category, is that of *social responsibility*, which takes the libertarian model to another plane. Introduced here are concepts of the public's right to know and the moral responsibility of the media. Although the libertarian media paradigm stresses the free market of ideas, including the free market of selling not just those ideas but also products and services as its central purpose, the social responsibility concept tempers that with responsibilities that accompany those privileges. As with libertarian structures, the media play a role in educating and enlightening the public, serving as a forum for public debate of the issues, monitoring government activities especially in regard to individual rights, supporting a free-market economy, entertaining, and, of course, making a profit. The added wrinkle under social responsibility theory is the recognition that the media have fallen short of carrying out those functions and require additional guidance and direction from some agency. That agency will ensure that the entertainment is suitable, that profit is reasonable and does not supersede serving the greater good, and so forth. This is a paradigm still under development but gaining momentum. In Chapter 2 we talked about the growing Corporate Social Responsibility (CSR) movement, and that movement is certainly influencing the shaping of the social responsibility theory of media structures; media companies are, after all, corporations. The social responsibility theory recognizes also that some media outlets deserve to be subsidized in order to provide a voice for messages and publics that might not otherwise enjoy access – hence the birth of government-supported public radio and television stations and networks and even public access channels. Public relations practitioners who position themselves at the vanguard of this development will be poised to serve their organizations and clients well in the area of media relations, and will be able to do so well within the high contemporary ethical bounds of the discipline.

Of course, there are other possible approaches to categorizing media systems. Hallin and Mancini (2004) propose a three-model framework. Their "liberal model" is dominated by marketing mechanisms and commercial media, and occurs currently in North America, Great Britain and Ireland. Their "democratic corporatist model" is typified by the commingling of commercial media with media conduits allied with social and political groups; this model is common in continental northern Europe. And their "polarized pluralist model" links media with the political party and includes a dominant state role; this model, say the authors, is typified in Mediterranean southern Europe.

2. *Who has access to the media?* This refers to the ability to place messages in mass-media channels. Access is what public relations practitioners seek, whether for news releases, interviews, public service announcements, talkshows, and so on. The answer to this question would be fairly obvious for the four different paradigms we just described: in authoritarian structures, whomever the crown permitted would have access; in radical-ideological settings, only the loyal and orthodox would have access; in libertarian settings, whoever could pay money or in kind for the privilege would have access; and, in social responsibility settings, whoever had something of value to say would have access. Of course, within those broad categories finer distinctions can usually be made. In developing your communication plan for another country, you will need to determine what, if any, strategies are appropriate. For example, in a libertarian setting, you may find that advertising may need to play a larger role. In a social responsibility setting, messages crafted to emphasize your company's or client's positive role in matters related to the environment, public health or the arts may improve your success.

3. *What audiences pay attention to the media?* Experienced public relations practitioners know that successfully placing messages in media channels is not the ultimate measure of merit when it comes to evaluating campaign success. The next gauge is whether those messages appear in media that reach target publics. Eventually, the practitioner will need to find ways to conduct detailed research related to his or her campaign program, but it is useful to begin with generalizations. Begin with simple exposure – this may include determining the saturation levels for broadcast radio and television, cable systems, satellite channels, newspaper and magazine distribution, Internet availability, and so forth. A related issue is a nation's literacy rate, and this may vary dramatically by age, gender, region or other factors. A public health communication campaign initiated in a highly developed nation, where the campaign relied heavily on print media and materials, may need to be significantly recrafted if it is to be introduced in a nation with a 20 percent literacy rate among the target public. In a poorly developed country, even if the families you're trying to reach with the campaign are literate, their income may be such that purchasing a newspaper or magazine is a major economic decision, and owning a radio or television may be out of the question.

A small but important audience that practitioners should sometimes consider even in campaigns and programs within their own national borders is the audience of expatriates living elsewhere. Practitioners should learn where those groups are concentrated and identify media channels that reach them. An obvious example is US service members and their families serving abroad; there are official and commercial media vehicles that can reach this substantial audience and that are receptive to public relations materials that meet other criteria for placement. Similarly, a campaign by the Polish government or another Polish organization that included as its target publics *émigrés* now abroad might consider including components of the plan that reach those audiences in Chicago, New York, London and elsewhere.

4. *Who or what agency controls the media?* Understanding the mechanisms within which media outlets must function will preclude errors in judgment by public relations practitioners and may boost credibility by demonstrating thorough awareness of unique national circumstances. In authoritarian settings, media outlets are likely to be subject to prior censorship enforced by strict or even capricious licensing or other controlling policies. In recent years, we have seen instances in even notional democratic settings, such as Russia, where severe sanctions have been exercised against media outlets deemed to challenge their sitting power. In authoritarian settings, this is normally associated with negative, propagandistic roles for media, but conceivably could be exercised in positive ways as well. In Asian nations such as Malaysia, Indonesia and Singapore, for example (as you will see in Chapter 7), authoritarian governments employed mass media under direct control for beneficial development campaigns in the earliest stages of their independence, then gradually permitted the loosening of central government control. Exercising control over mass media has, of course, become exceedingly difficult with the advent of satellite communication, the Internet, simplified publishing technologies, and so forth. Even so, governments are often able to enforce varying degrees of restraint through systems of laws and courts, prosecuting media outlets after the fact for infractions committed. This is often the case in libertarian settings. Public relations practitioners should familiarize themselves with pertinent statutory and case law that might affect their campaigns and programs.

In radical-ideological settings severe control may be exercised by government-supported or -sanctioned surveillance bodies, even to the point of controlling who may work at any level of the media sector. In this paradigm, the government exercises absolute power over resources necessary for media to function, the means of production, access to material and information, and means of distribution. Because fundamental decisions are made by the central controlling bureaucracy, the only avenue of public relations practitioners here is through contact with members of that controlling body. Further, communication material that does not in some way reflect the underlying ideological framework that defines and guides that society is unlikely to penetrate the media curtain.

Libertarian settings, having played the most prominent role in spawning the public relations profession, feature control structures quite conducive to our discipline. Control is exercised largely and increasingly by market forces, with few restraints on media content or distribution. Here, practitioners must craft materials and messages compatible with those market forces – and that has advantages and disadvantages. For example, messages about a company's new product or service may be construed as newsworthy if the media outlet judges that information to be of genuine value to consumers who are also members of the media audience, but risk being labeled merely marketing or advertising messages if the character of those messages is overtly commercial. This battle is in evidence in the United States, for instance, in the area of pharmaceutical companies' communication efforts. This industry has made aggressive use of video news releases; and television stations and networks have included these releases, often "doctored" to appear locally generated, in their newscasts ostensibly as a service to their viewers. The US Congress was so concerned with the ethical implications of the practice that it held hearings on the subject, but the practice continues. Sometimes, too, control is not applied uniformly across all media. Again, using the United States as an example, we find limited controls exercised over broadcasting channels through licensing and regulatory restrictions on content and ownership, but no parallel controls exerted over printed media; nor do broadcast controls extend to cable networks or the Internet. Even for broadcast channels, licensing requirements have been severely reduced, and content restrictions had nearly disappeared before a few noteworthy cases in recent years. The libertarian model, therefore, relies heavily on media self-policing, for better or for worse. This certainly has an impact on public relations practice, and changes in the control framework result in changes in appropriate public approaches. When licensing of broadcast outlets was more stringent in years past, public relations practitioners with non-profit organizations and government agencies could rely on those channels' cooperation in placing public service announcements, the airing of which helped media outlets bolster their case for license renewal. Loosening of licensing procedures has led to fewer "free" slots for PSAs in an environment that has seen rapid growth in the number of non-profits seeking these slots. The result has been much more vigorous competition, but far greater attention to production values – stations are more likely to air PSAs that reflect their own high quality standards.

The growing social responsibility movement, particularly in traditionally libertarian media settings, is one worth monitoring closely if public relations practitioners are to remain in the vanguard of their practice. Fortunately, the question of control in a social responsibility environment is matched perfectly to the principles of ethical, proactive public relations practice because control in this setting transfers to the community members in which the media outlet operates. Media decisions are driven in large part by consumer action and by community opinions. Well-educated and experienced public relations practitioners bring to this environment an appropriate array of tools and skill sets to identify, analyze and track these factors, providing advice and counsel to organizational leaders that will enable them to shape decisions and policies leading to a harmonious, synergistic relationship between the organization and relevant constituencies. That relationship, in turn, will benefit all parties. Those tools and skill sets include quantitative and qualitative research techniques, knowledge of programs designed to build those productive and lasting relationships, issue management, planning and programming, program evaluation, as well as fundamental management skills. In settings where media recognize and are motivated by a strong sense of responsibility to the communities they serve (local, regional, national and global), public relations practitioners should seek opportunities for useful partnerships with media – partnerships that address community needs and goals and that make strategic sense for both media involved and the organization. Following this course will lead to approval by the controlling agency – in the case of a social responsibility setting, that means the community.

5. *What content is permitted in the media?* It might be simpler to express this question in terms of what is not permitted. Certainly, in an authoritarian setting, anything even remotely critical of the government in power would never be published or broadcast. However, in such systems general debate of broad issues would be acceptable, so long as no criticism were explicitly or implicitly incorporated. In some settings – for example, newly independent Malaysia, Singapore and Indonesia as cited earlier – multinational corporations employed the technique of collaborating with the government in broad national efforts to improve conditions and lay the groundwork for national prosperity; doing so did not directly promote the corporations, but built large deposits of goodwill that often subsequently led to tangible benefits.

In radical-ideological régimes news is likely to be centered on the ideological implications of an event or issue. When the purpose of the media is largely propaganda, content must logically comply with the one model acceptable to that régime. Unlike in authoritarian settings, even broad debate of the issues is unacceptable here.

Sidebar: President Mubarak spoof

The advent of the Internet and its rapid spread is affecting the ability of nations to control information flow, especially through media, as they might have done in the past. Reports say that as early as 2004 a 33-second video clip was available on the Internet, a clip Egyptian law and leadership would consider treason, but which they were powerless to curtail. In the clip, an anonymous prankster – most assume he is a taxi driver – is seated at the wheel of a car and delivers his impersonation of Egyptian president Hosni Mubarak speaking (in Egyptian) about his "tough" stance in regard to relations with Israel. The narrative is straightforward, but the parody lies in the speaker's amusing imitation of the president's speaking style, including the set of his mouth, even his squint. Needless to say, it is rather unflattering, portraying the national leader as quite the dolt. It is an obvious insult, and Egyptian law prescribes severe punishment for anyone insulting the president; and President Mubarak, critics say, has used the law to silence opposition and even shut down newspapers. That is in stark contrast to the often merciless skewering delivered routinely through media satires and commentary in many nations with media freedom. Official reaction from the corridors of power has been to deny having seen the clip or to avoid comment all together. Meanwhile, the clip's cult-like popularity expanded rapidly thanks to thousands of text messages and e-mails sent by Egyptians and others reveling in this brief bit of Internet-enabled rebellion. At the time of writing, the clip may be found at www.youtube.com/watch?v=StpLny2dxlf (Allam and El Naggar, 2006).

Even in libertarian and social responsibility environments there are some limited restrictions on the media, but none likely to affect public relations practitioners as a matter of course. Prohibitions against obscenity, material that is libelous or slanderous, or material that could incite violence, crime or hatred are likely to be restricted to varying degrees, though practitioners are not likely to be engaged in activities that even approach such areas. During national emergencies, tighter restrictions may, of course, apply.

6. *What is news?* This question related to permitted content, but one with an even more direct application to public relations practice, addresses a difficult area. If you were raised in a single culture, exposed primarily to the media in your own country, you have been programmed to believe that you know what constitutes news; but those who have been exposed to multiple systems are aware of the subtle and not-so-subtle difference in the content of what we universally refer to as news media, including television, radio, newspapers, magazines, and so forth. Foreigners observing election campaign coverage in the United States may be surprised, for example, to note that the preponderance of the coverage is about who's ahead in the polls, who scored big in the televised debates, or even the comparative personalities of the candidates; much less coverage is devoted to the salient issues and where the candidates stand on them. Does that sort of coverage help citizens make informed decisions in the voting booth? In turn, US citizens traveling elsewhere might be puzzled by what they perceive as lengthy, boring reports about the contents of candidates' speeches or accounts of their record on foreign affairs and issues of national security. Practitioners faced

with an international assignment that will likely involve placement of material in media channels – typically as news content – will need to address this question in considerable detail.

In authoritarian and radical-ideological settings, news is what those in authority say it is, so anticipating what content to expect is simplified, even if the placement of public relations materials is challenging. News in those settings must be related to the goals that serve the leaders and power structures. In libertarian media structures news is a commercial commodity and, as such, far more difficult to anticipate, though most practitioners understand the basic principles that guide news selection in such settings. Negative news is common in Western cultures because it "sells", while negative news is rare in developing nations because it fails to serve the greater good. The same commercial motivation is present in social responsibility settings, though media experience the added control of community interest and well-being as judged by formal and informal agencies and processes. Martin and Chaudhary (1983) say that the key to understanding a culture or nation's definition of news is understanding the selection process: Who selects the news? When is it selected? To what extent does the audience matter in the selection? That last question is important – the role of the audience in the news selection process. Do news gatekeepers think about what the people want to know? Need to know? Care about? Identify those gatekeepers and discern their selection criteria and you will be able to prepare materials appropriate for that setting.

7. *To what extent and in what way do the media influence public opinion?* Media in all settings have the capacity to create demand for products and services and to help define social norms. In authoritarian and radical-ideological settings that is what the leadership counts on. In libertarian and social responsibility settings that is a natural result and perhaps the essence of economic dynamics. The greater role media play in this process, the greater benefit communication campaigns can achieve through careful, intelligent planning of the media component. The answer to this question should be segmented to match campaign aims. That is, find the extent to which *target publics* are influenced by media.

Questions for discussion

1. Compare your country to another country you are interested in. What are the similarities and the differences concerning how news is defined in each country? How might you adjust campaign media materials to manage the transition of the campaign from your country to the other successfully?
2. To what extent do the media influence product and service demand in your country? To what extent do the media influence social norms? Provide examples for each.
3. Some say *proximity* is a universal news value, meaning that localized information is most likely to achieve publication. Do you agree? Why or why not?
4. What are some of the ethical considerations that might come into play in attempting to devise media materials with the hope of placing them in the media in an authoritarian or radical/ideological setting?

Legal structures

Laws constitute a highly structured value system that reflects a society's culture. The same could be said of education systems, family systems, political systems and so forth. Hofstede (1980) says that these systems, once established, seldom change and tend to reinforce the cultural values that spawned them. He also correlates his metric of *uncertainty avoidance* with legal structures; societies scoring high in *uncertainty avoidance* are more likely to feel a need for more rules, more legislation. He cites Germany, with a high UAI (65), compared to the United Kingdom, with a low UAI (35). Germany, consequently, has laws governing emergencies that *might* happen, though the UK does not even have a constitution (p. 179).

The field of comparative law is an active one in many disciplines, such as economics, business and politics. Regrettably, there is scant research in the field of communication or, in particular, public relations. Ogus (1999) points out several tasks for comparative law scholars. He says research should "investigate differences between legal systems . . . distinguish between 'real' differences . . . and 'superficial' differences . . . and explore tendencies of convergence or divergence" (p. 405). In fact, he suggests that there has been a decided tendency toward global convergence of legal structures except in areas of moral and religious norms. He points out, too, that understanding the legal structures of another culture and country can be critical. When considering business activities in international settings, "The nature of the legal régime and its costs may have a substantial impact" (p. 408).

As we found for comparative media systems, we shall suggest a framework for conducting comparative law research, and it is straightforward enough to be managed by non-lawyers. Reitz (1998) put forward nine principles pertaining to comparative law, and we draw upon that framework to prescribe a simpler one more suitable to non-lawyers:

1. *Draw explicit comparisons.* Compare what you learn about a particular foreign law to what you know about the comparable law in your own country and express those comparisons in specific terms.
2. *Focus on similarities and differences of the legal systems involved.* Consider how the entire legal system works as a whole. Consider also interrelationships between and among various parts of the law, especially between law and procedure. For example, take into account the roles of various actors in the legal system: judges, attorneys, jurors.
3. *Suggest reasons that might explain differences and similarities between systems.* For example, consider social and cultural norms, comparative histories, religious and ideological issues. Consider also the country's placement on various cultural metrics such as *power distance, uncertainty avoidance* and *individualism/collectivism.*
4. *Compare the law on the books to the law as it is actually applied.* Do not limit research to reading the law; include a study of cases that invoke that law. Such a gap may stem from a variety of causes: ignorance, poverty, corruption, fear, and so on. As Reitz observes: "No legal system is entirely immune to this phenomenon" (p. 630).
5. *Retain respect for other legal systems.* You may experience a degree of fascination that goes beyond interest and curiosity; your response may even be one of amusement, condescension or derision. You must avoid that. Remember that different does not mean better, nor does it mean wrong. It is not your place to criticize, just to understand in order to provide advice and counsel.

What areas of the law are of interest to public relations practitioners? It might be easier to list laws that *do not* affect public relations practice! Still, there are areas of particular impact that warrant greater attention. Here is a suggested menu:

- *Freedom of speech:* To what extent does it apply in public relations contexts? Does it pertain to both the spoken and the written word?
- *Media censorship:* To what degree does the law impose prior restraint? What subjects are affected? How is censorship enforced? What penalties are involved? Are all media affected or is censorship limited to selected channels of communication?
- *Defamation:* What are the laws regarding libel and slander? What are the tests for defamation? Is this a civil or a criminal issue, or both? What are defenses against accusations of defamation?
- *Privacy:* What rights of privacy extend to individuals? What circumstances affect those rights? What are the subcomponents of privacy law (e.g., in the United States, intrusion, false light, and misappropriation).
- *Copyrights and trademarks:* What real and intellectual property is protected? What is exempt? What constitute exemptions from the law such as fair use?
- *Access and disclosure:* What are a journalist's privileges in regard to access? What records and procedures must be made available? What information must be disseminated and how must that be done (e.g., quarterly corporate earnings statements in the US)?
- *Commercial speech:* To what extent do individual rights, such as free speech, extend to organizations? Do organizations have unfettered access to advertising channels?
- *Contracts:* What laws pertain to formal agreements with clients, vendors, employees, printers/producers, and so on?
- *Agency law:* What government agencies exert controls over public relations and other organization activity that have the force of law? For example, in the United States a practitioner would have to become familiar with regulations enforced by the Security and Exchange Commission, the Federal Trade Commission, the Food and Drug Administration, the Federal Communication Commission, the National Labor Relations Board and others.
- *New media:* What regulations apply to the Internet, the Worldwide Web and social media?

Because so little has been written about comparative international law as it pertains to public relations practice, this is a fertile area for research. An obstacle is that research in this field would often require fluency in the languages of both countries being compared. Because the research would be delving into cases and manuscripts written in often esoteric legalese, language capability would need to be of the highest order, and a level of comfort in legal terminology would be extremely useful.

Comparative ethics

When we speak of ethics, we generally speak of a system for determining what is right or wrong and what is valued. That is clearly an oversimplification but it is not inaccurate, either. As you can imagine, there are likely to be vast differences from one culture to another on these scales. As you will discover, professional public relations associations around the globe establish codes of ethics as foundational dimensions of their disciplinary responsibilities, so clearly public relations leaders and aspiring leaders think ethics is important. In fact, a code of ethics is seen as one of the salient factors in determining the "professionalization" of any discipline. Of course, as Bowen (2007) points out, membership in these associations is voluntary, and many more public relations practitioners do not hold membership than do. Bowen also notes that, at least in the US, few practitioners have had meaningful academic training in ethics. That limitation is probably indicative of practitioners elsewhere as well and does not instill confidence in our discipline's ability to offer useful advice and counsel, especially when issues and events are complicated by international contexts. Further, as Gaither and Curtin (2006) observe, having a professional code of ethics is one thing, but enforcing the code appears to present problems, and public relations codes of ethics typically lack teeth. Kruckeberg (2000) adds that public relations practitioners, in the context of globalization and the increasing power of multinational corporations, bear an increased responsibility for "shaping the institutional culture, values and ideology" of the organizations they represent (p. 37). He bemoans the fact, too, that professional association codes of ethics are "grossly inadequate" because they are invariably limited to tactical issues of our practice; this, he says, does not serve us in our increasingly important role as "interpreter and ethicist and social policy-maker in guiding organizational behavior as well as in influencing and reconciling public perceptions" (p. 37). More useful would be a broader framework, similar to the cultural syndromes described in the previous chapter, for comparing the ethical paradigm of one culture to that of another. Understanding and accommodating differences in legal structures is difficult enough, but plumbing the somewhat amorphous arena of comparative ethics is highly problematic.

This section is concerned less with professional public relations ethics than with the overarching ethical frameworks that help define a culture and that most assuredly will affect public relations practice. There are a number of well-established rubrics that categorize and describe various ethical approaches and that may serve practitioners facing international engagements. Of course, the first important step in identifying ethical contrasts and similarities between your cultural paradigm and another is recognizing your own set of values. As is often said, "The last thing a fish notices is water". That means most of us are unaware of the values that guide our thoughts and behaviors, or of the underlying principles and prejudices that formed those values. That is a matter for deep contemplation and study; and, as important as that endeavor would be, it deserves far more consideration than we can possibly provide here, so please forgive the relative superficiality of this discussion. In fact, we're looking only at a tiny slice of the ethics pie. Comparative ethics is also sometimes called *descriptive* ethics and asks simply: "What do people say is right?" Above that level we would have *normative* ethics, which is prescriptive – suggesting what *is* right. Then there is *applied* ethics, which examines how those moral judgments are applied to real-world circumstances. Finally, there is *meta*-ethics, when we take a step further back and question what *right* even means. Philosophers dedicate lifetimes to unpacking these.

Comparative or descriptive ethics looks at groups of people – in our case, cultures – to determine what their values are, what they consider to be right and wrong, what is virtuous and what is abhorrent. Further, for the purpose of public relations practice, we would consider the issue in applied contexts. There are classical dilemmas that generate lively debate such as whether it would be *right* for a poor man to steal medicine needed to save his wife's life, or for a woman to compromise her moral standards to earn money to buy food for her child when she has no other options. We can take that a step further and ask whether the answers would vary depending upon the cultural setting. The classic example for public relations is whether it would be appropriate to bribe a journalist or editor for the placement of a news release; in most cultures that would be an abhorrent practice, but what if bribery were an accepted cultural practice? Kruckeberg and Tsetsura (2003) conducted exhaustive research on just this issue and report that the spectrum of positions on "cash for news" varies widely; practitioners venturing into international assignments may encounter attitudes very different from their own. Although the researchers argue strongly for a universal standard that dismisses this practice because of its obvious consequence of corrupting the channels of communication (assuming those channels would otherwise be perceived as fair and objective), Kruckeberg and Tsetsura acknowledge that in some settings bribery may be viewed as necessary to supplement poverty-level wages paid to journalists. The researchers also raise the potential argument calling for tolerance of other value systems as well as the need for patience in permitting media in developing or transitional nations to mature and reach a more robust and democratic stage. On the one hand, they say, an argument can be made that public relations practitioners from a culture in which "cash for news" is unacceptable have no right to impose that value on another culture in which the practice is the norm; however, the same sentiment could be expressed in the opposite direction: the journalist expecting a bribe has no right to impose that value on the public relations practitioner.

Sidebar: Bribery likelihood rankings

Here is a listing of sixty-six countries ranked in order of the likelihood that bribery in the form of "cash for news" occurs. Based on the scale the researchers used, there are a number of "ties" at some ranks. Those ranked nearest to first are least likely to practice bribery; those closer to 33rd are most likely to practice bribery:

1. Finland
2. Denmark, New Zealand, Switzerland
3. Germany, Ireland, the UK
4. Norway
5. Austria, Canada, the Netherlands, Sweden, Belgium, the USA
6. Australia
7. Ireland, Israel, Italy
8. Spain
9. Cyprus
10. France, Portugal
11. Chile, Greece
12. Estonia, Japan
13. Bosnia and Herzegovina
14. Brazil, Hungary
15. Puerto Rico (not a country, of course)
16. South Korea, Latvia, Russia, Slovakia
17. Bulgaria, Czech Republic, Hong Kong (also not a country), Lithuania, Singapore, Mauritius, Slovenia
18. Poland
19. Argentina, Mexico, Taiwan, Ukraine
20. Croatia
21. Turkey, Venezuela
22. South Africa, Thailand
23. United Arab Emirates
24. Malaysia
25. India, Kenya
26. Kuwait
27. Indonesia, Nigeria
28. Bahrain, Jordan
29. Egypt
30. Pakistan
31. Bangladesh, Vietnam
32. Saudi Arabia
33. China

Source: Kruckeberg and Tsetsura (2003)

What other applications for ethical frameworks might a public relations practitioner encounter? Consider the issue of conflict of interest. In many cultures it would be inappropriate to engage in activity while concealing the personal benefit to be derived by that activity. For example, representing two clients who are competitors would violate codes of ethics maintained by a number of professional organizations, but might be considered clever balancing in other cultures. Similarly, nepotism might be frowned upon in your culture but expected in another; you may deem it unethical to award a subcontract to a relative, but in another culture such an arrangement might be considered routine. How about making claims and promises you know are not supportable? In some cultures doing so might be viewed as pleasing customers by telling them what they want to hear. Along that line, you will read in the upcoming chapters that in many countries there is little distinction made among public relations, marketing and advertising; there is little question that marketing and advertising sometimes employ techniques and approaches that overstep the bounds of most public relations ethical codes.

These and other ethical issues pose a dilemma for us. Should we adopt the ethics of the culture and country we find ourselves in – *ethical relativism*? Or should we hold rigidly to our own standards, even at the risk of failure? Kruckeberg (1998) argues strenuously, and we agree, that professional ethics should supersede individual cultural and even organizational ethics, and as public relations becomes increasingly professionalized and global we expect there will be continuing movement toward universal standards. Further, those universal standards should be based upon principles that reflect social responsibility and the highest regard for elevating the human condition.

Conclusion

There are other structures that merit comparative analysis, such as religion, family, local and national government, and education system, each of which affects to some degree the conduct of public relations activities. Not surprisingly, there is little or no literature concerning how these structures might have an impact on practice, so the need for research is considerable. As Sriramesh and Verčič (2003) note: "The fledgling body of knowledge of global public relations consists almost exclusively of descriptive studies" (pp. xxvii–xxviii). They go on to delineate how political and cultural structures, plus degree of activism, conspire to transform public relations practice to suit each unique set of circumstances in terms of those factors. Of course, within each of those factors lies a host of subcomponents, each of which needs to be explored methodically in order to discover principles and theories that aid our understanding of the communication process as it pertains to public relations practice. After a sweeping overview in the following chapter, we shall begin exploring that interplay and demonstrating potential directions for tomorrow's scholars.

Questions for discussion

1. There is often dynamic tension between legal counsel ("say nothing") and public relations counsel ("be open and transparent"). Do you think that applies to all cultures? What factors might affect that tension?

2. Your CEO is going to be involved in significant business activity in another country, and there is a communication component to the issues involved. Who should take responsibility for backgrounding the CEO on relevant communication law – you or the legal counsel? Explain your view.
3. If your organization values environmentally responsible business practices, and you are establishing operations in a country in which lax environmental laws will permit you to increase profits sharply while still meeting and exceeding requirements, what recommendation will you make to the CEO?
4. Suggest ways in which other structures, not addressed here, such as family, religion, or educational system, might affect public relations practice.

Featured biography: Dean Kruckeberg

Dean Kruckeberg, APR, Fellow PRSA, is a professor in the Department of Communication Studies at the University of North Carolina, at Charlotte. As a Fellow of the Public Relations Society of America, Kruckeberg served as director-at-large on the national board from 2000 to 2002, as the 1993–4 Midwest District Chair, and as a 1996 national nominating committee member. He was also newsletter editor of the PRSA International Section and is the former National Faculty Advisor to the Public Relations Student Society of America. In addition, Kruckeberg is past Chair of the Public Relations Division of the International Communication Association, former Chair of the Public Relations Division of the National Communication Association, a charter member of the Commission on International Public Relations, and an active member of several other professional associations.

As a proponent and advocate of globalization, Kruckeberg has not only established a renowned global public relations curriculum at the University of Northern Iowa, but has also demonstrated sincere dedication to the advancement of international public relations. Kruckeberg has been a keynote speaker at an international conference sponsored by Ulan-Ude City, Buryatia, Siberia, and Russia, and has been an invited speaker to the Swedish Public Relations Association in Stockholm. He has also been a speaker at the *Teaching the Teachers* workshop in St Petersburg, Russia, which helps prepare communication faculty in the Baltic States and Russia to teach public relations. Kruckeberg has also participated in a review of the public relations and mass communication programs at the United Arab Emirates University and was also part of the project team that developed the public relations degree program at the university.

Kruckeberg observes that now, more than ever, public relations theory and practice is needed globally in business, in non-governmental organizations and in government. He explains:

> Global public relations has existed for as long as there have been professional public relations practitioners, for over a century. However, it is only during the past few decades that most US practitioners and scholars have given primary attention to the global environment that is of geometrically increasing importance regardless of a practitioner's client/employer or professional specialization.

He further contends that "problems evident in today's emerging global society have made it clear that public relations as practiced in one geo-political-socio-economic system and culture may not be effective or appropriate elsewhere".

According to Kruckeberg, globalism in itself makes no promise of a concurrent multicultural harmony among the diverse peoples of the world. He says:

If anything, the obverse may be true as publics from different cultures will be forced through globalization to live with those who have highly disparate beliefs and value systems that have resulted from these publics' different cultural heritages, traditions, belief systems, and value norms.

He also says that "organizations will be challenged in unprecedented ways, particularly in the clarification of their own ethical values and in the reconciliation of these values in the global arena". Kruckeberg is sure, however, that "as the level of public relations professionalism increases, multicultural perspectives will tend to become subsumed by a global professionalization that will tend to result in a commonality of professional best practices".

Kruckeberg advises future public relations practitioners to possess intelligence and a cosmopolitan worldview, as these are essential characteristics for success. He says: "The practitioner possesses excellent professional communication skills and is highly interested in lifelong learning to satisfy her fascination with her environment and the world in which she lives." He also believes that an exceptional breadth and depth in public relations theory is necessary for progress, as well as an overwhelming intellectual curiosity and a strong focus in public relations within the communication discipline. Kruckeberg refers to the public relations practitioner as the "point person" and "lead architect" in reconciling differences among the publics of organizations within the global arena and expects practitioners to "thoroughly understand the ethical ramifications of this awesome responsibility". Kruckeberg also makes clear that professional public relations is among the most competitive of career choices. There is no room for mediocrity; indeed, he suggests that future practitioners should "make wise decisions and engage in professional behavior".

To Kruckeberg, "global" not only denotes a professionalized occupation that shares best practices worldwide, but also connotes the need for a universal professional ideology as well as shared professional core values and belief systems. He recognizes the undeniable truth that in this day and age it is impossible for international public relations not to have a significant impact on the organizations they serve. It is Kruckeberg's earnest proposition that "as professionalization increases, the value of public relations will be increasingly recognized worldwide and practitioners increasingly will become influential members of an organization's dominant coalition".

Recommended websites

International Index of Bribery for News Coverage http://www.instituteforpr.org/research_single/index_of_bribery/

Online codes of ethics   http://ethics.iit.edu/codes/

Global Alliance Protocol Standards   http://www.globalpr.org/knowledge/ethics/protocol.asp

PRSA Code of Ethics   http://www.prsa.org/aboutUs/ethics/preamble_en.html

IABC Code of Ethics   http://www.iabc.com/about/code.htm

International Code (Code of Athens)   http://www.cerp.org/codes/international.asp

Center for Global Communication Studies   http://www.global.asc.upenn.edu/

References

Allam, H. and El Naggar, M., 2006. Net video spoofs Egyptian leader. *The Charlotte Observer*, September 15, p. 15A.

Bowen, S. A., 2007. Ethics and public relations. *Institute for Public Relations* [online]. Available at: http://www.instituteforpr.org

Gaither, T. and Curtin, P., 2006. International public relations ethics: a cross-disciplinary approach to the challenges of globalization, identity, and power. International Communication Association 2006 Annual Meeting. Dresden, Germany, June 19–23.

George, A. M., 2003. Teaching culture: the challenges and opportunities of international public relations. *Business Communication Quarterly*, 66 (2), pp. 97–113.

Hallin, D. C. and Mancini, P., 2004. *Comparing Media Systems*. New York: Cambridge University Press.

Hofstede, G., 1980. *Culture's Consequences: International Differences in Work-related Values*. Beverly Hills, Calif.: Sage.

Kruckeberg, D., 1998. Future reconciliation of multicultural perspectives in public relations ethics. *Public Relations Quarterly*, 43 (1), pp. 45–8.

Kruckeberg, D., 2000. The public relations practitioner's role in practicing strategic ethics. *Public Relations Quarterly*, 45 (3), pp. 35–9.

Kruckeberg, D. and Tsetsura, K., 2003. International index of bribery for news coverage [online]. Available at: http://www.instituteforpr.org/research_single/index_of_bribery/ [accessed February 20, 2008].

Martin, L. J. and Chaudhary, A. G., 1983. *Comparative Media Systems*. New York: Longman.

Ogus, A., 1999. Competition between national legal systems: a contribution of economic analysis to comparative law. *The International and Comparative Law Quarterly*, 48 (2), pp. 405–18.

Reitz, J. C., 1998. How to do comparative law. *The American Journal of Comparative Law*, 46 (4), pp. 617–36.

Siebert, F. S., Peterson, T. and Schramm, W., 1963. *Four Theories of the Press*. Urbana, Ill.: University of Illinois Press.

Sriramesh, K. and Verčič, D., 2003. *The Global Public Relations Handbook*. Mahwah, NJ: Lawrence Erlbaum.

Zaharna, R. S., 2001. "In-awareness" approach to international public relations. *Public Relations Review*, 27, 135–48.

Chapter 6

The state of the public relations profession

Summary

You have learned the basics behind public relations including definitions, theory, and the development of practice. You have also examined differences in cultural metrics and national structures to better understand the effects on public relations. This chapter expands your knowledge of international public relations by discussing where public relations stands today. With companies expanding globally and the development of an electronic culture, public relations is playing a larger role. The importance of learning a broad overview of worldwide practice deserves extra emphasis, which is why this chapter seems long. This chapter encompasses the history of international public relations as a whole and defines how the world practices, teaches and views public relations. By the end of the chapter you will be ready to explore public relations in specific regions of the world.

Chapter goals

- Distinguish development differences in public relations between countries.
- Describe various public relations functions and how they differ throughout the world.
- Explain how the discipline is achieving professionalization through professional organizations and other factors.
- Identify the education systems available to young practitioners and how education differs from region to region.
- Describe worldwide viewpoints on public relations.
- Identify different publics involved in international public relations.

Introduction

Most college students today have probably heard the phrase "global village". Originally referring to the Worldwide Web's ability to connect computer users around the globe, the phrase has come to signify life in an interconnected, cross-cultural, increasingly boundary-less society. Many professions have been altered radically by the opportunity to engage more easily the world's citizens and consumers in the global village. Public relations is no exception. More than a decade ago, noted international public relations practitioner Joe Epley (1992) predicted what the public relations profession would be like in this emerging era. As if gazing into a crystal ball, Epley suggested that public relations would play an important role in an increasingly interdependent global society. He predicted that communication technology, the realignment of economic power, the emergence of issues that recognize no political boundary, and the prospect of world peace would shape public relations fundamentally in the twenty-first century.

If you look around today, Epley's predictions were apt. Students learn of new products on Facebook. Cold Stone Creamery chose YouTube.com as the promotional channel for its latest ice cream flavor. Instead of faxing, many public relations practitioners now "e-blast" their latest news releases to a handpicked selection of journalists' e-mail inboxes. We now live in a world in which China is a major force in business and trade; not surprisingly, public relations is booming in its major cities. Issues do seem to know no boundaries: HSBC Bank is responding to the hotly debated global warming issue by publicizing "green" financial services to customers from Brazil to India. Finally, although the prospect of world peace still continues to be a daunting challenge, hopeful signs such as the agreement between the Protestant and Catholic groups in Ireland suggest progress. Public relations is seen here also in diplomacy efforts between the two sides.

This chapter builds on Epley's assessment of public relations in the global village to gain a better understanding of the status of the public relations profession today. Several scholars have suggested a variety of comparative metrics to aid in this task. As we noted, Sriramesh and Verčič (2001) suggest that four key infrastructural ingredients are important in understanding the status of public relations in a country: a nation's political system, its level of economic development, its legal system, and the level of activism present. Similarly, Botan (1993) suggested the following four factors in examining the status of international public relations: level of national development, primary clients, legal/political context, and the history of the practice. This chapter broadly explores these variables and others by reviewing the profession's typical functions; its professional organizations, licensing and accreditation; the status of public relations education around the globe; varying world publics' views of the profession; and public relations' relationships with media and other publics.

Recent developments in public relations

It is important to begin a discussion about the historical development of public relations by noting that since World War II the world economy has been integrating toward a single market (Hill 2002). International trade organizations such as the International Monetary Fund (IMF), the World Trade Organization (WTO), and the World Bank have monitored and developed this global economic system. This change in the world economy has been accelerated by new communication technologies. In public relations, the global economy means public relations practitioners now, more than ever, need to communicate internationally (Lee 2005).

In 1999, for example, two commuter trains in London's Paddington Station accidentally crossed tracks and collided, killing thirty people. A few days later, the listed share price of stock in a mid-sized US insurance company dropped sharply. Strange coincidence? It turned out that rumors circulating the week following the incident suggested that the trains' insurer, US-owned

St Paul International, stood to lose billions of British pounds. Until St Paul issued a news release to stem the tide of rumors and to comfort investors, the power of the international rumor mill caused wide and damaging speculation in the US stock market (Hirogoyen 2000). This illustrates how public relations can help organizations deal with competing global forces and viewpoints. Public relations practitioners can help companies communicate globally corporate social responsibility, citizenship, conflict resolution, and much more (Drobis 2002).

Yet even in light of the challenges and opportunities globalization presents for the public relations profession it is important to recognize, as we have already argued, that public relations in one country may not be the same in another (Turk and Scanlan 2004). Today many major US, European, and other nations' corporations conduct business in more than one country and are known as multinational corporations (MNCs). As a result, knowledge of particular characteristics and developments of public relations in host countries, along with understanding how it is conducted in the "home" country of the MNC, is critically important.

One area of interest lies in understanding the roots of the public relations profession in a given country or region. Although Chapter 2 described the roots of US public relations in democracy and capitalism, European discussions about public relations, for example, are guided often by social critic Max Weber. Meanwhile, in Asia, public relations is influenced more by Eastern theology and hierarchic relationships. In Thailand, for example, social status shapes public relations practices (Wakefield 2000). These differing origins of the profession can lead to differences in levels of public relations development. They give rise also to specific issues of concern in a given country or region. Although discussed in more detail later in the chapter, for now, note that the development of public relations and the *perception* of development vary by country. Australian practitioners, for example, believe that the US leads academic discussion of public relations theory and practice (Epley 2003). Canadian executives, meanwhile, believe US public relations practice may be a little more sophisticated in terms of market size and budgets. They believe, however, that their own use of technology may be more advanced. In terms of non-Western nations, Chinese public relations executives report that the profession is still maturing and developing as an industry, while Taiwanese executives note that more attention needs to be paid to measuring the effectiveness of their public relations programs (Epley 2003).

In any case, students of international public relations must begin to understand the differing development of public relations around the world. For US students in particular, successfully understanding and practicing public relations means not always relying on Western experience. Indeed, though US universities initially led the study of international public relations, international public relations practitioners the world over need non-Western examples of how public relations developed in a particular region in order to expand their knowledge. This section describes that process, looking at the development of public relations in Europe, Asia, Africa, Latin America, the Middle East, and Australia and New Zealand.

Public relations in Europe

According to public relations scholars David Miller and Philip Schlesinger (2001), public relations in Europe is unevenly developed. Some countries have very well developed public relations industries while others are continuing to establish the profession. This section explores the varying levels of development and provides insight into the historical development of the profession in the European Union (EU).

Public relations in Britain is the most developed in Europe. Between 1979 and 1997, British public relations consultancies expanded nearly tenfold (Miller and Schlesinger 2001). British firms dominate the market in most member states of the EU (Miller and Schlesinger 2001). In the United Kingdom (UK), the public relations profession remains on an upward growth path and is now the second most popular profession, worth £3.4 billion to the UK economy (Dickerson 2005; Nagvi 2007). Indeed, companies are now replacing advertising budgets with public relations. Health, food and sports public relations comprise the highest growth areas. Government public relations is on the rise, and crisis and risk public relations are also growing. In terms of a profile of the typical UK public relations practitioner, the average age is late twenties and is increasingly ethnically diverse. To be a successful public relations practitioner in the UK, one must have "specialty" knowledge in addition to his/her public relations skills: i.e. finance, medicine, or sports expertise (Dickerson 2005).

Elsewhere in Europe, the public relations profession developed differently according to region. Overall, for example, public relations in the EU is growing in scope and intensity (Miller and Schlesinger 2001). Public relations professionals target EU institutions, national and regional government in the EU member states, trade associations, corporations and interest groups (Miller and Schlesinger 2001). As in both the UK and the US, today the EU public relations profession enjoys educated professionals, advanced scholarship, and interested students. Public relations foci vary across the EU. In Western European countries, for instance, corporate social responsibility is particularly important in public relations work. Studies of European consumers often indicate a desire for quality and safe products, and they want to know that what they buy has been produced in a socially and environmentally responsible way (Weber Shandwick 2003). Indeed, seven out of ten European consumers are willing to pay more for the products of socially responsible companies (Weber Shandwick 2003). In Italy, for example, consumers are drawn to companies with social campaigns and were predicted to donate €1.1 billion to social causes in 2005 (Weber Shandwick 2003).

In contrast to Western Europe, public relations in Central and Eastern Europe has differing levels of development. These regions are historically different legally and politically from Western European counterparts, largely owing to their history of communism (Botan 1992). Nevertheless, public relations has burgeoned, academically and professionally, in these regions (Turk and Scanlan 2004). In terms of historical development, much has happened in the public relations profession here since 1998. Many Eastern Europe countries are joining the EU, and their public relations industries are being nourished by exposure to international markets and ownership (Weber Shandwick 2004). Public relations generally is viewed positively in the region, especially as it is helping nations to develop. Lithuania, for example, has become one of the fastest-growing economies in Central and Eastern Europe and is now a member of the EU. Public relations began to emerge in Lithuania after the fall of the Soviet Union. Along with growth in the economy and public sectors, Lithuanian public relations has become part of the corporate culture and marketing mix, operating today in larger organizations and government institutions. It is expected to grow and improve (Burneikaite 2004 cited in Turk and Scanlan 2004).

Public relations in areas of Central Europe once dominated by communism may also have some differences in development, but the industry clearly is growing in the region. Fees typically are lower here than in the US, the UK, Germany and Japan, yet prospects for future growth in Hungary and the Czech Republic are strong (Josephs and Josephs 1998). Many local offices of US or UK firms are located here, but there are also a number of sizable local and regional agencies. In this region, fewer public relations practitioners come from a media background – probably because, in totalitarian régimes, publications and broadcasting were often government-owned. Sometimes, client sophistication levels do not reach US levels, but this is changing as savvy clients demand more. Work typically involves media relations and print placements, though strategic planning and crisis communication are growing in importance (Josephs and Josephs 1998).

The nature of public relations in Poland illustrates the status of public relations in this region. Since the 1990s, the public relations market in Poland has been developing rapidly, with an annual growth rate of 12 percent (Ławniczak *et al.* 2003). Many of the first clients were large multinationals, and many other companies saw public relations as a subcategory of advertising (Laszyn 2001). Polish public relations saw a slowdown in the late 1990s because of an economic downturn. By 2001, however, a steadily growing market and acceptance into the EU generated a boost for Polish public relations practice.

Public relations in Asia

An area as large as Asia is bound to illustrate differences in how public relations developed. The first foreign public relations firm opened in China in 1984. By 1997, public relations courses were official and being offered at university. Local firms are now sprouting up to compete with the big multinational agencies there (Gorney 2005). Today, the public relations industry in China is experiencing a tremendous 33 percent growth rate (Gorney 2005). Indeed, throughout Asia, countries show high levels of public relations sophistication (Turk and Scanlan 2004). Asian public relations developed historically out of a collectivist cultural model. As a result, some US American assumptions about public relations cannot be applied to Asian cultures because of the differences in political systems, cultural values and media environment (Wu 2005). For example, the most important skill for Asian public relations people is different from the US, where writing is most important. Because of the collectivist nature of Asian culture, interpersonal communication skills can become most important in working with clients and publics.

Other differences surface when thinking about the relationship of Asian public relations with the media. In China, for example, the public relations industry still relies heavily on the concept of *guanxi* – good connections – and requires practitioners to have developed relationships with journalists (Weber Shandwick 2004). Similarly, in Korea, the media even has different names for public relations sources: "*hong bo*" for government sources and simply "public relations" for corporate publicity (Newsom 2007). Newspaper sources favor corporate sources over the government ones (Park 2001).

Many Asian nations have used publicity and promotion for nation-building, sometimes called development public relations (Newsom 2007). Such campaigns directed toward citizens are common both in Singapore, where government owns the news media, and in India, which has a free press (Newsom 2007). In Malaysia, government-inspired campaigns still account for much of the current public relations activity. This type of public relations work began in 1945 with the British establishing a Department of Publicity and Printing there to counter the appeal of communism. After Malaysia gained independence from Britain in 1957 (as the Federation of Malaya), its government concentrated on nation-building and conducting communication campaigns such as combating malaria and encouraging racial harmony. As national development continued, market-based public relations started, though even today "almost every major (public relations) consultancy in Singapore and Kuala Lumpur derives 20–30 percent of its income from one of the various government ministries" (Van Leuven 1996, p. 213).

Singaporean public relations also has roots in nation-building but has since expanded greatly. In Singapore, public relations began when the British set up a Department of Publicity and Printing following the end of World War II, hoping to instill a sense of loyalty to British rule (Lim *et al.* 2005). When Singapore began self-governance, a variety of campaigns were launched stressing good social behavior important to a young developing nation (Lim *et al.* 2005). After Singapore became independent in 1965, international public relations firms began to appear there. They were designed to keep Western countries informed about the health of MNCs located in the country. In the early years, public relations in Singapore was located in service industries such as hospitality, banking and retail. The public relations industry has grown significantly in the last two decades, as Singapore is one of Asia's leading financial, media and industrial hubs. Singapore's public relations industry is growing at a rate of 34 percent, outpacing Hong Kong, once the dominant public relations market in Asia. After the Asian financial crisis in 1997, Singaporean public relations has focused on corporate governance and transparency. Now emerging as one of the "Asian Tigers", there is great potential for Singapore's public relations industry.

Although Japan has a high level of national public relations development, and its primary clients are businesses, its historical roots are quite different from those of some of its Western counterparts. Japan traces its public relations roots to the role of press clubs, where each industry in the private sector has its own press club. All public relations announcements, whether from government or from industry, should come through these press clubs (Botan 1992; Ohashi 1984). Today, Japan's media environment would suggest a flourishing public relations marketplace. The country has a host of national and regional newspapers with a combined circulation of 70 million, the highest per-capita figure in the world (Weber Shandwick 2006). Yet the Japanese public relations industry is about a tenth of the size of the US industry and is worth around US$4 million per year (Weber Shandwick 2006). This status might be surprising, considering Japan's GDP is nearly half that of the US. Indeed, the Japanese public relations industry is still working to convince business leaders and politicians of the value of the profession. Japanese companies believed traditionally that public relations should be handled internally, so investor relations, CSR, issues management, and internal relations were handled within various corporate departments. Media relations was also handled by in-house staff and faced the challenge of the press club system. Recently, however, public relations in Japan has been maturing and gaining more visibility. Political parties have begun using public relations firms. Two major independent domestic public relations firms went public through initial public offerings. With the resulting rise in public awareness, college students are increasingly targeting public relations companies as their ideal employers (Weber Shandwick 2006).

Public relations in Africa

Today, Africa is both the originator and the focus of intense public relations efforts (Turk and Scanlan 2004). Although many African nations still see public relations primarily as a tool for national development or nation-building, the profession certainly is growing on the continent. Africa's need to attract foreign investors to aid in economic growth and political stability, as well as its looming debt and health crises, do present significant challenges to the developing public relations industry (Fobanjong 2004). Modern African public relations is modeled on European approaches, but there are distinct differences in a region with so many developing nations (Pratt and Okigbo 2004). In Kenya, for example, modern public relations developed partly out of the founding of the British

Broadcasting Company (BBC) in 1922. The network's need for journalists to fill the new medium and the channel's ability to develop public opinion began to form the beginnings of public relations practice there. Following independence, public relations in Kenya focused on implementing self-government, supporting Kenya's foreign policy, and supporting business owners and unions (L'Etang and Muruli 2004).

One key difference in African public relations entails understanding the public relations role in creating foreign investment. To attract these moneys, public relations practitioners must help improve governance and conflict management, increase equity and investment in its people, and attract better support from the international community (Pratt and Okigbo 2004). In Africa, then, government is a primary client. Public relations professionals work with governments to open public relations resources such as newspapers, radio and television stations (Fobanjong 2004). They work also with officials to help open régimes to political participation and economic competition (Fobanjong 2004).

Similar to the US, in many African countries the media were the primary originator of public relations (Sattler 1981). As a result, the media continue to be a primary communication channel for public relations messages. Reliance on mass media alone is typically insufficient, so traditional communication channels such as the gongman, the town crier, the market square, and the chief's courts still exist (Botan 1992; Pratt 1985). In Ghana, for example, folk media such as dance, song and storytelling still may be important channels for conducting public information campaigns (Riley 1991). The unique "(Product) Red" campaign illustrates how media and other channels may be used to help Africa solve one of its primary health challenges.

Questions for discussion

1. Do you agree that we are living in a "global village"? Support your answer with an example. How does living in a "global village" affect public relations practice?
2. It has been emphasized that public relations began in the US. Do you believe that the US is the leader in public relations? Explain your answer.
3. How do different development stages of public relations across the globe affect practice? How does one practicing public relations account for these differences?

Sidebar: Shop (RED) and save lives – a campaign to raise awareness and funds for the Global Fund to Help Fight AIDS in Africa

Health issues such as AIDS have reached crisis proportions in Africa. Rock singer Bono of the band U2 and Bobby Shriver, Chairman of DATA (Debt, AIDS, Trade, Africa), sought to partner private-sector businesses and the buying power of the public to help eliminate AIDS in Africa. Iconic companies such as Gap, Motorola, Converse, Giorgio Armani, and Apple were brought together to make long-term investments in Africa and build an exciting consumer brand. Each company made a five-year commitment to license (PRODUCT) RED™ retail, marketing and on-line activities, each contributing a significant percentage of sales or portion of profits into Global Fund-financed AIDS programs. Bono reminded consumers that red is the color of emergency and revolution. Consumers responded by buying products to "do the (RED) thing". The (RED) brand team partnered with OTX (Online Testing Exchange) to track brand recognition and its impact on (RED) partner brands. (RED) was launched with a series of high-profile US media relations events, including *The Oprah Winfrey Show*, a New York media blitz, coverage on CNBC, *The Today Show*, *Good Morning America*, *The Daily Show with Jon Stewart*, *The Rachel Ray Show*, *Martha* and E!. Myspace.com featured (RED) banner ads. On YouTube.com, a 90-second (RED) manifesto received nearly 300,000 views. In the end, more than 3,000 media hits were generated, with nearly $20 million in sales delivered to the Global Fund. In Africa, Global Fund-financed programs have reached more than 168,000 mothers with counseling/services to prevent mother-to-child transmission of HIV, trained more than a thousand healthcare providers, and provided anti-retroviral therapy for HIV/AIDS for almost 16,000 people. This far-reaching public relations branding effort shows the power of the (RED) brand team, OTX, celebrity, and corporate America working together to help solve one of Africa's greatest challenges. (Compiled from PRSA.org Campaign Profiles)

Public relations in Latin America

The Latin American public relations market is one of the fastest-growing in the world. Once associated with lobbying and events, the Latin American public relations industry is now evolving to meet the challenges of communicating across this vast region (Weber Shandwick 2005). In the past, the media environment was dependent on the current political administration and was tied closely to personal connections with journalists. Today, strong, independent media are developing. Media outlets are simultaneously consolidating and expanding, providing more avenues for brand and product promotion (Kotcher 1998). Many public relations professionals in Latin America have backgrounds in politics and the media; and, as a result, many firms are involved in political campaigning, public affairs, and government strategy. Unlike Western firms, politics is not considered a "specialized" area of Latin American public relations (Weber Shandwick 2005). Further, while crisis communication is a significant part of daily public relations work, consumer public relations is a more recent area of attention.

Ten years ago, public relations agencies in the region were small, and focused on political strategy and crisis communications. They also helped Western oil firms manage their presence in the countries. In addition, firms helped large financial institutions such as Citibank to deal with communication challenges. They helped manage privatization work for Latin American public utilities, airlines, and telecoms operators (Weber Shandwick 2005). Today, there are opportunities to work for regional brands, such as Wines of Chile, Petrobas, and the Costa Rican tourism board, both domestically and locally. Work on behalf of global clients such as Microsoft, Kraft and ExxonMobil also continues.

In Latin America, foreign investors even with strong corporate reputations may face an initial degree of distrust from local consumers. Because the region's public relations is developing in an area where publics faced corrupt governments and media institutions, public relations professionals must work to engender trust (Tilson 2004). Unfortunately, some public relations firms in the region were involved in representing violent and corrupt régimes. As a result, foreign and domestic corporations sometimes need to do better in promoting the welfare of employees or the local community (Tilson 2004). Understanding the region and building true corporate social responsibility programs is very important here.

Public relations in the Middle East

Public relations has ancient roots in the Middle East, dating from early Egyptian and Mesopotamian civilizations (Grunig and Hunt 1984). Public relations in Arab cultures is said to extend back 1,200 years. In the Middle East, practitioners carefully consider indigenous cultures when applying public relations theory and strategies (Ayish and Kruckeberg 2004). Public relations still must be considered in the context of Islamic ethical theory and Arabic laws. Generally, though the level of development of public relations in the Middle East varies, sometimes public relations is still thought to mean procuring visas, arranging transportation, and performing hospitality functions (Ayish and Kruckeberg 2004). However, public relations differences among nations are clear. The public relations profession in the United Arab Emirates (UAE), for example, has been affected tremendously by the socio-economic, educational and cultural development of that country (Kirat 2006). In some ways, UAE public relations agencies are virtually identical to their US counterparts, primarily focusing on product publicity and marketing public relations. Similarly, UAE ministries and government administrations established their in-house public relations departments to respond to the growing demands of their various publics. In this way, the profession in the Middle East is evolving. UAE agencies may use primarily one-way asymmetrical press agency and public information models of public relations, but internal government organizations are starting to approach more of a two-way model (Kruckeberg 1994). The future of public relations in the UAE and elsewhere in the Middle East is promising. Universities here have launched public relations programs to meet the need of the job market for qualified practitioners. Indeed, throughout the Middle East, universities are preparing students for public relations careers (Turk and Scanlan 2004).

Public relations in Australia and New Zealand

Public relations is also growing in Australia and New Zealand. In Australia the industry has grown tremendously from the establishment of professional public relations institutes in 1949 in the state of New South Wales and in 1952 in the state of Victoria. Australian public relations has been shaped by US developments but also displays differences in culture, language, geography, economics, politics and business (Singh and Smyth 2000). Australia saw its first major public relations firm, Eric White & Associates, open its doors in 1947. The firm began by specializing in government relations and was later bought by international public relations firm Hill & Knowlton (Sourcewatch 2007). Another early Australian firm, IPR, was acquired by the international public relations giant Weber Shandwick. Today, the Australian industry features both corporate and agency public relations and operates in all business sectors including healthcare, financial services, technology, community, and consumer relations (PRIA.com/au). Although data regarding the size of the industry are difficult to obtain, the ABS Labour Force Survey reported in November 2005 that more than 61,000 individuals were employed in public relations, marketing and advertising in Australia in 2005–6. Estimates suggest that around 15 percent (10,000+) of this number work in and around public relations, with around 1 in 4 (2,500) currently members of the Public Relations Institute of Australia (PRIA.com/au). Growth in public relations work is strong, with very good job prospects (PRIA.com/au).

In New Zealand, the public relations industry had no formal training until the mid-1980s but is now a growing, maturing profession (Prinz.org.nz). Seven major institutes around the country now provide specific communication and public relations degree and diploma courses. Previously, many practitioners came from a journalism background, but today many come from a public relations educational background. Responsibilities of New Zealand public relations practitioners are growing, too, from media relations to risk and issues management, community relations, corporate affairs, government relations, marketing communications and internal communications. As in other regions, many practitioners are female, and the country is working on addressing the gender imbalance. Although the profession is relatively young here, respondents in a public relations survey administered by the Public Relations Institute of New Zealand (Prinz.org.nz) expressed a desire to be regarded as a true profession. To do so, practitioners are working on helping the influence of public relations to be felt at decision-making levels, increasing entry-level qualifications, providing ongoing professional development, and broadening the function and scope of a professional's responsibility. The average public relations salary across New Zealand is US$83,000, with the average practitioner possessing ten years' experience.

Public relations functions

The previous section should provide students with a glimpse into how the public relations profession has developed and evolved. Worldwide, public relations practitioners are engaging in the main function of public relations: using communication to adapt relationships between organizations and their publics (Botan 1992). As we read, areas of emphasis vary. Professionals put the public relations process to work in government communication, entertainment, sports, crisis, marketing-related and risk communication. In the US, a 2006 PRSA survey reveals that public relations professionals spend most of their time on media relations, followed by marketing communications, corporate communications, community relations, event planning, and public relations counseling. In the US and around the world, however, the move away from public relations supporting marketing functions continues, with professionals providing their services in organizations including non-profit/foundation groups, privately held corporations, public relations agencies, publicly held corporations, government, and educational institutions (Stateman 2007).

This section of the chapter details some functions and challenges in managing international public relations. It is important to note that, though countries vary their areas of emphasis in public relations, there are some common foci (Epley 2003). In France, Portugal and Canada, for example, there is increased emphasis on targeting messages to smaller and more discrete segments of the population. Meanwhile, the UK, Australia, Canada, Argentina and Malaysia see a move toward corporate social responsibility work. The Netherlands finds an increase in integrated marketing communication; similarly, Turkey and Russia see an increase in marketing public relations. Both Argentina and Germany express a need to discover cost effectiveness while handling more complex projects. Russia and Denmark note that public relations is now being seen as a distinct profession. Turkey, Italy, Japan, Mexico and Taiwan note increased specialization in such areas as financial public relations, crisis communication, healthcare, travel, risk and environmental public relations. Besides these areas of commonality, what are some of the specialized functions of public relations work engaged in by members of the international community? There are four functions of particular interest in international public relations.

National identity and promotion

Some public relations efforts are focused on promoting the interests of various countries. In Latin America, for example, the PromPeru public relations agency works to attract foreign capital investment and tourism to Peru (Tilson 2004). Similar efforts are seen in Africa. Asian countries are also active in these types of public relations efforts, particularly targeting the US when promoting their countries' interests. Western European and Middle Eastern countries also promote their interests inside the US (Lee 2006). These countries employ economic campaigns, along with political, tourism, culture, education and communication strategy to promote their interests. Representatives from these countries tend to meet with government officials and members of their staff; media owners and journalists; private corporations and investors; tourism partners; and industry officials. In fact, these countries' public relations efforts are a significant predictor of their prominence in US news coverage (Lee 2006). An international campaign launched by the Chinese government in the US, for example, helped China gain coverage in major US newspapers, including the *New York Times* (Zhang and Cameron 2003).

Managing corporate reputation

Another important international public relations function is helping companies manage their corporate cultures both internally and externally. For example, public relations professionals helped RWE Solutions, a multinational company, to adopt change management strategies and establish a new corporate culture (Durig 2004). They helped RWE's management to formulate and articulate the core statements and the "mission" of the company, making sure its business model and strategy were comprehensible and communicable to external publics. Public relations managers also assessed whether the company's "emotional presence" was evident in its corporate design and made sure that the design matched the story, self-image and goals of the company. Public relations work of this sort is a critical component of international corporate strategy.

The RWE Solutions example illustrates the increasing need to include public relations professionals as part of the management team or dominant coalition. As discussed earlier in the book, public relations is moving away from the technician role to becoming an integral part of the corporate management team. When public relations professionals become part of management, they have the greatest impact on decisions made about public relations (Sriramesh *et al.* 1996). In fact, public relations practitioners who are not part of the dominant coalition "function more in the implementation of decisions about public relations than in their formulation" (Sriramesh *et al.* 1996). Of course, the inclusion of public relations professionals in the corporate management team also helps them meet the challenges of conducting international public relations campaigns more effectively.

Crisis communication

As it stands, public relations is still somewhat underprepared in terms of global public relations management. Coca-Cola's response to its tainting crisis in Belgium and France provides one notorious example. In 1999, 300 Europeans claimed to have become sick from drinking Coca-Cola beverages laced with dioxin. More than forty children in a Belgian town became ill, followed by dozens more in that country. As Belgian media jumped on the story and Belgian citizens demanded answers, the government ordered Coke to close its production plants. France then followed Belgium's lead and banned production of the drink (Cobb 1999). A full *week* after the European claims of sickness, Coke chief executive Douglas Ivester met with government officials and employees in Europe. Although ads placed in newspapers offered apologies and free Coke, the company was considered self-serving and late in its response to the tainted product crisis (Wakefield 2000). Sales have now recovered, but the crisis shows a misstep in global public relations preparation and management.

Although Coke executed the textbook US response to solve the crisis, that approach did not work in the Belgian market. There, Ivester's immediate presence, along with words of concern that the claims of illness were important to Coke, was necessary. Coke needed to understand the local environment better. Belgians needed empathy in addition to scientific data showing product safety (Cobb 1999). Often, then, global public relations management is a victim of benign neglect because practitioners are still working to become a greater part of the dominant coalition. That is, though Coca-Cola did not mean to fuel the crisis by its response, its lack of research and proactive public relations planning for the European market left it in the lurch when the crisis arose. In fact, many US firms continue to separate domestic and international public relations, which makes responding to crisis situations more difficult (Wakefield 2000). On the other hand, European firms are beginning to coordinate the function globally. The biography of Thomas Mattia at the conclusion of the previous chapter, though, shows that Coca-Cola has come a long way since the Belgian incident.

It is an increasingly necessary public relations function, then, to be able to manage conflicts on a world stage. In doing business abroad, the transnational corporation can run into a conflict that has the potential to affect its business in its home country and around the world where it operates. Molleda (2005) observes that the nature of the global environment often requires organizations to respond to crisis in many geographical locations. Strategic management of organizational actions and responses is necessary. The longer the conflict lasts, the more countries and news media become involved, and the likelihood of additional players, including activists, to express their views and participate in the conflict increases. This type of snowballing situation can result in greater damage to the reputation and operation for the organization responsible for causing the problem (Molleda 2005).

Communications locally

Finally, on the flip side, public relations professionals must still keep the concerns of local audiences in mind. Another important public relations function is in helping many MNCs open subsidiaries in several host nations (Bardhan and Patwardhan 2004). Although fears of neocolonialism and postcolonial anxieties are very real phenomena in parts of the world, MNCs can carefully practice public relations in once-resistant host cultures (Bardhan and Patwardhan 2004). For example, two MNC subsidiaries in India, Hindustan Lever Ltd (of Unilever) and Maruit Udyog Ltd (of Suzuki Motor Corporation), show that MNCs can be successful in potentially resistant host countries. These subsidiaries employed culturally attuned involvement, intervention, and respect for the local culture, proving their commitment to their host nations through socially responsible performance over time. Carefully cultivating these relationships is an important variable in practicing public relations in host nations around the world. As Harold Burson, CEO of Burson Marstellar, points out, successful management of the global public relations function may mean employing a two-tier structure: centralization for coordination and consistency of policies and messages; regional implementation for adaptation to local language, culture and politics. As he puts it, MNCs must possess a "global reach, local touch" philosophy: that is, "while world strategies evolve around a central point, the tactics must reflect local realities" (in Epley 1992).

Questions for discussion

1. In New Zealand, a gender imbalance is present. Do you think a gender balance is good? Is a gender balance present in your workplace or educational program?
2. Do you agree that public relations specialists should be part of a company's management team? Do you believe the profession should be elevated to a higher level? How long do you think it will take for the discipline to be raised this high nationally and internationally, and what measures are needed to achieve that?

Professionalization: Professional organizations, licensing and accreditation

Harold Burson's observation about the requirements of managing the global public relations function successfully makes a good deal of sense in today's multicultural landscape, but how well prepared are students and practitioners for such challenges? Data suggest that practitioners lack readiness for international work. In an international public relations survey, Southern Methodist University noted that only 10 percent of practitioners had more than three years of international experience, and 80 percent felt unprepared for the global marketplace (Wakefield 2000). Fortunately, the profession is working hard to support its practitioners and future professionals through professional associations, licensing initiatives and accreditation procedures.

The good news for future professionals is that, in terms of building a professional attitude and standards among public relations practitioners, the field is making progress (Coombs *et al.* 1994). Around the world, professional public relations associations work to empower professionals "to reach their fullest potential and provide development, knowledge, and support to different members" (Ravazzani 2006). In addition to empowering members, professional public relations associations can help promote diversity and interculturalism (Ravazzanini 2006). Diversity represents a major commitment and a strategic objective for professional associations such as the Public Relations Society of America (PRSA), the Federazione Relazioni Pubbliche Italiana (FERPi) and the Chartered Institute of Public Relations (CIPR). These associations help encourage people from diverse backgrounds and experiences to join the public relations sector to make practitioners as representative of society as possible (Ravazzanii 2006).

There is a wide range of professional public relations associations available to practitioners around the world. In Africa, the Federation of African Public Relations Associations (FAPRA) helps foster unity among public relations practitioners and helps set the standards for the burgeoning profession. In Asia, the China International Public Relations Association (CIPRA) supports Chinese professionals. India offers its practitioners membership in the Public Relations Consultants Association of India (PRCAI). Similarly, the Public Relations Institute of Australia (PRIA) represents professionals' concerns there. Like many professional public relations associations, PRIA helps ensure quality public relations education standards, accrediting various academic programs. PRIA also offers guest lectures, short courses, and teaching programs. Similarly, PRINZ (Public Relations Institute of New Zealand) promotes public relations and its practitioners in New Zealand.

Practitioners can belong also to associations that represent their interests regionally or worldwide. The International Public Relations Association (IPRA), for example, organized in 1955, is helping raise the standards of public relations practice in various countries and improving the quality and efficiency of practitioners (ipra.org). It has created an International Code of Ethics, informally known as the "Code of Athens", that has been promoted widely. It presents Golden World Awards for Excellence to recognize excellence in public relations practice worldwide. In addition to IPRA judges, a special UN panel assesses each year's entry. Today, IPRA places special emphasis on education and professional literature, and particularly promotes the public relations profession in the developing countries of Central and Eastern Europe (ipra.org). It offers also an informative public relations publication, *IPRA Frontline*.

Some countries and regions offer other very well developed professional associations that provide members with many public relations resources. In the United States, for example, the Public Relations Society of America (PRSA) forms the world's largest organization for public relations professionals and includes 28,000 professional and student members. The society has 112 chapters nationwide and 255 college and university chapters throughout the United States. Chartered in 1947, PRSA seeks to advance the standards of the public relations profession and to provide members with professional development opportunities. It provides continuing education programs, information exchange forums, and research projects conducted on the national and local levels. It seeks to advance the profession through professional development programs, works to strengthen the society by seeking new strategies to increase membership and enrich member services, and establishes global leadership strengthening alliances with other public relations organizations throughout the world (prsa.org). In addition to offering professional development and networking opportunities, the PRSA publishes *Public Relations Tactics*, *The Public Relations Strategist* and the recently revived *Public Relations Journal*.

In Europe there are several multicountry and country-specific associations. The Chartered Institute of Public Relations is the largest public relations institute in Europe, offering its 9,000 members a qualification diploma, training and development, policy guidance, and a Code of Conduct dedicated to raising the standards of European public relations practitioners (ipr.org.uk). The Chartered Institute of Public Relations publishes *Public Relations Strategy*, designed to explore strategic management theories in relation to public relations (ipr.org.uk). *Public Relations Strategy* also examines how globalization and the Internet are changing public relations practice.

In Latin America, professional organizations are also active. CONFIARP, the Latin American Public Relations Association, helped develop the region's public relations philosophy. It seeks to elevate the status of public relations in Latin America by promoting integration and professionalism among and within its member associations (Molleda 2005). Currently, fifteen association members in three geographical areas make up CONFIARP and include: Netherland Antilles, Costa Rica, Cuba, Mexico, Panama, Puerto Rico, Bolivia, Colombia, Ecuador, Peru, Venezuela, Argentina, Brazil, Chile and Uruguay. CONFIARP has had success in elevating the profession in the region, with, for example, Mexican public relations practitioners noting that the practice is becoming more professional (Epley 2003).

Although professional organizations are strong, the issues of licensing and accreditation for public relations practitioners around the world are still being debated. There are several reasons for the debate. In essence, the licensing discussion centers on whether public relations professionals should have to take a licensing exam in order to practice their skills, similar to the exams undertaken by prospective doctors, lawyers and psychologists. In the US, for example, practitioners do not have to be licensed. Some US practitioners argue against licensing on the grounds that the government would have too much control over practitioners; others argue that licensing curtails First Amendment rights (primarily freedom of speech and freedom of the press). Some practitioners support the licensing initiative but disagree about the criteria for licensure. Licensing is likely to continue to be a thorny issue (Cherenson *et al.* 2006) but remains uncommon. In Latin America, only two countries have legalized and licensed public relations as a profession: Brazil, in 1967, and Panama, since 1980. In addition, the judicial system in Argentina has recognized public relations professionals with a university degree as expert witnesses since 1996 (Molleda 2005). Although it seems that the issue of licensing is one that may take time to resolve, the accreditation process offered by several professional public relations organizations offers an alternative method to ensure quality public relations practitioners.

Accreditation involves pursuing voluntary public relations credentials. One of the best-known programs is administered by the PRSA. Passing its accreditation exam earns the practitioner the Accredited in Public Relations (APR) designation. About a quarter of PRSA's members are accredited (Graham and Hearle 1996). Proponents of accreditation believe the process allows them to pinpoint areas of strength and weakness; further, earning credentials keeps them current in today's public relations environment. Although many firms do not require the APR designation, some do so for their more senior staff. Accreditation can help ensure professional development and complement real-world experience, ultimately benefiting both employee and firm (Schmelzer 2007). Some public relations professionals argue that, to make the accreditation process more meaningful, PRSA members need to educate their clients about the exam and its high standards (Graham and Hearle 1996).

In summary, whether through professional organizations, licensing, or accreditation, practitioners and scholars seem to agree that increasing professionalization in the discipline is a worthy goal. Although the best method for accomplishing this goal is debated, many professionals agree that strengthening the educational system of public relations is crucial in the development of professionalism. Scholars argue that public relations education needs a greater emphasis on theory, research, and the value of learning to move practitioners out of technician roles to the more expansive outlook of public relations managers (Coombs *et al.* 1994). Let us take a closer look at public relations educational systems around the world.

Public relations education

Remember seeing a groovy lava lamp from the 1970s? The slowly moving lava bubbles, soft light and unique shape still earn this funky decorative object a place in some college dorm rooms today.

Strangely enough, lava lamps provide a way to think about the role of education in international public relations. Public relations scholar Erik Koper (CITE) suggests that the lava-lamp metaphor helps students see the relationships between organizations and publics. Imagine the public relations practitioner as a "connector" bubble that helps organizations and publics work together and interact. Alternatively, one could imagine public relations professionals standing outside the lava lamp, supporting different stakeholder and organizational bubbles. The public relations professional can help groups to establish their current "bubble" positions and predict their next ones. Either way, successfully serving as a "connector" bubble or a lamp "supporter" requires that students receive a broad education. Students of international public relations need to know more than just the mechanics of the profession. They need to be able to see the big picture, and this entails skills in global economics and politics, mediation, cultural anthropology, and other fields relevant to a global arena (Wakefield 2000). Students also need better training in foreign languages and international studies (Epley 2003). Although many countries lack the resources to train more qualified practitioners adequately, progress is being made in both quality of education and number of students served (Wakefield 2000).

One challenge in strengthening international public relations education is that the existing body of public relations knowledge remains highly ethnocentric. Scholars argue that, in some ways, public relations education has a US bias that has not kept pace with the rapid globalization that has occurred since 2002. Students need a comprehensive body of knowledge and qualified educators to impart and build a broader perspective. As it stands, for example, diversity is not included as a fundamental part of the profession. Textbooks do not often contain international case studies or effective strategies to communicate with global audiences living in different socio-cultural environments. Public relations education needs to become more holistic, inclusive and multidisciplinary. In doing so, public relations students and practitioners will become more effective cross-cultural communicators, better able to build and maintain relationships with multicultural and diverse contemporary stakeholder groups (Sriramesh 2002). We shall now examine how well various countries and regions are working on strengthening public relations education.

United States

In the late 1980s, there were more than 600 US university departments offering graduate and undergraduate courses in public relations (Neff 1989). By the end of the twentieth century, the US had more than 3,000 universities teaching public relations, more than the rest of the world (Verčič et al. 2001). As of 2003, conservative estimates noted in excess of 20,000 public relations students, including 7,730 PRSSA members in 234 campus chapters, a jump from 5,820 members on 209 campuses five years ago (Hallahan 2003). In 1999, the Commission on Public Relations Education (CPRE) released its report on the state of public relations education in the US. The panel recognized the US as the leader in public relations education, but strongly advocated that the US prepare students to be effective communicators in the "age of global interdependence" (CPRE 1999, p. 44). Students should now know how to analyze, as well as conduct, global public relations (Culbertson and Chen 1996). Scholars say it is critical for future public relations practitioners to prepare themselves to communicate with various countries and cultures and be able to design public relations strategies that take into account a specific country's culture, political ideology, economic system, activism, and media system (Verčič et al. 2001; Grunig et al. 1995).

To reach these goals, the 1999 CPRE report recommended that public relations courses for undergraduates comprise 25 percent to 40 percent of all university credit hours. Five courses should clearly identify public relations in the title and include classes such as Public Relations Case Studies, Introduction to Public Relations, Public Relations Research and Evaluation, Public Relations Law and Ethics, Public Relations Writing and Production, Public Relations Planning and Management, Public Relations Campaigns, and a Public Relations Internship. Although the study recommended that students master broad knowledge areas such as multiculturalism and global issues, a separate class was not recommended; however, fluency in a second language was. The report recommended further that graduate programs should help students acquire advanced skills and knowledge in public relations research, management, problem-solving and issues, and management-level expertise. A thesis and/or comprehensive exam and/or capstone project was recommended also (Fischer 2000).

Europe

European practitioners and scholars are working on creating a European Public Relations Body of Knowledge to account for US-centric educational issues (Verčič *et al.* 2001). They note, for example, that the PRSA and the IABC each has more members than the IPRA. Major textbooks emerge from the US as does the global marketplace for public relations services. Further, some scholars argue that a European view of public relations stresses more managerial, operational, reflective and educational roles for public relations practice (Verčič *et al.* 2001). As a result of these issues, the curriculum has more emphasis on the reflective and educational roles required of European practitioners (Verčič *et al.* 2001). Overall, though, European study of public relations is advanced through the CERP (Confédération Européenne en Relations Publiques), to which both national public relations associations and individual practitioners belong. European scholars and practitioners may be working on customizing education to their specific needs, but academic interest in public relations is high. In Germany alone, for example, there were 216 German-language theses and dissertations related to public relations from 1980 to 1990 (Signitzer 1990).

Latin America

Latin American public relations practitioners are working similarly on creating a Latin American approach to public relations knowledge and education. The Latin American School of Public Relations is promulgated by CONFIARP and the Latin American Association of University Careers in Public Relations (ALACAURP) through events, research, educational advancements, and publications. One main Latin American concern is the advancement of ethically and formally trained public relations practitioners who represent socially responsible organizations (Molleda 2005).

Asia

In Asia, too, the body of public relations knowledge is young and growing. Research about public relations in Asia has grown and evolved since 1992, but only a few countries are represented in scholarship. As a result, students in Asia sometimes still lack local examples of case studies highlighting successes and failures of various public relations strategies and techniques within the complex Asian social and cultural milieu. Scholars argue that Asian public relations students need to know how the definition of public relations in Asia is different. In Asia, parameters of public relations are often limited to maintaining good relations between the client/organization and one specific public: the government (Taylor and Kent 1999). Along with government relations, activism and media relations are different in Asian nations, because the media do not play as much of a watchdog function, and activist voices are not as present. As such, both Asian and public relations students worldwide need anthologies describing public relations practice in Asia, Africa, Latin America and the Caribbean to understand and account for these and other differences (Sriramesh 2002).

Nevertheless, academic public relations scholarship helps fill in these gaps and broaden the discipline's knowledge base. Public relations research experienced explosive growth in the early 1990s and at the beginning of the new century. To continue making progress, scholars need to address multinational corporations, supranatural organizations and public relations between nations, and compare public relations among different countries or regions (Molleda and Laskin 2005). Currently, the US and the UK still host the majority of international scholarship. Unfortunately, international collaboration among authors is rare (Molleda and Laskin 2005). By broadening research to regions beyond Europe and Asia, and working to develop theory, public relations scholarship can help students gain a fuller picture of the complexities and challenges involved in international public relations (Molleda and Laskin 2005).

Questions for discussion

1. What is your view on licensing and accreditation? Do you believe it should be required by law? Does it bring more credibility to the profession? What problems are associated with licensing? Defend your position.
2. Education programs need to focus on international aspects and need to be developed more. If you could develop an international public relations program, what would it look like? How can we best learn about international public relations?

Public view of the profession

If scholars can help international public relations students broaden their knowledge base and gain exposure to various case studies and cultures, future practitioners will become ever better equipped to solve public relations challenges in today's global world. We have looked a little at what practitioners and educators think about public relations, but we also need to examine the public's perception. Do international audiences understand what public relations is? Do they know how the profession can be beneficial in a global society? Similar to our discussion of public relations education, the public's view needs to broaden, and in some cases correct, in order to establish a fuller, more accurate understanding of the profession.

There remains a litany of public misperceptions about the profession. In 2004, for example, an article ran in the *Sunday Telegraph*, a respected newspaper in the UK, with the headline "Beware the Spin of an Invisible Public Relations". Clearly, some still view the profession with suspicion.

According to a 2005 PRSA survey, for example, many people in the US have mixed feelings toward the public relations industry. Although some recognize that public relations professionals help increase awareness of important issues, a majority still believe public relations takes advantage of the media in a negative manner (PRSA 2005). That is, public relations professionals are still seen sometimes as unethical spin doctors, "hired guns", or manipulators of the truth. In fact, in a 2004 agency survey, only 7 percent of Americans and 14 percent of Europeans thought company public relations spokespeople were "either extremely credible" or "very credible" (Weber Shandwick 2004). To many public relations professionals this perception of "spin" is distressing. One PRSA member remarked: "spin is a four-letter word, in my opinion. I'd actually like to remove it from our vocabulary as public-relations professionals . . . Spin doctors work with myths, not facts . . . They are not concerned with truth. They are concerned with results" (Lewis 2007, p. 1). Another commentator added that, for many people, "when they hear the term public relations, they know they are about to be spun. Something went wrong, somebody screwed up . . . and here comes the public relations team" (Elsasser 2007, p. 1). Unfortunately, the connection between spin and public relations professionals still persists, despite efforts to break the association. Indeed, witness recent movies such as *Thank You for Smoking*, where the movie's main character, Nick Naylor, was portrayed as a manipulative, deceitful spokesperson for the tobacco industry. Along with other members of the MOD (Merchants of Death) squad, he and fellow spokespeople from the alcohol, tobacco and firearms industries devised plans to deceive the public into consuming these products.

Another misperception contributes to the belief that public relations is a frivolous career. The media's glamorous, unrealistic portrayal of public relations professionals and their activities undercuts the profession's efforts to maintain a seat at the management table. Witness, for example, television programs such as MTV's *PoweR Girls*, ABC's *Spin City* and HBO's *Sex and the City* and their portrayals of public relations. *Sex and the City*, in particular, portrayed one of its main characters, Samantha, as a public relations executive who never appeared to be doing any work beyond attending parties, modeling fancy business attire, and drinking glamorous cocktails. Harmless, you might say? No. As one PRSA practitioner cautions, "media influence is enormously powerful and should not be discounted as a force in creating reality" (Frisina 2003, p. 1). As a result, on college campuses and elsewhere, it is important to convey to students and the broader public the real public relations. If the media present a misleading account of public relations, it is up to the profession to combat these impressions with more accurate ones.

Even among those who have a somewhat clearer idea of what public relations is, some still do not understand the full range of public relations work. Frequently, public relations is seen as a service industry, indistinct from marketing and advertising. It is very important for public relations professionals to be "fully aware (and also be prepared with convincing arguments to make their stakeholders fully aware) that their own professional activity is distinct from advertising and marketing" (Falconi 2006). Falconi argues that the public relations body of knowledge has developed and accumulated over the last twenty to thirty years and is solid enough to establish public relations as a profession of its own.

Correcting business perceptions about public relations is also necessary. Corporate management still encourages the public relations staff to emphasize product support over problem prevention, and public relations is said to be concerned only about getting messages out (Falconi 2006). In this way, public relations is still perceived as merely media relations. None the less, public relations people must continue to persuade business leaders of the importance of public relations to become part of the management team. In addition, it is important to help the public understand that public relations does not serve only the private sector and large companies such as Exxon Mobil, Shell, Procter & Gamble or General Electric; indeed, "the largest public relations investors in the world today are more likely to be the US Government, the UN, the EU or the World Bank" (Falconi 2006).

To combat these negative perceptions of the profession, Botan (1993) recommends closer attention to the public relations relationship between images and ethics. Public relations professionals are well aware of this challenge, calling ethical issues, individual privacy and organizational integrity the issues most important to the public relations industry (Stateman 2007). In fact, in a PRSA survey, respondents felt that the greatest single challenge facing the public relations profession is upholding credibility (Stateman 2007). And, as public relations professor Robert Jackall (1995) puts it: "Acting ethically – at all times, regardless of the circumstance – must be obligatory for any practitioner who cares about retaining personal and organizational credibility" (p. 1). Botan (1993) suggests that ethical problems may arise when images are used instrumentally by organizations in an attempt to manage publics. In *Thank You for Smoking*, Nick Naylor's attempt to deceive the public about smoking's dangers would be an example of this approach. Naylor's efforts are essentially one-way and unethical because they reduce the public's chance to use the tobacco industry's symbols and images rationally to make informed choices. Instead, Botan recommends that practitioners and their clients use two-way dialogical communication and accept the ethical responsibility to enhance, and not degrade, the humanity of all parties involved in public relationships. With this approach, for example, Nick Naylor would work with the public, as well as with health organizations and management, to represent smoking's health concerns more accurately. In using humanitarian approaches, public relations practitioners do not reduce publics to the service of their clients but join them in the process of interpreting the world together. Botan (1993) argues that this humanitarian approach is especially important in international public relations, where one culturally bound community deals with the interpretations of another.

Relationships with media and other publics

Whether through closer attention to questions about the relationship of public relations to images and ethics or other practices, it is important for the profession to find ways to address misconceptions and negative impressions. After all, groups of people constitute the publics with whom public relations works. Negative impressions are bad for business. It is true in public relations that there is no "general" or "mass" public any more. Public relations messages are not addressed "to the public". Instead, public relations professionals work with segmented groups of people who unify to represent a particular viewpoint about an issue or a concern. They may also address publics who may not be fully aware of an issue, those who support the public relations professionals' viewpoint, and those who do not. Sometimes, they may need to address publics who are apathetic or do not seem to care about the issue at all. For international public relations, there are three particular publics that need to be addressed frequently, as they can constrain multinational organizations: labor unions, stockholders and pressure groups (Grunig 1992).

According to Lee (2005), identifying these and other publics is crucial for an organization's operation on the global stage. Another important public that has emerged today is called the global public. But what exactly is a global public? A global public is active on various global issues and situations, and can form in response to either negative or positive issues or situations (Lee 2005).

Problems are global when they cannot be solved within the boundary of a single unit of decision or system-operation (Campanella 1993). Examples of parts of global publics might be multinational employees; investors and consumers in free trade and financial markets; satellite television or other high-tech media targeting worldwide audiences; foreign governments; and international organizations, including the United Nations, the World Trade Organization, the World Bank and international non-governmental organizations (NGOs). Identifying the global publics involved with a particular issue is critical for an organization's operation in the global arena. As the notorious example of Shell's public relations efforts in Nigeria (see Chapter 10) illustrate about global publics: "as more US businesses invest overseas and vice versa, the need for public relations and marketing campaigns to communicate an organization's message to their clients effectively cannot be understated" (George 2003). The worldwide ripples of dissatisfaction that Shell encountered in the wake of its Nigerian public relations efforts speak to the concept of a global public the international public relations practitioner may now face.

Questions for discussion

1. There is a view that public relations professionals are unethical spin doctors. How do you view public relations professionals? How does your country view public relations professionals? Are you ever criticized for studying public relations?
2. Can you think of other examples of how public relations professionals are portrayed in the media? How are they portrayed? Is it good or bad?
3. This chapter identified a variety of publics. Is any one more important than another? Why or why not? Which publics are important in your country?

Conclusions and looking ahead

Epley's 1992 predictions about public relations in the global village have become realities in the twenty-first century. No matter the public, successful students of international public relations should notice that a global communication stage means working with different cultures and sometimes changing assumptions. Dealing with activists, internal publics, and community members successfully means improving intercultural communication and revising culturally sensitive assumptions (Banks 1995). Again, although public relations may have historically developed most in the West, it is now necessary for all practitioners, including Western ones, to develop a global, multicultural perspective (Zaharna 2000).

How do budding practitioners develop this multicultural global perspective, now that they have been exposed broadly to the historical development of public relations, its functions, public perception, various publics, and progress in professionalization? Cultivating a multicultural perspective in light of all of these matrices may seem overwhelming at first. Yet culture is paramount in international public relations (Zaharna 2001). Practitioners able to increase awareness and cultural sensitivity will be head and shoulders above the crowd pressing to join the exciting and rewarding world of international public relations practice. The remaining chapters in this textbook will continue to help you master the requirements of this challenging profession.

Featured biography: Joe S. Epley

Joe S. Epley, APR, Fellow PRSA, founded Epley Associates, Charlotte, North Carolina's first public relations firm, in 1968. Before that, he worked successfully in mass media as an award-winning news reporter and editor for a Charlotte television station. He remembers that when he started his career in public relations few people understood the field. Epley recalls "he had few competitors in those early years, but that has changed dramatically over time". The public relations field has since developed greatly, playing an important role on national and international levels. Epley points out that, to succeed as a practitioner today, "Students interested in working in public relations should get special education or training and possess such qualifications as excellent writing and communication skills, critical thinking, and acute interest in what is happening in the world".

Epley argues that understanding countries' historical development is crucial for success in public relations practice. Understanding historical development means knowing countries' political and economic trends, and appreciating their cultural and religious differences. Such valuable knowledge can help public relations practitioners communicate effectively and successfully achieve clients' goals. One of these goals may be in successfully managing crises on an international level. Here, learning a country's history and culture is important in developing efficient communication and building understanding among parties. To manage crises successfully, public relations specialists should ask such questions as what the crisis is about; what area/who is affected by the crisis; what needs to be understood about the people, region and country affected; and what tools and techniques apply to the situation. With this information, public relations specialists then need to develop a strategy and act quickly.

Working on a global level may be quite a challenge for public relations specialists. Epley advises to "never stop learning". He has successfully applied this philosophy to the practice of public relations in Charlotte, the US and internationally. Thanks to Epley's inquisitive mind and command of tools and techniques, he has achieved great success. Epley is proud of being one of the founders of the Worldcom Public Relations Group, the world's leading network of independent public relations consulting firms. Today, this organization operates in thirty-nine countries and serves national and international clients. Another professional achievement is Epley's consulting work with the University for International Relations (MGIMO) in Moscow. As president of the Public Relations Society of America, Epley helped put in place the public relations curriculum needed for a country entering the free market economy. After being tested at MGIMO, the curriculum was introduced over the next decade to more than a hundred universities, helping further develop public relations in Russia. The Russian Public Relations Association was created with the help of Epley's guidance.

Epley sees public relations in Russia and Eastern European countries improving, but development has matured in Western Europe. He says: "In general, public relations in Western and Central Europe has become more sophisticated." Epley cites the United Kingdom's public relations practices where extensive effort has been made to achieve high professional and ethical standards.

Epley also praises public relations development in South America. This region boasts a strong public relations community with considerable potential. And, among Asian countries, Epley points to China as a country in which many positive changes took place during the last ten to fifteen years. China has experienced a transition from government-controlled public relations to numerous independent public relations firms working hard to develop the field further. Conversely, the conditions for public relations growth are currently unfavorable in the Middle East and Africa. Epley suggests that the reason for this is that these societies "are still highly controlled by governments and cultural restraints".

Despite many differences in countries' public relations practices, Epley recognizes that business crosses political boundaries. The world is now a "global village" where all spheres of our lives are interdependent. Epley recommends that future and present public relations specialists keep in mind that today's environment brings both opportunities and challenges. That is why impeccable ethics and high professional standards are key components of success. Epley says that there is always room for improvement in this field. In his opinion, the main challenge in public relations is to work at a much higher level and become more counselors than technicians.

Recommended websites

Public Relations Society of America   http://www.prsa.org

International Association of Business Communicators   http://www.iabc.com

(PRODUCT) Red   http://www.joinred.com

International Public Relations Association   http://www.ipra.org

Public Relations Institute of Australia   http://www.pria.com.au

Public Relations Institute of New Zealand   http://www.prinz.org.nz/

Burson-Marsteller   http://www.burson-marsteller.com

Chartered Institute of Public Relations   http://www.ipr.org.uk/

Federation of African Public Relations Associations   http://www.fapra.org/

China International Public Relations Association (English version)   http://www.cipra.org.cn/english/about-us/main-us.htm

Public Relations Consultants Association of India   http://www.prcai.org/

European Association of Communication Directors   http://www.eacd-online.eu/

Commission on Public Relations Education   http://www.commpred.org/

Platform Online Magazine, student-run publication from the Plank Center for Leadership in Public Relations   http://www.platformmagazine.com

References

Ayish, M. and Kruckeberg, D., 2004. Abu Dhabi National Oil Company (ADNOC). In J. V. Turk and L. H. Scanlan, eds. *The Evolution of Public Relations: Case Study from Countries in Transition*. 2nd edn. Gainesville, Fla: The Institute for Public Relations Research and Education.

Banks, S. P., 1995. *Multicultural Public Relations: A Socio-interpretive Approach*. Thousand Oaks, Calif.: Sage.

Bardhan, N. and Patwardhan, P., 2004. Multinational corporations and public relations in a historically resistant host culture. *Journal of Communication Management*, 8 (3), pp. 246–63.

Botan, C., 1992. International public relations: critique and reformulation. *Public Relations Review*, 18 (2), pp. 149–59.

Botan, C., 1993. A human nature approach to image and ethics in international public relations. *Journal of Public Relations Research*, 5 (2), pp. 71–81.

Burneikaite, I., 2004. Tell me the story too. In J. V. Turk and L. H. Scanlan, eds. *The Evolution of Public Relations: Case Study from Countries in Transition*. 2nd edn. Gainesville, Fla: The Institute for Public Relations Research and Education.

Campanella, 1993. The effects of globalization and turbulence on policy-making processes. *Government and Opposition*, 28 (2), pp. 190–205.

Chartered Institute of Public Relations. ipr.org.uk.

Cherenson, M. G. *et al.*, 2006. September is PRSA's ethic month – topic is licensing PR practitioners a practical solution? *Public Relations Tactics*, pp. 1–6.

Cobb, C., 1999. The aftermath of Coke's Belgian waffle. *Public Relations Tactics*, pp. 1–2.

Commission on Public Relations Education, 1999. *Public Relations Education for the 21st Century: A Port of Entry.* New York: Public Relations Society of America.

Communication Director. *Idea.* Online posting. Available at: http://www.communication-director.eu/magazine/idea.php [accessed July 19, 2007].

Coombs, W. T. and Holladay, S. *et al.*, 1994. A comparative analysis of international public relations: identification and interpretation of similarities and differences between professionalization in Austria, Norway, and the United States. *Journal of Public Relations Research*, 6 (1), pp. 23–39.

Culbertson, H. M. and Chen, N., 1996. *International Public Relations: A Comparative Analysis.* Mahwah, NJ: Lawrence Erlbaum.

Czarnowksi, P., 2003. The transition of Polish PR. *IPRA Frontline*, 1.

Dickerson, M. A., 2005. One example of a successful international public relations program. *Public Relations Quarterly*, Fall, pp. 18–22.

Drobis, D. R., 2002. The new global imperative for public relations: building confidence to save globalization. *Public Relations Strategist*, pp. 1–3.

Durig, 2004. Public relations and change management: the case of a multinational company. *Journal of Communication Management*, 8, pp. 372–82.

Elsasser, J., 2007. General session summary: Tavis Smiley – stop the spin. *Public Relations Tactics*, 1–2.

Epley, J. S., 1992. Public relations in the global village: an American prospective. *Public Relations Review*, 8 (2), pp. 109–16.

Epley, J. S., 2003. *Perspectives from 17 Countries on International Public Relations.* WORLDCOM Public Relations Group.

Falconi, T. M., 2006. *How Big Is Public Relations (and Why Does It Matter)? The Economic Impact of Our Profession.* Gainesville, Fla: The Institute for Public Relations Research and Education.

Fischer, R., 2000. Rethinking public relations curricula: evolution of thought 1975–1999. *Public Relations Review*, pp. 16–20.

Fobanjong, J., 2004. The quest for public relations in Africa: an introduction. In D. J. Tilson and E. C. Alozie, eds. *Toward the Common Good: Perspectives in International Public Relations.* Boston, Mass.: Pearson Education.

Frisina, E. T., 2003. Addressing the "Sex and the City" syndrome. *Public Relations Tactics*, 1–2.

George, A. M., 2003. Teaching culture: the challenges and opportunities of international public relations. *Business Communication Quarterly*, 66 (2), pp. 97–113.

Gorney, C., 2005. China's economic boom brings a PR explosion. *Public Relations Strategist*, 1–3.

Graham, J. D. and Hearle, D. G., 1996. Face off: why accreditation makes sense/why accreditation doesn't make sense. *Public Relation Strategist*, 1–4.

Grunig, J. E., 1992. Communication, public relations, and effective organizations: an overview of the book. In J. E. Grunig, ed. *Excellence in Public Relations and Communication Management.* Hillsdale, NJ: Lawrence Erlbaum.

Grunig, J. E. *et al.*, 1995. Models of public relations in an international setting. *Journal of Public Relations Research*, 7 (3), pp. 63–86.

Grunig, J. E. and Hunt, T., 1984. *Managing Public Relations.* New York: Holt, Rinehart & Winston.

Hallahan, K., 2003. Challenges confronting PR education. *Public Relations Tactics*, 1–2.

Henderson, T. and Williams, J., 2002. Shell: managing a corporate reputation globally. In D. Moss and B. Desanto, eds. *Public Relations Cases: International Perspective.* London: Routledge.

Hill, 2002. In S. Lee, 2005. The emergence of global public and international public relations. *Public Relations Quarterly*, 14–16.

Hirogoyen, P., 2000. Postcards from international public relations. *Public Relations Strategist*, 1–4.

Howard, E., 1998. Swooshed! What activists are teaching Nike. *Public Relations Strategist*, 1–3.

International Public Relations Association. ipra.org.

Jackall, R., 1995. Practical moral reasoning in public relations. *Public Relations Strategist*, 1 (2), 1–4.

Josephs, R. and Josephs, J., 1998. The public relations in Central Europe. *Public Relation Tactics*, 1–2.

Kirat, M., 2006. Public relations in the United Arab Emirates: the emergence of a profession. *Public Relations Review*, 32 (3), 254–60.

Kotcher, R., 1998. Public relations south of the border. *Public Relations Strategist*, 1–3.

Kruckeberg, D., 1994. A preliminary identification and study of public relations models and their ethical implications in select internal public relations departments and public relations agencies in the United Arab Emirates. Paper presented in the Association for Education in Journalism and Mass Communication conference, Atlanta, Ga, August.

Laszyn, A., 2001. Poland's PR slowdown. *FrontLine*, March 11.

Ławniczak, R. and Rydzak, W. and Trebeski, J., 2003. Public relations in an economy and society in transition: the case of Poland. In K. Sriramesh and D. Verčič, eds. *The Global Public Relations Handbook: Theory, Research, and Practice*. Mahwah, NJ: Lawrence Erlbaum.

Lee, S., 2005. The emergence of global public and international public relations. *Public Relations Quarterly*, 14–16.

Lee, S., 2006. An analysis of other countries' international public relations in the US. *Public Relations Review*, 32, pp. 97–103.

L'Etang, J. and Muruli, G., 2004. Public relations, decolonization, and democracy: the case of Kenya. In D. J. Tilson and E. C. Alozie, eds. *Toward the Common Good: Perspectives in International Public Relations*. Boston, Mass.: Pearson Education.

Lewis, A., 2007. Isn't PR a synonym for BS? *The Denver Post*, July 20, p. C-01.

Lim, S., Goh, J. and Sriramesh, K., 2005. Applicability of the generic principles of excellent public relations in a different cultural context: the case study of Singapore. *Journal of Public Relations Research*, 17 (4), pp. 315–40.

Luer, C. and Tilson, D., 1996. Latin American public relations in the age of telecommunications, JC Penney and CNN. *Public Relations Quarterly*, 41 (2), pp. 25–7.

McDonald's. 2004. "I'm loving it" global brand campaign launch. Campaign profile of a Silver-Anvil Award, [online posting]. Available at: http://www.prsa.org [accessed July 13, 2007].

Miller, D. and Schlesinger, P., 2001. The changing shape of public relations in the European Union. Globalizing public relations. In R. Heath, ed. *Handbook of Public Relations*. Thousand Oaks, Calif.: Sage, pp. 675–84.

Molleda, J. C., 2005. International paradigms: the Latin American school of public relations. *Journalism Studies*, 2 (4), pp. 513–30.

Molleda, J. C. and Laskin, A. V., 2005. *Global, International, Comparative and Regional Public Relations Knowledge from 1990 to 2005: A Quantitative Content Analysis of Academic and Trade Publications*. Gainesville, Fla: The Institute for Public Relations Research and Education.

Nagvi, S. 2007. Putting a spin on art of good PR. *Birmingham Post*, Feb. 22, p. 8.

Neff, B., 1989. The emerging theoretical perspective in PR: an opportunity for Communication Departments. In C. Botan and V. Hazleton, eds. *Public Relations Theory*. Hillsdale, NJ: Lawrence Erlbaum.

Newsom, D., 2007. *Bridging the Gaps in Global Communication*. Malden, Mass.: Blackwell Publishing.

Ogbondah, C. and George, A., 2004. Fire at Nigeria's treasure base: an analysis of Shell Petroleum's public relations strategies in the wake of the Niger Delta crisis. In D. J. Tilson and E. C. Alozie, eds. *Toward the Common Good: Perspectives in International Public Relations*. Boston, Mass.: Pearson Education.

Ohashi, S., 1984. Public relations in Japan. *Public Relations Journal*, 41, pp. 11–16.

Park, J., 2001. Images of "hong bo (public relations)" and PR in Korean newspapers. *Public Relations Review*, 27 (4), pp. 403–20.

Pratt, C. B., 1985. The African context. *Public Relations Journal*, 41, pp. 11–16.

Pratt, C. B. and Okigbo, C., 2004. Applying reconstructed and social responsibility theories to foreign direct investment and public relations for social change in sub-Saharan Africa. In D. J. Tilson and E. C. Alozie, eds. *Toward the Common Good: Perspectives in International Public Relations*. Boston, Mass.: Pearson Education.

Public Relations Institute of New Zealand. PRinz.org.nz.

Public Relations Society of America. PRSA.org.

Public Relations Society of America, 2005. China's economic boom brings a PR explosion. *Public Relations Strategist*, spring. Public Relations Institute of Australia. PRIA.com/au.

Ravazzani, S., 2006. *Communicating for Diversity, with Diversity, in Diversity: Main Implications and Summary of the Contents*. Gainesville, Fla: The Institute for Public Relations.

Riley, M., 1991. Indigenous resources in a Ghanaian town: potential for health education. Paper presented to International Communication Association conference, Chicago, Ill.

Sattler, J., 1981. Public relations in Africa: impressive strides. *Public Relations Journal*, *37*, pp. 28–9.

Schmelzer, R., 2007. The agency business: accreditation receives high marks from most firms. *PR Week*, May 28, p. 7.

Shop (RED) and save lives, 2007. Campaign profile of a Silver-Anvil Award winner, [online posting]. Available at: http://www.prsa.org [accessed July 15, 2007].

Signitzer, B., 1990. Aspects of the production of public relations knowledge: PR research in German-language theses and dissertations. Paper presented to special conference on public relations as a science. Salzburg, Austria, December 6–8.

Singh, R. and Smyth, R., 2000. Australian public relations: status at the turn of the 21st century. *Public Relations Review*, 26 (4), pp. 387–401.

Sourcewatch (2007) Eric White Associates, [online]. Available at: http://www.sourcewatch.org/index.php?title=Eric_White_Associates [accessed July 13, 2007].

Sriramesh, K., 2002. The dire need for multiculturalism in public relations education: an Asian prospective. *Journal of Communication Management*, 7 (1), pp. 54–70.

Sriramesh, K., 2003. The mass media and public relations: a conceptual framework for effective media relations in Asia. *Asian Journal of Communication*, 13 (2), pp. 1–20.

Sriramesh, K. Grunig, J. E. and Dozier, D. M., 1996. Observation and measurement of two dimensions of organizational culture and their relationship to public relations. *Journal of Public Relations Research*, 8 (4), pp. 229–61.

Sriramesh, K. and Verčič, D., 2001. International public relations: a framework for future research. *Journal of Communication Management*, 6 (2), pp. 10–117.

State of the PR Profession Opinion Survey 2006 (2007). Public Relations Society of America: Bacon's information.

Stateman, A., 2007. The 2006 State of the Profession survey. *Public Relations Tactics*, 14 (3), p. 24.

Taylor, M. and Kent, M. L., 1999. Challenging assumptions of international public relations: when government is the most important public. *Public Relations Review*, 25 (2), pp. 131–44.

Tsetsura, K., 2003. The development of public relations in Russia: a geographical approach. In K. Sriramesh and D. Verčič, eds. *The Global Public Relations Handbook: Theory, Research, and Practice*. Mahwah, NJ: Lawrence Erlbaum.

Tsetsura, K., 2005. Bribery for news coverage: research in Poland. *The Institute for Public Relations*.

Tilson, D., 2004. Latin America: a perpetual land of the future? In D. J. Tilson and E. C. Alozie, eds. *Toward the Common Good: Perspectives in International Public Relations*. Boston, Mass.: Allyn & Bacon.

Turk, J. V. and Scanlan, L. H. eds, 2004. *The Evolution of Public Relations: Case Study from Countries in Transition*. 2nd edn, Gainesville, Fla: The Institute for Public Relations Research and Education.

Van Leuven, J., 1996. Public relations in Southeast Asia. In H. Culbertson and N. Chen, eds. *International Public Relations: A Comparative Analysis*. Mahwah, NJ: Lawrence Erlbaum.

Verčič, D. et al., 2001. On the definition of public relations: a European view. *Public Relations Review*, 27, pp. 373–87.

Wakefield, R. I., 2000. What's wrong with multinational public relations? *Public Relations Strategist*, 1–3.

Wakefield, R. I., 2005. The emergence of global public and international public relations. *Public Relations Quarterly*, 50 (2), pp. 14–16.

Weber Shandwick, 2003. Corporate communications role increase in complexity and stature, survey finds, [online]. Available at: http://www.webershandwick.com [accessed April 5, 2005].

Weber Shandwick, 2004. The challenges of public relations in China, [online]. Available at: http://www.weber-shandwick.co.uk/outcomes/issue6/story2.html [accessed July 24, 2007].

Weber Shandwick, 2005. Latin America: a fast growing PR market, [online]. Available at: http://www.weber-shandwick.co.uk/outcomes/issue8/article4.html [accessed July 24, 2007].

Weber Shandwick, 2006. Embracing PR in Japan, [online]. Available at: http://www.webershandwick.co.uk/outcomes/issue10/article3.html [accessed August 30, 2007].

Wu, M., 2005. Can American public relations theories apply to Asian cultures? *Public Relations Quarterly*, 23–7.

Zaharna, R. S., 2000. Intercultural communication and international public relations: exploring parallels. *Communication Quarterly*, 48, pp. 85–100.

Zaharna, R. S., 2001. "In-awareness" approach to international public relations. *Public Relations Review*, 27 (2), pp. 135–48.

Zhang, J. and Cameron, G. T., 2003. China's agenda building and image polishing in the US: assessing an international public relations campaign. *Public Relations Review*, 29 (1), pp. 13–28.

Part 3

Using the comparative framework presented in Part 2, regions and selected nations are examined in greater detail. Contexts for national public relations development and practice are presented. Challenges and approaches for cross-border and cross-cultural campaigns are proposed. A model for developing country profiles as they relate to public relations practice is presented. The section begins with those cultures most easily differentiated from that of the US, used as a baseline, then moves purposefully toward those regional cultures that are often mistakenly viewed as basically similar to the US. In each chapter, brief case studies provide illustrations of comparative metrics.

Several chapters in this section are written by scholars closely associated with the regions and countries addressed, so the reader benefits both from firsthand knowledge of these scholars as well as from their unique approaches to analyzing the development and application of public relations in those regions. The value lies in the reader's exposure to different ways of thinking about public relations – ways that are informed presumably by the contexts in which these contributing scholars were and are immersed.

Chapter 7

South and Southeast Asia

Summary

In earlier chapters, we addressed the classic evolutionary model of public relations: press agentry, public information, two-way asymmetric and two-way symmetric, as well as a mixed-motive model. This framework has been a mainstay of public relations research for decades, but does it serve equally well in non-Western cultural contexts? As you will see, there is evidence to suggest that other paradigms may be necessary to describe and explain development of public relations in those settings. In this chapter, we shall examine the emergence and application of public relations strategies and tactics in several unique but representative nations and discover fresh perspectives on the discipline.

Chapter goals

- Establish broad principles to aid in understanding and appreciating public relations practice in the region and recognize unique national variations within those broader principles.
- Describe the peculiar regional cultural dynamics that commingle with historical trends and forces, described in Chapter 2, that have shaped perceptions of public relations in the three countries addressed here.
- Observe at least one systematic method for exploring, describing and analyzing public relations in a given nation and/or cultural setting.

Certainly the student or practitioner appreciates the folly of assuming that all of Asia could be embraced in a simple single cultural profile that would apply to each of the varied countries that comprise this vast region. Similarly, it would be beyond the scope of this text to address each of those countries in detail. Here is a list of the countries we would have to include: Afghanistan; Armenia; Azerbaijan; Bangladesh; Bhutan; Brunei; Burma (Myanmar); Cambodia; China; Georgia; Hong Kong; India; Indonesia; Japan; Kazakhstan; Korea, North; Korea, South; Kyrgyzstan; Laos;

Malaysia; Maldives; Mongolia; Nepal; Pakistan; Philippines; Singapore; Sri Lanka; Taiwan; Tajikistan; Thailand; Turkmenistan; Uzbekistan; Vietnam. In fact, all the nations of the Middle East could rightfully be included in the vast continent of Asia as well, but that special region is the subject of Chapter 9. Russia, too, has considerable territory in what could be considered Asia, but we shall cover that country in Chapter 12. And Japan, China and South Korea are subjects of Chapter 8.

Among Asian countries you will find the most populous in the world (China and India), the most populous Islamic country (Indonesia), and some of the most highly developed and least developed in the world. Political systems range from the democratic, featuring free press and expression, to the authoritarian, marked by repression and strict state control. There are monarchies, military rulers, and democratically elected governments. Literacy rates and socio-economic development run the gamut, as do telecommunication and transportation infrastructures. Much of Asia suffered development setbacks during colonial experiences that ranged from the sixteenth to the twentieth centuries. Those setbacks, coupled with some of the highest population densities in the world, contribute today in parts of Asia to chronic underdevelopment, low literacy, lack of quality healthcare, food shortages, poor nutrition, and dreadful environmental conditions. Add to this a substantial list of religious and ethical systems from Buddhism, Christianity and Confucianism to Islam, Taoism, Shintoism and Hinduism.

Because of wide variances in cultural patterns and economic development, it follows naturally that there would be wide variances in Asian public relations practice from one nation to another. In developing nations, what we typically find is a public relations model working in concert with government agencies, NGOs and even corporations toward long-term common goals aimed at achieving socio-economic progress. A term often used to describe this type of activity is *development communication*. While Western public relations is usually described in terms of the four traditional models (press agentry, public information, two-way asymmetric, two-way symmetric), development communication is certainly a legitimate model of public relations in other settings. The concept views public communication much less in a business context and more in a social responsibility context. Public relations becomes, in this setting, more of a catalyst for positive change on a national or regional scale. Through strategic partnerships among government agencies, NGOs, universities, media, and private-sector institutions, programs (including a substantial communication component) might be conducted in areas such as public health, sustainable development, literacy, improved agricultural practices, women's rights, and so on The idea is to encourage public participation in these pervasive efforts. In this model, one could argue that public relations activities follow an asymmetric vector; but, unlike in the Western models, the imbalance is not necessarily a negative factor. Several universities have established academic programs in development communication, and it is an area in which public relations can contribute significantly.

Because of their recent colonial or semi-colonial past, several Asian nations, achieving independence, were faced with tremendous challenges of integrating peoples from disparate backgrounds while striving to establish infrastructures, national identities, and concepts of responsible citizenship. Some Asian countries, too, sought through communication campaigns to retain Eastern values despite the lure, generally through mass media, of Western cultural trappings. We shall look at several south and southeast Asian nations shortly, examining representative communication efforts and describing the environment in which public relations practice is evolving. First, though, let us outline some generalizations about Asian culture as it might affect communication at all levels.

A broad cultural profile

In contrast to Western cultures, Asians are likely to identify with only a few social or professional groups, and to maintain strong ties to those groups for a lifetime. This would include immediate and extended family, neighborhoods, friends and work groups. In short, Asians tend to establish only a few close relationships, to nurture, retain and value those relationships for a long time, and to avoid making distinctions between personal and professional relationships. The Westerner who lands at Beijing airport hoping quickly to obtain a signature on a contract then return immediately to his or her home office in the West is likely to encounter subtle but formidable resistance. The Asian counterparts will expect to establish at least a rudimentary personal relationship before they would deem it appropriate to enter into any business arrangements. Also, to a greater extent than in the West, a person's position in life is strongly influenced by the birth family's position and status. This is changing, rapidly in some quarters, but remains a factor to be considered. A Western practitioner would also find in some Asian cultures more socially defined and acceptable gender roles than he or she may be accustomed to, with women often relegated to limited responsibilities. Interpersonal communication in Asian cultures is less direct than in the West; the tendency is to avoid the risk of disharmony by employing a far more subtle approach to conveying messages. Similarly, Asian communication patterns generally reflect Hall's high-context orientation, indicating that meaning is implied and internalized using shared codes based on values, context, non-verbals, setting and other cues.

Using Hofstede's taxonomy of power distance, individualism/collectivism, uncertainty avoidance and masculinity/femininity, central tendencies in Asian countries basically share similar tendencies on the indices for these metrics. On his power distance scale, Hofstede considered a score of "0" to be average or neutral, with positive scores reflecting a preference for high power distance – an emphasis on unequal distribution of power, or a stress on stratification. On that scale, Hofstede listed, among Asian nations, Malaysia (leading all nations at +218), the Philippines (+172), Indonesia (+98), India (+93), Singapore (+79), Hong Kong (+52), Thailand (+33), South Korea (+15) and Taiwan (+5) as above average. Arab countries (+107) and Turkey (+42), not addressed in this chapter but part of Asia, were also above average according to Hofstede's research. Among Asian nations, only Pakistan (–8) and Japan (–13) were below average in emphasizing social distance between strata. Also, Israel, considered part of the Asian continent as well, earned a score of –203.

On individualism/collectivism, Asian nations reflect a tendency toward the collective. With "0" representing the average, negative scores representing collectivism and positive scores representing individualism, just three Asian countries garnered positive scores (individualism valued): Israel (+43), India (+20) and Japan (+12). Far more Asian countries place varying degrees of emphasis on the value of collectivism: Iran (–8), Arab countries (–20), Turkey (–24), the Philippines (–44), Malaysia (–68), Hong Kong (–72), Singapore (–92), Thailand (–92), South Korea (–100), Taiwan (–103), Pakistan (–115) and Indonesia (–115). Therefore, Asian practitioners and other professionals are more likely to base decisions on collective good, looking beyond individual and even company or organizational benefit. Loyalty to the group will be a hallmark.

The uncertainty avoidance scale is far less definitive for Asian countries, with scores ranging from high positive to high negative, though the tendency is clearly toward the negative end of the scale. Once again, "0" is average or neutral, and positive scores suggest a desire to avoid uncertainty, while negative scores suggest comfort with ambiguity. Positive scores are listed on Hofstede's scale for Japan (+110), Turkey (+81), South Korea (+81), Israel (+65), Pakistan (+19), Taiwan

(+15) and Arab countries (+11). Scoring in the negative range, indicating tolerance of ambiguity and uncertainty, were Thailand (–6), Indonesia (–72), the Philippines (–89), India (–106), Malaysia (–122), Hong Kong (–157) and Singapore (–239). Those Asian nations with negative scores would be more comfortable with an unpredictable future and would accept and adapt to changes more readily. Practitioners in these countries would require fewer rules and rituals, and would accept more in the way of risk-taking. Be careful, though, about making generalizations about Asian culture; as these scores indicate, not all countries on the continent share characteristics on this index. A practitioner in India, for example, may view a practitioner in Japan or South Korea as being too structured and uncompromising, and the Indian practitioner might be viewed by the Japanese or South Korean practitioner as too willing to accept risk.

Similarly, on the masculinity/femininity scale, Asian nations range from highly masculine to moderately feminine. Recall that this has nothing to do with *feminism*, but rather the degree to which members of the society value achievement and assertiveness (masculinity) or nurturance and social support (femininity). Hofstede's scale ascribes positive scores to masculinity and negative scores to femininity, with "0" the average or neutral score. Leading the list for all nations surveyed is Japan (+255), with several other Asian nations following on the positive side of the scale, though at a considerable distance: the Philippines (+84), India (+40), Arab countries (+23), Malaysia (+7) and Pakistan (+7). Other Asian nations value feminine qualities as defined by Hofstede: Singapore (–4), Israel (–10), Indonesia (–15), Turkey (–21), Taiwan (–21), Iran (–32), South Korea (–59) and Thailand (–98). One consequence of this syndrome, Hofstede suggested, is that the high-masculinity countries tend to place more restrictive roles upon men and women and consider sexual inequality as beneficial to societal order. Conversely, countries with large negative scores would hold gender roles to be far more fluid, to place less emphasis on individual achievement, and to view gender equality as the norm. Hofstede says teachers in masculine societies are more likely to praise students for academic performance, and perhaps that extends to the work environment. Feminine societies would be characterized by more cooperative effort, more modesty, and less emphasis on financial success.

Other tendencies in Asian cultures, broadly speaking, include the tradition of children being taught to lower their eyes when in conversation with an elder, especially a teacher; direct eye contact, considered appropriate listening behavior in Euro-American cultures, would constitute poor manners, even confrontation, in most Asian cultures. Similarly, silence during a conversation is viewed positively in Asian cultures, signifying respect and consideration of the conversation partner's ideas. Silence by a participant here suggests the participant is carefully pondering the pros and cons and carefully formulating a suitable response. Silence in Western cultures, on the other hand, may be construed as confusion or disengagement.

Questions for discussion

1. Based on scores for Hofstede's cultural taxonomy, brainstorm key messages that might form the core of a public health campaign such as encouraging citizens to have their children immunized against polio. How might messages differ between, say, Japan and India? Between the Philippines and South Korea? Explain your answers.

2. If you are not from an Asian culture, describe how you might approach a planning meeting with your counterparts from several Asian countries aimed at outlining a plan to invite tourism from those Asian countries to your own. If you are from an Asian culture, what might be the goals and strategies of a campaign to encourage Western tourists to visit your country?
3. Hofstede conducted his surveys in the late 1970s. Looking at the scores reported here, do you think that they are still valid? Why or why not? What factors might be affecting those scores? If you think some scores may have changed – in which direction?

The influence of Confucius

Hofstede accounted for differences within Asian cultures along the continua representing his cultural dimensions by distinguishing between more developed Asian cultures and those less developed. Because his initial research dates from the late 1970s, Hofstede listed only Japan as a more developed cultural setting and counted among less developed settings countries such as India, Indonesia, Malaysia, Pakistan, the Philippines, Singapore, South Korea, Taiwan and Thailand. Certainly a number of those "less developed" nations would by now be described as more developed, but the phenomenon suggests that Bond may have a point when he notes that these cultural syndromes have a built-in Western bias, devised as they were by Western scholars using Western terms, Western research paradigms and Western viewpoints. Bond (1987), therefore, had Asian researchers (he himself lived in Asia for more than two decades) develop and conduct a survey of twenty-three countries. The results, in large part, were similar to Hofstede's findings, but one different and important dimension emerged – a dimension that described a person's orientation to life and work, a dimension that Bond said described an orientation based on Confucian cultural patterns. We shall talk more about the centrality of Confucianism in Asian cultures in Chapter 8 when we talk about China, but Confucian influences permeate most, if not all, of Asia, so a summary of its tenets is appropriate here.

Confucianism is not a religion, but rather a set of principles and rules of ethics intended for practical application to daily life. Here are the basic tenets:

1. Social order and stability are supported by a system of unequal relationships between people. Respect and obedience are accorded based on these relationships. These relationships are determined by family position (father/son, husband/wife, older sibling/younger sibling, and so on), friendship, and leader/follower (such as in a work setting). Age also affects relationship status and direction. This system can obviously become enormously complex.
2. The family is the model for all other social relationships. Principles of relationships are learned in the family, then applied throughout life to other personal and professional relationships.
3. Proper behavior should be based on not treating others in ways in which you would prefer not to be treated yourself. This is not quite the *Golden rule* because the Confucian approach extends to choosing your associates and friends based upon reciprocal behavior and avoiding those who do not meet that criterion.

4. Teaching and learning are held in high esteem, and all people should develop skills, pursue education and work hard while exercising thrift, modesty, patience and perseverance.

Bond says Asian cultures vary along a Confucian dynamic ranging from a long-term orientation to a short-term orientation, but the important point is that they remain within the Confucian paradigm, an orientation not necessarily shared so strongly in other cultures. The short-term Confucian orientation – prevalent, Bond says, in Pakistan and the Philippines (and reflected in Western nations such as the United States, Great Britain, Canada, Germany and Australia) – is characterized by respect for tradition, stability and *face* (described in more detail in Chapter 8). The short-term orientation places more emphasis on giving gifts and receiving favors. The long-term Confucian orientation is more descriptive of China, Taiwan, Japan, South Korea, India and Thailand, and is characterized by a highly developed sense of shame, status distinctions, thriftiness and persistence. Throughout the Confucian dynamic spectrum, however, the stress is on virtue; the differences from one end to the other are subtle and could easily be lost on the ill-informed public relations practitioner in professional settings.

With the preceding as foundation, let us turn our attention to what researchers have reported about public relations practice in several nations in this region.

India

The second most populous country in the world, and the largest democracy, India is rapidly growing as an economic power, manifesting a number of the trends described in Chapter 2 that led to the emergence of the public relations profession in the United States. But, with India's population plus advances in communication, transportation and other infrastructure changes, the effect is occurring on an unprecedented scale and at a far more rapid pace. Half its 1.1 billion population is under the age of 25. More than 2 million Indians graduate from college each year, with many of those receiving degrees in engineering or management. India's exploding information technology sector is creating high-wage jobs for skilled software engineers and other professionals. In a land often associated with poverty, glass high-rises and suburban communities are becoming a hallmark along with condominium complexes and shopping malls (Fang 2006). The Indian Postal Service now handles more than 14 billion pieces of mail daily. It is a popular choice for business because, among other appeals, one-third of its population speaks English – the language of business. The rapidly growing middle class in India now numbers more than 300 million – approximately equal to the entire US population. It clearly presents economic opportunities on a massive scale, both as a global base and as a domestic market, with some predicting that India's economy will be second only to the United States by the middle of the twenty-first century. On the other hand, India has a long way to go, with more people living in poverty than in any other nation, and 70 percent of the population still living in rural or village settings. The 30 percent of the population living in cities produce 60 percent of the nation's wealth. The nation is highly regional, with some states having average incomes five times the level in other states. Cultures and languages vary sharply regionally as well.

Economic growth sometimes clashes with cultural traditions. Indians have historically been reluctant to get into debt, but credit cards are becoming increasingly popular. The spread of television has bolstered awareness of the Western world, and with that awareness comes increasing acquisitiveness, in turn creating conflicts. For example, the increasing popularity of modern washing machines conflicts with a strong tradition of a large service sector devoted to providing washing and pressing of clothes. Similarly, fast-food franchises such as McDonald's are finding that they must still provide ample vegetarian options; and, unlike Westerners who gobble their meals at these fast-food restaurants, Indians often go as a family, lingering and visiting as they enjoy their meals. And the spread of Internet access is facilitating a deeply valued tradition by permitting online arranged marriages. A major change is that the housewife can no longer be stereotyped as uneducated and unaware. Many cultural changes, though, remain subtle. The concept of consumer rights, for instance, remains nascent, and bartering is still common. And one tradition continues unabated – neighborhood tea shops are where people discuss politics and other issues; consequently, magazine and newspaper readership is at high levels, offering public relations practitioners an excellent conduit for organizational messages.

Mass media in general have flourished in India since independence, and the media enjoy a high degree of independence as well. More than 5,000 daily newspapers are published in more than a hundred languages across the country; most are published in Hindi, but English is the second most common language for these newspapers, followed by a dozen or so other languages. The *Hindi Daily Press* distributes more than 23 million copies daily. Many of the newspapers are consolidated under publishing groups. And new newspapers, magazines and cable news channels are constantly being added to the mix, creating an atmosphere of increasingly intense competition. Media penetration is understandably higher in urban areas. Although print media reach 25 percent of the total Indian population, that number jumps to 46 percent for urban areas. For broadcast television, the overall Indian penetration is 53 percent, but 80 percent of urbanites receive those signals. For cable and satellite television the figure is 20 percent for all of India, but 46 percent in urban areas. Radio is more equitably distributed, with 22 percent penetration for all of India and 25 percent in cities. The Internet still lags far behind, with an overall penetration of 1 percent, 3 percent in cities (2003 figures), though that is likely to rise precipitously.

No discussion of Indian media could be complete without reference to "Bollywood", India's phenomenally prolific motion picture industry. The wild national popularity of Indian-produced films makes the industry a leader in creating fashion trends, musical hits and celebrity status. However, films such as *Bend It like Beckham* and *Bride and Prejudice* have helped to acquaint the rest of the world with Indian culture and even to popularize it.

The Press Information Bureau of India points to their nation's extensive history of great communicators beginning with their great philosophers such as Gautama Buddha and Sankaracharya, who spoke to the common people in idiomatic language listeners found easy to understand. The emperor Ashok (third century BC) sent his children to (now) Sri Lanka to spread the message of Buddhism, making Ashok's daughter, in the eyes of the Press Information Bureau, the first woman public relations executive in history! More recently, but in the era preceding independence, newspapers were used largely to convey messages on behalf of the rulers that they were working for the good of the people and that the people should support their continued rule. In the European rulers' defense, newspapers were also used to educate and enlighten the people, especially on socially important issues. Of course, the great Indian communicator of the twentieth century was Mahatma Gandhi, whose tremendously effective communicative style catalyzed hundreds of thousands of citizens to push for and achieve independence.

The development of modern public relations in India can be linked to a great extent to the expansion of the Indian Railways. Not only did the railways conduct campaigns promoting tourism, but the Publicity Bureau of the Great Indian Peninsular Railways also introduced a traveling cinema and conducted fairs and festivals. The Bureau proactively participated in exhibitions abroad to promote tourism in India, especially by rail. Early in the twentieth century, India's government established the Central Publicity Board, later renamed the Central Bureau of Information and ultimately the Bureau of Press Information. It served as a link between the federal government and the media. It was not until 1938, though, that the bureau was headed by an Indian. With independence in 1947, the government established a more comprehensive Ministry of Information and Broadcasting, and today all state governments and territories operate similar bureaus (Sardana n.d.).

India has enjoyed the attention of several public relations scholars. Among leaders in this area is Sriramesh, who has published extensively on Indian public relations. Historically, Sriramesh (1996) says, India viewed public relations practitioners as "fixers" – those who could make things happen for the client, generally by questionable methods. Wining and dining were traditionally seen as part and parcel of effective practice. Sriramesh cites an early work by Kaul, published in India, that describes a four-phased historical sequence of public relations practice there. According to that profile, during the first phase, prior to World War II, the practice was characterized by simply disseminating information, with a focus on community relations. There was no organized function that could be construed today as formal public relations. During and following World War II, Indian public relations experienced a second stage, one driven by the need to mobilize public opinion to support the war effort; at the same time there was rapid growth in mass-circulation newspapers with a commensurate elevation in the influence of media in general. India, during this second phase, saw the first establishment of formal public relations functions.

The major event in recent Indian history, independence from Great Britain in 1947, ushered in a third stage in public relations development, this one marked by multinational corporations, already established in India, suddenly faced with the need to build and nurture relationships with government leaders and agencies quite different from their British predecessors. As democracy took root not only at the national level, but also at regional and local levels, organizations elevated public relations to this third phase as structures and dynamics changed radically. The fourth stage (we would never say "final" because the development of the public relations profession is constantly evolving) might be traced to the establishment of the Public Relations Society of India (PRSI) in 1958, about the same time that the first course in public relations was offered in Calcutta. In 1968, Indian public relations practitioners met for their first professional conference in New Delhi, and it was at that conference that participants agreed to develop a code of ethics.

A representative campaign in the 1970s, referenced by Sriramesh, involved an effort by the government of the city of Hyderabad to encourage citizens to work toward a cleaner city. The campaign blended strategies and tactics familiar to Western practitioners with those strategies and tactics that recognize the unique characteristics of Indian culture and communication preferences. The campaign coordinated broadcast and print media, outdoor advertising, exhibitions, brochures and fliers, plus folk media such as dance dramas and songs in the poorer areas less penetrated by traditional mass media.

One of his (Sriramesh's) earliest studies was based upon an ethnographic study of organizations in Bangalore, a major city in southern India – a study the author argues is generalizable to India as a whole (1996). Sriramesh, by the way, is a firm believer that culture has a profound impact on the individual worldviews and communication patterns of public relations practitioners and managers. In this study, the researcher adopted an ethnographic approach, performing as a participant observer, spending several days observing activities in each of eighteen representative organizations in Bangalore, home to a host of high-tech industries. He found that most practitioners there carried the title of manager, but their responsibilities were far from managerial. More likely, they were involved in scheduling meetings and making sure snacks and meals were properly arranged. They engaged principally in administrative chores and behind-the-scenes "spade work". Top executives in the organizations equated public relations with marketing and sometimes advertising, and felt public relations involved establishing and maintaining a positive image for the organization. The strategic function of public relations was not evident.

Sriramesh said that media relations figured heavily in the public relations scene in Bangalore. Interestingly, he reported that practitioners often met with journalists outside office hours in social settings, hoping, apparently, to bolster personal relationships that would ultimately benefit the practitioner's work on behalf of the organization. News conferences, he said, were as much to build the practitioner's reputation as they were to disseminate important news. Media junkets were fairly common, and largely to pamper journalists, hoping that doing so would engender positive stories.

Sriramesh's research suggests that Indian public relations practice falls mainly within the press agentry model, though one government agency studied exercised a public information model. Beyond that Western paradigm, though, the research revealed a strong added dimension of interpersonal relationships as an essential component of public relations practice in India. This would, of course, coincide with the central tendency generally prevalent in Asia for considering interpersonal relationships a prerequisite for professional relationships.

Also, practitioners observed in the study were almost invariably younger than their supervisors, in keeping with the cultural propensity for marked power distance structures. Consequently, practitioners felt little autonomy and were reluctant to express this or other ideas to their superiors; they simply followed the directions of their superiors. They would certainly never express views different from those of their superiors. Interestingly, subordinate practitioners appear comfortable with this arrangement, even so far as expressing disrespect for a boss who would consult them before making a decision. Sriramesh says, though, that the former caste system based on birth is gradually being replaced by an equally stringent structure based on class, with class being based on wealth and political power.

Sidebar: High-tech farm markets

At a farmer's home in a rural Indian village, a computer on the table links an undereducated community with the latest in agricultural science and the complexities of commodity pricing. This is one of several thousand "e-choubals" – a word combining the Internet with the Hindu word for a rural gathering-place. They serve nearly 2 million farmers in nearly 20,000 villages and are an initiative of the International Business Division of ITC Ltd. The Division trades commodities such as soybeans, coffee and shrimp that it obtains from small-scale farmers. ITC is among India's biggest businesses, with interests in hotels, paper, apparel and packaged foods.

S. Sivakumar, the Division's chief executive, decided to use technology to aid farmers who were struggling to grow food to eat plus a crop to sell. These farmers lacked irrigation and other resources, and knew little about even basic advances in agricultural science. Limited access to loans, and then only at high interest through a middleman, further worsened the cycle of poverty. Often, unscrupulous agents who ran local and regional markets charged inflated commissions and priced commodities unfairly. At the same time, buyers such as ITC are stuck with substandard produce and lack a reliable supply source. Now ITC provides selected literate farmers in target villages with solar-powered computers coupled with a satellite Internet link. The farmer, dubbed a "sanchalak" – conductor of information – takes an oath of honesty before accepting his charge. ITC provides computer training along with lessons in crop improvement, inspection and pricing. Each sanchalak becomes a link between ITC and roughly a thousand farmers who travel miles to use the e-choupal. The sanchalak, in turn, receives a commission on each transaction.

Through the e-choupal, farmers can track weather patterns, compare prices, and gauge the best times to plant and take produce to the right market. Crops have improved, economically benefiting the community. Now, too, ITC has made its e-choupal system a conduit for farm supply vendors it rates as ethical. Similarly, micro-credit providers, insurance companies, and healthcare and educational organizations have been granted access.

ITC has spent $250 million on the e-choupal system but expects to recoup that investment. Its goal is to reach 100,000 of India's 600,000 villages by 2010 (Melcer 2004).

Bardhan and Patwardhan (2003), two Indian-born scholars teaching in the United States, examined multinational corporations Lever and Suzuki and found that it is possible for major companies to establish a presence successfully in India despite the country's fears of neocolonialism, provided that they respect the culture and perform in a socially responsible manner. They say that India's fairly recent independence means that there is a lingering fear of "cultural and economic imperialism". This, plus a history of protectionist markets, suggests that foreign companies must tread carefully when seeking to establish operations in India. The two authors conducted extensive interviews with Indian practitioners and qualitatively analyzed public relations products including brochures, presentation materials, and websites. Reinforcing the notion that personal relationships are of considerable importance in Asian cultures, Bardhan and Patwardhan demonstrate how this might be borne out on a larger scale – building and sustaining a "personal" relationship between an organization (a multinational corporation) and the Indian community in which it operates. The relationship is built and enhanced if the organization is attuned to local needs, values and goals. For example, establishing operations that create job opportunities in depressed areas, supporting community development programs in areas such as health and nutrition, and engaging in projects related to conservation and the environment all contribute to a business–community relationship upon which a working relationship can be built. The same is true of employee communication – relationships between workers and managers should be based upon demonstrated concern by management for the welfare of the employees. Companies that emphasize two-way symmetric communication structures are likely to gain the acceptance, trust and loyalty of the Indian public.

The most prominent issues facing public relations in India include the remnants of the caste system, establishing the practice as a legitimate and vital component of organizational success, and developing the educational programs to generate the professional practitioners capable of elevating the discipline in India. The efforts of the PRSI, coupled with responsible actions by multinational corporations, should propel Indian public relations in the proper direction.

Malaysia

Malaysia is growing rapidly as it continues its transition from developing nation to industrialized nation, an inviting place for multinational corporations to expand into the Asian market. Along with growth comes the development of the public relations profession, but practitioners face challenges. The 24 million people of Malaysia represent four distinct ethnic groups: Malay (the dominant group), Chinese, indigenous and Indian. Although the Chinese have enjoyed the most success in business and in education, they have not attained commensurate political power. Additionally, the Chinese seek to maintain their traditional beliefs and cultures, creating something of an obstacle to Malay–Chinese relations (Taylor 2000). Although Islam is the dominant religion, Buddhism, Taoism and Hindi are also prominent. Similarly, a host of languages are in use. Consequently, making assumptions about a general description of cultural communication patterns in Malaysia would lead to difficulties.

From the late eighteenth century, the area of current Malaysia was under British colonial rule until Japanese occupation from 1942 to 1945. Following World War II, the British-ruled territories of the Malay peninsula became the Federation of Malaya, which achieved independence in 1957. The nation now called Malaysia was established in 1963 with the addition of Singapore, Borneo and the two states of East Malaysia. Efforts to control or claim parts of the Federation by Indonesia and the Philippines led to Singapore's secession in 1965. In the last decade, Malaysia has been in transition from a producer of raw materials to an emerging multisector economy, though agriculture continues to outpace second-place industrial technology as the main source of national wealth.

Van Leuven (1996) and Van Leuven and Pratt (1996) peg the beginning of public relations in Malaysia to the return of British colonial rule after World War II and say early practice was "characterized by government-run, nation building campaigns" (Van Leuven 1996, p. 209). These campaigns, influenced by the British psychological warfare model, aimed to enhance development efforts and engender a culture of development. The authors say the goal of these campaigns was generally to educate citizens on national issues and government programs and to affect citizens' behavior in some way. Often, too, the purpose was to showcase government achievements. An important concept promoted in those days was the principle of *rukunegara*, "the national ideology which insures that all people are fully informed of the aims and objectives of government policies and which encourages the peoples' participation in the various measures undertaken by the government to help achieve the goals of unity, integration, and national development" (Van Leuven and Pratt 1996, p. 96). The government saw this practice as important in building trust with its citizens.

In those early years, one of the primary aims of the Malaysian Department of Publicity and Printing was to discredit communism. In 1960 came the Rural Development Plan to expand roads, water supplies, power supplies and community centers vastly; the plan included an ambitious communication component. Low literacy and a dispersed population dictated campaigns that included folk media and presentations in community gathering centers. Traditional media were employed primarily to reach opinion leaders and multinational companies.

With the New Economic Policy of 1969 came an effort to disengage the links between race and specific occupations, and to address poverty across all sectors. To support these important communication initiatives, government information staff strength grew to 2,500 – quadruple the number of their counterparts in the private sector. This substantial information force launched campaigns concerning food production, drug use, hoarding, Dengue Fever and road safety. Other campaigns aimed to bolster various economic sectors such as agriculture, the rubber industry and commercial fishing, though the campaigns were more accurately described as marketing and advertising than as public relations. In the early 1970s, private-sector public relations efforts began to emerge, but even then private-sector activity sought government favor by extending financial support to government campaigns. Foreign companies often sought to curry national favor by conducting special events, hoping to deflect attention from their foreign status and profit goals – concepts they feared might engender distrust among the population.

During the 1990s, government campaigns centered on a "Look East" policy designed to fashion the Malaysian economy more on the Japanese and Korean models than on Western models. And, as the Malaysian economy shifted from a heavy emphasis on agriculture to more of a balance with manufacturing, the tone of government communication campaigns shifted from one of influencing individual behavior to one of enlisting public support of and participation in government efforts. This, say Van Leuven and Pratt (1996), stems from Islamic values, officially the national religion.

As Venkateswaran (2004) describes, the most distinctive difference between public relations practice in Malaysia today and the practice in other developed democracies is the relationship between media and the government. She notes that the government exercises control over print media through the 1984 Malaysian Printing Presses and Publications Act, which requires all publications to renew their licenses annually. Under this legislation, the government can withdraw a newspaper's license, suspend its operations, and even arrest anyone who stands in violation of the act. Consequently, mainstream newspapers are owned or controlled directly or indirectly by the National Front. Major newspapers include titles printed in Malay, Chinese and English. In addition, there are roughly twenty radio stations in Malaysia, six free broadcast television channels, more than seventy pay channels, and two government channels. Like newspapers, television and radio stations are available in a variety of languages. All media, like the private sector in general, are expected to cooperate with the government in its effort to build an informed citizenry – simply pursuing profit and growth is not compatible with national aims.

The Institute of Public Relations Malaysia (IPRM) was established in 1962 and adopted its constitution in 1965 (http://www.iprm.org.my). The organization has published a book on Malaysian public relations, *World Class PR in Practice*, edited by Tun Dr Mahathir Mohamad, but the Institute still lacks a code of ethics. According to its website, officials with the Institute cite several contemporary challenges to the practice in Malaysia:

Challenge 1: To gain government support in pushing for recognition of public relations as an essential contributing factor to excellent strategic management and positioning process for social, political and economic success of Malaysia.

Challenge 2: The right fit – Personality, Attitude and Aptitude, Professional Skills to match the era of globalization.

Challenge 3: Win recognition for the profession among key decision makers via benchmarking.

Challenge 4: To educate and gain acceptance for PR. Debunking many myths.

Challenge 5: A focus on Public Relations Ethics and raising ethical conduct to enhance professionalism. Documenting the role of PR in societal and national development.

Challenge 6: AFTA/WTO/Globalisation? Are we ready?

These challenges are formidable in light of Taylor and Kent's (1999) observation that high power distance and the importance of personal influence still permeate Malaysian society. This, along with dominance of the government as the most important public for private-sector public relations, renders Western public relations theories and concepts less applicable in Malaysia's current public relations environment.

Thailand

This Southeast Asian nation of roughly 65 million people is unique in the region in that it has never been occupied by a European power. Known as Siam until 1939, Thailand retains a constitutional monarchy and features a well-developed, free-enterprise economic infrastructure. Thailand appears to have fully recovered from the 1997–8 Asian Financial Crisis and has become one of East Asia's best economic performers.

Hofstede's cultural metrics would gauge Thais to be low in masculinity characteristics such as shows of manliness and external achievement, and more focused on service to others and sympathy for the less fortunate. Here you could expect to find more equality between the sexes and less stress on gender-specific roles. Thais also lean heavily toward collective rather than individual tendencies. However, the Thai power distance index is above average. Relationships in Thailand have subtle differences in comparison to Western values in this area. To be considered a friend is to be accepted entirely, as a whole person; friendships cannot be compartmentalized or limited. If any aspect of someone's behavior is objectionable or in some way conflicts with another's values, the two are unlikely to establish a close relationship. Thais, too, are measured and restrained in their expressions of emotion, either positive or negative. For example, a Procter & Gamble television commercial for one of its shampoo/conditioner products featured the time-saving attribute of the all-in-one item, an attribute illustrated by a woman racing into a locker room and slamming the locker door. When the ad was broadcast in Thailand, that sequence was cut from the television ad because Thais would have been uncomfortable with such an outward expression of emotion (Full of Western Promise 1992).

Something that can be said about Thailand that is also true of other countries with similar demographic characteristics is that there is a considerable chasm between urban and rural populations. The mass media and other cultural manifestations that permeate urban areas have not necessarily reached rural sectors. Consequently, as Silverblatt and Zlobin (2004) observe, people living in an urban setting such as Bangkok have more in common with residents of large, bustling cities in other countries than they do with their citizen counterparts in rural Thailand. The authors also point out an interesting and revealing insight into Thai views of the Chinese. In 1993 a Thai adaptation of Tennessee Williams's play *A Streetcar Named Desire* featured a Chinese character as Stanley, the brutish protagonist, suggesting the lower-class status attributed to Chinese people in Thailand.

As in other Asian nations, formal public relations practice appears to have originated with the government with the establishment of the Publicity Division in 1933. The agency's charge was to improve understanding about democratic administration and parliamentary democracy among the public as Thailand made the transition from an absolute monarchy to a constitutional monarchy. The office grew rapidly, and its name was changed to the Public Relations Department in 1952. Its mission is to promote the national interest and national security through informing domestic and international publics of Thailand in general and its policies. The department has three main areas of responsibility: (1) operating a television network, a radio network and shortwave broadcasts, plus conducting media relations on behalf of the Thai government; (2) planning and conducting communication campaigns, providing public relations advice and counsel to government leaders and other government agencies, including offering public relations training for personnel in other agencies, and monitoring and evaluating the agencies' public relations activities; and (3) managing a network of eight subsidiary offices throughout Thailand and overseeing international public relations programs aimed at building Thailand's reputation abroad. A visit to the department's website (http://thailand.prd.go.th/index.php) will reveal that much of its effort centers on promoting the Thai royal family and on highlighting national progress along a variety of fronts.

Ekachai and Komolsevin (1996) point out that most Thai practitioners – at least in the public sector – lack formal education in public relations, and that press agentry and public information models of practice dominate the sector. They found an emphasis on the technical role of public relations even at the measurement level – counting clips, and so on. However, the researchers also found, even in the public sector, a focus on rural development, though in campaigns characterized by one-way asymmetric communication. On the other hand, they observe that little effort is made in determining needs of relevant publics, nor in assessing whether campaigns are successful in addressing those needs.

Indonesia

This Muslim nation of 17,000 islands, 14 languages, 500 dialects, and 245 million people covers about 2 million square miles of the Earth. It is susceptible to floods, droughts, tsunamis, earthquakes, forest fires, volcanoes and even terrorism. Like other Asian nations, it still struggles to overcome the financial crisis of the 1990s, a struggle evident in high unemployment, corruption, inadequate infrastructure, and vastly unequal distribution of wealth. Additional economic strain is caused by Indonesia's becoming an oil importer in 2004. Still, the nation continues to overcome a difficult past and will certainly play a pivotal role in the region and globally.

Colonized by the Portuguese in the sixteenth century, by the Dutch in the seventeenth century and by the British in the eighteenth century, then again by the Dutch, Indonesia was subsequently occupied by Japan during World War II. Indonesia declared independence when the Japanese left, but the Dutch contested it, and it was four years later, in 1949, that the UN recognized Indonesia as an independent nation. During the 1950s, the country was run by what might be dubbed a benevolent dictatorship; print media during this period were associated exclusively with political groups, and broadcasting emerged solely as an instrument of the government. A military dictatorship followed a failed communist *coup* in 1965, followed by increasingly tight control over broadcasting (a period known as Orde Baru, or New Order, a period that would last until 1998). Print media were given more freedom, but the government still required licenses for all print outlets and curbed any journalistic efforts that threatened the *status quo*. Reformation (*reformasi*) began to emerge in the wake of the 1997 Asian financial crisis, and several independent television networks have become firmly established, though a law passed in 1996 required that 80 percent of programming be domestically produced. In 1999, media were granted total freedom, and the controlling agency, the information ministry, was dissolved. Since then, television has become a medium important for public political discourse; and Chinese-language programs, previously restricted, have become more common (Thomas 2004).

In the post-New Order Indonesia, public relations needs to play an important role, according to the Public Relations Society of Indonesia. That role will include contributing to good governance and respect for human rights. That will mean public relations in Indonesia, as it is elsewhere in Asia, will engage in development efforts as well as with public diplomacy, improving relations with other nations in the region. The Society stresses the need to transcend politics in order to address issues of common welfare, peace and stability. The Society also sees a responsibility for public relations practitioners to help build Indonesia's reputation internationally, employing new communication technologies to engender a cooperative spirit. This, says the Society, will be a challenge given Indonesia's difficult history and recent natural disasters, but those in the public relations discipline are ideally positioned to face that challenge. Doing so means, of course, embracing tenets such as two-way communication, honesty, mutual understanding and cooperation, all based on research. To illustrate the importance the Indonesian public relations profession places on this lofty vision, the Public Relations Society of Indonesia was included as a partner in the 2005 Asian Forum on Corporate Social Responsibility, a gathering in Jakarta of more than 400 CEOs and senior managers from corporations, NGOs and government agencies from across the Asia-Pacific region. As we have pointed out in other nations in this region, public relations practitioners are seen here as required to play a greater role than simply contributing to the prosperity of their organizations; they also represent a greater purpose and are expected to apply their unique skills to that purpose.

Singapore

The last nation we shall look at in this chapter is Singapore, though there are certainly other nations worthy of examination. The point, however, is to demonstrate to the reader the initial information one might gather in preparation for research or projects to be conducted in selected nations. Singapore shares some similarities with other regional nations, but presents some unique challenges as well. Similarities include the gradual transition from a profession dominated by government campaigns designed to bolster the nation-building process to a profession with a strong private sector presence, but still contributing in some degree to nation-building. Its colonial history is linked to that of Malaysia, and Singapore became part of the Malaysian Federation in 1963, but separated in 1965, becoming independent. Since then, Singapore has become one of the world's most prosperous nations, characterized by vibrant international trade and *percapita* GDP commensurate with nations of Western Europe – this despite its size of less than 700 square kilometers, about 3.5 times the size of Washington, DC. Its 4.5 million people live under a parliamentary republic with a government unscathed by corruption. Economically, Singapore is continuing to recover from the 2001–3 global recession and from the SARS outbreak in 2003.

Initial challenges Singapore faced following its independence centered on its disparate population. Early nation-building programs aimed at developing shared values and a national identity out of a mixture of Malay, Chinese and Indian citizens, according to Van Leuven (1996). Early government campaigns such as "Lungs for Singapore" and "Anti-Litter" helped engender a sense of citizenship in the new nation-state. As private-sector public relations emerged in the 1970s, the aim was often to curry government favor by providing support to government nation-building efforts. Media in those early days were largely complicit with government efforts to disseminate development communication messages, even to the point of embellishing government news releases. As in other regional nations, too, Singaporean campaigns combined mass media with community presentations and events, as well as the organization of "Citizens Consultative Committees" that localized national development efforts; examples include the Singapore Environment Council and the Waterways Watch Society, each of which matches government education efforts in the schools with citizen council efforts aimed at the adult population. Still, for the last couple decades of the twentieth century, public relations practitioners had roots in journalism, and their efforts reflected that, based largely on news releases and media relations activities. Also, public relations is broadly defined, often considered interchangeable with advertising and marketing. Gradually, though, public relations is moving more toward a management function as Singapore's economy continues to diversify and subsectors of public relations such as consumer and investor relations become increasingly important. It means, for example, a gradual shift away from campaigns aimed at a single amorphous mass public toward segmentation of publics and more careful crafting and targeting of messages and other program elements.

Of course, another reason to take a closer look at Singapore is its unique approach to issues related to traditional freedoms such as freedom of speech and freedom of assembly. On the one hand, the government has wired every home for the Internet, for example, but this altruistic measure is tempered by the fact that the government owns almost all housing – at least apartment housing – and individual Internet use is subject to government scrutiny. Similarly, the Singapore government controls the media, and satellite dishes are banned.

Any research on Singapore, either for academic or practical public relations purposes, would need to include study of the Singapore 21 Report, the government's report based on extensive research in the late 1990s on how the nation should respond to societal and global changes. The entire report is available at http://www.singapore21.org.sg/s21_reports.html. Highlights include:

- Singapore should plan for a system of lifelong learning for its citizens.
- Citizens' ties to their homeland need to be strengthened.
- Singaporeans should have a greater say in national affairs.
- Women should be conscripted into military service just as the men are.
- Singapore's economy is increasingly global and outward.
- Ideas should flow up from the workforce.

Of course, there's a lot more to the substantial report, but a key to understanding its importance is understanding how it conflicts with embedded cultural traditions. For example, conscripting women into the military contradicts traditional gender roles that have resulted in very few women achieving management and/or leadership roles, especially in the government. The recommendation for ideas flowing upward from the workforce contradicts the Asian tradition of saving "face", as does the notion of citizens taking an increasing role in national affairs, according to Newsome (2004). She says both activities would imply, in Singaporean culture, the suggestion that employees and ordinary citizens would be pointing out mistakes or registering complaints, however mild. Doing so could result in loss of "face" for the employee or citizen for violating the unspoken order of things, and for the employer or government official toward whom the communication is aimed. Clearly, implementation of the 21 Report will be evolutionary rather than revolutionary.

Still, Newsome predicts that Singapore is poised on the cutting edge for public relations excellence because of its embrace of English as the lingua franca, the city-state's well-developed and efficient infrastructure, and its inherent expertise in the public relations profession. Chay-Nemeth

(2003), however, cautions that public relations in Singapore retains an excessive focus on media relations and publicity, elements associated with pre-professional levels of practice. So the establishment of public relations as a strategic function at management level remains a goal to be achieved, though the practice in Singapore is certainly poised for that leap forward.

Chay-Nemeth adds that preparing for and understanding the environment for public relations practice in Singapore requires an awareness of *kiasuism* – a word literally meaning "to be afraid to lose out". In practice it means that Singaporean culture generates members committed to conformity, cautious but focused on material success. Ambition is curbed, and paranoia and self-censorship become the norms. Criticism is inappropriate. Oddly, though, when Hofstede conducted his massive research project, Singapore led the list of all nations, posting the most negative score on the index for uncertainty avoidance. That would mean, at the time (the 1970s), Singaporeans reflected a high tolerance for uncertainty and ambiguity, and the low score suggests a culture that abhors rules and rituals affecting human behavior. That would seem to be incompatible with Singapore today, where gum-chewing is outlawed, stiff penalties greet anyone caught littering, and placing flower pots in shallow dishes containing water is forbidden under the country's strict mosquito-control rules.

Questions for discussion

1. What factors might account for the disparity between Singapore's score on Hofstede's Uncertainty Avoidance Index in the 1970s and the strict regimen of rules governing Singaporeans today?
2. Scholars studying the development of public relations in Asia have encountered and reported on the phenomenon of public relations taking an active role in nation-building. Is that an appropriate role for the discipline? In what ways might the same role be useful in Western societies? What historical factors created the need for the role in Asia?
3. If you are from a non-Asian culture and you were assigned to develop a public relations program for your organization's new operations in Asia, describe how you would approach the challenge.
4. If you are from an Asian culture and you were assigned the task of designing a public relations campaign in North America or Europe, what would be some of the cautions you would convey to your staff?

Featured biography: Kapil Rampal

Kapil Rampal is head of one of the leading public relations agencies in India – Creative Crest. Chief Executive Officer for the past six years, Rampal has expanded the agency to major states, developed a partner network with countries such as Sri Lanka and Nepal, and worked with such clients as the Department of Information Technology of India, Sahara Computers & Electronics, IBM, Wipro Technologies and others. Before his current position, Rampal was a consultant for LiveWorld. At LiveWorld, which is based in California and focuses on social networking and community solutions, he managed public relations activities for many Fortune 500 companies. Rampal has also contributed and developed content for many leading media companies in the country as well as consulting for About.com, Inc. He received his postgraduate degree in Public Relations and Advertising from the Indian Institute of Mass Communication, New Delhi. Rampal also holds a post-graduation diploma in computer science and is a member of the Public Relations Society of America.

Rampal points out several Indian cultural characteristics that should be kept in mind in order to communicate effectively in the country. Indians are very proud of their culture. According to a recent Pew Global Attitudes Project, 74 percent of Indians believe their culture is far superior. Another unique characteristic of Indian culture is the role of the media. Rampal says that the Indian media are very strong and powerful. Indians trust the media and usually read or watch the media choice of their family. Public relations in India needs a lot more message localization that includes "translation into regional languages, modifying releases to media requirements and giving it a personalized delivery", Rampal advises. Many media professionals still prefer fax, snail mail and in-person delivery to e-mail. A localized message ensures better coverage, less editorial work for the media, and an ability to reach out to the target audience. For example, Creative Crest developed a campaign for Hughes, an American company providing e-learning solutions. Creative Crest took over some of their courses and promoted them through personalized stories in Indian media. The courses were offered in English, but the campaign was done also in regional languages. That resulted in the growth of enrollments by 400 percent.

Rampal notes that public relations is a young industry in India. A large percentage of Indian companies see public relations as "a tool for getting low-cost publicity using mass media with media endorsement", he observes. Nevertheless, the awareness of the positive role of public relations is increasing every day. The Public Relations Society of India plays an important role in the process, providing "a platform for public relations specialists to interact and network, and gives guidelines and high standards for effective and professional work", according to Rampal. Indian public relations professionals also face many challenges. Rampal cites lack of a proper structure for the public relations industry *per se* in India as well as lack of information available about the industry and rankings on the top-performing companies. "Unfortunately, there are some public relations firms with no proper public relations background," he says. "They pitch clients with low and unsustainable retainers that reflect the other agencies poorly."

Rampal thinks the future development of public relations will "give rise to agencies that specialize in a particular sector (such as healthcare and pharmacology)". He predicts an increase in companies specializing in public affairs, investor relations, and crisis management. Social issues will also receive more attention. In Rampal's opinion, social problems are best-addressed with public relations. He lists social campaigns promoting sustainability projects, fuel conservation, and awareness for paying taxes that Creative Crest has successfully executed. Rampal believes such social programs can be effectively promoted through public relations all over the world.

With the fast development of public relations in India, the need for public relations professionals is growing as well. Rampal says that there has always been a lack of good public relations specialists. Now that shortfall is being addressed by new public relations courses offered by several good institutes. Most courses insist on an internship before students earn a certificate. The faculty in universities is comprised of academics and industry professionals who allow students to get a combination of academic preparation and practical experience. To become good public relations specialists, Rampal advises students to acquire some important qualities: sound communication skills using any medium, relationship management skills, and stress management.

Recommended websites

Center for Development Communication www.cendevcom.org
Asian Institute for Development Communication www.aidcom.com
Public Relations Society of India http://www.prsi.co.in/

Press Information Bureau of India   http://pib.nic.in

Institute of Public Relations Malaysia   http://www.iprm.org.my

Thai National News Bureau Public Relations   http://thainews.prd.go.th

Thai Government Public Relations Department   http://www.prd.go.th

Public Relations Society of Indonesia   http://www.pr-society.or.id

Singapore 21 Report   http://www.singapore21.org.sg/s21_reports.html

Institute of Public Relations of Singapore   http://www.iprs.org.sg

Blog on Indian Public Relations   http://www.indiaprblog.com/

References

Bardhan, N. and Patwardhan, P., 2003. Multinational corporation and public relations in a historically resistant host culture. *Journal of Communication Management*, 8, pp. 246–63.

Bond, M. H., 1987. Chinese values and the search for culture-free dimensions of culture. *Journal of Cross-cultural Psychology*, 18, pp. 143–64.

Chay-Nemeth, C., 2003. Becoming professionals: a portrait of public relations in Singapore. In K. Sriramesh and D. Verčič, eds. *The Global Public Relations Handbook: Theory, Research, and Practice*. Mahwah, NJ: Lawrence Erlbaum, pp. 86–105.

Ekachai, D. and Komolsevin, R., 1996. Public relations in Thailand: its functions and practitioners' roles. In Hugh M. Culbertson and Ni Chen, eds. *International Public Relations: A Comparative Analysis*. Mahwah, NJ: Lawrence Erlbaum, pp. 155–70.

Fang, B., 2006. Spending spree. *US News & World Report*, May 1, 140, pp. 42–50.

Full of Western Promise, 1992. *The Economist*, 325, pp. 83–4.

Goenka, V., 1996. Journalism in India: a changing perspective. *Editor & Publisher*, 129, pp. 68–9.

Hofstede, G., 1991. *Cultures and Organizations: Software of the Mind*. London: McGraw-Hill.

Melcer, R., 2004. Rural e-commerce can break down the caste system. *St Louis Post-Dispatch* June 13. The Lexis-Nexis Academic database [accessed August 9, 2006].

Newsome, D., 2004. Singapore poised for prominence in public relations among emerging democracies. In D. J. Tilson and E. C. Alozie, eds. *Toward the Common Good: Perspectives in International Public Relations*. New York: Allyn & Bacon, pp. 363–86.

Popping corks: far more news than is fit to print? 2005. *The Economist*, 376, July 30, 55.

Reynolds, S. and Valentine, D., 2004. *Guide to Cross-cultural Communication*. Upper Saddle River, NJ: Pearson Prentice Hall.

Sardana, C. K., n.d. Public Relations in India, [online]. Available HTTP: <http://pib.nic.in/feature/fe0999/f1509991.html> [accessed June 29, 2006].

Silverblatt, A. and Zlobin, N., 2004. *International Communications: A Media Literacy Approach*. New York: M. E. Sharpe.

Sriramesh, K., 1996. Power distance and public relations: an ethnographic study of Southern Indian organizations. In H. M. Culbertson and Ni Chen, eds. *International Public Relations: A Comparative Analysis*. Mahwah, NJ: Lawrence Erlbaum, pp. 171–90.

Taylor, M., 2000. Toward a public relations approach to nation building. *Journal of Public Relations Research*, 12 (2), pp. 179–210.

Taylor, M. and Kent, M. L., 1999. Challenging assumptions of international public relations: when government is the most important public. *Public Relations Review*, 25 (2), pp. 131–44.

Thomas, A. O., 2004. The media and *reformasi* in Indonesia. In D. J. Tilson and E. C. Alozie, eds. *Toward the Common Good: Perspectives in International Public Relations*. New York: Allyn & Bacon. pp. 387–404.

Tilson, D. J. and Alozie, E. C., 2004. *Toward the Common Good: Perspectives in International Public Relations*. New York: Allyn & Bacon.

Van Leuven, J. K., 1996. Public relations in South East Asia from nation building campaigns to regional interdependence. In H. M. Culbertson and Ni Chen, eds. *International Public Relations: A Comparative Analysis*. Mahwah, NJ: Lawrence Erlbaum. pp. 207–22.

Van Leuven, J. K. and Pratt, C. B., 1996. Public relations' role: realities in Asia and in Africa South of the Sahara. In H. M. Culbertson and Ni Chen, eds. *International Public Relations: A Comparative Analysis*. Mahwah, NJ: Lawrence Erlbaum, pp. 93–105.

Venkateswaran, A., 2004. The evolving face of public relations in Malaysia. In D. J. Tilson and E. C. Alozie, eds. *Toward the Common Good: Perspectives in International Public Relations*. New York: Pearson Education, pp. 405–25.

Chapter 8

Evolutionary public relations in China, Japan and South Korea

A comparative analysis

Contributed by: Ni Chen

Summary

By now you will appreciate that today's world is becoming increasingly integrated, economically and socially. Although offering marvelous opportunities, economic globalization has risks as well. Political, economic, cultural and religious conflicts are spreading, creating an urgent need for discourse and cooperation among peoples with different basic beliefs and ways of thinking (Culbertson 1996). Modern public relations, with communication and management as its core, provides guidance, as we have seen, in building/managing/softening relationships across borders and cultures. As businesses are competing in a global market, global ambitions must be supported by global marketing and global communication. The practice of public relations has subsequently spread rapidly around the world, and "practitioners are identifying best practices and applying them as soon as poss-ible in their own countries" (McElreath et al. 2000, p. 665). Indeed, public relations has grown fast in East Asia, first in Japan, then in South Korea, and now in China. Not until recently have empirical studies been conducted about the nature of public relations in the region. This chapter attempts to describe, analyze and synthesize how public relations is practiced in China, Japan and South Korea, exploring the unique patterns of its evolution and development. To this end, this study examines each country's political, economic, cultural and media systems, which serve as a context within which public relations practice has evolved in these countries (Culbertson and N. Chen 1996; Sriramesh 2004). This study also ventures to predict the future development of public relations in the region.

Evolutionary changes of public relations in China

With about 1.3 billion people, China is the world's most populous nation, constituting 21 percent of the global total. China has, since the 1980s, been developing rather rapidly, with an average double-digit GDP growth rate in the past two decades (*World Almanac and Book of Facts* 2006). Its government is one of the few remaining communist régimes, even as the country is transforming itself from a command economy to a market economy with "Chinese characteristics". The social transformation in China is also breathtaking: a centuries-deep agricultural society is advancing directly into an information age. It is with similar rapid change that public relations practice has evolved in China.

Political, economic, cultural and media systems

Following a socialist model, China has been governed by the Communist Party of China (CCP) since 1949. As economic and administrative reforms have dominated public policies since the early 1980s, state power is being relatively augmented. The primary organs of state power are the National People's Congress (NPC), the president and the State Council. The NPC constitutionally enjoys the highest authority, while the State Council is the executive body, exercising unified and hierarchical leadership over all state administrative organs at the central, provincial, autonomous regional and municipal levels.

China's administrative system has been élite-governing, authoritative and bureaucratic. The central government is entitled to impose strict control over local bodies. However, administrative reforms toward decentralization since the 1980s have helped loosen ties between central and local governments, introducing increased freedom to local officials (economic planning, taxation, social welfare) as well as to activists (consumer and environmental protection). As resistance to bureaucracy and corruption intensifies, stress has increasingly been placed on political and social reforms: free election at village level is extending to townships, and the number of CCP authorities has been greatly reduced at provincial, municipal and county levels. Promoting the idea of "political democracy" (*zhengzhi mingzu*) – not democratic politics – since 2002, the central authorities have adopted a less ideological and more pragmatic policy toward China's modern transformation.

Economic reforms have been the most significant driving force behind China's dramatic changes since the early 1980s. The economic reforms have, however, experienced three stages: first, the trial stage (1980s) in which an export-oriented economy supported largely by foreign capital was successfully tested in four "special economic zones" along the eastern coast (Shenzhen, Zhuhai, Shantou and Xiamen); second, the expansion stage (1990s) characterized by a large number of Chinese state-owned enterprises turning private and with a market economy spreading in the rest of the country; third, the stabilizing stage (since 2002) with free-market systems penetrating all types of economic sectors, manufacture and service alike. Consequently, as nearly half of China's economy has been privatized in the past two decades, the traditional command economy is being transformed into a market economy.

Without doubt, China's success has benefited greatly from economic globalization, which has, in turn, integrated the Chinese economy into the international competitive system. Over the years, direct foreign investment has seen fast growth, ranking China among the top countries in the world; China's foreign trade has expanded, serving as the most dynamic engine driving the country's economy, and foreign technologies and managerial talents have moved into China, upgrading almost all types of industry. China's entry into the WTO marked yet another milestone, not only motivating "Fortune 500" corporations to establish long-term operations in China, but also leading China's top companies toward further overseas expansion (National Bureau of Statistics of China 2005). Going global, China's economy has slowly but surely acquired a role in shaping the world economy; the ups and downs of stock prices in Shanghai and Shenzhen are instantaneously felt in the New York, London and Singapore stock markets.

Although lifting millions of people out of poverty, China's economic reform entails serious challenges. For one, agriculture has lagged far behind all other sectors. Farmers, who make up more than 80 percent of the population, are only slightly better off (rural incomes are less than a third of urban incomes – a difference much higher than in most countries), keeping much-needed consumption power consistently low (Wang and Hu 1999). Additionally, the unprecedented growth in manufacturing has not only turned China into a major "factory of the world" but also, more seriously, ruined a large part of the country's environment, rendering the development hardly sustainable. Worst of all is the continuous state interference in the economy. Still seeing themselves in the driver's seat, government officials are too proactive in shaping economic activities both at macro and micro levels.

Despite moving fast toward a modern society, Chinese traditions remain largely in effect. With a culture spanning more than 5,000 years, Confucianism, for example, continues to serve as a secular ideology to maintain the social order. Many traditions are kept intact. They include: near-universal marriage, close family ties, traditional arts (handicrafts, music, cuisine, medicine, and so on), natural respect for education, matrilineal family structure, male dominance, a China-centered perspective, disdain for most other cultures, deference to individuals of higher status, and a preference for functioning in hierarchical systems.

Scholars (Sriramesh and White 1992; Culbertson and N. Chen 1994; Sriramesh 1996; Sriramesh *et al.* 1996) have argued that a nation's culture shapes its public relations practice, and this text supports that contention. N. Chen and Culbertson (2003) discussed several cultural dimensions proposed by Hofstede (2001) and their implications in relation to public relations practice in China. You have read about these in earlier chapters, but the following paragraphs place them in a Chinese context.

First, *power distance*. China's high power distance stems largely from its imperial tradition, in which emperors and/or upper-level people are viewed as sons of God and superiors, and low-level people owe their superiors respect and obedience in exchange for protection and consideration (Hofstede 2001, p. 114; Ng 2000, pp. 51–2). It is the Chinese philosophy on governance that has subordinated "ordinary people" to powerful leaders. In a Confucian society, government is the heart of civilization.

Second, *collectivism versus individualism*. Chinese people highly value collectivism, which regards the group's well-being and interests as superior to those of the individual. Harmony through the advocacy of benevolence (*ren*), rituality (*li*) and fidelity (*yi*) is highly desired, often at the expense of individual interests. A major aspect of Chinese collectivism is *guanxi* – one's network of connections and friendships – which is emphasized in both personal and business relationships. For example, a good *guanxi* can help a company get positive coverage in media, acquire favorable policy from officials, or even provide a protection umbrella (N. Chen and Culbertson 2003, p. 27).

Third, *masculinity versus femininity*. Chinese society has been male-dominated. Confucius once said that women and children are artfully immature and hard to deal with. Thus, men are viewed as superior to women. In a masculine society such as China, male egos ought to be stroked and their strength respected in negotiations. Masculine stubbornness resists compromise and may even lead to violence (Hofstede 2001, p. 436). Consequently, women are perceived as weak and soft, subject to skepticism and confined to marginal roles in society.

Fourth, *long-term orientation*. One aspect of such an orientation reflected in Chinese attitudes is the focus on patience, hard work and perseverance. Taken together, collectivism and long-term emphasis on virtue contribute to a major idiosyncrasy of Confucian societies, namely, preserving face. Loss of face is often considered to be worse than loss of a limb (Hofstede 2001, p. 354). On the one hand, this motivates people to work hard and be virtuous; on the other hand, it may lead them to conceal problems and withdraw from relationships to avoid embarrassment.

Against this backdrop, the communication pattern in Chinese society relies on high context. Information is thus not explicit but embedded in the context or internalized in the communicators. This means that people may use ambiguity and silence to deliver a message, contrary to common practice in low-context Western culture. In a high-context culture, open, direct and honest communication may be viewed as distasteful.

Chinese media have long served as the official and authoritative mouthpiece. Government and the Party censor the media both formally and informally. However, the landscape of media has been changing fast, partly as a result of economic reforms. In the market economy, media competition has shaken the connection between the Party and the media organs and, in some cases, changed media ownership structure (N. Chen 2003, p. 119). To increase readership or rating to maximize advertising income, many media have increased their volume and changed the nature of media content. A growing number have become media conglomerates by expanding into other businesses. Journalists have adjusted their roles with increased awareness of professionalism and sense of social responsibility.

Media in China today have gradually expanded their functions. Although retaining their role as the Party's "propaganda tool", they have begun to provide news, information, knowledge and entertainment, and increasingly to voice public opinions and criticize the government's wrongdoings, playing somewhat of a "watchdog" role. In addition, traditional media are continuously losing ground to new media. For instance, newspapers in 2005 were hit hard by falling circulation for the first time after consecutive growth for over a decade. New media such as the Internet, blogging, podcasting and mobile phones have become an emerging force (Zhu and Wang 2005). Media diversification and fragmentation are expected to continue.

The evolution of public relations practice

It was not until the 1980s that Western public relations concepts and practice moved into China. Although often attributed to changes in the economic system, the evolution of public relations in China has much deeper roots – earlier changes in political ideology and later in the political system (N. Chen 1994, p. 122). Public relations development in China must, however, be seen as a multidimensional process. The field first underwent a vertical development, gaining as much acceptance and growth as advertising and marketing by Chinese business organizations. After being introduced in some key industries such as tourism and banking, public relations practice spread horizontally to other areas such as government institutions. Both vertical and horizontal moves followed the same geographical pattern: starting from the southern coastal regions around Guangzhou (the city adjacent to Hong Kong and pioneering the economic reform), via the commercial and cosmopolitan city of Shanghai, to the country's capital of Beijing, and finally into the more conservative inland cities (N. Chen 1994).

Vertically, the evolution of public relations in China has undergone several stages: introduction, upsurge, rethinking, declining, and toward professionalism. The *introduction* stage lasted from 1980 to 1985, paralleling China's initial opening-up period. Much as with other newly introduced concepts and practice, the roles and functions of public relations were often misunderstood and confusing. It was thought of virtually as a substitute for interpersonal relations and networkbuilding – *gao guanxi* – and as a new scheme to help get things done. It was also viewed stereotypically as a glamorous occupation because most of the first-generation practitioners were young and beautiful ladies but with little training, usually playing a role of "guest relations" to keep the guests/clients accompanied and entertained, or the so-called "Ms. PR" (N. Chen and Culbertson 1996).

From 1986 to June 1989, public relations practice saw an *upsurge*. During the period, more and more people became aware of and interested in public relations, which was even turned into a buzzword. Public relations offices/departments and associations were set up. More important, universities began to offer training and courses in public relations. At the same time, public relations books and articles from the West were translated into Chinese, which further helped diffuse the concept. Earlier misunderstood principles and concepts became somewhat focused.

The third stage was termed a *"rethinking"* stage from June 1989 to 1992, triggered primarily by the famous student pro-democracy movement in Tiananmen Square. Looking for the "evil influence" behind the movement, the Chinese leadership blamed imported ideas and practices from the West and thus called for "rethinking" of them. Under this circumstance, "socialist public relations with Chinese features" came into being, which discouraged copying Western public relations into Chinese practice and required close state supervision and guidance of the practice. Although not banned altogether, modern public relations practice visibly slowed in China, owing to the political confusion and power struggle between liberals and conservatives.

The years 1992–2000 saw evident *declining* of public relations in China. Approximately a third of the public relations firms and departments in large business organizations were eliminated. Public relations associations suddenly shrank. The number of newspapers and journals dedicated to public relations declined from thirty-three in 1989 to just two. The Ministry of Education refused to accredit public relations as a course for study in universities, allowing only Zhongshan University in Guangzhou to offer a public relations program on a trial basis (N. Chen and Culbertson 2003). The political "rethinking" about Western ideas and practice certainly had its impact on public relations practice. Certainly, state-owned enterprises, the centrally controlled media, and state university professors remained cautious about allowing public relations to rebound. Also, as China's economy was severely affected by the Asian financial crisis and subsequent economic slowdown in the late 1990s, business organizations began to cut budgets on public relations programs. Moreover, many blamed public relations practitioners and their practices for widespread government corruption and business fraud as a few public relations people were found to be helping cover up scandals (X. Wu 2002).

Sidebar: China loses reputation in Mattel recall

In August 2007, toy company Mattel recalled 1.5 million toys worldwide tainted by lead paint, the first of a series of recalls leading to deep investigations of China's manufacturing plants. Subsequent recalls of Pixar car toys, Fisher-Price toys and Barbie accessories followed on August 14 and September 4 involving different Chinese toy-manufacturing companies who used cheaper, unapproved paint-suppliers (D'Innocenzio 2007). An additional, smaller recall of 55,000 Go Diego Go toys followed on October 25 because of lead paint. All of these recalls created a crisis in the capital of toys – China.

The first August 2 recall involved Fisher-Price toys with characters such as Dora the Explorer and Elmo. The toys tested positive for lead paint, forcing Mattel to face a massive recall. After investigating its China manufacturing plants, Mattel found that Lee Der Industrial Co.'s paint supplier, Dongxing New Energy Co., ordered 330 pounds of yellow pigment powder from Dongguan Zhongxin Toner Powder factory when Dongxing ran low on yellow pigment (Lee and Magnier 2007).

While the recall created havoc in the US for Mattel, the head of Lee Der, Cheung Shu-hung, felt pressure and guilt in China. The day after the recall, Shu-hung was found dead after hanging himself inside his factory (Lee and Magnier 2007). He was not the only person responsible for the recall, but apparently felt his reputation was ruined and that he had failed the public. His suicide during the toy crisis con-

trasts with Mattel's communication efforts in the US and reveals profound cultural differences.

Mattel's Vice-President of Corporate Communications, Lisa Marie Bongiovanni, took a proactive approach and used many communication vehicles to handle news of the recall. As Bongiovanni (in Bush 2007) pointed out: "It takes a very big effort to communicate with as many parents as possible and as quickly as possible, so they understand and are not confused about what the issues are" (p. 1). Mattel bought ad space in major newspapers across the US to address parents with a personal letter from Bob Eckert, Mattel's chairman and CEO. It also worked with public relations agencies Weber Shandwick and Cone to make its consumer website more interactive with a videotaped message from Eckert (Bush 2007). Eckert also did a satellite media tour on the morning of the recall, and on the evening news Mattel executives were interviewed on CNBC, CNN, ABC and Fox News, among others. The company also did interviews for print outlets and wire services, including the AP, the *Wall Street Journal*, the *New York Times* and *USA Today*. Because Bongiovanni wanted to convey the facts and issues to parents to help them determine if they owned the toys in question and to prevent the media from breaking inaccurate news stories about the recall, Mattel's media outreach was critical. Mattel CEO Eckert agreed: "I thought it was important for us to be transparent, to provide information openly and quickly. The alternative is to stick your head in the sand and hope it goes away. It never does" (in Goldman and Reckard 2007). Eckert's observation is particularly true in light of the global nature of the recall. Mattel's staffers answered media and consumer inquiries from Europe, Latin America, Asia and the US. As Bongiovanni summarized, "Our goal was to make sure we had as close to a 100 percent response rate as possible" (p. 1). Response to Mattel's efforts has been positive overall. Parent Johanna Gutlay of Santa Monica, California, said: "They're doing a good job in the sense that they're telling people. Now I think they're going to be careful and safer" (in Goldman and Reckard 2007).

In China, manufacturers still caught the blame for the defective toys. On September 21, 2007, Mattel's Executive Vice-President for Worldwide Operations, Thomas A. Debrowski, attempted to save face by apologizing to China's product safety chief, Li Changjang. Debrowski said: "Mattel takes full responsibility for these recalls and apologizes personally to you, the Chinese people, and all of our customers who received the toys" (Veiga 2007). The first recall involving lead paint was not the only recall, and the second and third recalls involving magnets were a Mattel design flaw, for which China was not responsible. Over a month later, the apology failed to satisfy China's toy manufacturers because it did not recover the loss the companies had suffered. The tarnished reputation is leading Chinese toy manufacturers to file suit against Mattel. Mattel's reputation is also damaged, and it was one of four companies awarded the International Bad Product Award by Consumers International.

Mattel's toy crisis demonstrates global crisis techniques and the importance of "face" in Chinese culture. It also provided an opportunity for Mattel and Chinese companies to tighten production regulations. With 80 percent of toys worldwide exported from China, China will still be making toys, but this episode will long affect perceptions of China's manufacturing sector.

Entering the new millennium, public relations practice in China has finally been *revitalized*. Two major success stories have helped elevate the level of public interest in public relations. In 2002, Beijing was selected by the International Olympics Committee as the sponsoring city for the 2008 Summer Olympic Games. The competition campaign was assisted by Burson Marsteller, one of the world's leading public relations firms, whose creative strategy – "isolation versus engagement" – to refute the criticism of China's human rights status seemed very effective: the Committee members were persuaded that China should be "engaged" rather than "isolated"; thus, awarding the Games to Beijing was the best way to engage and integrate China. The second event occurred in 2003, when SARS epidemics created a terrifying public health crisis first in Beijing and soon affecting the rest of China. The situation posed a serious challenge to the new Chinese central leadership headed by Hu Jingtao. The administration was able to pacify the panicking public, partially by conducting open and direct communication with the public via the "spokesperson" system. The system has since been institutionalized at almost all governmental levels. What stands out is that political leaders came to realize that public relations programs, if executed properly, can help (N. Chen 2003, pp. 112–13).

Ni Chen and Culbertson (2003, pp. 31–2) identified five other factors that may contribute to the revitalization of public relations in China. First, growing public pressure for transparency has compelled government and business to rely more on public relations in response to public skepticism and criticism. Procurement, recruitment, accounting, among other operating functions, would have to be made public. Such publicizing, government and business leaders soon realized, requires public relations expertise. Second, as media systems became less shackled, so has media relations become more of a priority for both government officials and business executives. Especially with new media coming into full play, online public relations provides a cheaper but more effective communication conduit. Third, the internationalization of Chinese business has convinced business executives that public relations practice is at least as important an element as advertising in the marketing process. Integrated marketing communication (IMC) has consequently gained attention (Y. Wu and N. Chen 2007). Fourth, with Chinese business further diversified and government more decentralized has come the intensification of public advocacy (X. Wu 2002). Nongovernmental organizations for consumer rights, environmental protection, "migrating labor" rights, anti-fraud, anti-corruption, and medical care are on the rise. Although each has its own public relations concerns, they have together driven the need for public relations to be further specialized and professionalized. Fifth, the field of public relations has been formally incorporated by the government into general higher education. The Ministry of Education has accorded considerable flexibility to public relations programs in universities. In Shanghai, four universities are offering bachelor-degree programs in public relations, and one offers a master's degree. These programs will produce around 200 graduates each year for the public relations profession in Shanghai (Mao 2007).

After more than a decade of ups and downs, public relations is moving toward professionalism in China. To date, it has become a profession that has employed thousands of people. By the end of 2006, in Beijing alone, there were approximately 2,000 public relations/marketing counseling firms in operation, tripling the number of ten years ago. The political system in China, however, predetermines media functions, thus constructing the basis of public relations practice. As government rather than the consumer has been the key public, one major function of Chinese public relations has been government relations. It is likely, though, that the promotion of a "harmonious society" by the central leadership may inspire further public concerns over issues associated with justice, ethics, sustainable development, law and order, each of which would require public relations practice to tackle and push it to grow toward sophistication.

Questions for discussion

1. With the cultural dimensions of power distance, collectivism, masculinity and long-term orientation, how should foreign practitioners approach public relations in China?
2. Seeing examples of success and failure in China, does failure suggest that public relations does not work or does it encourage the need for good public relations crisis techniques?
3. China has already undergone many stages in developing public relations. What do you see as the next stage for public relations in China? What steps does China need to take to reach this stage?

Evolutionary changes of public relations in Japan

Although introduced as a Western concept, public relations practice in Japan was found in a 1996 study to have developed "a nonwestern ethos". The same study also forecast that six changes in Japanese society would have significant implications for public relations practice in Japan into the twenty-first century. These were: (1) the disappearance of lifetime employment, consumer complacency and quiet stakeholders; (2) the beginning of true multiparty politics; (3) increasing foreign pressure to open domestic markets; (4) female dissatisfaction with male-dominated society; (5) environmental awareness; and (6) disillusionment with public scandals and corruption (A. C. Chen 1996). It has been almost a decade since the study, and Japan has since undergone numerous changes, as has its public relations practice. This section focuses on contextual factors and their impact on the evolution of public relations in Japan.

Political, economic, social, cultural and media systems

The term "uniqueness" has appeared more than any other in outsiders' observations about Japan's political, economic and social life. An island country comprising the four islands of Honshu, Hokkaido, Kyushu and Shikoku plus a number of smaller islands, Japan forms an arc in the Pacific Ocean to the east of the Asian continent. Japan has a population of 127 million as of July 2007 and is ranked as the tenth-largest in the world. Since the end of World War II in 1945, Japan has seen a profound transformation. Politically, Japan has moved from foreign occupation as part of the international arrangement upon its defeat to a democratic government. In less than twenty-five years, Japan moved from being a less-developed country to the second-largest economy in the world, making up roughly 15 percent of the world's GNP.

But Japan is a country full of contradictions in politics. Although its Western-based constitution is democratic, its imperial tradition is widely cherished. Emperor Akihito took the throne as Japan's 125th emperor in 1989, and the monarchy remains strong. Although the upheaval in politics in 1993 led to the end of Liberal Democratic Party (LDP) rule, true multiparty politics has become more or less a political reality only at local levels. With Prime Minister Koizumi in office in 2001–6, new-conservatism dominated Japan's public affairs. As a result, liberal movements for environmental protection, women's rights, and social responsibility are taking a back seat in politics. Aspiring for true great-power status not only in the region but also in the world, Tokyo participated in the "coalition of the willing" in the invasion of Iraq in 2003, reinforced its security alliance with the US to balance China in 2004, and played a big part in reining in a nuclear North Korea in 2005–6 (Pekkanen and Krauss 2005). Working meticulously for a permanent seat on the UN Security Council, the Abe government (2006–7) threatened to do away with the peaceful constitution of 1947 (Pilling 2006). Prime Minister Yasuo Fukuda, chosen by the governing Liberal Democratic Party in September 2007, is a moderate who has stressed the need to build strong ties with China and other Asian nations.

Japan's postwar economy, based solidly on industrial development and international trade, has often been described as a miracle. From the 1950s to the 1970s, its average annual growth rate was 8 percent, making it the first country to be moved from "less developed" to "developed" status in the postwar era. The fast economic growth was attributed to high rates of both personal savings and private-sector facilities investment, ample supply of cheap oil, innovative technologies, and effective government intervention in private-sector industries and, most important, a labor force with a strong work ethic. In fact, employees in Japan are known to have a strong sense of belonging and loyalty to their employers. Although the economic boom continued in the 1980s, by the end of 1990 the Tokyo stock market had fallen 38 percent, wiping out 300 trillion yen (US $2.07 trillion) in value; and land prices dropped steeply from their speculative peak, symbolizing the "bursting" of the "bubble economy". The post-bubble recession lingered into the new millennium. Addressing deflation, debt problems and the budget deficit as structural problems in the Japanese economy, the government implemented a wide range of structural and regulatory reforms, public company privatization, and administrative reforms. Major changes are also taking place in the corporate world as companies strive to increase competitiveness. It becomes inevitable, however, that lifetime employment is fast disappearing, while consumer confidence is severely weakened and stakeholders become more alert to market changes than ever before.

Although the younger generation is becoming more Westernized in Japan, traditional culture, which is characteristic of Confucian values and beliefs, still affects people's way of thinking and behavior. Although its economy reaches almost every corner of the world, the society is insulated, and the nation remains highly homogeneous. With long Chinese influence, Japanese culture continues to emphasize collectivism, harmony and concord (*wa*), and is categorized as high-context. With patience as a way of life, Japanese place emphasis on avoidance of direct conflict and stress group welfare over individual desires (A. C. Chen 1996). In this sense, organizations prefer either covering up or doing nothing to going public with negative news. Taciturnity or nonverbal communication (*ishin denshin*) is morally accepted; and nontalkativeness is socially encouraged. The level of implicitly conveyed meaning in communication is high, resulting in a proportional limit on the extent of tangible information exchanged. Meaning depends on the interpretation, with communicators having to take into account the circumstances under which the communication is conducted. In addition, boundaries between in-group and out-group members are highly visible. In exchange for loyalty, groups look after their own members. Thus, open, direct, or honest communication is regarded as inappropriate.

Japan's communication infrastructure, though well developed, helps to keep the traditional pattern of communication intact. Transmission of information is both fast and dependable, but the media are by no means free or diverse. For instance, major newspapers are owned by tightly knit groups of family members of the paper's founders and top management. Each of the five television networks based in Tokyo is connected to a major national newspaper, a link that not only enables it to share news facilities, but has also over the years given it distinctiveness. And these television networks are privately owned and highly commercialized. The Japan Broadcasting Corporation (Nippon Hoso Kyokai – NHK) is the only noncommercial public radio and television broadcasting network. Contrary to the overall decline of print media worldwide, Japanese newspapers enjoy high saturation with 587 copies per 1,000 people. Japanese newspaper circulation ranks first in the world, but the papers are distinctively conservative in design and layout. They put more emphasis on text than on visuals, and only one major newspaper, *Mainichi*, has a color front page (Asian Media Project, Japan). Moreover, the relationship between media and organizations seems significantly smooth, as media simply refuse to see themselves as "watchdogs" over government and large corporations. Reporters seldom investigate government and business affairs. Even in news conferences, reporters rarely ask sensitive, probing or challenging questions.

The use of new technologies, including the Internet for communication, is gaining currency in Japan. There are reportedly 47 million people using the Internet. Also, the usage ratio of mobile phones is comparatively high. It is believed that, with the communication infrastructure becoming more intensive and diversified, messages can reach a large audience quickly and easily, bypassing the traditional "gatekeepers" and thereby transforming the traditional mode of communication in Japan.

Evolution of public relations practice

Although modern public relations practice is found to have its beginning in 1945 (A. C. Chen 1996), its early appearance can be traced back to 1925 (Inoue 2003), when the Japanese government was pushing for military expansion in Asia. From 1925 to 1945, public relations was mainly a propaganda function serving war mobilization, building up the nation's military strength, manipulating public opinion to support Japan's armed forces and securing people's compliance with the government's wartime policies. Communication, thus, was strictly one-way and manipulative.

Following Japan's surrender in 1945, the United States and Allied forces occupied Japan and used public relations in support of that occupation. US forces set up central and regional offices to disseminate information promoting allied objectives for reforming Japan. Thus, from 1946 to 1952, modern public relations was practiced in Japan but with a distinct focus on government information dissemination via media (A. C. Chen 1996). Although establishing a linkage between public relations and publicity, such a focus invariably brought about misunderstanding of public relations functions; people tended to mix public information with public relations. As a result, the communication became predominantly one-way, functioning as an information provider via media. Given such a tradition, public relations practice has been perceived by the public chiefly as "media relations" even to this date.

With Japan's fast economic development in 1952–90 came high growth of public relations. Starting from the late 1950s, government institutions as well as corporations began to realize that the public's approval was vital to an organization's success. And, to gain the public's approval, organizations had to carry out good deeds in order to pave the way for positive publicity to take place. It was found, though, that the public's approval could be easily obtained via the use of such controlled media as corporate advertising and advertorials (A. C. Chen 1996). This further fueled the misunderstanding about the function of public relations. As a result, people tended to mix public relations with advertising and advertorials.

Meanwhile, as industrialization led to mass production of consumer goods, public relations functions were naturally extended to the areas of sales and marketing promotion and product publicity. The domestic market soon proved too small for Japanese companies to survive and succeed; Japan had to go regional and global. Corporate leaders began to realize that, if they had to pursue an international ambition, they were compelled to have an international communication program. Public relations was to be used to provide tactical support to international marketing communication, first to help sell products/services, and then to nurture favorable feelings and combat resentment in overseas markets. Moreover, domestic customers started to consider the company's level of corporate citizenship when buying its products. Social responsibility became an issue to be addressed and managed by public relations practitioners (A. C. Chen 1996).

Although public relations practice saw a rapid development in scope in Japan, the fundamental nature of communication efforts was limited. They were one-way and persuasive in nature. Public relations was used mainly both in-house and externally to help solve image and reputation-related problems brought on persistently by corruption, scandals, pollution, product deficiencies, and financial mismanagements. However, Japanese corporations did not see the need to beef up their public relations staffs, but instead began to seek professional services provided by public relations agencies mainly as troubleshooters. As a result, agencies started to flourish in Japan.

Haruta and Hallahan (2003) conducted a case study contrasting the organizational responses to two major airline crashes that happened in 1985, one in Japan and the other in the United States. The study revealed significant differences in crisis communication and management by Japan Air Lines and Delta Air Lines regarding the use of public apology, media strategies and litigation concerns. Interestingly, the differences can be mainly attributed to culture-bound differences.

First, as the cornerstone of JAL's handling of the crisis, President Takagi of JAL was quick on his feet to apologize publicly to the victims' families and the survivors long before the investigation into the cause of the crash was completed. JAL, indeed, did what was expected by the Japanese public and what was perceived to be right in Japanese society. Even though an apology does not imply guilt, as it does in Western culture, it is a gesture containing multiple meanings such as concern, remorse, reparation, compensation, and a request for forgiveness in Japan. Making a public apology is also a moral obligation the Japanese public would expect JAL to fulfill, guilty or not. In addition, in a culture with strong uncertainty avoidance, people tend to avoid ambiguity, and JAL met its expectations by claiming responsibility publicly even if the cause of the crash was unknown at the time. Also, according to the principles of Confucius, "what works" is more important than "what is true". Thus, virtue rather than truth is stressed in Japanese culture, requiring JAL to make an apology to show it cared. Further, in a culture with high power distance and strong masculinity, it is a social norm that the head of the organization shall make the apology and make himself visible in a crisis situation. On the other hand, though expressing some sympathy for the loss of lives, US-based Delta made no public apology, purposely avoiding what it perceived as potential legal responsibilities.

Second, in terms of media strategies, JAL exercised highly centralized control of information to preserve hierarchical harmony. Such a strategy reflected its greater emphasis on collectivism, strong power distance, and face-saving in Japanese society. In a collectivistic culture such as Japan, groups' interests and well-being outweigh those of individuals. The large power distance encourages centralized management systems and vertical communication networks (Hofstede 1980; 1991). These culture attributes dictate that crisis communication strategies be adopted to ensure the protection of a group's well-being, not that of the individual. These characteristics also demand that media inquiries shall be handled by a male spokesperson who is perceived to be strong, assertive, decisive and in control. In addition to high-level information control, JAL deliberately appointed a male to be the spokesperson, one whose face and voice appeared as frequently as possible in the media. Delta, on the other hand, engaged in open and direct communication with the media with no intent to dominate or manipulate the information. To provide a "motherly" face and a sympathetic voice, a middle-age female spokesperson was at the center of Delta's communication with the public.

Third, JAL was not nearly so concerned about the litigation issue as was its US counterpart, Delta. In a culture in which collective concord is emphasized, restoring harmony is viewed as the most important agenda item in the aftermath of a crisis. And litigation is viewed only as contributing to the creation and worsening of disharmony in relationships. Moreover, Japanese value social harmony so much that they resolve disputes through compromise and conciliation. This may also help explain why Japan has one of the lowest numbers of court cases and lawyers *per capita* among all industrialized nations (Dean 1990). On the contrary, avoiding potential litigation was a key issue in Delta's crisis communication responses.

This case study reveals that, although Japan's economy is profoundly linked with the West, the country's traditional culture still greatly affects the practice of public relations. Within this unique social and cultural context, it is thus highly desirable to incorporate cultural and social factors as key variables in designing and executing public relations programs and campaigns in Japan.

Sidebar: Japanese press clubs

To gain quick and easy access to news conferences conducted by the government and various businesses, journalists must join a "press club", or *kisha*, in Japan. Each government and business has its own press club, amounting to hundreds of press clubs nationwide in Japan.

To become a member of a press club, an organization must first belong to the Japan Newspaper Publishers and Editors Association or a similar organization. In addition, the organization must receive two recommendations from existing press club members. Once established as a member, the organization pays a monthly fee to stay in.

There are a few problems associated with press clubs. First, often foreign journalists feel left out. Because so much information is available only through press clubs, or press clubs are given news first, foreign journalists have limited access to information. Foreign journalists can attend press club events, but only through approval by press club members. Magazine writers and Web reporters are also left out of press clubs.

The second controversy concerns press clubs dealing closely with government and businesses. By participating in élite clubs, the government can limit what is said in media outlets. Also, close relationships may discourage reporters from doing investigative reports or shedding bad light on a company or the government.

Despite exclusiveness and controlled information, press clubs are often the only way for media outlets in Japan to gain information.

It is also interesting to note that Japanese culture seems to shape politicians' understanding of, and attitude toward, public relations practice. Japanese politicians do not seem to have much faith in the utility of public relations, especially in an image crisis situation. Once they are involved in a scandal, instead of taking active measures in crisis communication and management, they tend to resign, usually with an open apology, and in extreme cases even to commit suicide. Two recent cases are illuminating examples. On May 28, 2007, the Japanese agricultural minister, Toshikatsu Matsuoka, killed himself only hours before he was to face parliamentary questioning on a political funding scandal (Fackler 2007). Less than two months later, defense minister Fumio Kyuma resigned only a few days after making public remarks suggesting that the 1945 US atomic bombings of Hiroshima and Nagasaki were inevitable. The statement varied from the Japanese stance on the use of nuclear weapons. Kyuma came under intense criticism from A-bomb survivors, opposition lawmakers and fellow members of the Cabinet who make up the core of Japan's pacifist sector. Instead of managing the crisis, he elected to step down, and his decision was accepted by the prime minister (Kana 2007). In both cases, neither the two troubled ministers nor the embattled Abe government used public relations in dealing with the crises.

The history of modern public relations in Japan is relatively longer than that of China and South Korea. Interestingly, though, its development – especially in regard to the scope and nature of public relations functions – lags behind that of China and South Korea. For example, despite its status as second-largest economy in the world, there are only about ten major public relations agencies operating in Japan (Inoue 2003). Public relations roles have largely been confined to gaining publicity via media relations. Indeed, the term "public relations" in Japan continues to imply "press relations", as newspapers remain the predominant source of information for the public in Japan. In this sense, public relations practitioners still maintain the technician mentality. More surprisingly, the infrastructure for public relations education and professional training has yet to be established, as modern programs in public relations are still waiting to be incorporated into university curricula.

Nevertheless, there is reason to believe that future development of public relations in Japan is promising. The demand for public relations services in the areas of risk communications, investor relations, brand management and global communication is increasing. As Japan managed successfully to recover from the collapse of the bubble economy, corporate and opinion leaders have gradually realized the importance of two-way communication, and the sense of social accountability has taken a firm hold within the corporate world and society. Public relations practice has, thus, improved and will increasingly fulfill management functions in the areas of crisis communication, employee relations, community relations, global marketing and integrated communication.

Questions for discussion

1. A good economy drove the evolution of public relations in Japan. How does the economy continue to affect public relations practice in your country?
2. The government controls to some extent information given to media sources. How does freedom of the press in other countries allow investigation of the government? What effect does controlling information have on public relations practice?
3. What steps does Japan need to take to change public relations from serving media relations functions to serving other functions such as strategic planning?
4. Compared to other countries, why do you think Japan is behind in developing public relations practice?

Evolution of public relations in South Korea

Located in the southern part of the Korean peninsula, South Korea has been a dynamic country economically and politically. For most of the twentieth century, South Korea was hardly "the Land of the Morning Calm". Since the end of Japanese colonial rule in 1948 and the Korean War in 1953, life there has mostly been about calamity. The country, however, seems to have finally left its troubles behind. With a population of 46 million (ranked eighth in Asia), it has developed into the world's eleventh-largest economy and the seventh-largest in foreign trade at the beginning of the twenty-first century (S. Jo and J. Kim 2004). Meanwhile, South Korea has increasingly consolidated its market economy and democratic system.

Political, social, cultural and media systems

Dating back to 2333 BC, the Korean people have gone through a tortuous path in building a nation-state. Their modern history is characteristic of fighting tenaciously for political independence and cultural identity as well as resisting foreign invasions. After repelling the Khitans, the Mongols and the Manchus since the fourteenth century, Korea was annexed by Japan in 1910. The occupation ended with the conclusion of World War II in 1945, but the peninsula was plunged once again into an international conflict in June 1950. The Korean War came to a halt in July 1953, but the Korean peninsula remains nationally divided to this day: the Republic of Korea – a democratic system – in the south and the Democratic People's Republic of Korea – a communist régime – in the north.

South Korea's government follows a republican model, where political power is shared by the presidency, the legislature and the judiciary. Constitutionally, the president is the head of state, elected to serve for a single term of five years. Major political parties include the Uri Party (Uri), Grand National Party (GNP), Democratic Labor Party (DLP), Democratic Party (DP) and People Centered Party (PCP). From 1945 to 1992, however, the political system was basically authoritarian, largely ruled by military dictators. Western-style democracy in South Korea was not cemented until 1992 when the first free elections were held (D. C. Shin 1999) and has since been firmly consolidated (Diamond and Kim 2000, pp. 21–52).

The economic system in South Korea is market-oriented. Its economy has achieved an incredible record of growth since the 1960s: *per capita* GNP in 1963 was about $100, but exceeded $14,000 in 2004. As a result, South Korea has often been referred to as one of the "Four Dragons of East Asia" (along with Taiwan, Hong Kong and Singapore) for its fast economic development. Through the late 1980s, the economic miracle in South Korea was achieved primarily through a system of government–business partnerships, with a strong labor effort, and via an ever-growing international outreach. Although the Asian financial crisis of 1997–9 inflicted a big setback upon its economy, South Korea has recovered and rebuilt its financial stability, turning decline in 1998 into strong growth, made possible by consistent governmental efforts to reshape and restructure the nation's economy (Kwon *et al.* 2003).

Socially and culturally, South Korea retains influence from its immediate neighbors. As the dominating philosophy, Confucianism serves to guide people's thinking and behavior; it has been so prevalent in Korea that it casts more influence on its culture than any other religion or philosophy, Western or oriental (Hong 2003; H. S. Kim 2003). People in South Korea tend to respect and follow the orders of the old and the authorities. High-ranking individuals usually have more power over their subordinates than do their counterparts in the West. Decision-making in Korea follows a formal and rigid procedure in which senior approval is desirable (Microsoft® Encarta® Online Encyclopedia, 1997). In addition, hard work, obedience to the head of the family, protection of the family, and proper decorum among family members are commonly held values. Furthermore, South Korea is characterized as a society by its culture of high power distance, high collectivism, high masculinity, and high Confucian dynamism (H. S. Kim 2003). Information is most effectively delivered and received if it is passed through personal channels (J. O. Yum 1991).

The media in South Korea are well developed and diversified. Most print media are privately owned. As of December 2003, there were 124 daily newspapers across the country. For broadcasting, there are four nationwide television networks, including two public broadcasting networks (KBS and MBC), one private (SBS), and one state-owned educational broadcasting network (EBS).

Public broadcasting networks receive funds from the government which, in turn, collects revenues from mandatory license fees. The government thus exerts controls over the management of national networks primarily through the Korean Broadcasting Commission (KBC).

South Korea's media, however, have been acquiring more and more freedom and independence since the democratic movement in 1987. The media now are said to be more or less free of governmental pressure and interference (Jo and Y. Kim 2004). Freedom of the press did not come easily, though. Before the political liberalization in South Korea in the late 1980s, the government tightly controlled the press and suppressed criticism of the government with the Press Ethics Law (Y. Kim 2003a). In 1975, for example, the National Assembly enacted a criminal law that called for imprisonment of up to seven years for people found guilty of "slandering" Korean constitutional organizations at home or aboard. Also, in the same year, the government canceled the license for the Journalists Association of Korea, terminating the assembly for journalists. Through a New Year's address in 1976, then President Park Jeoung-hui publicly affirmed his commitment to maintaining national security as the country's top priority, even at the cost of freedom of the press (J. K. C. Oh 1977). These measures virtually eliminated public demand for political transparency, limited the activities of opposition parties, and rendered free press impossible. It is only since 1987 that the media in South Korea have, slowly but steadily, been released from rigid government control (Korean Overseas Information Services 1999).

The rapid development of new media technologies in recent years has accelerated freedom of the press. Internet, electronic newspapers, cable television and satellite broadcasting provide people with more options to access information. Recent studies show that more than 80 percent of the 15 million households in South Korea have a personal computer (Korean Online Marketing Association 2002). Inspired by such development, most organizations begin to see the Worldwide Web as a cheaper and more effective medium to reach audiences without going through the traditional gatekeeping process.

Evolution of public relations practice

The introduction of public relations into South Korea is closely related to Western influence in East Asia. As part of the Allied occupation of Japan at the end of World War II, US armed forces stationed in the southern part of the Korean peninsula set up the first public relations office (Office of Civil Information) in 1945 to publicize its activities via media (D. B. Oh 1991). That was the introduction of contemporary public relations in South Korea with a strong orientation toward press agentry and public information. This also explains why public relations is commonly known as *Hong Bo*, meaning "publicizing widely". The term, however, carries a negative connotation in Korean because it suggests a scheme to gain publicity through self-promoting and self-serving information. At the initial stage, public relations practice in South Korea was characterized solely as publicity via media relations (Park 2001).

Economic advances in South Korea in the 1960s and through to the 1980s paved the way for public relations to grow. During this period, public relations functions began to widen. Expanding rather rapidly, Korean corporations invariably utilized public relations to sell products and services at home and abroad. However, it was the marketing function of public relations that was emphasized by the corporations. In the mean time, the authoritarian government also intensified its use of public relations in curtailing criticism and in image-refurbishing. As the authoritarian political environment prevailed, the emphasis of government public relations was placed almost exclusively on managing negative publicity and on image protection. In both cases, the one-way communication model had been followed by both government and corporations.

Prompted perhaps by eventful challenges since the late 1980s, public relations practice in South Korea has undergone further functional changes. The sponsorship of the Seoul Olympic Games in 1988, the establishment of a true representative government in 1992, the Asian financial crisis in 1997, along with the emergence of activist groups derived from college student movements and the rise of social demands for ethical practices, have rendered a rare opportunity for public relations to develop further. Gradually but surely, such modern functions of public relations practice as event management, relationship management and crisis management have been recognized and employed by government, corporations and other organizations. As a result, the public relations communication model has become more and more two-way. Corporations have, for example, started to consider activists as important stakeholders, acknowledging that negative media coverage initiated by activist movements can affect the reputation and success of organizations.

Meanwhile, with free elections now conducted at all government levels in South Korea, public relations practice plays an increasingly important role in political campaigns. Campaign managers rely more and more on public relations to make the candidates known to the publics and to enhance voters' understanding and support. Uniquely, though, because "regionalism" is the critical variable affecting South Korean politics (S. Jo and J. Kim 2004), political candidates are supported by voters from the same regions so consistently that their characters, ideology, and policy orientations are not of that great a concern compared to regional identities and affiliations (D. C. Shin 1999). Operating within this reality, political campaign managers tend to apply public relations strategies and tactics to strengthen "regional" ties and associations between candidates and voters. Once in office, candidates who have benefited from this function of public relations continue practicing it, subsequently shifting the focus of government public relations from executing propaganda and managing negative publicity to enhancing understanding and building mutually beneficial relationships with publics.

There can be little doubt that the South Korean government successfully applied public relations in combating the financial crisis in 1997–8. What stands out is that effective government public relations showcased its ability to mobilize hundreds of thousands of overseas Koreans in assisting their mother country in surviving the crisis. Many of them donated much of their assets to the Seoul government to protect the currency from collapsing altogether (M. Y. Oh 2001). In the aftermath of the crisis, the measures taken by the South Korean government brought about not only more problems for public relations to tackle but also more chances to mature. For instance, job security that came from lifelong employment was hopelessly disappearing, leading to high anxiety, low morale and diminished loyalty in the workforce. It is in this area that the internal communication component of public relations has been strengthened. Organizations have widely recognized modern public relations as an important tool, especially in the area of employee relations, to smooth the relationship between management and employees.

Increasingly public relations is taking on a global scale in South Korea. To coordinate its international outreach best, South Korea set up the Government Public Relations Department in 1999 mainly to help rehabilitate international trust in the Korean economy. The move is viewed as a landmark decision as it gives the public relations profession recognition as a national-service activity. In the same year, public relations practice was "officially classified as a profession by the government" (S. Jo and J. Kim 2004, p. 243). The field of public relations in South Korea has, therefore, experienced gradual expansion to include employee relations, investor relations, community relations, government relations, international and global public relations and marketing. Although media relations remains an important part of public relations practice, organizations have also begun to recognize the importance of research and strategic communication management in building relationships with various stakeholders, both domestic and international.

Several points regarding the recent development of public relations in South Korea are worth highlighting. First, a number of local and international public relations agencies/firms have established a footing in South Korea. Among major international public relations agencies, Burson-Marsteller, Edelman, Ogilvy & Mather, and Shandwick are in full operation. In 2000, revenue generated by a hundred independent public relations firms and twenty-three advertising/public relations agencies reached an equivalent of US$175 million (Y. Kim and Hon 2001).

Second, public relations associations are able to play a major role in overseeing public relations practice in South Korea. Among them, the International Public Relation Association's (IPRA's) Korean chapter was the first to be established (1988), followed by the Korean Public Relations Association (KRPA) founded in 1989. In addition, professional organizations such as the Korean Academic Society of Public Relations (KASPR), formed by academic scholars in 1997, publishes the quarterly *Korean Journal of Public Relations Research* and conducts public relations seminars and conferences regularly, providing professional training to public relations practitioners. And scholars have learned to measure the efficacy of public relations practice scientifically (H. C. Shin 1997). In 2000, public relations agencies founded the Korean Public Relations Consultancy Association (KPRCA). Both KRPA and KPRCA have established codes of public relations ethics.

Third, South Korean institutions of higher education have positively responded to the increasing demand for public relations education. Bachelor, master, and even doctoral programs in public relations are offered to both full- and part-time students. Public relations curricula are incorporated into all major colleges and universities, with most housed in either mass communication/journalism departments or advertising/public relations units. A large number of scholars who have received their advanced training in public relations and mass communications in the US and the UK have formed the backbone of the public relations faculty in South Korea.

Fourth, pioneering in communication technology development and application, especially the use of the Internet in public relations, has become prevalent in South Korea. The Public Relations Team (2000) pointed out that the Internet represents a paradigmatic shift in communication, creating the possibility of full two-way communication, thus having a unique impact on the way public relations is practiced. According to a 2006 survey, South Korea had the highest penetration rates for broadband in the world. And a 2002 survey on Internet usage in Korea showed that the impact of the Internet on public relations practice was strong and positive, with, for example, boundary-spanning improved and facilitated through the use of the Internet (Jun 2002).

Fifth, although gaining more professional recognition than ever before, the status of public relations practitioners in organizations remains low compared to those working in advertising, management consulting firms and the media. This is so mainly because of the strong influence of a "technician mentality". Practitioners often consider themselves as technicians (rather than as communication managers), in charge of writing, editing, speaking, graphic designing, and media relations. Many of them tend to follow one-way models more than two-way models (Y. Kim and Hon 2001). A survey by KRPA revealed that the majority of corporate public relations practitioners still regarded media relations as the most important public relations function. In fact, more than 95 percent of agency public relations practitioners were more familiar with media relations than with other public relations functions, according to J. Y. Jo (2002).

Evidently, modern public relations practice in South Korea has not yet reached its maturity. Culture seems to have stood as a delaying force (S. Jo and J. Kim 2004). Although public relations in the West stresses open communication, the relatively closed Korean society had difficulty in embracing the concept; traditional particularism, reciprocity, and in-group and out-group distinctions demanded vertical, not horizontal, relationships. Further, as a society of intermediaries, there is much overlap of personal and public relationships (J. C. Yum 1987). Personal influence and connection still shape public relations practice in all areas, especially in media relations and public affairs, as "who you know" in the media and government holds the key to successful media and government relations (J. Y. Jo 2002). Park (2001) and Hong (2003) indicated, in particular, that public relations practitioners in South Korea prefer personal networks with members of the media to organizational influence. As a result, many veteran journalists with personal connections to media and government officials are encouraged to join the public relations profession (Y. Kim 1996).

In this connection, four cultural attributes have proved useful in explaining the pattern of public relations evolution in South Korea. They also seem to be obstacles public relations practitioners may have to overcome in the years ahead.

High Confucian dynamism. Confucian dynamism is comprised of long-term versus short-term orientations. Public relations practitioners in South Korea tend to value a long-term, future-oriented vision, emphasizing relationships directed more toward the future with their clients. Unlike the short-term orientation reflected in Western culture, public relations practice of long-term orientation stresses thriftiness, ordering relationships by status, tradition, saving face, exchanging favors, and personal stability (Hofstede 1980; 1991).

High power distance. South Korea's adoption of Confucian élitism has warranted a high power distance between the upper and lower classes. The upper orders are born to rule and cultivate enlightenment and learning, while the lower are born to obey and serve. This makes it extremely difficult for genuine two-way symmetric communication to take place. One-way and downward communication prevails with top management often issuing orders without seeking feedback. This communication mode consequently leads to lower-quality decisions, resembling that of "group-think" – a mode of thinking that people engage in "when they are deeply involved in a cohesive in-group, when the members' striving for unanimity overrides their motivation to realistically appraise alternative courses of action" (Janis 1982).

Collectivism. The oriental collectivism featured in Korean culture generates pressure on individuals to conform to group demands. Collectivistic value systems, goals and aspirations trump those of individuals, and the group is viewed as the most important part of society. Thus, organizations or people with close ties to famous families or groups (*Chaebols*) would receive extra favor and enjoy comparative advantages. In this sense, Korean culture can be viewed as a "relationship culture". Personal networks, developed into a unique practice of personal relationship building and maintaining, encourage nepotism in organizations. Practitioners sometimes give gifts or *chonji/ ddukgab* (money for buying Korean cakes) in personal network building (Hong 2003).

Saving face for harmony. The ultimate purpose of communication for many Koreans is to create harmony, which is found in the maintenance of an individual's *face*, referring to one's dignity, self-respect and prestige. Thus, saving not only one's own but also another's face often defines public relations practice in South Korea. Instead of direct/honest/open communication, practitioners have to "beat around the bush" to show respect and value for a harmonious relationship, or they often try to take negative news out of the media and place only positive news to protect their client/organization. This, in part, also explains why Korean practitioners seldom take advantage of competitors' vulnerabilities because saving another's face is a prime consideration (Kim 2002). The "face-saving" requirement in interpersonal relationships has thus been extended to professional relationships.

Modern practice of public relations has been much shaped by the dynamic political, economic, social, cultural and media circumstances in South Korea. As such, the major functions public relations plays were confined to publicity and media relations dominated by one-way communication at its initial stage of development (1940s–1970s), but extended to marketing-related activities in the 1980s. It has since the 1990s been moving toward relationship-building and strategic planning and management, placing more emphasis on two-way communication. Continuous changes in South Korea's economic, social, political and media systems have not only helped put public relations on a fast track, but have also inspired expansion of its functions. Although now widely recognized as a profession, public relations in South Korea still has a long way to go to command respect.

Questions for discussion

1. Because South Korea relies on personal channels to gain information, which interpersonal techniques do outsiders need to develop to form personal informational relationships?
2. In South Korea public relations received the *Hung Bo* nickname, which has a negative connotation. Does public relations practice have negative connotations in your culture? How do practitioners overcome this negative stigma?
3. South Korean culture saves face for harmony by putting a positive light on negative messages. How is truth perceived and constructed in audiences?
4. Of the three countries studied, which is closest to developing public relations programs resembling practice in the West?

Conclusion

As we have seen, a society's political system, economic structure, cultural heritage and media infrastructure tend to shape people's social behavior and communication patterns. Such is the case with the evolution of public relations practice in China, Japan and South Korea.

In all three countries, the evolution of public relations as a modern profession is driven by both outside and inside trends toward modernity. After several thousand years of being rigidly closed to the outside world, Japan was the first to open to the West, followed by South Korea shortly after its formation, with China joining only in the early 1980s. Each nation's embrace of modern public relations concepts and practice has basically followed the same chronological order. Economic globalization has been the most important catalyst behind the maturation of public relations in all three. Together, the three economies rank as the largest in the world. Interestingly, however, the public relations industry in the region lags significantly behind that of the other two worlds' economic centers, North America and the European Union.

Long-sustained traditions have left their imprint on the development of public relations in China, Japan and South Korea. Inhabited by the largest number of people in the world, and representing one of the oldest civilizations, the region shares one common cultural attribute – Confucianism. Although emphasizing social stability through proper human relationships, Confucianism acknowledges inequality of human beings and requires social relationships to precede individual interest. Forming a high-context culture, social trust rests largely with social relationships. Public relations practice in China, Japan and South Korea, therefore, blends professional and social relationships. Also, in a culture characterized by high power distance between the masses and the élites, excellent public relations programs are hard to come by in the three countries (Sriramesh and White 1992).

In addition to seeing different stages of public relations development in China, Japan and South Korea, we see a degree of *imbalanced* development in the three countries. Still in an authoritarian political system, public relations practice in China leans more toward government relations than in either Japan or South Korea. Functioning in a highly sophisticated democracy but a homogenous society, public relations in Japan focuses predominantly on marketing-related and promotion-oriented activities. With communication technologies developing most quickly in South Korea, public relations practice there consistently places heavy emphasis on media relations. One encouraging trend, however, is that as activist groups emerge as one of the most important publics in all three countries, most notably in South Korea followed sequentially by Japan and China (Yap 2005), public relations practice has a good chance of being further specialized and increasingly professionalized.

Featured biography: Y. K. Chung

Y. K. Chung is considered to be one of the founders of public relations in Asia. After receiving a Master's degree in journalism and public relations at the University of Iowa in the US, Chung took the public relations skills he had acquired back to China and Taiwan. Highlights of his career include serving as chief public relations officer for the Taiwan Provincial Government, Counselor and Public Relations Officer at the Premier's Office, President of NOEC Corporation, national chair and council member of the International Public Relations Association, and chair of the Public Relations Department at the World College of Journalism and Communications. He now teaches at Shih Hsin University and is the standing director of the Chinese Public Relations Association in Taiwan.

Chung bases his approach on many public relations concepts. Typically, public relations is described as trying to influence those who can influence others; but an alternative description, in Chung's view, is cultivating understanding and harmony to achieve prosperity. Chung recommends a balance of theory and practice in public relations. In addition to encouraging this balance, he advises: "Don't be a frog living in the bottom of a well." He uses this Chinese proverb to suggest that practitioners look beyond their countries and envision expanding their practice globally.

Chung views the US as the first country to establish public relations as a discipline and historically the worldwide resource for public relations education, innovation and practices. Chung maintains that the basics of public relations practice in other countries remain the same but cautions: "Practitioners have to adapt new techniques to parallel the ever evolving environment" (Chung 2007). Other countries such as China and Taiwan have different cultures and cannot simply copy US methods. They must adapt US concepts to fit their culture. Chung uses the phrase "Select American and redirect local" to explain this idea (Chung 2007).

Two cases illustrate how merely copying US methods does not work. The first case explains how Beyer, a German chemical manufacturer, tried to open a factory in Taiwan. By using US textbook lobbying and governmental public relations methods, it failed. Not only did it fail, but Taiwan's image was also harmed because it was seen as a bad foreign-investment site. The second example concerns the Taiwan Postal Administration's issue of a stamp with a picture of a pig; that offended Islamic nations, and mail bearing the stamp was refused in those countries. These examples have led to Chung's views on adapting lobbying and "textbook" public relations. Instead, Chung advises using third-party endorsements and avoiding uniformity in grassroots lobbying. Indeed, in applying standard public relations methods, he suggests, it is OK to break the rules if methods are failing, because methods need to adapt to the situation.

Public relations education programs in Taiwan are helping practitioners there develop culture-sensitive approaches to the discipline. Since 1953, the Chinese Public Relations Association in Taiwan has produced seminars, publications, training programs, and international exchanges. The first college program began in 1963, but today formal public relations education can be found in Taiwanese schools up to the doctorate level. Taiwan may have learned public relations practice from the US, but now employs its own professionals and educators.

Like other countries discussed in this chapter, public relations practice in Taiwan evolved from governmental needs. By 1958, public relations units in state-owned facilities and some government agencies were established. Industries followed the government in employing public relations, paving the way for public relations organizations and consultancies to form. As Taiwan became a powerful market economy, the need for public relations practice increased.

During the development of public relations practice in Taiwan, Chung has witnessed the growth of public relations, held both government and professional positions in the practice, teaches, and contributes to the spread of the discipline. From his experience, he urges practitioners to learn more about China and Taiwan. His final advice is this:

Understanding the history and culture, traditions and taboos, business practices, government, and the relationship with Mainland China is most essential. Learn the country by studying cases, participating in seminars and meetings, Chamber of Commerce events. If one can learn enough communicable Mandarin and Taiwan dialect, it would be a plus.

(Chung 2007)

It is clear from Y. K. Chung that learning about and immersing oneself within a culture or country is the best way to improve international public relations practice.

Recommended websites

International Communication Association – PR division   http://www.icapr.org/

International Public Relations Association   http://www.ipra.org/

China International Public Relations Association   http://www.cipra.org.cn/english/about-us/main-us.htm

Fortune China (Chinese firm)   http://www.fortunechina.com.hk/

Kyodo-PR (Japanese firm)   http://www.kyodo-pr.eu/

Public Relations Society of Japan   http://www.prsj.or.jp/english/index.html

Korean Public Relations Association   http://www.koreapr.org/

Korean Academic Society of Public Relations   www.kaspr.or.kr

Korea Public Relations Consultancy Association   www.kprca.or.kr

Korea Association for Advertising and Public Relations   www.kadpr.or.kr

KPR (Korean firm)   http://www.kpr.co.kr/eng/index.aspx

References

Anon., 2002. Abacus to China. *Encyclopedia of Modern Asia.* Volume 1. New York: Berkshire Publishing Group.

Anon., 2003. *Korean Advertising Yearbook.* Seoul, South Korea: [s.n.].

Anon., 2004. *Consumer Market of South Korea.* Hong Kong: Hong Kong Trade Development Council.

Bae, J., 2007. Interview with Dr Ahn, Jong Bae, professor of Hansei University, Hawaii, USA. January 8.

Bush, M., 2007. Pet food industry unites in crisis. *PR Week,* [online]. Available at: http://www.prweek.com/us/news/article/657951/Pet-food-industry-unites-crisis/ [accessed May 29, 2007].

Chen, A. C., 1996. Public relations practice in Japan: beginning again for the first time. In H. Culbertson and N. Chen, eds. *International Public Relations: A Comparative Analysis.* Mahwah, NJ: Lawrence Erlbaum.

Chen, N., 1994. Public relations education in the People's Republic of China.

Chen, N., 2003. From propaganda to public relations: evolutionary change in China. *Communications of the ACM,* 48 (4), pp. 49–53.

Chen, N. and Culbertson, H., 1996. Guest relations: a demanding but constrained role for lady PR practitioners in mainland China. *PR Review,* 22 (3).

Chen, N. and Culbertson, H., 2003. Public relations in mainland China: an adolescent with growing pains. In K. Sriramesh and D. Verčič, eds. *The Global Public Relations Handbook: Theory, Research, and Practices.* Thomson.

Chinese government. *Asian Journal of Communication,* 13 (2), pp. 96–121.

Chung, Y. K., 2007. Email discussion on his biography. Personal communication, October.

Culbertson, H., 1996. Introduction. In H. Culbertson and N. Chen, eds. *International Public Relations: A Comparative Analysis.* Mahwah, NJ: Lawrence Erlbaum, p. 1.

Culbertson, H. and Chen, N., eds, 1996. *International Public Relations: A Comparative Analysis.* Mahwah, NJ: Lawrence Erlbaum.

Culbertson, H., Chen, N. and Alanazi, A., 1996. In H. Culbertson and N. Chen, eds. *International Public Relations: A Comparative Analysis.* Mahwah, NJ: Lawrence Erlbaum.

Dean, M., 1990. The Japanese legal system: a step into the unknown. *New Law Journal,* February.

Diamond, L. and Kim, B. K., eds, 2000. *Consolidating Democracy in South Korea.* Boulder, Colo.: Lynne Rienner.

D'Innocenzio, A., 2007. Mattel recalls 800,000 toys worldwide. *Associated Press Online,* September 5.

Fackler, M., 2007. Japanese cabinet minister commits suicide. *International Herald Tribune/Asia-Pacific,* May 28.

Goldman and Reckard, 2007. *LA Times,* [online]. Available at: http://www.latimes.com/business/printedition/la-fi-pr18aug18,0,3471349.story?page=1&coll=la-headlines-pe-business [accessed October 13, 2007].

Grunig, J. E. and Hunt, T., 1984. *Managing Public Relations.* New York: Holt, Rinehart & Winston.

Haruta, A. and Hallahan, K., 2003. Cultural issues in airline crisis communications: a Japan–US comparative study. *Asian Journal of Communication,* 13 (2).

Hofstede, G., 1980. *Culture's Consequences: International Differences in Work-related Values.* Beverly Hills, Calif.: Sage.

Hofstede, G., 1991. *Cultures and Organizations: Software of the Mind.* New York: McGraw-Hill.

Hofstede, G., 2001. *Cultural Consequences: Comparing Values, Behaviors, Institutions, and Organizations across Nations.* Thousand Oaks, Calif.: Sage.

Hong, Y., 2003. Influence of culture on public relations practitioner roles: a cross-national study, the United States and South Korea, [online]. Available at: http://0-proquest.umi.com.hkbulib.hkbu.edu.hk/pqdweb [accessed October 3, 2006].

Inoue, Takashi, 2003. An overview of public relations in Japan and the self-correction concept. In K. Sriramesh and D. Verčič, eds. *The Global Public Relations Handbook: Theory, Research, and Practice.* Thomson.

Janis, I. L., 1982. *Groupthink.* Boston, Mass.: Houghton Mifflin.

Jo, J. Y., 2002. Media relations in Korea and recent trends. Paper presented to the pre-conference meeting of the Public Relations Division at the Annual Conference of the International Communication Association, Seoul, Korea.

Jo, S. and Kim, J., 2004. In search of professional public relations. In K. Sriramesh, ed. *Public Relations in Asia: An Anthology*. Mahwah, NJ: Lawrence Erlbaum.

Jo, S. and Kim, Y., 2004. Media or personal relations? Exploring media relations dimensions in South Korea, [online]. Available at: http://proquest.umi.com/pqdweb [accessed November 6, 2006].

Journalism Education, spring, pp. 36–41.

Jun, M. C., 2002. Internet usage in Korea: a survey of public relations practitioners, [online]. Available at: http://0-proquest.umi.com.hkbulib.hkbu.edu.hk/pqdweb_[accessed November 20, 2006].

Kana, I., 2007. Kyuma resigns over A-bomb comments: defense minister slammed for suggesting 1945 attacks were inevitable, [online]. Posted July 3, 2007. Available at: http://news.aol.com/story [accessed July 25, 2007].

Kim, H. S., 2003. Exploring global public relations in a Korean multinational organization in the context of Confucian culture. *Asian Journal of Communication*, 13 (2), pp. 65–95.

Kim, Y., 1996. Positive and normative models of public relations and their relationship to job satisfaction among Korean public relations practitioners. MA, University of Florida.

Kim, Y., 2002. Cultural and relationship management in South Korea. Paper presented to the pre-conference meeting of the Public Relations Division of the Annual Conference of the International Communication Association, Seoul, Korea.

Kim, Y., 2003a. *Ethical Standards and Ideology among Korean Public Relations Practitioners*. Netherlands: Springer.

Kim, Y., 2003b. Professionalism and diversification: the evolution of public relations in South Korea. In K. Sriramesh and D. Verčič, eds. *The Global Public Relations Handbook: Theory, Research, and Practices*. Thomson.

Kim, Y. and Hon, L., 2001. Public relations in South Korea: applying theories and exploring opportunities. *Journal of Asian Pacific Communication*, 11 (2), pp. 263–86.

Korean Online Marketing Agency Association, 2002. The status of internet use in Korea, [online]. Available at: www.adcr.co.kr/archives/html.

Korean Overseas Information Services, 1999. News and medias, [online]. Available at: http://www.korea.net/korea/kor_loca.asp?code=C0101 [accessed November 10, 2006].

Kwon, O. Y., Sung, H. J. and Kyung, T. L., eds, 2003. *Korea's New Economic Strategy in the Globalization*. Edward Elgar.

Lee, D. and Magnier, M., 2007. Trouble in Toyland: safety problems bear down on Chinese manufacturer. *Los Angeles Times*, August 24, p. C1.

McElreath, M., Chen, N. and Azarova, L., 2000. The development of public relations in China, Russia, and the United States. In L. R. Heath, ed. *Handbook of Public Relations*, pp. 665–6.

Mao, J., 2007. *Gonggong guanxi de zuixin fazhan qushi* (*New Trends in Public Relations*). Shanghai: Shanghai Foreign Languages Education Press.

Microsoft® Encarta® Online Encyclopedia, 1997. South Korea, [online]. Available at: http://encarta.msn.com/encyclopedia_761562354_6/South_Korea.html [accessed November 20, 2006].

National Bureau of Statistics of China, 2005. *China Statistical Yearbook – 2005*. China Statistics Press.

Ng, R. M., 2000. The influence of Confucianism on Chinese conception of power, authority, and the rule of law. In D. R. Heisey, ed. *Chinese Perspectives in Rhetoric and Communication*. Stamford, Conn.: Ablex, pp. 45–55.

Oh, D. B., 1991. *PR Communication Theory*. Seoul: Nanam.

Oh, J. K. C., 1977. South Korea 1976: the continuing uncertainties. *Asian Survey*, 17 (1), pp. 71–80.

Oh, M. Y., 2001. South Korea attitudes towards foreign subsidiaries of multinational corporations (MNCs): the influence of corporate image and country of origin image, and the presence of halo effect, [online]. Available at: http://0-proquest.umi.com.hkbulib.hkbu.edu.hk/ [accessed November 20, 2006].

Park, J. M., 2001. Images of "hong bo (public relations)" and PR in Korean newspapers. *Public Relations Review*, 27, pp. 403–20.

Pekkanen, R. and Krauss, E. S., 2005. Japan's "coalition of the willing" on security policies. <u>Orbis</u>, summer.

Pilling, D., 2006. Abe aims to secure Japan's world status. *The Financial Times*, October 31.

Public Relations Team, 2000. Annual report: challenge the limit [brochure]. Seoul: Samsung Munhwa.

Shin, D. C., 1999. *Mass Politics and Cultural in Democratizing Korea*. New York: Cambridge University Press.

Shin, H. C., 1997. Media relations and public relations. *Hong-Bo Hak*, 1.

Sriramesh, K., 1996. Power distance and public relations: an ethnographic study of southern India organizations. In H. Culbertson and N. Chen, eds. *International Public Relations: A Comparative Analysis*. Mahwah, NJ: Lawrence Erlbaum.

Sriramesh, K., 2004. Public relations practice and research in Asia: a conceptual framework. In K. Sriramesh, ed. *Public Relations in Asia: An Anthology*. Thomson.

Sriramesh, K., Grunig, J. E. and Doizer, D., 1996. Observation and measurement of two dimensions of organization culture and their relationship to public relations. *Journal of Public Relations Research*, 8, pp. 229–61.

Sriramesh, K. and White, J., 1992. Societal culture and public relations. In J. Grunig, ed. *Excellence in Public Relations and Communication Management*. Hillsdale, NJ: Lawrence Erlbaum.

Veiga, A., 2007. Mattel apologizes to China over recalls. *Associated Press Online*, September 22.

Wang, S. and Hu, A., 1999. *The Political Economy of Uneven Development: The Case of China*. New York: M. E. Sharpe.

World Almanac and Book of Facts, 2006. New York: World Almanac Books.

Wu, X., 2002. Doing PR in China: a 2001 version – concepts, practices and some misperceptions. *Public Relations Quarterly*, 47 (2), pp. 10–18.

Wu, Y. and Chen, N., 2007. *Zhenghe yinxiao: lilun yu shijian (Integrated Marketing Communication: Theory and Practice)*. Shanghai: Shanghai Foreign Languages Education Press.

Yap, F., 2005. *Citizen Power, Politics, and the Asian Miracle*. Boulder, Colo.: Lynne Rienner.

Yum, J. C., 1987. The practice of uye-ri in interpersonal relationship in Korea. In D. L. Kincaid, ed., *Communication Theory: Eastern and Western Perspectives*. San Diego, Calif.: Academic Press.

Yum, J. O., 1991. International culture: understanding diversity. In L. Samovar and R. Porter, eds *Intercultural Communication*. 6th edn. Belmont, Calif.: Wadsworth, pp. 68–71.

Zheng, N., 2007. Interview with vice president of Chinese International Public Relations Association, Zheng, Nianlong, Beijing, China, May 15.

Zhu, J. and Wang, E. H., 2005. Diffusion, use and impact of the Internet in China. *Communications of the ACM*, 48 (4), pp. 49–53.

Chapter 9

The Middle East

Summary

The nature of the public relations profession, its role and function, as well as its contribution to society and to organizations, has been a controversial issue in the Middle East for many years. Sometimes, the public relations function constitutes the core of some organizations, accounting in considerable measure for their success or failure. On the other hand, many organizations here have not yet established a public relations department at all. Unfamiliar with the nature and function of the discipline, owners and managers of such organizations may not believe there is a genuine need for it in their organizations.

In a world of vastly expanding access to information and of accelerating technology innovation, nations and peoples are metaphorically within a stone's throw of each other. Consequently, looming questions arise: What is the status of public relations now, and what is its projected role and anticipated function in a rapidly changing environment? What does the future hold for it and its practitioners and managers, especially in the enigmatic Middle East? (Rizk 2005). This chapter aims to cast light upon the role, function and future of public relations in this important region.

Chapter goals

- Appreciate the characteristics of Middle Eastern cultures that enhance the richness of communication but that also complicate the establishment of shared meaning across cultural divides.
- Understand the importance of the context within which public relations practice is conducted in the Middle East.
- Examine several countries in the region to discover the range of communication styles and consider how one might best prepare for public relations assignments involving counterparts from the Middle East.

Scope and diversity

The Middle East Institute defines the Middle East as a region encompassing southwestern Asia and northeastern Africa, from Morocco to Pakistan, including the Caucasus. This region is home to the beginning of civilization and of the world's three dominant monotheistic religions. The region's history has been influenced by Persian, Greek and Roman empires, Crusaders, Mongols, Mamluks, Ottomans, Europeans, and many others. The majority of the countries that comprise the region gained independence only in the last century or so. Since then, the Middle East has been profoundly changed by the discovery of oil, the reconstitution of the state of Israel, Islamic revival and the Iranian Revolution, the Iran–Iraq War, the Arab–Israeli conflict, the Persian Gulf War, and the wars in Afghanistan and Iraq. The future of the Middle East remains uncertain as it struggles to balance the importance of religion, development and stability in an ever-democratizing, interconnected world.

The Middle East area encompasses the following countries: Afghanistan, Algeria, Armenia, Azerbaijan, Bahrain, Djibouti, Egypt, Georgia, Iran, Iraq, Israel, Jordan, Kazakhstan, Kuwait, Kyrgyzstan, Lebanon, Libya, Mauritania, Morocco, Oman, Pakistan, Palestinian Territories, Qatar, Saudi Arabia, Sudan, Syria, Tajikistan, Tunisia, Turkey, Turkmenistan, United Arab Emirates. This area occupies around 20.5 million square kilometers and is home to more than 700 million people.

Although some countries in the Middle East are among the richest in the world, many of their societies suffer from high illiteracy, food shortages, poor nutrition and a lack of quality healthcare, in addition to severe unemployment that creates the problem of migration of minds and talents. A large number of well-educated people are forced to emigrate or travel to other nations to find suitable jobs. This movement deprives their home societies of the skills and expertise needed for undertaking developmental programs.

Hofstede and Hofstede (2005) combined all Arab countries into a single block for the purposes of their cultural analyses. Collectively, data suggest that Arabs score quite high in *power distance* (top 20 percent of seventy-four cultures evaluated), meaning that there is a perception that power is distributed unequally within the culture, indicating an autocratic, paternalistic environment. You would not expect to experience consultative decision-making here. The Arab culture appears in the middle of the *individualism/collectivism* measure, though Hofstede and Hofstede concede that there are considerable variations from one Arab nation to another, which could account for the composite central tendency to appear ambiguous. For example, they note that Saudi Arabia leans more heavily toward the collective, while Egypt and Lebanon are more individualistic. Regarding *masculinity/femininity*, the composite Arab culture is in the top third of cultures, stressing masculine values of assertiveness and clearly delineated gender roles. Arab countries are once again found in the middle of the *uncertainty avoidance* measure; but, again, variations among Arab nations probably account for this ambiguous result. Zaharna (2002), testifying before the US Congress, highlighted the difficulty of communicating across the US American and Arab cultures: "For [US] Americans, facts, figures, rational and logical arguments are the way one builds a compelling persuasive case . . . In the Arab world, emotional neutrality, in an emotionally charged context, can be perceived as deception. If one hides their emotions, what else are they hiding?"

Because Middle East countries are located on the continents of Asia and Africa, it is no surprise that the cultures of these two continents influence the practice of public relations there. And, because of the diversity of cultures, traditions, values and political systems that typifies this area, the practice of public relations differs to a commensurate degree from one nation to another and from one society to another. These factors result in different conceptions, definitions, roles, functions and objectives of public relations. Differences stem from varying government structures, the degree of freedom, and the strength or weakness of public opinion. Financial factors affect public relations programs, too. More important is the degree to which higher management in the organization perceives public relations as a need that may help in advancing the organization.

One condition influencing the practice of public relations here is the dominant theory of the press, as discussed in Chapter 5. In most parts of the Middle East, the authoritarian theory is in effect, so public relations operates within the constraints of this model. Even in relatively progressive Jordan, which enacted a Press Law in 1993 that overturned earlier restrictions on the media, there has been a renewed shift toward government control; a "temporary" law passed in 1997 continues to place extensive restrictions on news media (Najjar 1998). That is why Al-Enad (1990) questioned whether we really need public relations in many parts of what is called the Third World or the Developing World. Most communication is controlled by the government, and that communication is one-way and unbalanced, the author says, and adds that factors that ordinarily create the need for public relations in Western societies are not always found in developing societies. Public opinion, an essential influence in the evolution of public relations, lacks weight or consequence in many Middle East countries.

Although many Middle East countries face similar problems, each country has its own goals and varying ways of applying public relations programs to help achieve those goals. Often it is seen merely as the function of a receptionist, but public relations specialists may also serve as communication agents in information offices of various ministries and government agencies. In a broad sense, though, the function is applied toward one or both of two goals: (1) to educate the public on subjects related to the client's field of work, increase public knowledge about pertinent issues, and persuade the public to behave or act in a way that achieves the goals of the organization; and (2) to publicize the achievements of the client and/or society as a whole, and to make the public feel content and gratified.

Sidebar: Afghan soap opera aims to rebuild

For ten minutes a day, many Afghani fans are glued to their radios to hear the latest developments in the soap opera *Let's Build Our Village*. The serial's characters encounter plot twists that address topics considered controversial in Afghanistan these days: condom use, child brides, multiple wives. It is part of the government's effort to rebuild villages ravaged by war. In many parts of Afghanistan, electricity is intermittent at best, and a sizable proportion of the population is illiterate, so radio can be an effective conduit supporting nation-building efforts. *Let's Build Our Village* is helping to educate Afghanis about the new Community Development Councils, elected by secret ballot and charged with improving rural towns through projects such as building bridges and establishing health clinics. More than a hundred actors play characters from five fictional villages in the land of "Chamanistan" (literally, "Greenland"). Episodes describe, in story format, how democracy works, and there are lessons addressing public health issues. One village's friendly barber, for example, becomes addicted to hashish and gambles away his means of livelihood, but eventually discovers the error of his ways. The delicate topic of birth control is raised when a young couple in the village is advised by the doctor to wait, for the mother's health, before having more children, though they may continue to share a bed. The couple asks how this is possible, and the idea of condoms is introduced. Some stories have tragic endings. One depicts a feud between two village families that is settled when one provides a daughter to marry a member of the opposing family. The bride is miserable and commits suicide. Still other stories touch on family rifts when the father turns to growing poppies or on domestic problems when a man takes a second wife. This soap-opera approach capitalizes on the Afghani rural tradition of relying upon gossip to obtain the latest news and information.

Source: Mulrine (2007)

The majority of Middle East countries are Arab countries. Kruckeberg and Vujnovic (2004) note that Arab culture has endured and thrived for thousands of years, and Arab societies have a proud history, but the people and their cultures have never been challenged as they are today. This may be the principal public relations challenge for Arab diplomacy, corporations and non-governmental organizations throughout the world, a challenge that has arisen and is propelled in part by globalization. In such a global environment, no nation, state or people can totally preserve its identity or values from outsiders. So, just as do other countries, Arab nations face difficult issues in forging helpful relationships, and the first task is to recognize the importance of contemporary, strategic public relations in addressing those relationship issues without sacrificing their own history and traditions. They need to develop a theoretical foundation upon which to construct an Arab model of public relations and actively practice that model. This practice must be supported by high-quality education for aspiring practitioners as well as continuing education for those already engaged in diplomacy, corporate public relations and NGOs. To that end, the Confederation of Public Relations Associations of Islamic Countries was established in 2006. Of course, the CPRAIC encompasses non-Arab Middle Eastern nations such as Iran and Turkey as well. The Confederation's goals call for increasing professionalization of the public relations discipline, building professional networking opportunities, incorporating concepts of social responsibility into public relations activities, and supporting public relations research. These goals are often expressed in terms reflecting traditional Islamic values.

Despite these efforts, public relations in the Middle East is still associated with ceremonies and advertising. Communication channels between senior organizational leadership and the public relations function are almost nonexistent. Public relations tasks are generally confined to answering media queries, handling ceremonial and administrative tasks, event planning, and receiving guests and delegations. Seldom does a public relations officer take part in administrative meetings with other officers at the organization. We often find that the public relations department has little effective role in the decision-making process or in developing general policy and strategic planning of the institution. The press agentry model prevails, with a dominant view toward polishing the image of the institution or its principal/director. Research, analyzing publics and gauging opinion are not in play. The emphasis is on distributing news releases and achieving publicity. Even in the event of a crisis, the public relations function tends to ignore the crisis and refrains from discussing it. At best, the crisis is addressed for the purpose of blaming others or uncontrollable factors instead of accepting responsibility and seeking solutions.

Kirat (2005) notes with dismay that public relations in the Arab world suffers from a lack of professionally trained specialists and must struggle to develop in the absence of a culture of democracy. He laments that planning and research are largely missing and that the public relations discipline is still viewed as a means to foster organizational image through publicity and propaganda. He especially remarks that since September 11, 2001, "Arabs and Muslims have been portrayed as initiators of terrorist acts and responsible [for] all the ills that target the West". He says: "The event [terrorist attacks on New York's World Trade Center and the Pentagon in Washington, DC] painted the entire Arab World with a broad brush of terrorism, the region seen as a war zone, and Al Qaeeda as dominating the region's perception" (p. 324). Worse, Kirat says: "Arabs . . . failed to defend themselves, and to convey their true image, their history, their civilization and true meaning of Islam and its universal principles, values, virtues, and humanness". He concludes: "International Arab public relations [has] not met the challenges" (p. 324). Those are strong words, but Kirat balances that assessment with equally strong words of promise. He notes, for example, that higher-education programs in public relations are spreading throughout the Arab world, and democratization is gaining purchase which, he says, will call for increased transparency and two-way communication. He reports that organizations are responding to these developments, and public relations is gaining in recognition and value in politics and business.

The rapid diffusion of communication and information technology, the emergence of a nascent civil society, the spread of democracy – all of which call for a public relations function – are increasingly evident. Still, when Curtin and Gaither (2004) conducted a research project to analyze official websites of Middle East nations, they were disappointed to find that more than half of them do not have websites and are therefore neglecting a powerful conduit for conducting international relations. Of those with websites, the researchers found, most do well conveying information to individuals, but fail to provide sophisticated online areas and materials for media. This, they surmise, follows the Middle Eastern cultural preference for a personal influence model rather than Western typologies. It appears that public relations, though gaining ground in many Middle East countries, is still in its embryonic stages.

However, Vujnovic and Kruckeberg (2005) find in Middle Eastern traditions the seedbed for their *organic theory* of public relations – one in which the process supersedes the outcome and in which relationship-building is more important than persuading. Consequently, the scholars recommend that Arab public relations models would be better-understood through the windows of interpersonal communication theories rather than through the Western tradition of stressing mass communication theories. So perhaps the difficulty in increasing the prominence of public relations in the Middle East stems in part from the common practice of viewing the discipline throughout the globe through the same set of Western filters. In support of that contention, Zaharna (1995) mapped variations in communication patterns between Western (US) and Arabic models. Here is a summary of what she described:

- The West stresses accuracy, technical and concrete language; Arabs prefer symbolic language, poetry and abstract language that creates experience.
- The West leans toward explicit language, details (*low context*); Arabs place meaning within context (*high context*).
- Western models tend to the direct and the objective; Arabs are indirect and can use circular, ambiguous patterns as well as embellishments.

■ The West stresses *doing*, action, and linkage between word and deed; the Arab model is more about *being* and emphasizes relationships and the social impact of discourse.

■ In the West, arguments are linear and limited in theme; Arabs are non-linear and do not feel obligated to structure arguments with clear beginnings and endings.

■ Western message patterns are simple, often understated and stress actions; Arab messages may be repetitious and include imagery, exaggeration and symbols (p. 247).

With that foundation, let us examine more closely several nations in the region, beginning with Saudi Arabia.

Saudi Arabia

It is where Islam was born and the site of the faith's two most important shrines – Mecca and Medina. The government, in fact, is a monarchy, and the monarch's official title is Custodian of the Two Holy Mosques. In 1902, Abdul Aziz Ibn Saud captured the current capital of Riyadh and waged a thirty-year campaign to unify the Arabian peninsula, founding the modern Saudi state in 1932. Ibn Saud's son rules the nation today. The country is bordered by the Red Sea on the west; the Persian Gulf and the United Arab Emirates on the east; Yemen and Oman to the south; and Iraq, Jordan and Kuwait on the north. Its population of 27.6 million includes nearly 5.6 million non-nationals who play an important role in the Saudi economy, though guest workers may never become citizens.

This is an oil-based economy with considerable government control over major economic activities. It boasts the largest petroleum reserves in the world (26 percent of known deposits), and this sector accounts for roughly 75 percent of total budget revenues, 40 percent of GDP, and 90 percent of export earnings. Vast gas reserves also help define the Saudi economy. Less well known is Saudi Arabia's rich mineral deposits such as gold, silver and copper. To reduce its dependence on oil, the Saudi government has launched a program to privatize some public institutions such as power generation and telecommunications. Further, the government has encouraged the development of a wide range of manufacturing industries, providing incentives to private-sector entrepreneurs.

Still, non-Muslims require an invitation to enter Saudi Arabia – typically that means the involvement of a prominent Saudi. Once in the country, visitors are subject to Saudi Islamic law, dictating modest dress and appropriate behavior, including particularly strict limits for women (e.g., no driving). Visitors also require an exit permit – no exceptions. Morrison and Conaway (2006) caution that "public activities in Saudi Arabia are strictly segregated by gender. Do not try to change traditions through any controversial behavior" (p. 427). Do not expect punctuality, and Saudis may set appointments only for non-specific periods between prayer times. Do expect to be kept waiting, so do not schedule more than one appointment each day. Your meeting is likely to be interrupted by phone calls and visits by others as well. The work week is from Saturday to Wednesday. Conducting any business can be a long and laborious journey requiring considerable patience, especially for Westerners. You may talk about sport in casual conversation, but never raise the topic of women (even the health of one's wife or daughter) or the subject of Israel. Transparency in government activities is nearly nonexistent, and there are no checks and balances in that arena. The official religion is Wahabi, a strict, puritanical sect of Islam. Criticizing

Islam or the Saudi royal family is forbidden. Visitors must not wear any visible symbols of non-Islamic faiths.

Cognitive processes, negotiations and value systems cannot be separated from Islam among Saudis. Faith and feelings within the Islamic concept overcome all other considerations. Western ideas simply do not penetrate. Morrison and Conaway (2006) note that Saudi society is clearly male-dominated, but the individual is subordinate to the family, tribe or community. Status comes from lineage, not from achievements.

Origins of public relations

As we noted in Chapter 2, some scholars see the Middle East as the cradle of public relations going back thousands of years. Cuneiform tablets found in Iraq date to 4,000 years ago and appear to be bulletins telling farmers how to grow crops better – a sort of news release; some maintain. Hammurabi used the sheep-shearing season to gather his people for "town hall meetings". Pharaohs used the irrigation season to celebrate the Nile river and disseminate information and news to farmers. In Arab culture, even before Islam, the Okadh Souk was an event where people would meet, discuss and debate, recite poetry and deliver public speeches. With Islam, communication concepts were encouraged, especially to convert new followers and spread Islamic teaching. The *Hajj*, the annual pilgrimage to Mecca by Muslims from throughout the world, is a means to build and nurture those relations. And it would be impossible to discuss public relations in the Middle East without considering the *majlis* – open forums at which any citizen may meet with high officials, present a grievance or make a speech (Alanazi 1996).

In Saudi Arabia, it would be impossible to discuss the emergence of contemporary public relations without considering the Arab–American Oil Company (ARAMCO). ARAMCO began to search for oil in Saudi Arabia in the 1930s. Because US managers and workers failed to appreciate and accommodate Saudi cultural issues, serious communication problems quickly emerged. To its credit, ARAMCO established a public relations function and charged it with two principal tasks: (1) to train Arabs to work with US Americans, and (2) to teach US Americans to understand, respect and adapt to Saudi culture. The company established research tools to permit more effective communication across the two cultures, and facilitated learning of language and history of the nation by US employees and their families. For a thorough description of ARAMCO's impact on the history and development of modern Saudi Arabia, as well as other dimensions of that process, visit the website for a documentary entitled *The House of Saud*, at http://www.pbs.org/wgbh/pages/frontline/shows/saud/.

In the decades since ARAMCO's appearance in Saudi Arabia, and with the developed world's growing thirst for oil, the nation's economy has grown considerably, and the kingdom has increasingly become a modern state. It has not all been smooth sailing for public relations, however. As Alanazi (1996) points out, innovation and progress were often in conflict with some Saudi religious leaders. For example, he relates the problem of introducing radio to the country when some religious leaders were convinced the medium was satanic, relenting only when the king persuaded them that the radio, as well as the telephone and the automobile, was an innovation that could be used to serve religious purposes as well. Nevertheless, public relations and advertising firms are being established with some speed, and those firms are increasingly calling upon advanced technology to conduct their activities. A leading aim is to change the world's stereotype, regularly perpetuated by Western media, of the Saudi kingdom and its people. Saudi efforts often use

Western media to pursue that goal, signing a contract, for example, with former United Press International correspondent Crawford Cook and his firm to conduct a public relations campaign on the Saudis' behalf in the United States. Al-Hazmi (1990) found that public relations efforts to build a favorable image of Saudi Arabia could lead to the establishment of business relationships and consequently concluded that every government ministry should have a public relations function to counteract negative attitudes abroad.

Although the public relations role is gaining momentum in Saudi Arabia, limited support from top management and squeezed budgets continue to limit progress. Hussein *et al.* (1991) found, too, that most public relations research focuses on one crisis or another and fails to move the discipline forward by developing and exploring theories and models suitable to the Saudi context. Al-Arabi (2004) observed, in addition, that top Saudi managers continue to see public relations predominantly as a propaganda function rather than as a valued contributor to decision-making. In summary, Saudi public relations is characterized by:

- Misunderstanding of the concept, role and function of public relations
- Lack of expertise and training
- Limited financial resources
- Rapid growth in higher education programs in public relations
- The seeds of professional standards of practice

Factors that will continue to propel Saudi Arabia from a society distrustful of foreign (especially Western) influence toward a more integrated approach to international relations and commerce include the presence of foreigners in the country and the annual *hajj* and other pilgrimages. Foreigners are present because of the vast oil and gas industries as well as to supplement the workforce. This cross-pollenization is bound to influence both Saudi acceptance of external influence and the outside world's perception of the kingdom and its people. Because of Saudi Arabia's considerable influence on oil supplies and stable prices, and the resultant impact on the global economy, it is in the interest of the rest of the world to understand and respect its culture. Public relations professionals obviously play a major role in that process.

Questions for discussion

1. How would you propose designing a media campaign aimed at several Middle Eastern countries? For example, imagine that you have been charged with developing a campaign to encourage the use of pre-natal vitamins.
2. If you were training your CEO to prepare for a series of interviews with Saudi Arabian media in advance of establishing operations in the Saudi capital, Riyadh, what advice would you provide?
3. What challenges might you face if you were planning to conduct primary research in the Middle East as part of your planning for a major communication campaign?

United Arab Emirates

The UAE provides an interesting counterpoint to the Kingdom of Saudi Arabia. This federation of seven emirates is on the northeast part of the Arab peninsula and borders Saudi Arabia to the west, Oman to the east, the Persian Gulf to the north, and the Gulf of Oman to the south. It is roughly the size of the US state of Maine. Abu Dhabi is its capital. Although Arabic is the formal language, English is commonly used in business. The UAE has embarked on an ambitious program to build international partnerships, and the number of foreign embassies there has risen from three in 1971 to around 120. Strategic partnerships are now in place addressing economic, educational, political, scientific, health and trade issues. Data suggest that the UAE leads regional counterparts in attracting foreign investment and in tourism. Unlike Saudi Arabia with its monarchy, the UAE delegates some authority to the federation and retains other powers within each of the member emirates. The president and the vice-president are elected by the Federal Supreme Council; citizens do not vote. A complex electoral college elects members to the Federal National Council (or *majlis*), and it is important to note that the roughly 6,700-member electoral college includes more than 1,000 women. There is one woman in the 40-member Council. The country enjoys a high *per capita* income as well as a large trade surplus, though 40 percent of GDP is directly attributed to gas and oil output. It was the discovery of oil in the 1970s that helped propel the UAE to become a modern state (CIA World Factbook 2008). The country comprises an eclectic mix, however. As Kirat (2006) points out, expatriates constitute two-thirds of the population, and more than 160 nationalities and thousands of foreign and international companies are found there.

The UAE is a model of communication technology diffusion, and it leads the region in terms of Internet usage and adoption; this is exemplified by the establishment in 2000 of the Dubai Internet City housing regional operation bases for hundreds of computer and technology companies. A study of twenty websites of public and private institutions in the UAE reveals extensive use of the Internet as a public relations tool (Ayish 2005). A National Media Council oversees and supports media initiatives and development but also has the power to rescind or suspend media operating licenses for a variety of infractions. Radio and television are largely consolidated under the government-operated Emirates Media, with satellite, broadcast and Internet operations, and Dubai Media, Inc., a semi-government company that runs major radio and television services. The Emirates News Agency provides national and regional news of Arab affairs; the agency retains a cadre of correspondents outside the UAE as well, and offers service in both English and Arabic. The UAE's 20+ radio stations top the Arab world, and 40 television stations, including some with Western-style programming, constitute a considerable presence. A recent list of headlines found on the official UAE news and information website suggests the lively media environment there:

- "New internet TV channel to hit air today"
- "Sharjah TV set to launch new sports channel soon"
- "Gulf Craft supports launch of first 24-hour Marine TV channel"
- "Sharjah launches satellite channel"
- "Dunia TV starts DVB [digital broadcasting] from Fujairah"
- "Sharjah to launch the first visual radio channel"
- "Fujairah to host 28 TV channels"
- "TV channel on way to spread awareness about labour issues"
- "E-Vision to showcase top Hollywood blockbusters"
- "Dubai One launches English-language daily news bulletin" (UAE Interact 2008)

With such an ambitious agenda for development and a confusing population mix, there is clearly a need for effective communication in support of awareness, education and behaviorally focused campaigns. Public relations in the UAE is quickly emerging to meet those challenges, in both the public and the private sectors. Kirat (2006) says that public relations growth can be traced to the 1970s and 1980s and followed the rapid expansion of print and broadcast media, but was also influenced by growth in a variety of other sectors such as education, agriculture and tourism. Creedon *et al.* (1995) credit the UAE's first president, Sheik Zayed bin Sultan Al Nahayan, with a progressive view toward vast and rapid expansion of the nation's education system, and especially for extending educational opportunities to women. Part of that effort, the researchers describe, was a well-planned initiative to establish a public relations program at United Arab Emirates University at Al-Ain in the mid-1990s. That effort, they say, was not without resistance; some at the university were concerned that introducing Western-style public relations was a manifestation of "ideological or educational 'imperialism'" (p. 66). Several leading scholars from the US, though, during a consultative visit to the university, were able to overcome any reluctance by demonstrating the compatibility of the dominant public relations model with the overarching goals of the rapidly developing nation.

As multinational corporations began to seize upon business opportunities in the UAE, so, too, appeared leading global public relations and advertising firms. By the mid-1980s, according to Kirat, roughly two-thirds of government agencies had established public relations departments, and those that had not simply assigned that function to other departments such as human resources. It is important to note that adult literacy was around 15 percent in the 1970s but had reached 91 percent by 2007 (UAE Yearbook 2007). The burgeoning of print media sources during this period has influenced and been influenced by the rising educational levels of the population. The first higher education programs in journalism and mass media appeared in 1980, but it was not until 1995 that a public relations track was offered. By 2004, more than 250 students were enrolled in the course at United Arab Emirates University at Al-ain (interestingly, the majority were female). Now a number of UAE universities offer programs in public relations. At the University of Sharjah alone, more than 550 students were studying public relations in the 2004–5 school year.

Headquartered in Dubai, UAE, the Middle East Public Relations Association was established in 2001. Here is its mission:

> The Middle East Public Relations Association (MEPRA) is a non-profit organisation that represents the interests of the Middle East public relations industry. MEPRA endeavours to highlight the strategic role of public relations in the Arab world and help set high standards for quality and ethical conduct by consultancy firms. The Association provides a single point of contact for government, the business community and the media to talk to the region's growing PR industry. MEPRA's full membership currently consists of almost 20 public relations firms with more than 100 offices in more than 16 countries across the region (December 2006). MEPRA is registered at Dubai Media City in the United Arab Emirates and is a member of the International Committee of Public Relations Consultancies Associations (ICCO), which represents leading PR consultancies across 29 countries (MEPRA 2008).

Its structure includes a rigorous "Code of Practice"; but, unlike with the CPRAIC, this code does not include a context of Islamic tradition.

Although the conditions are suitable for continued growth in public relations in the UAE, Kirat (2006) suggests a number of lingering barriers in the public sector:

- Misunderstanding of the discipline by top management
- Limited budget allocations
- Small staffs
- Poor qualifications and limited experience among practitioners
- Lack of clarity regarding roles and functions
- Ongoing emphasis on publicity and press agentry
- Lack of scholarship and research
- Exclusion from the decision-making process

It is comforting to know that the obstacles our profession faces appear to unify us! The strength of private business in the UAE supports a commensurately strong public relations presence in the private sector, with the majority of businesses actively conducting in-house public relations efforts or contracting with the many public relations firms operating there. In fact, 60 percent of all Middle East public relations contract activity is conducted by UAE firms (Kirat 2006).

The conditions in the UAE are well suited to a burgeoning public relations profession provided, as Kirat (2006) cautions, that practitioners and organizational leaders employ a "systematic, professional and ethical use of public relations" (p. 259). In fact, the author predicts that public relations can contribute in significant ways to the ongoing effort to make the UAE a "cosmopolitan, tolerant, successful country where everybody can live in a clean, safe, secure and prosperous environment" (p. 259).

Sidebar: Business reconciled with Islamic law

In the United States, a popular fried chicken restaurant has removed bacon from the menu, and a leading chain of coffee shops has vowed never to sell pork or pornography. Dow Jones, financial publishing giant, has created an Islamic investing index. A company in Texas issued more than US$160 million in "Shariah-compliant" investment bonds to support natural gas operations in the Gulf of Mexico. The German state of Saxony-Anhalt offered a €100 million note to be managed by Citicorp and that complied with Shariah rules. What has happened is that booming oil revenues in the Middle East have created considerable wealth among many Muslims whose faith dictates significant restrictions on how they might invest that wealth. For example, collecting or paying interest is contrary to Islamic law. Consequently, investment instruments must be packaged in ways to avoid that; investing in precious metals and other commodities is one way to make money and still comply with Shariah, as is the pledge of income from an asset. Western investment and banking firms are scrambling to design investment opportunities compatible with Muslim restrictions. Also prohibited are profits related to alcohol, gambling and weapons. Muslims may own shares in a company, but only if that company is complying with Shariah; technology stocks are a favorite because they are generally "clean" and do not carry debt. Young, affluent Muslims are eager to let their investments reflect their commitment to their faith. As a result, investment firms are retaining the counsel of Islamic scholars to analyze transactions and determine their compatibility with the restrictions. These developments illustrate the importance of understanding Muslim culture that so permeates the Middle East – whether you expect assignments to the Middle East or not.

Source: Freed (2006)

Israel

Before we leave the region, it is appropriate that we spend a few moments examining the development of and environment for public relations in this unique Middle Eastern country. The only Jewish state in the world, this country of roughly 7 million people is approximately the size of the US state of New Jersey. It is a Western-style nation surrounded by generally less developed and sometimes unstable nations, and maintains high democratic ideals. It may surprise many to know that both Hebrew and Arabic are official languages here, though English is commonly used in business settings. Despite the importance of Judaism to the culture, Morrison and Conaway (2006) report that international business is addressed from a secular viewpoint (there is no official state religion), and Israelis may seem to others to be particularly informal in their business dealings, not reluctant at all to ask quite personal questions. Further, Israelis tend to proceed either quite slowly or immediately, so be patient, but be prepared to respond quickly when the time is right.

Morrison and Conaway (2006) caution that several considerations are paramount in cognitive, communication and negotiation processes: the needs of the state; problems that must be solved; and that security must be maintained. Objective truths serve largely to supplement and support these principles. Individual initiative is valued, and the right to private opinions is jealously guarded. On the other hand, the family is the central source of security, and Jewish history is revered. With level educational opportunities and universal military obligations, Israel is an egalitarian society, though biases against Palestinians and other Arabs are present as well. Gender equality is well entrenched.

You may be kept waiting at an appointment, so do not schedule more than two a day, Morrison and Conaway (2006) advise. No business is conducted on the Sabbath, which begins at sundown on Friday and ends at sundown on Saturday. Consequently, the work week is traditionally Sunday to Thursday.

Gannon (2004) says Israel is a nation of tribes, of a variety of religious and ethic groups finding challenges in living together comfortably. He cites the fact that there are ten or more political parties vying for attention and power at any given time. For example, visitors to Israel should be aware that even among Jewish citizens there are a number of divisions. Perhaps most prominent is the distinction between Ashkenazim, Jews from Europe, and Sephardim, Jews from the Middle East including North Africa. Friction between these two groups has diminished in recent years because of ongoing campaigns to address differences and to improve conditions for Sephardic Jews.

Gannon (2004) uses the *kibbutz*, the collective farm so vital to the settlement and development of the Jewish state, as symbolic of Israel's character and culture. The community ownership of property, the absolute egalitarianism, the collective decision-making, and communal responsibility are emblematic of Israel's ideals. Power is not allowed to accumulate with any individuals. However, each *kibbutz* is small enough to permit a feeling of individual value. It is a unique blend of socialism and individualism with strong democratic elements. On the other hand, *kibbutzim* (plural form) account for just 3 percent of the population and retain a high degree of isolation, even élitism.

Media in Israel basically follow tenets of the press in a democratic environment, providing accuracy in news reporting to the extent possible and offering a spectrum of viewpoints largely independent of government interference. Prior to the Yom Kippur War (1973), though, newspapers generally supported the government. Since then, and especially since the 1980s, newspapers have become more openly analytical and often critical of the government. A tumultuous period for the press ensued, and just three national newspapers have survived (plus one business daily), owned by a few influential families. Still, editors and journalists adhere to the Western approach to news, ensuring principles of responsibility. Newspapers continue to serve as a check on government and business, preventing or exposing excesses. Israelis are avid newspaper-readers and, unlike European and other Western readers, have little tolerance for sensationalism (Jewish Virtual Library 2008).

For a number of years, into the 1960s, Israel had just two radio stations: Kol Yisrael (the Voice of Israel) and Galei Tzahal (military radio). In 1965, Israel introduced educational television even before it offered commercial television, reflecting the country's view of broadcasting as an educational medium. Now a network of cable television channels and additional radio channels are available, including regional stations. Satellites also beam a wide variety of channels into the country. An interesting phenomenon in Israel is the proliferation of pirate radio stations, illegal but viewed with leniency by the authorities. These pirate stations range from religious to commercial and amateur to professional (Jewish Virtual Library 2008). Of course, the Internet provides access to hundreds of global newspapers, and Internet access is widespread.

About 250 members constitute the Israel Public Relations Association, associated with the International Public Relations Association, and members are expected to adhere to the Code of Athens. Founded in 1960, most of its members are divided between corporate and agency affiliations, though government specialists participate as well. As in many other nations, the profession here struggles to shrug off the publicity and press agentry image and replace it with a strategic management identity. Although media relations dominate practitioners' activities, minority sectors of the population, such as ultra-Orthodox Jews and Russian immigrants, generally limit their media exposure to their own internal channels of communication. Consequently, it can be challenging to achieve success in reaching those segments. Still, with just three daily newspapers and three national television networks, building and sustaining relationships with media representatives is manageable. Large Israeli companies – technology firms, for example – are faced with the unique circumstance of having extremely limited local sales opportunities, so most communication is directed abroad. With a growing economy, investor relations is becoming an increasingly desirable specialty (ISPRA 2008).

An important term in the context of Israeli public relations is *hasbara*, which means basically "to explain" or "to account for". It is used to refer to the effort to explain to the international community Israel's situation and endeavors to be free of perceived media bias. There is a *hasbara* website that describes itself as the Israel Citizens Information Council and serves as a word-of-mouth effort to bypass traditional media filters. It says:

> Our goal is to provide diversity to official Israeli government positions by using citizens from all walks of life and political persuasions. Our 'citizen diplomacy' allows the presentation of mainstream Israeli thinking as represented by the grass roots. ICIC speakers are academicians, professionals and community activists who can provide communities with an authentic voice reflecting the mainstream in Israeli opinion.
>
> (Hasbara 2008)

We must not leave Israel without noting the public relations dimension of the ongoing Israeli–Palestinian conflict. Without entering the minefield of the underlying issues, the public relations approaches taken by each side provide fascinating and instructive insight. Israel treats public relations as a critical and integral part of its effort in this conflict. *The Economist* (The

Palestinians 2005) noted that Israel maintains a press officer in each of its ministries and embassies, and provides annual public relations training in Washington, DC, for its spokespersons. The foreign ministry conducts round-the-clock media monitoring in several languages and distributes realtime analytical reports to ministry officials. Even Israel's soldiers are trained in appropriate behavior when the cameras are rolling. In contrast, the Palestinians have no real press offices, but only an information ministry with no clearly delineated role. There is no coordination of messages on the Palestinian side and no media monitoring. Even top officials generally lack media training, and occasionally non-government figures appear to speak officially on behalf of the government. It is hard to conduct public diplomacy without the necessary infrastructure to do so successfully.

Questions for discussion

1. What factors do you perceive as most important in permitting the United Arab Emirates to develop such an advanced level of public relations professionalism?
2. If you could predict that technological advances would make the world less dependent on oil, what recommendations would you make, as communication counselor, to Middle Eastern leaders?
3. Examine recent media coverage in your area on Israel and the Palestinians. Based on your analysis, what recommendations would you make to either party if you were called upon to provide public relations counsel?

Conclusion

There are other countries in the region making important contributions to public relations through excellence in practice, scholarship and educational programs. Turkey, for example, boasts a highly advanced professional cohort. Egypt, Georgia, Armenia and Azerbaijan are making strides as well. As communication technology, market economies and democratic structures continue to move forward, though in unique ways in different cultures and settings, we can expect to see our discipline increasingly recognized and valued. There are longstanding and overarching problems to be faced in the Middle East, and effective, collaborative communication is essential to managing those problems today and for the long term. With such cultural variety coupled with vast disparities in resources and opportunities, that will be a challenge. Nevertheless, communication seems to be a promising tool if applied responsibly and fairly.

Featured biography: Sadri Barrage

Married with three children, Sadri Barrage is a 49-year-old Lebanese national who completed his Bachelor's degree in Marketing from the Lebanese American University (Beirut) in 1982. He began his publishing career as Marketing

Manager for *Sport Auto* magazine, the leading Arabic motoring magazine, in 1980, where his responsibilities included identifying promotional and advertising opportunities in Jordan, Kuwait, Bahrain, Qatar, Oman and the UAE.

Sadri's insight into the region earned him a promotion to full partner in 1985 when a new publication, *Al Faez*, was started by the group. This allowed Sadri to prove his leadership talents and journalistic skills, soon rising to become Editor-in-Chief and Associate Publisher.

In 1991, armed with his comprehensive knowledge of the region and in view of the growing demands for public relations services, Sadri launched Headline Public Relations in Dubai. Today, the company has established offices in the United Arab Emirates, Saudi Arabia, Lebanon and Jordan.

His contribution in highlighting the Middle East as a key player in the international public relations profession contributed to the formation of the Middle East Public Relations Association in December 2000, with Sadri elected by his peers as the founder-chairman. Since then, Sadri has become a regular lecturer on public relations for various universities and conferences across the Middle East and North Africa. In 2007, Sadri was elected chairman of IPRN, a global network of independent agencies in more than thirty-five countries on six continents.

Recommended websites

The House of Saud documentary   **http://www.pbs.org/wgbh/pages/frontline/shows/saud/**

News on the UAE   http://www.uaeinteract.com

Middle East Public Relations Association   http://www.mepra.org

Israel Public Relations Association   http://www.ispra.org.il/

Hasbara – Israel Citizens Information Council   http://www.hasbara.com/

References

Alanazi, A., 1996. Public relations in the Middle East: the case of Saudi Arabia. In H. M. Culbertson and N. Chen, eds. *International Public Relations: A Comparative Analysis*. Mahwah, NJ: Lawrence Erlbaum, pp. 239–56.

Al-Arabi, A., 2004. Public relations practice in the Kingdom of Saudi Arabia: a descriptive study of the Ministry of Culture and External Communication. The International Conference on Public Relations in the Arab World: Current Realities and Future Prospects. Sharjah, United Arab Emirates, May 4–5.

Al-Enad, A., 1990. Public relations' roles in developing countries. *Public Relations Quarterly*, 35 (1), pp. 24–6.

Al-Hazmi, W., 1990. The development of public relations in Saudi Arabia. Unpublished doctoral dissertation, Wayne State University, Detroit, Mich.

Ayish, M. I., 2005. Virtual public relations in the United Arab Emirates: a case study of 20 UAE organizations' use of the Internet. *Public Relations Review*, 31, pp. 381–8.

CIA World Factbook, 2008. United Arab Emirates. (Country profile), [online]. (Updated February 12, 2008). Available at: https://www.cia.gov/library/publicaions/the-world-factbook/index.html [accessed February 25, 2008].

Creedon, P. J., Al-Khaja, M. A. W. and Kruckeberg, D., 1995. Women and public relations education and practice in the United Arab Emirates. *Public Relations Review*, 21 (1), pp. 59–76.

Curtin, P. A. and Gaither, T. K., 2004. International agenda-building in cyberspace: a study of Middle East government English-language websites. *Public Relations Review*, 30, pp. 25–36.

Freed, J., 2006. Companies courting Muslims with money. *The Charlotte Observer*, October 13, p. 3D.

Gannon, M. J., 2004. *Understanding Global Cultures*. 3rd edn. London: Sage.

Hasbara, 2008. Israel Citizens Information Council, [online]. Available at http://www.hasbara.com/ [accessed February 27, 2008].

Hofstede, G. and Hofstede, G. J., 2005. *Cultures and Organizations: Software of the Mind*. London: McGraw-Hill.

Hussein, S., *et al.*, 1991. *Public Relations Management in Governmental Institutions in the Kingdom of Saudi Arabia.* Cairo: Alem El Koutoub (in Arabic).

ISPRA, 2008. Israel Public Relations Association, [online]. Available at http://www.ispra.org.il/ [accessed February 27, 2008].

Jewish Virtual Library, 2008. The Media in Israel, [online]. Available at http://www.jewishvirtuallibrary.org/jsource/Society_&_Culture/mediatoc.html [accessed February 27, 2008].

Kirat, M., 2005. Public relations practice in the Arab world: a critical assessment. *Public Relations Review*, 31 (3), pp. 323–32.

Kirat, M., 2006. Public relations in the United Arab Emirates: the emergence of a profession. *Public Relations Review*, 32, pp. 254–60.

Kruckeberg, D. A. and Vujnovic, M., 2004. The imperative for an Arab model of public relations as a foundation and framework for Arab diplomatic, corporate and nongovernmental organization relationships: challenges and opportunities. Conference on Public Relations in the Arab World: Current Realities and Future Prospects, Sharjah, United Arab Emirates, May 4–5.

MEPRA, 2008. Code of Practice, [online]. Available at http://www.mepra.org/about1.php [accessed February 25, 2008].

Morrison, T. and Conaway, W. A., 2006. *Kiss, Bow, or Shake Hands.* 2nd edn. Avon, Mass.: Adams Media.

Mulrine, A., 2007. In Afghanistan, it takes a soap opera to build villages. *US News & World Report*, June 18, pp. 30–1.

Najjar, O. A., 1998. The ebb and flow of the liberalization of the Jordanian Press: 1985–1997. *Journalism & Mass Communication Quarterly*, 75 (1), pp. 127–42.

The Palestinians are not only outgunned, but outmessaged, 2005. *The Economist*, March 26, p. 48.

Rizk, A., 2005. Future of public relations in United Arab Emirates institutions. *Public Relations Review*, 31, pp. 389–98.

UAE Interact, 2008. News Stories: The Media – Radio & Television (summary and links), [online]. Available at http://uaeinteract.com/news/default.asp?ID=45 [accessed February 25, 2008].

UAE Yearbook, 2007. Social Development, [online]. Available at http://uaeinteract.com/uaeint_misc/pdf_2007/index.asp [accessed February 25, 2008].

Vujnovic, M. and Kruckeberg, D., 2005. Imperative for an Arab model of public relations as a framework for diplomatic, corporate and nongovernmental organization relationships. *Public Relations Review*, 31 (3), pp. 338–43.

Zaharna, R. S., 1995. Understanding cultural preferences of Arab communication patterns. *Public Relations Review*, 21 (3), pp. 241–55.

Zaharna, R. S., 2002. Views of the Arab public, [online]. Testimony before US Congress, October 8, 2002. Available through MasterFILE Premier database.

Chapter 10

Public relations in sub-Saharan Africa

Contributed by: Isaac Blankson, PhD

Summary

In this chapter we expose public relations students and professionals to the practice of public relations in sub-Saharan Africa. We first discuss the historical, political, economic and socio-cultural factors that have contributed to the evolution of public relations in sub-Saharan Africa. This is followed by a discussion of what scholars have identified as general characteristics applicable to public relations across Africa. We must, however, be mindful of the fact that Africa's diversity and complexity have also allowed for variations in public relations in individual countries. Additionally, recent political and economic reforms in many African countries are transforming their institutions, including public relations, in ways that caution against generalizing about "Africa's" public relations. We conclude the chapter with a discussion of public relations in three African countries: Ghana, South Africa and Kenya. We start with the historical, political, economic and socio-cultural factors that provide the background knowledge for understanding public relations in sub-Saharan Africa.

Chapter goals

- Comprehend how the study of public relations in sub-Saharan Africa compares with the study of public relations in other countries and nations.
- Develop sensitivity for the sub-Saharan culture in order successfully to understand and integrate their practice of public relations.
- Understand the history of sub-Saharan Africa and use that knowledge as a base for understanding public relations practices in the country.

Background characteristics

The term "sub-Saharan Africa" is used to describe the vast area of the African continent that lies south of the Sahara desert. It comprises forty-eight countries usually grouped into five geographic regions. East Africa refers to Kenya, Tanzania, Uganda, Rwanda, Burundi, Sudan and Somalia. West African countries are Benin, Burkina Faso, Cameroon, Chad, Côte d'Ivoire, Equatorial Guinea, Gabon, The Gambia, Ghana, Guinea, Guinea-Bissau, Liberia, Mali, Mauritania, Niger, Nigeria, Senegal, Sierra Leone and Togo. Central Africa includes the Democratic Republic of Congo, Republic of Congo, Central African Republic, Rwanda and Burundi. Southern African countries include Angola, Botswana, Lesotho, Malawi, Mozambique, Namibia, South Africa, Swaziland, Zambia and Zimbabwe. Additionally, African island nations include Cape Verde, São Tomé and Príncipe (in West Africa), Comoros, Madagascar and Mauritius (in Southern Africa), and Seychelles (in East Africa). The region north of the Sahara desert, commonly referred to as North Africa, is not addressed in this chapter because of its marked socio-cultural differences from the rest of the continent.

The United Nations Human Development Report (2006) classifies sub-Saharan Africa as the poorest region in the world. Twenty-five of its countries are ranked poorest in the world. Table 10.1 provides a summary of economic and human development data on the region. In 2004 there were about 726 million people living in the region. However, the region suffers from high poverty, low life expectancy, low adult literacy, poor health and nutrition, and a high incidence

TABLE 10.1 Basic human development indicators for sub-Saharan Africa (during 2004 unless otherwise stated)

Population	726.4
Gross Domestic Product (GDP) Annual Growth Rate (2000–4)	4.0
Life Expectancy at Birth	46 years
Adult Literacy Rate	63%
Urban Population (% of total)	34%
Fertility Rate	5.5
Population Undernourished	30%
HIV Prevalence	6.1%
* Telephone subscribers per 1,000 inhabitants (2006)	9.9
* Mobile phone subscribers per 1,000 inhabitants (2006)	129
* Internet users per 1,000 inhabitants (2006)	31.6
Number of countries classified as Low Human Development Index	18
Number of countries classified as Medium Human Development Index	11

Sources: Data compiled from the United Nations (UNDP) 2006 Human Development Report retrieved from http://origin_hdr.undp.org/hdr2006/pdfs/report/HDR_2006_Tables.pdf.
* Data obtained from International Telecommunications Union (ITU), World Telecommunication Indicators 2006. United Nations. Retrieved from www.itu.int/ITU-D/ict/statistics/at_glance/af_ictindicators_2006.html.

of diseases, especially malaria and, more recently, HIV/AIDS. Despite variations among the countries, scholars agree that certain historical, political, economic and cultural experiences are common to the region.

Colonial legacy

It is difficult to have a meaningful discussion on Africa without first examining the legacy of European colonization. According to Adi (2005) and Fobanjong (2004), colonization of the continent started in the early 1800s and lasted well into the 1990s. By 1884, European countries, including Britain, France, Germany, the Netherlands and Portugal, had divided the African continent into a patchwork that showed no regard for ethnic or linguistic boundaries. These colonial boundaries still serve as modern boundaries between African nations. Many blame colonialism as the source of Africa's problems. For example, Walter Rodney, in his influential 1972 book *How Europe Underdeveloped Africa*, argued that colonial policies are directly responsible for Africa's modern problems. The policies were designed to exploit the continent's mineral resources and to create economies geared solely to the production and export of raw materials, cash crops and mineral resources to Western nations. The policies did not promote the development of adequate infrastructure but rather discouraged the development and use of indigenous African institutions and ways of life, especially native languages. Similarly, Frantz Fanon (1967), the late anti-colonial revolutionary writer, further argued that the true effects of colonialism are psychological and that domination by a foreign power created a lasting sense of inferiority and subjugation that has created a barrier to growth and innovation. Today, many African economies still mirror the institutional structures left by their colonizers.

Political profile

Political stability establishes the necessary conditions for public relations to flourish in any society. The more stable the government, the greater the opportunities for the dialogic communication that characterizes contemporary practice. Unfortunately, since independence in the 1960s, many sub-Saharan African countries have been plagued by political instability and oppressive civilian and military dictatorships with notable civil wars in countries such as Sierra Leone, Liberia, Côte d'Ivoire, Rwanda, Uganda and the Democratic Republic of Congo as well as a succession of military coups in Ghana, Nigeria and Burkina Faso. Only a handful of countries, such as Kenya and Tanzania, have enjoyed stable governments. The more stable governments are usually tolerant of dissent and attentive to public opinion, pressure groups, and citizen involvement in nation-building campaigns. Many governments, on the other hand, use political power purely for their own benefit, and thereby create a culture of greed, corruption and self-aggrandizement – conditions that perpetuate a cycle of political unrest and economic stagnation. However, since the mid-1990s, many African countries have opened up to democratic governance and have begun to experience political stability. This is providing one of the necessary conditions for the growth of professional public relations in Africa.

Economic profile

Sub-Saharan Africa is well endowed with natural resources including gold, diamonds, platinum, uranium, and oil reserves. Yet, owing to poor governance, damaging global trade policies, political unrest, and other factors, few countries have benefited from their mineral wealth. Many countries are saddled with heavy foreign debt and spend from 15 to 41 percent of their annual gross domestic product (GDP) on servicing their debts (World Bank 2007). The poorest countries are those engaged in or just emerging from civil wars. They include the Democratic Republic of Congo, Sierra Leone, Liberia, Burundi and Somalia. While mining produces most of Africa's revenues, the industry employs less than 10 percent of the labor force compared to about 60 percent by the agricultural sectors and 15 percent by the industrial sector. Nearly all the continent's natural resources are controlled by the state or by foreign multinational corporations.

Communication and technology

Effective public relations practice thrives on the availability of and access to communication technologies. Unfortunately, most Africans are on the far side of the digital divide and are cut off from communications technologies, including the Internet. The United Nations (2006) reports that only 14 million Africans had phone lines in 1999. The region, however, has the largest growth rate of cellular subscribers in the world. In 2004 nearly 80 out of every 1,000 Africans subscribed to a cellular service and only 19 out of every 1,000 people had access to the Internet. Historically, many African governments have placed major communication and media outlets in their societies under their control. The lack of access to communication technologies and the state control of the media have affected public relations on the subcontinent.

Socio-cultural profile

The practice of public relations anywhere can be influenced and constrained by larger social and cultural forces, as we have seen in earlier chapters. Sub-Saharan Africa is no exception. Appreciation of layers of formal and informal cultural constructs is essential to the understanding of public relations practices in the region. For example, among Africans there is a high sense of communalism, group loyalty and solidarity, and mutual self-help. Social interdependent relations and social responsibility are well respected and serve as guiding principles for individual and corporate activities.

Cultural scholar Geert Hofstede (2001) has provided us with major cultural constructs for understanding differences in societies and described in greater detail in Chapter 4. To summarize, cultures differ in power distance (the extent to which the less powerful members of organizations and institutions accept and expect that power is distributed unequally), uncertainty avoidance (how well a society tolerates uncertainty and ambiguity, and the extent to which its members are programmed to feel either uncomfortable or comfortable in unstructured situations), and individualism/collectivism (the degree to which individuals are integrated into groups). Using Hofstede's cultural dimensions, African societies are high power distance, high uncertainty avoidance, and collectivist cultures (see Table 10.2). On the power distance scale, East African and West African regions each scored high – 64 and 77 respectively – compared to the United States (49) and the United Kingdom (35), both considered to be low power distance cultures. This implies that African practitioners are likely to accept and respect power differences in their organizations, such as between themselves and top management. On the uncertainty avoidance scale, East African and West African regions each scored high – 52 and 54 respectively – compared to the United States (46) and the United Kingdom (35), both considered to be low uncertainty avoidance cultures. This implies

TABLE 10.2 Cultural dimensions

Region/Country	Power Distance Index	Individualism Index	Uncertainty Avoidance Index
East Africa (includes Ethiopia, Kenya, Tanzania, Zambia)	64	27	52
West Africa (includes Ghana, Nigeria, Sierra Leone)	77	20	54
United States	40	91	46
United Kingdom	35	89	35

Source: Adapted from Hofstede Cultural Dimension at http://www.geert-hofstede.com/hofstede_dimensions.php

that African practitioners are likely to tolerate uncertainty and ambiguity as part of their practice. On the individualism scale, East African and West African regions each scored very low – 27 and 20 respectively – meaning that they are collectivist, compared to the United States (91) and the United Kingdom (89), both considered to be highly individualistic societies. This implies that African practitioners and their publics are likely to give higher priority to communal needs over individual needs and also likely to think and behave in ways consistent with group norms and thought patterns – a kind of groupthink. It means, too, that communication programs and campaigns need to take this characteristic into account.

As described in Chapter 4, cultural anthropologist Edward Hall (1959) notes that societies can be distinguished as high- or low-context cultures. In high-context cultures, such as African societies, much information is left implicit and unstated, group harmony is valued more than individual desires, and relational prestige is more important than logical arguments. African practitioners and the publics with whom they communicate are likely to mirror these characteristics in their day-to-day actions and activities. In low-context cultures, such as the United States and European countries, communication is explicit, and information flows freely. As you have read, cultures can be differentiated by their time orientations into monochronic or polychronic categories. African societies fit the polychronic orientation, meaning that plans are changed easily and often, and schedules and budgets are just guidelines but not strictures. Countries such as the United States are considered monochronic because deadlines and schedules are considered firm, privacy is respected, and promptness is expected and rewarded.

Language is another important social factor with significant implications for public relations practice in sub-Saharan Africa. Communication, through verbal and written language, is the primary instrument of public relations in every society. Communication in sub-Saharan African countries is made complex by the more than 2,000 languages spoken in the region. Six of the world's ten most linguistically diverse countries are in sub-Saharan Africa. It has been argued that African languages can be harnessed for civic engagement, education, and development of the continent and its people, but have been neglected. Indigenous African languages are either eliminated or marginalized. Instead, English, French or Portuguese, the languages of the former colonial powers, are primary languages of government and political and academic discourse. Ironically, only an educated minority speak these European languages fluently.

The complexity of Africa's political, economic, social and cultural systems has contributed to shaping the form of public relations practiced on the continent. Below, we discuss the major characteristics scholars have observed about the practice, specifically before the mid-1990s. Later in this chapter, instances of public relations transformations resulting from the 1990s political and economic reforms will be examined.

Public relations in sub-Saharan Africa

Public relations practitioners in sub-Saharan Africa face a terrain vastly different from that of their counterparts in Western countries. Though there are very few studies on the practice, it has been unfairly characterized and evaluated (using Western standards) as ineffective. None the less, public relations in Africa continues to evolve. Scholars such as Cornelius Pratt (1985), Jim Van Leuven (1996 with C. B. Pratt), Sattler (1981) and Al-Enad (1990) have observed that public relations in Africa, prior to the mid-1990s political and economic reforms, had the following common characteristics:

- It is a European import that has been adapted to African societies and structures. Even so, there are marked differences between public relations in Africa and in Europe or the United States. Professional public relations, in the Western sense, is yet to be realized, and its full responsibilities to African society and peoples are still untapped.
- It is synonymous with national public communication campaigns or nation-building programs. This is because development and nation-building goals continue to occupy government, organizational and individual attention owing to the region's endemic poverty, civil unrest, economic decadence and ethnic diversity. Governments usually assume responsibility for national development plans and expect loyalty and compliance from communication practitioners. Organizations have to develop programs to demonstrate their unwavering support of the government.
- African practitioners play a socially responsible role when they contribute directly to national development. This expectation is even emphasized by the Federation of African Public Relations Associations (FAPRA), the umbrella organization for African practitioners (to read more about FAPRA, visit http://www.fapra.org).
- African practitioners play largely a communication and information-generating function. They follow what Grunig and Hunt (1984) refer to as press agentry, publicity, and public information models. Most act as the information officer in ministries or other government agencies and play a largely functional role – informing and persuading people. This focus makes communication more of a conduit for communicating "programmed" development news than for nurturing development-oriented norms among the public.
- Public relations campaigns in Africa generally involve one-way, persuasive messages from the government to the people, using whatever media are available, but mostly a large network of field staff including agricultural extension agents, public health workers, community development specialists, and public relations officers. Traditional communication techniques such as radio broadcasting, storytelling, drama, and mounting loudspeakers on cars or vans are still common and effective for communicating campaign objectives (see Case Study below).

Sidebar: *Wetin Dey*: New Nigerian drama launch

The BBC World Service Trust has launched a ground-breaking television drama about the social realities facing people in Nigeria today. *Wetin Dey* (*What's Up?*), which was launched in Nigeria in April 2007, is designed to raise HIV and AIDS awareness across all of Nigeria, reaching its diverse population.

Many of the international television, film and advertising directors working on *Wetin Dey* are members of the African Diaspora. They have a strong commitment to the issues and to developing creative industries in Nigeria. The majority of the drama is shot on location, close to the capital city, Abuja.

The Trust has a large presence in Nigeria, home to two of its largest projects: "Voices" and the HIV and AIDS Awareness project. The "Voices" project, established in 2003, aims to stimulate debate about rights and responsibilities and increase civic participation in governance and resource allocation. "Voices" consists of a popular radio drama, *Story Story*; a discussion program, *Talk Talk*; and a comprehensive training initiative for local Nigerian broadcasters.

Talk Talk recently won the "Best Producer Radio" category in the pan-African awards, organized by the Union of National Radio and Television Organizations of Africa (URTNA). The program was also nominated in the Best Radio Program category. *Gatanan Gatanan Ku*, the Hausa-language version of *Story Story*, was also nominated for "Best Producer Radio".

The HIV and AIDS project was launched in early 2005, and seeks to improve sexual and reproductive health by incorporating educational messages into a range of entertaining media formats, including radio spots, talkshows, TV spots and a TV drama. Both projects are funded by the UK government's Department for International Development (DFID) and are carried out in partnership with Nigerian broadcasters, NGOs and government partners.

Source: BBC World Service Trust http://www.bbc.co.uk/worldservice/trust/news/story/2007/02/070227_wetin_dey_launch.shtml

---

Though these generalizations help us understand public relations in sub-Saharan Africa, it is worth noting that, like everywhere else, the practice is not static but reflects significant changes in the society and cultures within which it operates. Since the mid-1990s, several African countries have embarked on serious democratic and liberal economic policies that are transforming civil society institutions, including public relations. Next we discuss the impact of these policies on public relations in what Blankson (2004, p. 300) calls "emerging African democracies".

The 1990s reforms and opportunities

In the 1990s, a new era of political pluralism and neo-liberal economic policies began to sweep across the African continent. The World Bank and foreign donor countries mandated that African governments implement democratic and economic reforms if they wanted continued loans. At the same time, trade unions, students, the business community and the academic community in individual countries began to put pressure on their governments to allow for democracy, media pluralism and freedom of speech. The intensification of international and internal pressure forced governments reluctantly to allow (most for the first time) for political elections, public participation in civic discourse, private media ownership, and opening up of their economies to the free market system. The significance of the reforms is captured in a 1999 statement by former US trade representative Charlene Barshefsky, when she noted:

> In many African nations, governments have adopted economic reforms, from liberalizing exchange rates, to privatizing state enterprises, reducing subsidies and cutting barriers to trade and investment. These have been joined by free elections in many countries, and our own exports to Africa are up by nearly 50 per cent, African exports to the US have risen as well.
>
> (C. B. Pratt and Okigbo 2004, p. 283)

The effects of the reforms are evident at many levels of African society. They have ushered in multiparty democracy, stable political systems, and moderate economic growth in countries such as Ghana and Kenya that have been successful in implementing the policies. The media landscape has also been drastically transformed with the growth in independent and private media operations, especially radio and print. Between 1990 and 2006, the number of privately owned radio stations rose from zero to more than a hundred in many African countries, giving Africans more avenues through which to participate in state affairs and practitioners more conduits to carry their messages to their publics. Today, practitioners have access to alternative sources of information that range from the Internet to cable and satellite communications. There has also been renewed interest from private and corporate investors (mostly multinational corporations) in African economies – those that have developed necessary structures and infrastructures for political stability and economic growth. These transformations have created new expectations and opportunities for public relations in some countries. We first look at the case of Ghana, an example of public relations transformation resulting from political stability, economic growth, good governance, and media independence.

Questions for discussion

1. Reflect on Hofstede's (2001) cultural dimensions and how they apply to African societies. How can African public relations practitioners manage these cultural complexities in their daily activities?
2. Scholars have argued that Africa's cultural complexity and linguistic diversity hinder the implementation of effective public relations campaigns. Do you agree with this assertion? Can you think of how the continent's cultural complexity and linguistic diversity could be harnessed in public relations activities?
3. Why do you think public relations in SSA countries is generally considered propaganda or information programs? Do you think it is fair to evaluate their effectiveness using Western definitions and standards of public relations practice? How should the effectiveness of public relations in developing countries be evaluated?
4. Do you think public relations in sub-Saharan Africa should be considered a "process" or a "program"? Justify your answer.

Ghana

In 1957, Ghana, a former British colony known then as the Gold Coast, became the first black nation in sub-Saharan Africa to achieve independence from colonial rule. The US Central Intelligence Agency (2006) estimated Ghana's population to be 23 million. The population is divided into seventy-five ethnic groups with distinctively different ethnic languages. English is the official language, a legacy of British colonial rule. Nine other ethnic languages are used in the media. The people practice a variety of religions including traditional religions, Christianity and Islam. Like every African country, Ghana has sprawling urban centers with modern, colonial and traditional structures and a contrasting deprived rural sector. Primary and secondary education is free and compulsory. Until recently, higher education was provided only by state universities. Since 2000, a number of private universities have sprung up.

Ghana has roughly twice the *per capita* income of the poorest countries in Africa. In 2006, the country's *per capita* income stood at US$600, up from US$450 in 2004 and US$270 in 2000 (World Development Indicators 2006). The country has a diverse and rich resource base. Minerals – principally gold, diamonds, manganese ore and bauxite – are produced and exported. Cocoa exports are an essential part of the economy – Ghana is the world's second-largest producer. None the less, the domestic economy revolves around subsistence agriculture, which accounts for 60 percent of the workforce compared to 15 percent in industry and 25 percent in the service industry. Compared to other African countries, Ghana's industrial base is relatively advanced. It has a variety of import-substitution industries that include textiles, steel, tires, and oil refining. Tourism is one of the largest foreign-income earners. Even so, Ghana remains heavily dependent on international financial and technical assistance.

The Ghanaian social order is based on locality, kinship/family, and clan structures. Extended family systems serve as effective mutual aid groups, especially in the rural areas. Matrilineal, patrilineal and double-descent systems of social organization as well as villages and chiefdoms contribute to the national mosaic. These have historically provided the framework of social, political, religious and economic organization. However, the social and cultural systems continue to undergo profound changes as a result of modernization.

Ghana's political history between 1966 and 1980 revolved around a succession of military dictatorships and civilian governments. However, since the early 1990s, Ghanaians have been experiencing political stability and freedom of speech, a consequence of the government's successful political reforms toward democratic polity. The country is well administered and is often cited by the World Bank and the United States as a model for successful political and economic reforms in Africa. These factors have contributed in shaping the evolution of Ghana's public relations.

History of public relations

Very little research has been conducted on public relations in Ghana. The most comprehensive accounts of the history of public relations were provided by Gyan (1991) and Osam (1989). According to Gyan, public relations was introduced into Ghana by the British colonial administration. During the colonial days, public relations activities were performed solely by British and European expatriate practitioners. Their primary function was to serve as the communication and information ministry for the colonial administration. They also served the interests of the multinational corporations operating in the country.

The face and nature of public relations began to change immediately after Ghana obtained its independence in 1957. The new government of Kwame Nkrumah gradually began to replace expatriate administrators in key sectors of the civil service and government ministries, including public relations, with local Ghanaians. The Ghana Information Services Department (ISD) was charged with the sole responsibility of providing information, press and public relations services for all government ministries and departments in the country. To accomplish this task, the ISD sent officers known as "press secretaries" or "information officers" as attachments to government ministries to perform public relations functions, a practice that continues today. The majority of these officers had a journalism background. Several multinational corporations followed the government's lead and began to localize parts of their management positions. Some local organizations also employed people with all sorts of backgrounds, education, and training to serve as press and information officers. However, replacing departing expatriate practitioners with Ghanaians was a difficult task because of the lack of qualified Ghanaian practitioners. To solve this problem, journalists were employed as public relations officers. Their recruitment into public relations fields created a situation in which public relations became synonymous with journalism. The lack of qualified Ghanaian practitioners led Harold Macmillan (then British prime minister) and Jimmy Moxon (then District Commissioner and Mayor of Accra, the Director of ISD, and Public Relations Advisor to Ghana's President Nkrumah) to establish the Ghana Institute of Journalism (GIJ) to train public relations officers. Since then, the GIJ has been, and continues to be, one of the major institutions for public relations education in Ghana.

The 1970s was a period of significant developments for Ghana's public relations. In 1971 the Public Relations Association of Ghana (PRAG) was formed (it has since changed its name to the Institute of Public Relations, Ghana). Both Osam (1989) and Turkson (1986) record that the association was the brainchild of Hermann Alah, one of the early practitioners, and a small group of retired and practicing journalists employed as public relations officers. These officers met as a social group to discuss issues they were facing and to share their experiences. As their numbers increased, the social gatherings turned into weekly club meetings. By the late 1960s, some of the officers had become members of foreign public relations organizations, notably the British Public Relations Association and the Public Relations Society of America. They saw membership in foreign public relations organizations as impetus to transform their weekly meetings into a public relations association, which they considered would gain local recognition for their profession. The pioneer practitioners received a big boost from expatriate practitioners, particularly Dennis Buckle (then Head of Public Relations for Unilever) and Frank Jenkins (then British public relations educator and practitioner), who organized training courses and seminars for the public relations officers and those interested in public relations as a career. Their efforts helped create awareness and recognition for PRAG and for public relations in general. Membership of the association increased from 200 in 1975 to 342 in 1982 and comprised older journalists turned public relations officers and younger trained public relations practitioners from the GIJ. As a result of the increased recognition for public relations, businesses, organizations, educational institutions and not-for-profit organizations began to establish public relations departments.

In contrast to the 1970s, the 1980s was a period of turmoil and inactivity. PRAG became dysfunctional between 1984 and 1991 largely because of membership and leadership disagreements. Many of the older journalists turned public relations officers left the association when their younger GIJ-trained counterparts began to doubt their credibility and professional skills and questioned their legitimacy in leading PRAG. Their departure created a power vacuum that led to constant power struggles over who should lead the association. The crisis eventually plunged the association into disintegration.

The country's political and economic problems during the 1970s and 1980s hindered the growth of public relations. The period was marked by a succession of political and economic crises, tight government control, especially of media, and the suppression of the rights and freedoms of Ghanaians. From the 1960s to late 1980, the country had gone through ten changes of government, including five military coups. During times of military dictatorships and civilian governments, public relations activities were either directly or indirectly mandated to promote the government's agenda and to cultivate a positive image for the government. While military dictators typically favored the authoritarian press model with heavy government control and censorship, the democratically elected civilian governments practiced a *quasi*-liberal and developmental press model that allowed for some press freedom and public participation. Ghana's public relations had no choice but to follow these shifts, to its detriment. The state, because it had monopoly control over national resources, became the target of most public relations activities. Thus, to gain access to the state-controlled media, practitioners resorted to payment of financial or material incentives to government officials or journalists who could grant them access. These practices contributed to the low regard for practitioners in Ghana.

The studies by Osam (1989) and Boachie-Agyekum (1992) of the demographic composition of the Ghana public relations industry before the mid-1990s reported the following: there was a male dominance of twenty-three men to three women; a well-educated practitioner profile with 53 percent having some university education; the overwhelming majority occupying low- to mid-level positions in their organizations with little or no policy decision-making power; most working in very small departments and performing press agentry, publicity and protocol roles, typically monitoring the media, writing speeches and reports, arranging and attending meetings, and occasionally responding to public complaints. They also organized parties, ran personal errands for top management, renewed passports for senior personnel, and made traveling arrangements for institutional heads; very few counseled management.

Sidebar: China's role in Africa

In early November 2006, the Forum on China–Africa Cooperation (FOCAC) declared a strategic partnership featuring political equality and mutual trust, economic win–win cooperation, and cultural exchanges. The FOCAC, developed in October 2000, has organized three ministerial meetings and one summit since its establishment, and has provided an opportunity for China and the countries of Africa to conduct collective dialogues, enhance mutual trust, exchange experience in running the country and managing state affairs, and carry out pragmatic cooperation.

China and Africa have both reaped the benefits of this relationship. For example, China has invested a total of US$6.27 billion dollars in Africa over the past six years and has set up more than 800 non-financial enterprises, with investment projects spreading over forty-nine African countries involving trade, processing, resource development, telecommunications and agriculture, among other areas. The effect can be seen in trade volume between China and Africa. In 2000, trade between the two nations totaled US$10.6 billion and by 2005 had reached US$39.8 billion. China has also played an active role in seven UN peacekeeping operations in Africa.

On the one hand, the steady development of China–Africa cooperation is not only beneficial to the development and progress of China and Africa, but also promotes the cooperation and unity of developing countries, enhances global development featuring harmony and prosperity, and encourages the establishment of a moral and coherent new international political and economic order.

However, a realistic analysis would necessarily recognize that China's self-interest is a factor propelling this cooperation. Although China's share of world trade was less than 1 percent in 1980, it had risen to 6 percent by 2003 as a result of China's processing and assembly of raw materials and parts that come from other countries, namely Africa. Because China needs to continue expanding its economy and provide for its 1.4 billion citizens by adding more Chinese content to their exports, they need to secure and obtain sources of raw materials; that is where Africa comes in. Although the China–Africa relationship has been touted as founded on trade and aid, it is also driven by the nature and needs of Chinese development.

Transformations in public relations: The 1990s to the present

The most recent published report on Ghana's public relations industry was conducted by Blankson in 2004. According to Blankson, Ghana began serious implementation of democratic and liberalization policies in the mid-1990s. Pressure from international donor agencies, such as the IMF and the World Bank, and the Ghanaian academic community forced the then National Democratic Congress (NDC) government to begin, reluctantly, to implement democratization and liberalization policies. Over the years, the intensification of these policies began to pay off. Ghana began to experience multiparty democracy and political stability, economic growth (the economy became attractive to foreign private investment), media pluralism and independence, and freedom of speech.

The public relations profession began to feel the impact of these developments. First, the emerging political and economic climate created the need to reorganize the defunct Public Relations Association of Ghana (PRAG). In 1992, under a new executive, PRAG changed its name to the Institute of Public Relations, Ghana (IPR), set up a new secretariat, and launched major initiatives to revamp the association (see http://iprghana.com). These included, among other things:

- Redefining its mission to focus on promoting professionalism among practitioners and improving the image of public relations in the country;
- Educating management and the public about what public relations is and what its roles are in the emerging democracy;
- Establishing proper educational standards and professional criteria for practicing public relations;
- Seeking legal recognition as the professional body responsible for all public relations practitioners in Ghana;
- Defining what constitutes the body of knowledge in public relations in the country and setting standards for public relations practice and conduct;
- Preventing people from practicing public relations without the necessary education and professional training.

The IPR also obtained legal status as a professional organization, which allowed it fully to regulate and monitor the activities of public relations practitioners and to mandate every practitioner to register with the Institute. The IPR managed to get the Ghana parliament to authorize it to enforce its by-laws and to prevent non-qualified individuals from practicing public relations. In addition to these initiatives, the IPR organizes workshops and seminars, and sponsors studies and research on public relations (see http://iprghana.com). To identify with, and conform to, international public relations standards, the IPR instituted membership and accreditation examinations and adopted the International Public Relations Association's Code of Professional Conduct (see http://www.ipranet.org/codes.htm). Through the IPR's efforts, public relations in Ghana is gradually gaining respect and recognition. Its membership has grown from 276 in 1999 to 400 in 2004 and to more than 670 in 2007 (Blankson 2004; see http://iprghana.com).

Second, corporate relations is fast becoming a major function of public relations in Ghana. The country's political stability and economic growth have attracted local and foreign investment, particularly in mineral exploration, telecommunications, and the service and consumer industries. Multinational corporations from the United States, Japan, Korea and Europe such as Malaysia's TV3, Motorola Communications and Sprint Communications have entered the Ghanaian business landscape. The emerging economic reality has required organizations to find effective strategies to communicate and develop relationships with each other and their publics. This responsibility has fallen on Ghanaian public relations practitioners. The keynote speaker during the 2000 IPR Week conference in Accra made the following observation:

> The current business climate in Ghana demands that we [Ghanaian practitioners] attach greater importance to inter-corporate communications, both local and foreign. More importantly, we have to re-examine the way we have done business in the past and probably adopt the western-style, two-way communication and relationship building practices.
>
> (IPR 2001, p. 12)

Another speaker, an executive of a bank, commented that:

> Events in recent times had instilled in almost all organizations a sense of obligation to give public relations its rightful place. Success of any corporate body depends largely on the public's perception of it and also the kind of relationship that exists between the organization and its publics.
>
> (IPR 2001, p. 8)

Today in Ghana the primary mission of public relations continues to be redefined to focus more on the management of relationships between organizations and between the organizations and their publics.

Third, the media relations function has taken a central role in the daily activities of practitioners. The introduction of media independence and pluralism in 1994 has created a media environment characterized by diversity, competitiveness and open criticism. Print and radio are the most affected. For example, there are currently more than 200 private FM radio stations operating alongside the state media compared to only the state network prior to 1995. In Ghana today, the private media serve as gatekeepers and control information flow between organizations and their publics. Practitioners now use these media to report information to their publics, to mobilize public support for their activities, and to influence public policy. The plurality of media avenues has also made it easier for practitioners to develop and maintain media contacts, arrange for news conferences, place news releases, and determine what the media find newsworthy about their organizations. Media and public opinion monitoring are becoming critical activities for practitioners. Prior to 1995, practitioners could rely only on the state-controlled media for communicating their messages.

Finally, practitioners are becoming more sensitive to public opinion about their organizations and clients. Vocal, critical and discerning publics and advocacy groups have emerged and are using their newly found freedom of speech, via the diverse media platforms, to demand information, transparency and accountability from organizations and the government. Organizations and state officials are now forced to rethink the way they relate to the public and to communities. Ghana's practitioners are gradually embracing this important role in their new democracy, something they had historically ignored. Despite these significant developments, public relations in Ghana continues to face many challenges.

Challenges facing Ghanaian practitioners

Public relations in Ghana still suffers from lack of adequate recognition from both management and the public. Some in management refuse to recognize its importance to their organizations and continue to place public relations under departments such as marketing, personnel and advertising with no well-defined functions, responsibilities or job descriptions. Even in organizations where management recognizes the importance of public relations, practitioners are not accorded management functions. They struggle with a small staff, inadequate budget, and limited freedom and flexibility to plan and implement their programs. Similarly, the Ghanaian public continues to hold a negative view of, and low regard for, the profession. Many perceive practitioners as corrupt. Lack of adequate education and professional training opportunities continue to be major obstacles. The majority of Ghana's practitioners do not have education beyond a two-year diploma degree in public relations. Additionally, the educational standard for practicing public relations in Ghana is very low and not well structured. The growth of public relations is also hindered by the lack of access to modern communication technologies. Communication technologies such as the Internet and the Worldwide Web are still not readily available or accessible to the majority of the practitioners. Several organizations and public relations agencies in Ghana do not have websites. The IPR's website was set up in 2007 (see http://iprghana.com).

In spite of these challenges, public relations in Ghana has a positive future outlook, especially as the country continues its path to a true democratic and liberal economy. These are conditions within which public relations can flourish as a profession in every society, and Ghana is no exception.

Questions for discussion

1. Ghana is emerging as a stable democratic country, and its economy continues to grow, making it increasingly attractive to multinational corporations. However, the country still mirrors the cultural and linguistic diversity common to many African

nations. Now, assuming you have been offered a job as public relations officer in Ghana, how would your education and training in public relations help you to be effective? What skills will you need? What challenges and opportunities do you see?

2. Ghana is currently enjoying media pluralism/diversity and a vocal and critical public. Ponder how a public relations practitioner in Ghana might launch a public relations campaign to promote national unity in Ghana? What challenges and opportunities are likely to be faced by the practitioner?

3. What meaningful contributions can public relations make to the future of emerging African democracies such as Ghana?

South Africa

South Africa offers us an understanding of the role public relations can play in highly diverse societies and during times of major social and political change. The country's colonial and political history and its cultural composition offer a unique opportunity to study role-related issues in public relations, especially international public relations. Of course, before we discuss the history and character of South African public relations, we first have to understand the social, cultural, economic and political forces that shaped and continue to shape public relations in the country.

Background

South Africa is considered by many as both a developing and a developed society (Pahad 2001). Although it is a major player in the world economy, it is still addressing issues typical of the African continent. The South Africa Yearbook 2006–7 estimates that there were about 47 million people living in the country in 2006. Of these, native Africans were in the majority (79.5 percent), followed by whites (9.6 percent), the colored (8.9 percent), and then the Indian/Asians (2.5 percent). Despite this simplistic classification, the population is much more diverse, and many different cultural groups co-exist within these broader groups. South Africa is commonly called the "rainbow nation" because of its multicultural and multilingual nature. The 1996 Constitution of the Republic of South Africa (Act 108) recognizes eleven official languages. Although English is the mother tongue of only 8.2 percent of the population, it is the official language and the most widely understood and used.

Economically, South Africa is the leading power in sub-Saharan Africa. Its estimated GDP in 2006 of US$576 billion was the highest in Africa (CIA 2006). It is an emerging market with an abundant supply of natural resources and well-developed financial, legal, communications, energy, infrastructure and transport sectors. The country's economic sphere was transformed toward a capitalist-oriented, free-market and free-enterprise system after the country's transition from apartheid rule to democratic polity in 1994. State assets and previously state-run industries were rationalized and privatized. However, the country suffers from high unemployment (25.5 percent), high poverty (50 percent below the poverty level) and daunting economic problems from its apartheid legacy. The majority disadvantaged groups, especially native blacks, lack economic empowerment.

Crime, corruption and HIV/AIDS are prevalent. According to De Beer and Mersham (2004) and Skinner and Von Essen (1991), this economic reality has partly driven public relations practice during the apartheid and post-apartheid periods.

South Africa's political history is one of the most remarkable political transformations of the twentieth century. It began with the Dutch colonizing the country in 1656. Then, in 1806, the British seized the Cape of Good Hope area and forced many of the Dutch settlers (the Boers) to move north to found their own republics. The discovery of diamonds in 1867 and gold in 1886 spurred wealth and immigration. The Boers unsuccessfully resisted British encroachments. The sub-jugation of the native black inhabitants also intensified. During this time, South Africa was alternately ruled by the Dutch and the British until it unilaterally declared its independence from Britain in 1961. However, the new Union of South Africa operated under a policy of segregation and apartheid – the separate development of the races – until 1994 when it was dismantled and replaced with democratic rule. The political transition occurred in an atmosphere of open communication and freedom of speech (Mersham and Skinner 1998). The country had its first democratic election in 1994, which was won by the African National Congress (ANC) under the leadership of Nelson Mandela. Since then, the ANC has been governing the country.

The transition to democracy transformed South African society. South Africans refer to the South Africa that existed before 1994 as the "Old" South Africa and the post-1994 nation as the "New" South Africa (Holtzhausen *et al.* 2002). To promote successful political and social change, civil institutions, organizations and business communities had to confront issues such as human rights, freedom of association, freedom of speech and a basic concept of humanity. In terms of communications and organizational change there has been a shift toward consensus-seeking at all levels of government and between the government and the business communities. There is also growing recognition of the voice of local communities and the majority black population. Internationally, the political transformation has opened up a range of opportunities for the country and its people. Currently, South Africa is characterized by a healthy debate on issues of democracy, media freedom, freedom of speech, and particularly between the media and the government. These developments have had a significant impact on the evolution and character of public relations practices in the country.

History and characteristics of public relations

Many scholars have written extensively about public relations in South Africa (e.g., De Beer and Mersham 2004; Mersham 1993; Mersham *et al.* 1995; Mersham and Skinner 1998; Overton-De Klerk 1994; Pahad 2001; Holtzhausen *et al.* 2002; and Skinner and Von Essen 1991). These scholars agree that public relations in South Africa was influenced by a combination of Western public relations practices and indigenous African communication practices. It was primarily influenced by the country's ties with Britain and the United States. For instance, Senator Robert Bliss of New York was the guest speaker at the first public relations convention in Johannesburg in 1965. This connection ensured the predominant use of the English language and the simulation of Western practices. According to De Beer and Mersham (2004), the first public relations officer in South Africa was appointed by South African Railways in 1943, and the first public relations consultancy was established in Johannesburg in 1948. The introduction of several public relations departments in the private sector followed soon after, especially in the mining industry.

In the past, public relations was not considered a serious form of communication. Holtzhausen *et al.* (2002) report that practitioners were often portrayed as members of the wine-and-dine club. The 1994 peaceful transition to a democratic society and the new social, political and cultural realities exerted positive influences on public relations practice. Today, it is acknowledged as an important management function with a wide range of communication activities. Skinner and Von Essen (1991) wrote: "public relations has emerged in South Africa today as a sophisticated, multi-faceted discipline able to help forge effective two-way communication between an organization and its various publics" (p. 1). Public relations activities are evident in every sphere of the country's commercial, social and political life. Practitioners operate on two distinct levels: externally as consultants or advisors to their clients or to company management, or internally as inhouse corporate public relations officers performing multiple functions that include programming and counseling, media relations, organizing, writing, production of media messages, research and evaluation, training and advising executives and management on dealing with the media, and management. Holtzhausen *et al.* (2002) again note that public relations is also practiced within the context of development communication. After the collapse of apartheid, the previously marginalized and ignored black communities became an important focus for practitioners. An increasing number of native blacks entered the field of public relations. Most perform the development communication activities in the homelands created during apartheid rule to separate blacks from the developed provinces of the country.

South African practitioners also play a very important social role in the new democratic South Africa. They are involved in promoting the democratic process and explaining changes to both the public and organizations. As communicators, they have the task of building trust between the majority poor and the few wealthy groups, and between those with growing political power (especially blacks) and those with existing economic power (mostly whites). Consequently, the role of media relations has increased in order to take the various messages to the people. Mersham *et al.* (1995) and Overton-De Klerk (1994) all claim that corporate and government social responsibility/investment is a key driving force in South Africa's public relations. Organizations, through public relations, are required to demonstrate sensitivity to the needs and practices of developmental pursuits. Corporate social investment has become very important, and the corporate practitioner is often at the center of efforts toward assisting workers and senior management to accept substantial changes in the workplace and in society in general.

Sidebar: The Oprah Winfrey Leadership Academy for Girls

In 2002, popular US television personality and wealthy entrepreneur Oprah Winfrey unveiled plans to construct a leadership academy for girls in South Africa. Oprah's original interest in this project was sparked by both her own childhood and an inspirational conversation she had with former president of South Africa and anti-apartheid activist Nelson Mandela. After five years of intensive planning and construction, the doors to the Oprah Winfrey Leadership Academy for Girls were opened.

The Academy, based in Henly-on-Klip, is about forty miles outside Johannesburg, and consists of twenty-eight buildings including a theater, a library, a dining hall, classrooms and dormitories. One hundred and fifty-two South African girls were chosen, based on their leadership potential, to attend the Academy where they can garner the necessary skills to lead their country, which is still healing from apartheid, out of poverty and into glory.

Initially, the South African government was involved with assisting Oprah with the Academy, but they later pulled out of the project because they felt Oprah was doing too much. They reasoned that, because the country is so obviously poor, Oprah's extravagant means (i.e. a US$40 million dollar Academy) was going overboard. Oprah decided to continue with the project on her own and made it clear that she wanted to surround the girls of the Academy with beauty in order to give them an opportunity to feel important and make a difference in the world.

Public relations education and scholarship

South Africa has a long history of public relations education and scholarship. Over the years, a number of individuals have made substantial contributions to the field of public relations practice, education and scholarship. The pioneers involved in establishing public relations in the field of education and publishing include Jacques Malan and J. A. L'Estrange, who published the first handbook of public relations in South Africa in 1965, and Bob Krause. Recent contributors include Chris Skinner, Llew Von Essen, Arnold de Beer, Gary Mersham and several others. Their collective effort has ensured that public relations has a place not only within the scope of the newly democratic South Africa but also in serving as a powerful communication tool.

According to the Public Relations Institute of South Africa (http://www.prisa.co.za), the education and training of public relations practitioners is done within a well-organized and structured system that reflects the country's advanced education system. Public relations is taught at the tertiary level (higher education in South Africa is normally described as tertiary education) in either a university or a *technikon* (vocational school). Almost all universities with communication departments or schools teach public relations to some degree, with some offering it as a major leading to master's and doctoral degrees (e.g., North-West University at Potchefstroom, Rand Afrikaans University, University of the Free State, University of Zululand). At *technikons*, public relations is offered within its own school (e.g., Technikon Pretoria, Technikon Natal, and Port Elizabeth Technikon). In addition to the universities and *technikons*, a large number of private colleges (e.g., Damelin remedial college) and organizations, such as the Public Relations Institute of Southern Africa, offer public relations education, mainly in the form of one-year or short courses. In 1985 the Public Relations Ethics and Accreditation Council of South Africa (now the Ethics and Accreditation Council of PRISA) was formed as an independent and autonomous body to monitor the practice of public relations and to prevent malpractice. However, in recent years, public relations has started to lose its independent position as a separate field of study because the trend is to combine it with, or see it as part of, corporate communication or marketing communication (e.g., University of Pretoria). None the less, the driving force behind public relations education and professionalism in the country is the Public Relations Institute for South Africa.

The Public Relations Institute for South Africa (PRISA)

Founded in 1957 by twenty-three South African practitioners, PRISA has grown into a sophisticated discipline and professional organization with more than 3,500 members (see http://www.prisa.co.za). South Africa was one of the first countries to evolve a formal body of knowledge of public relations – an attempt by PRISA to define the theoretical and practical knowledge required by a professional practitioner (Malan and L'Estrange 1965). The Institute is guided by the following mission:

- To establish PRISA as the authority for the public relations profession;
- To foster the professionalization of public relations and communication management in Southern Africa;
- To set and maintain professional ethics and standards among members of the Institute;
- To provide dynamic value-added services to members of the Institute and thereby to its stakeholders;
- To establish public relations as a strategic management function;
- To transform the Institute continually to stay ahead of the dynamic changes in the social, political and economic environment.

Until recently, PRISA ran professional development courses, seminars and workshops in major centers around the country with the assistance of its regional chapters. It offered short or medium courses to new practitioners, mid-career professionals and managers. Through the process of accrediting university or other courses, as well as its own courses, PRISA developed a system whereby its members could obtain the highest public relations ranking, namely that of APR (accredited in public relations). Then, in June 2007, the South African Education Department announced that it had cancelled the registration of PRISA's training program, the PRISA Education and Training Center. The decision, which took effect in January 2008, prevented the center from offering courses. The department deregistered the center's certificate in public relations, higher certificate in public relations and diploma in public relations because professional bodies were not allowed to offer training directly when they were also responsible for endorsing other providers' training programs. This move broke PRISA's unfair monopoly over certification. ProVox, an organization with no ties to PRISA, except membership of the professional body, took over the PRISA short courses. It has already instituted two accredited courses in public relations, a certificate and a full diploma. The ProVox courses have been endorsed by PRISA and the Chartered Institute of Public Relations in the UK.

In conclusion, the South African environment offers the public relations scholar or practitioner the opportunity to explore not only generic public relations roles, but also culturally specific roles different from those experienced in any other sub-Saharan African country.

Questions for discussion

1. Despite the fact that South Africa has eleven official languages, English (mother tongue for only 8.6 percent of South Africans) is the primary language used for publicity and public relations campaigns. In view of this, it is often argued that the reality

that some practitioners have to write in a language other than their mother tongues might have an effect on preferred models of practice and, therefore, on the roles they perform. To what extent do you agree or disagree with this argument? Do you see the language issue influencing the choice of public relations models and strategies? Justify your answer.

2. In many ways, South Africa's public relations practitioners can be considered "change agents" during the post-apartheid era. The practitioners still have significant social and political roles to play in their society. What do you perceive these roles to be?

Kenya

The experience of Kenya provides a good example of how public relations is an outgrowth of deeper political and economic structural features of a society in the international context and also a consequence of change in these structures (L'Etang and Muruli 2004). It also provides an insight into the role African practitioners play in promoting corporate social responsibility and in advancing international public relations.

Background

Kenya was ruled by the British from 1890 until 1963, when it achieved full independence. Since then, it has maintained remarkable political stability. From 1964 to 1992, the country was ruled as a one-party state by the Kenya African National Union (KANU), first under Jomo Kenyatta and then under Daniel arap Moi. Demonstrations and riots pressured the Moi government to allow multiparty elections in 1992. But, in early 1995, President Moi moved against the opposition and ordered the arrest of anyone who insulted him. He stepped down in December 2002 following fair and peaceful elections. A coalition of opposition parties, led by Mwai Kibaki, won the 2002 presidential election. According to Opukah (2004), the elections marked an important turning-point in Kenya's democratic evolution in that power was transferred peacefully from the single party that had ruled the country since independence to a new coalition party. It also marked the end of twenty years of political torture, detention without trial, the plunder of the country's natural resources, scandals and massive corruption. The new government promised to put an end to the country's rampant corruption. In his first few months, President Kibaki initiated a number of reforms, ordered a crackdown on corruption, and instituted free primary school education. By 2004, disappointment in the government had set in as it made no real progress on the president's mandate to stem corruption. Today, there is a big change in Kenya's political landscape. It has brought with it a new dynamic in the public relations environment, one that calls for commitment to effective management and corporate social accountability. Of course, there has lately been a period of unrest in Kenya following questions concerning the legitimacy of recent presidential elections. However, at the time of writing it appears that a power-sharing agreement has been arranged with the help of former UN Secretary General Kofi Annan.

Economically, Kenya is the regional hub for trade, finance and communications in East Africa. After independence, the government promoted rapid economic growth through public investment, encouragement of smallholder agricultural production, and incentives for private (often foreign) industrial investment. However, Kajwang (2002) believes that weak commodity prices, endemic corruption, low investor confidence, meager donor support, and political infighting have limited Kenya's economic growth. The economy did not flourish under President Moi's rule. In the 1990s, Kenya's economic infrastructure began to disintegrate. The IMF and the World Bank suspended loans to Kenya because of the government's poor economic practices and its failure to institute several anti-corruption measures. Kenya is regularly ranked among the ten most corrupt countries in the world, according to the watchdog group Transparency International (2007). In 1993 the government began a major program of economic reform and liberalization. Under the directives of the World Bank and the IMF, a series of austere economic measures were undertaken. Consequently, since 2002, the country has been experiencing economic growth of nearly 6 percent. According to Opukah (2004), Kenya's economic landscape has changed significantly. In the past, businesses did not have to care about environment issues, human rights labor standards, community involvement, and the views of stakeholders. A realization has emerged that failure by businesses to engage in corporate social responsibility and to account positively for their conduct will be a recipe for the collapse of their new democracy and capitalism. This realization has created a new urgency and recognition for public relations practitioners. Kenya is also the primary communication hub of East Africa. It enjoys the region's best transportation linkages and communications infrastructure, though these advantages are less prominent than in past years. Although access to land telephones is very low (estimated 281,000 people in 2006), over 6.5 million people have mobile cellular phones, and nearly 2 million have access to the Internet. Private media operate alongside state media. A wide range of foreign firms maintain regional branches or representative offices in the cities.

Kenya is a diverse and multilingual country with many different cultures represented. There are sixty-two languages spoken in Kenya (Gordon 2005); most are African languages with a minority of Middle Eastern and Asian languages spoken by descendants of settlers. The official languages are Kiswahili and English. The United Nations estimates the current population of Kenya to be 37 million. Life expectancy is fifty-three years. A majority of the adult population is employed in agriculture (75 percent) compared to 25 percent in industry and services. Unemployment was estimated at 40 percent in 2001, and 50 percent of the population lives below the poverty line. These are the conditions within which public relations has evolved in Kenya. We now discuss the history, development and nature of public relations in the country.

History and characteristics of public relations

Not much has been published about public relations in Kenya, except for the work of scholars and practitioners such as Jacquie L'Etang and George Muruli (2004) and Opukah (1992). Others, such as Colin Church, a founding member of the Public Relations Society of Kenya, have given extensive speeches on the practice. According to L'Etang and Muruli (2004) and Muruli (2001), the emergence of public relations in Kenya was largely the consequence of the desire of powerful interest groups, particularly the British colonial administration, to create and manage public opinion. The colonial administration established the Kenyan Information Office (KIO) to handle its information and press functions. In 1942, the post of principal information officer (PIO) was created to take over the information and press duties from the KIO. Then, in 1944, a specialized post of public relations officer was created within the KIO with greater strategic responsibility for producing and supplying publicity materials.

Muruli (2001) asserts that private-sector public relations emerged as a consequence of labor conflicts and the important role that international capital played in the Kenyan post-independence economy. Businesses such as Kenya Power and Lighting, Kenya Shell, Unilever, the East African Post and Telecommunication Corporation, the Kenya Maize and Produce Board, East African Breweries, and the East African Harbors Corporation became aware of the virtues of publicity in the late 1940s. Their charge was primarily to develop personal relationships in the Kenyan communities to win friends and influence people, particularly during Kenya's labor conflicts and Mau Mau emergency. After independence in 1963, the need for planned public relations was recognized both by business and by unions. For example, Kenya Power and Lighting Company developed their communications to include areas like internal communication. Kenya Shell also developed a wide range of corporate social responsibility programs in areas such as environmental conservation and philanthropy work. According to L'Etang and Muruli (2004), though the first public relations consultancy in Kenya was established in 1955, it became a feature of public relations practice in Kenya after independence. Most of the firms were foreign-owned and employed native Kenyans as technicians, and then only when recommended by a non-African friend or "godfather" (L'Etang and Muruli 2004, p. 231).

Sidebar: Shell Oil in Nigeria

The "Royal Dutch/Shell Group", best-known as Shell, is a worldwide oil conglomerate comprising more than 1,700 companies. Shell Nigeria, as one of the largest oil producers in the Shell Group, has provided over US$30 billion to the economy of Nigeria, and it provides over 50 percent of the income that allows the Nigerian dictatorship to remain in power.

The Niger Delta in the southeast region of Africa accounts for 80 percent of oil extraction in Nigeria. This location also happens to be home for many small ethnic groups, including the Ogoni. Since 1958, oil from the Ogoniland has provided significant funds to the Nigerian economy, but Shell is often accused by its detractors of having done nothing to benefit the Ogoni people. For example, in 1996, Shell employed only eighty-eight Ogoni – just 2 percent of Shell's employees in Nigeria. As a result of Shell's oil-drilling, the Ogoni have suffered from significant environmental degradation and health impacts including natural gas flares, widespread oil spills, devastating acid rain, contamination of their land and water, mass construction and pipelines throughout their villages, and an increase in respiratory diseases and cancers.

Although the Ogoni and many other minority ethnic groups from the Niger Delta have tried to raise local awareness of their circumstances, the Nigerian government has remained in power, critics maintain, by violently repressing anyone trying to claim environmental and economic justice.

According to Church (2001), public relations in Kenya owes its development and growth to the Public Relations Society of Kenya. As one of Africa's earliest national bodies, the PRSK has consistently reflected the development of public relations in Kenya and wider Eastern Africa. It is a key player in both African and global public relations. The Society dates back to 1971 when its founders felt a need to establish the professional body to guide and bring together public relations practitioners in Kenya. The founders include Isaac Lugonzo (former Mayor of Nairobi) and Jesse Opembe (considered the father of public relations in Kenya). Others are Patrick Orr, Michael Dunford, James Smart, Muthoni Likimani and Colin Church (president of IPRA in 1996). These saw the need to build standards and develop a national voice.

The PRSK's broad objective is to advance excellence in public relations in Kenya and to ensure that the practice continues to thrive within the ethical framework defined by the profession (PRSK 2007). Within a few years of its formation, it demonstrated a commitment to international public relations by hosting the first African gathering of public relations practitioners in Nairobi in 1975. It was the first ever International Public Relations Association (IPRA) Council meeting in Africa. This event witnessed the founding of the Federation of African Public Relations Associations (FAPRA), the continental body for all national associations in Africa. It was a meeting of high tension as well as it witnessed the expelling of South African delegates over their government's apartheid policy (Church 2001). In the last three years, the society has hosted two major conferences under the auspices of the East African Public Relations Association (EAPRA) and FAPRA. To keep abreast of the global dynamics of the profession and to create networking opportunities for its members, the PRSK affiliates itself with regional, continental and global public relations bodies. Within the East African region, the PRSK is a member of both the EAPRA and the FAPRA. At the global level, the PRSK is a founding member of the Global Alliance for Public Relations and Communications Management. Also, its members subscribe to IPRA. To promote the highest degree of respect, practitioners are held to a Code of Professional Conduct based on IPRA's code of ethics founded on the Universal Declaration on Human Rights. The PRSK recently adopted the Global Alliance Universal Protocol, which aims to achieve a unified profession and industry worldwide. The PRSK was also involved in the establishment of IPRA's Environmental Communication Charter launched at the United Nations Environmental Program Headquarters in 1991 and which today is the cornerstone of global public relations practices in environment communications. These are testimony to Kenya's role in international public relations.

Apart from its international efforts, the PRSK has been the cornerstone of the growth of public relations in Kenya (PRSK 2007). The Society's mission is to promote excellence in public relations and communication management in Kenya by providing a forum for practitioners to exchange skills, knowledge and ideas. Its core values include developing the public relations practice, facilitating sharing of professional excellence for members and being a valuable resource base. To achieve these, the PRSK organizes conferences for practitioners, and students, a competitive exhibition, and Excellence Awards. Through the guidance of the PRSK, the public relations industry in Kenya has grown. According to its chairperson, Fatuma Mohamed (2007), Kenyan practitioners have made great strides in communicating deeply ingrained principles of the profession to top corporate management. Managers now appreciate the impact and value of public relations on the bottom line and contributions it makes to corporate social responsibility programs. Practitioners play a vital role in shaping the overall image of Kenya's organizations, corporate or otherwise, and this has made the practice one of the most dynamic in the country. Today, in Kenya, public relations is being adopted by more organizations. It has particularly gained relevance because Kenya is at the point at which corporate social responsibility has become a major concern. Both Opukah (2004) and Mohamed (2007) agree that in past years Kenyans understood public relations to mean propaganda and press agentry. Today, other professions (e.g., marketing and advertising) are integrating public relations in their communication plans. More organizations are beginning to make use of public relations. The practice is redefining itself and has taken a key position in improving organizational performance and sustaining the success of organizational objectives.

Driven by the need for specialized communicators, more colleges and universities offer public relations as a course. According to the PRSK's website (http://www.prsk.co.ke), about twelve educational institutions offer public relations education in Kenya. These include universities such as Nairobi, Maseno, Kenyatta, Moi, Daystar, and the United States International University in Kenya. Other colleges and institutes that offer public relations education include Kenya Institute of Management, School of Professional Studies, Makini, Zafrica Business School, Air Travel and Related Studies, and Kenya Polytechnic.

Despite its achievements, public relations in Kenya faces several challenges. Church (2001) points out that Kenya's own slow steps toward an open society and a multiparty democracy have constrained the profession's desire for great change. Mohamed (2007) has observed that public relations practitioners continue to be "everything to everybody" instead of carving out their niches and developing areas of specialization. Practitioners are yet to receive the recognition they deserve, though their practice has evolved both in depth and in width. Public relations is still not seen as a vital tool by some organizations. Practitioners continue to fight the misperception that public relations can be guided or replaced by marketing or advertising. Kenya's practitioners also struggle with the difficult task of selling the message of sustainable development for political expediency and corporate social responsibility and accountability to their companies. This task is made difficult by the ingrained political experience and financial corruption in the society. PRSK recently commissioned a study to help it understand the status and challenges of practitioners in Kenya. It is awaiting the findings. Nevertheless, public relations is making great strides. Practitioners understand that they have a big commercial, moral and political contribution to make to ensure that stability and sustainability are maintained. They also appreciate a need to embrace standards and indicators that will enable organizations to project a positive corporate reputation and move them forward.

Questions for discussion

1. Some scholars, particularly Western scholars, have characterized the public relations practice in African countries such as Kenya as ineffective because they use persuasive messages to promote national development programs rather than building relationships. Do you agree or disagree with this characterization? Justify your answer.

2. To whom is the public relations practice in Kenya most responsible – the government, the private businesses, or the people or communities? Outline the responsibilities Kenya's practitioners have to each of these constituents or publics.

Featured biography: Cornelius B. Pratt

Dr Cornelius B. Pratt is one of the prominent scholars of African communication, particularly in the fields of public relations, health and intercultural communication. His current research interests include international and intercultural communication, ethics, public relations, and health communication. Originally from Nigeria, Dr Pratt is a professor of communication and public relations in the Mass Media and Communication Studies department at Temple University, USA. He also serves on the staff of the National Office of Communication of the USDA Forest Service, Washington, DC, as Presidential Professor of Strategic and Organizational Communication. Prior to his current posts, Dr Pratt held academic positions at Howard University (2005–6), at Michigan State University (1991–2002), at Virginia Tech (1983–91) and at Weber State University (1981–3). He holds a master's and a doctorate from the University of Minnesota–Twin Cities.

Dr Pratt is a pioneer in research on public relations in Africa. In an area where very little, if any, research exists, he took the lead in publishing *Public Relations in the Third World: The African Context* in 1985. The significance of this contribution was that it set the agenda and tone for subsequent scholarship on Africa. He was among the pioneers to isolate the social responsibility and national development functions of Africa's practitioners – a significant contribution to the body of knowledge on public relations. In 1996, he collaborated with James Van Leuven to publish "Public relations' role: realities in Asia and Africa south of the Sahara". Dr Pratt's research is not confined to Africa's public relations alone. He has also made several significant contributions in other areas such as health and media in Africa. For example, in the area of African health communication, his 1997 work (with Irma Silva-Barbeau and Charlotte Pratt) titled "Toward a symmetrical and an integrated framework of norms for nutrition communication in sub-Saharan Africa" that appeared in the *Journal of Health Communication* is commendable. In the field of media in Africa, Dr Pratt's scholarship on *Cultural Memory and Senegalese Media: Analyzing the Relationship between Media and Culture in a Sub-Saharan African Context* investigates how Senegalese societal–cultural memory shapes their television media.

Dr Pratt believes that, though conflicts are commonplace in Africa, they have been under-reported in the media. In this regard he has made his research meaningful to solving Africa's health, civil unrest, and communication issues. Most recently, in May 2007, Dr Pratt participated in the International Health Conference titled *Unite for Sight Conference 2007* in Palo Alto, California, where he delivered his research "Mobilizing war-torn African communities to improve public health". Dr Pratt explains how the mobilization model for public health is a process, rather than an event, that transforms communities and builds positive interaction between warring groups. He hopes that public health initiatives will not only be concerned with clinical outcomes, but will also consider ways to reduce fear and improve security for health workers, especially in Africa.

As a "global scholar", Dr Pratt has not confined his research endeavors to Africa but has extended it beyond the continent. His works on public relations ethics, crisis communication, and international public relations are examples. In 2004, he examined the empirical literature on public relations ethics and concluded that serious doubts and concerns exist about the ethics of public relations practice. Prior to that, in 1994, Dr Pratt published "Applying classical ethical theories to ethical decision making in public relations" in *Management Communication Quarterly*. In this article, he argues for the adoption of an eclectic approach to problem-solving because no single theory in itself is sufficient to guide the complex decision-making process that precedes the public conduct of the strategic communication manager.

Dr Pratt has an impressive portfolio of collaborative endeavors with other scholars. The list includes such works as "Ethical inclinations of public relations majors" with Gerald McLaughlin (1989) in the *Journal of Mass Media Ethics*; "An integrated symmetrical model for crisis-communications management" with Alfonso Gonzalez-Herrero (1996) in the *Journal of Public Relations Research*; "International public relations education: US issues and perspectives" with Chris Ogbondah (1996) in an international public relations book; to name just a few. His solo publications are equally impressive and include such works as "Issues management: the paradox of the 40-year US tobacco wars" (2001) in *Handbook of Public Relations*; "Critique of the classical theory of situational ethics in US public relations"

(1993) in *Public Relations Review*; "Correlates and predictors of self-reported ethics among US public relations practitioners" (1992) in *Psychological Reports*; "PRSA members' perceptions of public relations ethics" (1991) in *Public Relations Review*; and "Public relations: the empirical research on practitioner ethics" (1991) in the *Journal of Business Ethics*.

Dr Pratt continues to make meaningful contributions to the field of communication both in Africa and to the discipline in general. Among the projects he is currently working on are "Ethical inclinations of tomorrow's advertising practitioners: then and now"; "Communicating stroke prevention in Philadelphia's African American communities"; and "The People's Republic of China and FAPRA: catalysts for theory building in Africa's public relations", soon to be published in the *Journal of Public Relations Research*.

Recommended website

Hofstede's cultural dimensions   http://www.geert-hofstede.com/hofstede_dimensions.php

Federation of African Public Relations Association (FAPRA),   http://www.fapra.org

International Public Relations Association's Code of Professional Conduct   http://www.ipranet.org/codes.htm

Public Relations Institute of South Africa   http://www.prisa.co.za

Global Alliance for Public Relations and Communications Management   www.globalpr.org.

International Public Relations Association   www.ipra.org

Public Relations Society of Kenya (PRSK)   http://www.prsk.co.ke

West Africa Public Relations News   http://www.cinnews.com/west-africa/newsfeed-west-africa-public-relations

Institute of Public Relations Ghana   http://iprghana.com

References

Adi, B., 2005. The moral economy and prospects of accumulation in sub-Saharan Africa: how the IFIS can help. *West Africa Review 7*.

Al-Enad, A. H., 1990. Public relations roles in developing countries. *Public Relations Quarterly*, 35 (2), pp. 24–8.

BBC World Service Trust, 2007. *Wetin Dey*: new Nigerian drama launch, [online]. Available at: http://www.bbc.co.uk/worldservice/trust/news/story/2007/02/070227_wetin_dey_launch.shtml [accessed July 13, 2007].

Blankson, I. A., 2004. Public relations in emerging democracies: the case of Ghana. In D. J. Tilson and E. C. Alozie, eds, *Toward the Common Good: Perspectives in International Public Relations*. Boston, Mass.: Alyn & Bacon, pp. 300–19.

Boachie-Agyekum, F., 1992. A comparative study of PR practices in selected state and private establishments. A case of Ghana Commercial Bank, Standard Chartered Bank, State Insurance Corporation, Great African Insurance Company, Ghamot, and Japan Motors. Unpublished thesis submitted to the School of Communication Studies, University of Ghana, Legon.

Church, C., 2001. Which way for PR in Africa. *PR Arena*, 1, p. 11.

CIA (Central Intelligence Agency), 2006. The World Fact Book 2006, [online]. https://www.cia.gov/library/publications/the-world-factbook/geos/sf.html [accessed July 10, 2007].

De Beer, A. S. and Mersham, G., 2004. Public relations in South Africa: a communication tool for change. In D. J. Tilson and E. C. Alozie, eds, *Toward the Common Good: Perspectives in International Public Relations*. Boston, Mass.: Alyn & Bacon, pp. 320–40.

Fanon, F., 1967. *Towards an African Revolution*. New York: Grove.

Fobanjong, J., 2004. Around Africa: the quest for public relations in Africa. In D. J. Tilson and E. C. Alozie, eds, *Toward the Common Good: Perspectives in International Public Relations*. Boston, Mass.: Alyn & Bacon, pp. 203–14.

Gordon, R. G., Jr, ed., 2005. *Ethnologue: Languages of the World*. Dallas, Tex,: SIL International.

Grunig, J. E., ed., 1992. *Excellence in Public Relations and Communication Management*. Hillsdale, NJ: Lawrence Erlbaum.

Grunig, J. E. and Hunt, T., 1984. *Managing Public Relations*. New York: Holt, Rinehart & Winston.

Gyan, M. I., 1991. A profile of public relations practice in Ghana. An unpublished thesis submitted to the School of Communication Studies, University of Ghana, Legon.

Hall, E. T., 1959. *The Silent Language*. Garden City, NY: Bantam Doubleday Dell.

Hofstede, G., 2001. Cultural dimensions, [online]. Available at: http://www.geert-hofstede.com/hofstede_dimensions.php [accessed June 10, 2007].

Holtzhausen, D. R., Petersen, B. K. and Tindall, N., 2002. Public relations models in the new South Africa. In the Public Relations Division, International Communication Association Conference. Seoul, South Korea, July 15–19.

Institute of Public Relations, Ghana (IPR), 1999. *IPR Newsletter*, 3 (1), pp. 1–3.

Institute of Public Relations, Ghana (IPR), 2001. *IPR Newsletter*, 5 (1), pp. 1–9, 16–17.

Kagwe, M., 2006. Public relations: the driver during major change. Speech delivered on May 26, 2006, during a PRSK luncheon at the Nairobi Safari Club Hotel, Kenya. Available at: http://www.prsk.co.ke [accessed July 13, 2007].

Kajwang, O., 2002. What is the political, social and economic way forward for Kenya after 2002 election?, [online]. Available at: http://www.prsk.co.ke/img/Kenya [accessed June 12, 2007].

L'Etang, J. and Muruli, G., 2004. Public relations, decolonization, and democracy: the case of Kenya. In D. J. Tilson and E. C. Alozie, eds, *Toward the Common Good: Perspectives in International Public Relations*. Boston, Mass.: Alyn & Bacon, pp. 215–38.

Malan, J. and L'Estrange, J., 1965. *Public Relations Practice in South Africa*. Cape Town: Juta.

Mersham, G., 1993. Public relations, democracy and corporate social responsibility. *Ecquid Novi*, 14 (2), pp. 107–26.

Mersham, G., Rensburg, R. and Skinner, C., 1995. *Public Relations, Development and Social Investment: A Southern African Perspective*. Pretoria: Van Schaik.

Mersham, G. and Skinner, C., 1998. Public relations: a vital communication function of our times. In A. De Beer, ed., *Mass Media – towards the Millennium*. Pretoria: Van Schaik, pp. 347–74.

Mohamed, F. H., 2007. Public Relations has come of age, [online]. Available at: http://allafrica.com/stories/printable/200705161091.html [accessed June 10, 2007].

Muruli, G., 2001. Public relations in Kenya: the missing link 1939–71. Unpublished master's thesis, University of Sterling.

Opukah, S., 1992. Challenges for public relations in Africa. *International Public Relations Review*, 15 (2), pp. 14–17.

Opukah, S., 2004. The dynamic nature of PR in the 21st century. *PR Arena*, 1, p. 4. Available at: http://www.prsk.co.ke/article10.htm [accessed June 12, 2007].

Osam, V., 1989. Public relations outfits in private and public institutions. Unpublished thesis submitted to the School of Communication Studies, University of Ghana, Legon.

Overton-De Klerk, N., 1994. Corporate social responsibility. In B. Lubbe and C. Puth, eds, *Public Relations in South Africa*. Isando, South Africa, pp. 173–90.

Pahad, E., 2001. South Africa is bridging the developmental divide. *The Sunday Times*, June 24, p. 19.

Pratt, C., 1985. Public relations in the Third World: the African context. *Public Relations Journal*, 41 (2), pp. 11–12, 15–16.

Pratt, C. B. and Okigbo, C., 2004. Applying reconstructed and social responsibility theories to foreign direct investment and public relations for social change in sub-Saharan Africa. In D. J. Tilson and E. C. Alozie, eds, *Toward the Common Good: Perspectives in International Public Relations*. Boston, Mass.: Alyn & Bacon, pp. 271–40.

PRISA (Public Relations Institute of South Africa), 2000. *Code of Professional Conduct and Standards for Accreditated Public Relations Practitioners*. Johannesburg: Public Relations Council of South Africa.

PRSK (Public Relations Society of Kenya), 2007. PR status survey in Kenya, [online]. Available at: http://www.prsk.co.ke/status.htm [accessed June 12, 2007].

Rodney, W., 1972. *How Europe Underdeveloped Africa*. Dar es Salaam: Tanzania Publishing House.

Sattler, J. E., 1981. PR in Africa: impressive strides. *Public Relations Journal*, 37 (6), pp. 28–9, 39.

Skinner, J. and Von Essen, L., 1991. *The South Africa Handbook of Public Relations*. Johannesburg: Southern Books.

South Africa, 2007. South Africa yearbook 2006/2007, [online]. Available at: http://www.gcis.gov.za/docs/publications/yearbook.htm [accessed July 10, 2007].

Transparency International, 2007. Global Corruption Report 2006, [online]. Available at: http://www.transparency.org [accessed June 12, 2007].

Turkson, D., 1986. PR section of the University of Cape Coast. Unpublished thesis submitted to the School of Communication Studies. University of Ghana, Legon.

United Nations, 2006. *Human Development Report 2006*. New York: United Nations Development Program.

Van Leuven, J. and Pratt, C. B., 1996. Public relations' role: realities in Asia and in Africa south of the Sahara. In H. M. Culbertson and N. Chen, eds, *International Public Relations: A Comparative Analysis*. Mahwah, NJ: Lawrence Erlbaum, pp. 93–106.

World Bank/World Development Indicators, 2006. *International Bank for Reconstruction and Development*. Washington, DC: The World Bank Development Data Center.

World Bank, 2007. African Development Indicators 2007, [online]. Available at: http://siteresources.worldbank.org/INTSTATINAFR/Resources/adi2007_final.pdf [accessed February 13, 2008].

Chapter 11

Latin America

Summary

This chapter addresses the range of public relations practice in Latin America. It provides an introduction to public relations in the region and contextualizes its growth in light of Latin America's history, cultural norms, and political challenges. The chapter also presents a more detailed analysis of public relations in Brazil, Mexico and Colombia, with some attention devoted to other countries' efforts in the region. It is important to differentiate Latin America's public relations philosophy from others in this textbook. The emphasis of the Latin American School of Public Relations on social integration and collaboration is explained, highlighting how this philosophy corresponds to the unique public relations needs in the region. A sampling of important public relations issues in the region is also presented. As you will see, understanding the significance of culture in public relations continues to be paramount. You will explore some cultural preferences for media relations, government relations, and the like, which will help to continue to build your education in global public relations.

Chapter goals

- Gain a broad historical understanding of the Latin America region.
- Understand the political, economic and social challenges facing public relations in Latin America.
- Differentiate the Latin American School of Public Relations philosophy from other public relations perspectives.
- Gain an appreciation of the types of public relations practice in Brazil, Mexico, Colombia and other Latin American countries.
- Learn about some of the contemporary Latin American public relations issues facing international practitioners.

Introduction

In 1959, Walter Lemmon had a warning for US public relations practitioners seeking Latin American clients. He observed that campaigns might be planned well for US standards but needed to get closer to the pulse of Latin American culture. Otherwise, he said, campaigns might fail because they would not be designed for effectiveness in that culture. Lemmon warned that US public relations practitioners needed to understand better the countries' communication needs, media preferences, and relationships. Later, in 1968, US public relations practitioner John M. Reed offered an analysis of the state of the profession in Latin America. Reporting from the Fourth World Congress of Public Relations, held in Rio de Janeiro, Reed noted efforts to help focus more attention on public relations in Latin America. The Congress represented a good cross-section of public relations in the region, with delegates representing major international companies, government, and independent public relations agencies. Even in 1968, delegates debated topics ranging from professionalism to the need for government control of the practice. Reed also reported about national public relations associations that existed in many Latin American countries and the PRSA's decision to affiliate with the regional public relations organization, Federacion Interamericana de Relaciones Publicas.

Surprised at this level of public relations activity in Latin America at the time? You should not be. Public relations in Latin America has a long, complex history that continues to inform the practice's exciting future today. As we shall see in this chapter, understanding the origins of public relations in Latin America will help today's practitioner be better-prepared for a dynamic public relations environment. Flash forward to today and it may be surprising that many Latin American public relations professionals still note the same interests and concerns as in previous decades.

Overview

Latin America continues to become a vibrant public relations market. Indeed, public relations practitioner Ray Kotcher (1998a) says the catchphrase for US Americans in the nineteenth century may have been "Go West, young man", but today the phrase may be "Vamanos a la Patagonia!" (colloquially, "Let's Go South") (p. 26). Once known by the "banana republic" stereotype, Latin America has become a major player in the global marketplace (Kotcher 1998b). With some exceptions, former state-controlled industries are becoming privatized, exports are rising, and foreign investment is increasing. Democratic and economic reforms continue. Economic growth, democratization, changing media environments, and increasing consumerism are creating opportunities for public relations in Latin America (Kotcher 1998a). For example, by 2010, more US exports (in dollar value) are expected to flow to the region with a market of 470 million consumers. These US exports to Latin America are more than to Europe and Japan combined (Kotcher 1998a). Trade barriers are also diminished or eliminated. Media, too, are moving from an informal system in which editors and reporters were paid to place stories to a system based on quality, fact-filled presentation of information. Journalists are also freer to express themselves, and the number and types of media outlets are expanding. Print and television media have embraced the region. As of 1998, for example, Brazil had almost 1,000 magazines, 1,200 daily newspapers, thousands of radio stations, and multiple television networks. CNN and other networks are creating Spanish-language channels to compete with Latin American networks. Print media such as *Time, Newsweek, Business Week* and *Fortune* are establishing regional, English-language distribution. Targeted media are also beginning to reach consumers, as trade and specialized publications are increasing. The reach of public relations firms has also increased with US agencies establishing offices in major Latin American capitals. Latin American universities now feature public relations programs. Many Latin American countries boast organized public relations associations, including the Association of Public Relations of Costa Rica, the Association of Public Relations of Nicaragua, and the College of Public Relations of Venezuela. The region also hosts public relations congresses through La Asociacion Latinoamericana de Investigadores de la Comunicacion, most recently held in Bolivia (2002) and Argentina (2004). As you can see, there is a lot of public relations activity and opportunity in Latin America.

For all the excitement and enthusiasm about public relations growth in Latin America, students and practitioners need to be aware that many difficulties arise as the area continues to adapt Western free-market economic reforms to its particular regional realities. Even as early as 1970, scholars noted that the growth of internationalism and globalism was paradoxically met with increasing regionalism in various parts of the world (Shaker 1970). Indeed, scholars of the time pointed out that Latin American citizens can be skeptical of private enterprise and a competitive system and instead place emphasis on quality of life, concerns about the environment, equitable economic distribution and maintaining cultural identity (Shaker 1970). As a result, foreign investment and government support may have contributed to economic growth in some sectors, but political, diplomatic and cultural initiatives were needed to support cross-cultural understanding and goodwill (Shaker 1970). Particularly in Latin America, this observation continues to be the case, as countries have met with varying success trying to implement economic and democratic reform.

Understanding Latin America's public relations context requires an appreciation of the region's complex historical and governmental legacies. Many Latin American countries are still considered to be "emerging democracies" in which nations struggle to implement the institutions and processes associated with that governmental system. Mexico, for example, has been independent from Spain since 1821 but was ruled by one dominant party from 1930 to 2000 (Tilson and Alozie 2004). Peru gained independence from Spain in 1924, ending an oppressive and paternalistic régime but implementing a forty-year chaotic structure featuring thirty-four different presidents (Freitag 2004). In Peru, as in other areas dominated by the Spanish colonial experience, society continues the legacy of a feudal system favoring white leaders and oppressing indigenous peasants (Freitag 2004). The Spanish colonies in Latin America featured governments that compensated low salaries by profiting from government service, appointed family members through nepotism, and favored their own interests over Spain when new laws were introduced (Sharpe and Simões 1996). The result was an overemphasis on family ownership and self-interest in social, political and economic interests that continues today (Sharpe and Simões 1996).

As countries in the region implement democracy and capitalism's free-market reforms, social problems such as poverty, unemployment and underemployment can be exacerbated. Tilson (1996) notes that, since 1990, Latin America has moved to privatize communication and other industries, with economic development and promotional activities simultaneously increasing. Following the 1994 Miami "Summit of the Americas", Latin American leaders emphasized the development of the region's telecommunication and information technology infrastructure as key in the area's economic development (Tilson 1996). As industries privatize and develop, the need for public relations grows. Nevertheless, corruption still plagues some Latin American nations as free-market reforms increase, leading to multiple challenges for practitioners. Ecuador, for example, has a long history of *caudillos*, who view communication as an end in itself, rather than representative government. Deception can be used to advance special interests rather than the common good (Tilson 2004). *Caudillo*-style governments in Ecuador institutionalized political corruption, with efforts to modernize and privatize industry met with mixed results. Peruvians also face high unemployment now that industries have been privatized (Freitag 2004). As a result, throughout Latin America, support for democracy is eroding in light of rising poverty, ongoing corruption, and insufficient social services (Tilson and Alozie 2004).

In hindsight, though scholars agree that market-oriented economic reforms adopted in most Latin American countries since the 1980s succeeded in curbing inflation and bringing a measure of economic stability, they have not as successfully boosted economic and social development (Leiras 2007). Each country's success with free-market reforms varied instead of resulting in region-wide economic success. Unemployment rose in many Latin American countries, and inequality among citizens remained high. Free-market reforms may have helped stabilize economies on a macro-level but did not fully sustain growth or reduce poverty.

As a result, as of 2007, some scholars argue that Latin American citizens are turning away from market-oriented policies. The region is witnessing the emergence of policies that seek social and democratic reform and emphasize resource distribution, programs that address poverty and inequality, more autonomy from the US, and efforts to embrace globalization on its own terms. Indeed, as Latin America is the most unequal region in the world, efforts in reducing social inequality are paramount to many of its citizens (Lynch 2007). Some nations continue to struggle with régimes that support democracy but economies that benefit only some segments of the population, generally represented by oligopolies (Lynch 2007). Many citizens seeking to reconcile their economies with politics are looking to new and, in some cases, more Leftist-leaning leaders, who appear more favorable to social equality (Lynch 2007). Nevertheless, Latin American citizens appear to seek democratic social reform rather than the national–popular administrations of the 1930s or the guerrilla romanticism of the 1960s and 1970s (Lynch 2007). Leaders are less likely to promise democratic reforms but practice unequal economic policies (Lynch 2007). Scholars argue that today's historical context is more promising than that of a decade ago. Now we shall explore what this brief discussion of political, economic and social challenges means for public relations. Above all, we shall find a need for ongoing sensitivity to the region's specific economic needs and social and political expectations.

Sidebar: Agency profile – Burson-Marsteller Latin America

The president of Burson-Marsteller for Latin America, Santiago N. Hinojosa, is excited about the opportunities for public relations in the region. Miami is the base for Burson-Marsteller's offices in Mexico, Puerto Rico, Venezuela, Colombia, Brazil, Argentina and Chile. Hinojosa notes the broad range of client work available in the region: "From Aeromexico to Zephyrhills, we have collaborated with local, regional, and world clients representing a large variety of industries" (Kenny 1999, p. 1). Some past clients include: Americatel, the Chilean Salmon Raisers Association, AT&T, Carnival Hotels and Casinos, Cigna, Citibank, Discovery Channel Latin America, Enterprise Florida, Esso Inter-America, Fidelity, Florida Power Corporation, Ford Motor Company, Greater Miami Chamber of Commerce, IBM, Kodak, Ryder

System, Texaco and Travel Channel (Kenny 1999). Burson-Marsteller Latin America offers a number of examples of successful Latin American public relations projects. In Mexico, the agency successfully attracted middle-class and affluent patrons to the Ringling Bros. Barnum & Bailey circus, an activity once associated with lower-income people. In Chile, after several cases of typhoid fever were reported, Burson helped McDonald's to overcome a ban on lettuce. Hinojosa also cites the campaign created for the Colombian Coffee Growers Federation and its personification of Juan Valdez as an example of positive worldwide perception. Hinojosa plans to draw on Burson's worldwide experience to capitalize on the region's growing opportunities: "We keep an open mind to the opportunities that may arise in Latin America. If the image of a person or a company is not handled correctly, much damage can be done. What we do is make sure the adequate and correct information reaches the media" (Kenny 1999, p. 1). (See www.bm.com for more information about Burson-Marsteller.)

Latin American public relations philosophy

The philosophy of public relations in Latin America reflects the region's varied history and attempts to combine economic reform with social concerns. Indeed, Simões (1992) identifies six different approaches to public relations in Latin America. For example, in Brazil, public relations was originally viewed as a specialty within journalism. Public relations can also be viewed as an activity that supports the selling of a product or organization. A third approach considers public relations to be the best performance of the organization; that is, public relations boosts the legitimacy of an organization through its ethical actions. Another approach to public relations is motivational and is concerned with organizational morale. Another model reduces public relations to an individual professional's social, technical and political contacts. Finally, another approach sees public relations as organizing social and cultural events as ends in themselves. Simões (1992) points out that throughout Latin America most of these approaches intertwine and rarely appear in their pure form. He also suggests integrating and expanding these philosophical approaches to create a new paradigm of public relations practice that is more complete.

Practitioners and scholars are attempting to foster this new paradigm. In this view, public relations people are encouraged to work for the needs of their respective societies in addition to client objectives. Molleda (2000) argues that Latin American scholars and professionals have cultivated a School of Public Relations that works for justice and equality along with citizen participation and integration. The first manifestation of the Latin American school of thought was expressed in the declaration of principles of the Inter-American Federation of Public relations (FIARP) founded in Mexico in 1960, then renamed the Inter-American Confederation of Public Relations (CONFIARP) in 1985. CONFIARP has helped develop the philosophy of public relations in Latin America. Its main objective is to elevate the status of public relations in Latin America by promoting integration and professionalism among and within its member associations. Currently, fifteen association members in three geographical areas make up CONFIARP: Netherland Antilles, Costa Rica, Cuba, Mexico, Panama, Puerto Rico, Bolivia, Colombia, Ecuador, Peru, Venezuela, Argentina, Brazil, Chile and Uruguay. In the 1980s, CONFIARP signed cooperation agreements with IPRA and the IABC to further the Latin American public relations philosophy throughout the world.

The idea of collaboration is important in the Latin American School of Public Relations. It sees public relations professionals as "social intermediaries" between organizations and publics, especially in societies where there are disproportionate rates of inequality, as in many Latin American countries (Molleda and Ferguson 2004). In essence, the Latin American School of Public Relations stresses the interests of the community and responds to the economic, social and political realities that influence public relations practice (Molleda and Ferguson 2004). Many scholars consider this perspective to be more humanistically and socially oriented (Molleda and Ferguson 2004). Indeed, the core assumption of the Latin American School of Public Relations is that organizations have a responsibility to contribute to the wellbeing of the social environments in which they operate (Molleda and Ferguson 2004). As a result of decades of social crises, failed democratic régimes and inefficient bureaucracies that have frustrated many Latin American citizens, public relations scholar Corredor-Ruiz argues that: "The main concern in Latin America is to allow publics to communicate with organizations; that is, to establish an equilibrium (symmetry) between organizations and publics" (Molleda and Ferguson 2004, p. 331).

To understand better the unique Latin American public relations philosophy, this section highlights several countries' public relations efforts and concerns. We shall take a look at public relations in Brazil, Mexico and Colombia. We shall also briefly examine public relations in other areas including Venezuela and Chile, as well as in Central America. In all cases, students and practitioners should attempt to adopt the tailored approaches discussed here for each Latin American country they address.

Brazil

Public relations in Brazil has a long history. The practice began in the country in 1914 with the creation of a public relations department in the São Paulo Tramway Light and Power Company Ltd (Kunsch 2007). Formal public relations education began in 1967, with the University of São Paulo School of Communication and Arts offering the first four-year public relations program. Today, seventy-eight undergraduate and twenty-four graduate programs are offered across the nation. The profession is more valued, despite ongoing controversy regarding the definition of the practice and debate about the meaning of public relations and its approach. The profession has become institutionalized, with legal support, civil associations, educational systems, and scientific and technical research studies (Kunsch 2007).

In keeping with the Latin American School of Public Relations discussed previously, public relations practitioners in Brazil view their roles as practitioners concerned with ethics and social responsibility, employee well-being, community well-being, and government harmony (Molleda and Ferguson 2004). As Brazilians tend to put relationships with people before money, and value the environment, practitioners identifying with these public relations roles is not surprising (Gannon 2001). Further, Brazil's transition from colonialism to a federal republic and from a dictatorship to a democracy perhaps highlights the importance of Brazilian public relations practitioners serving in these roles (Molleda and Ferguson 2004). Ultimately, Brazilian practitioners seem to be concerned with the betterment of their political and social environments (Molleda and Ferguson 2004).

In Brazil, foreign companies looking to enter the market should take note of a number of cultural preferences to boost success. Vale (1978) provided a number of suggestions for public relations practitioners working in Brazil and in Latin America in general. Practitioners should look for local partners, work with these local partners to gain government and public opinion support, and participate in local cultural and social activities. This suggestion echoes the Latin American Public Relations philosophy discussed in the previous section. Public relations in Latin America must include this social component. Further, practitioners might consider beginning a speakers' bureau the better to share the company's story with the government and publics. Social responsibility is also important in Brazil; for instance, practitioners should respect environmental concerns. Practitioners interested in the Brazilian market should also realize the importance of image-building in addition to merchandising.

In 1967, Brazil became the first country in the world to legalize public relations as a profession; and today professionals there continue to refine the law surrounding public relations practice. Brazilian public relations professionals must have a public relations degree and be licensed by their state's regional council to practice legally (Molleda and Athaydes 2003). As the scope of public relations work has diversified over the years, enforcement of the law has been difficult. In 1998, after a four-year debate about making changes in the law to help raise the profession's status in Brazil, several changes were proposed to the law, including provisions to clarify definitions of public relations and efforts to set educational standards of the discipline. Molleda and Athaydes (2003) point out that, though public relations has legal status in Brazil, it has not yet acquired legitimacy in society. As such, CONFIARP is working with universities and professionals to help ensure high-quality practice. In a survey designed to capture Brazilian professionals' opinions about licensing, professionals agreed that licensing should be maintained, although they differed on how best to manage the diffusion and enforcement of the legislation. Nevertheless, Brazil's experience with licensing serves as a guide to other countries considering licensing public relations. Molleda and Athaydes (2003) point out that, as interest in global public relations continues to grow, Brazil's experience may guide discussions about the licensing issue.

Many well-known US companies face poor brand awareness when they enter Brazil and the larger Latin American market. Lucent Technologies, for example, an independent company born out of an AT&T trivesture, had little brand awareness in Brazil and Mexico. Business executives in these areas thought Lucent to be a subsidiary of AT&T and did not know Lucent's scope of business. As a result, Lucent's public relations team formed regional brand councils in Brazil and Mexico to guide and integrate communication about the Lucent global brand position (PRSA). The brand councils planned aggressive media relations, special events and trade shows, customer events, internal communication, and philanthropy efforts, to name just a few. These efforts resulted in a tripling of brand awareness in Brazil and similar gains in Mexico. The brand council's united approach in each country helped to secure these results (PRSA). In other words, it was important for Lucent to recognize that it did not have a well-known image in Brazil. For it to assume it could do business without ensuring knowledge of the company and its objectives would have been a public relations mistake.

Mexico

Mexico has a bright future in public relations. International public relations firms, growing business media, more cause-related marketing, and increased NGO activity are helping the public relations and advertising industries to thrive (Newsom 2004). In the past twelve years there have been big changes in the country, and it is a particularly exciting market. Mexican public relations practitioners note that the practice is becoming more professional (Epley 2003). Indeed, in 2006, the PRSA awarded Manuel Alonso its Atlas Award, which celebrates the lifetime achievements of global public relations leaders (PRSA). Alonso is one of the first public relations practitioners in Mexico. He began working at the age of 11 for the Mexican States Editor's Association. He also served as an apprentice journalist at United Press International in Mexico City, but eventually switched his career focus to public relations. Alonso's firm, Imagenes Nte, secured accounts with clients such as American Express, Procter & Gamble, and Pfizer. He has also been honored by the Mexican Public Relations Academy for his influence on the Mexican public relations profession.

Public relations in Mexico continues to evolve. In addition to economic changes due to its North American Free Trade Agreement (NAFTA) membership, Mexico's evolving democracy, improving information technology and strengthening media system cultivate its public relations development (Molleda and Moreno 2006). Public relations in Mexico has been accelerated by the establishment of NAFTA. NAFTA helped Mexico embrace openness, the democratic process, and greater professionalism and expansion of public relations across diverse organizations (Johnson 2005a). NAFTA and other trade-related public relations also influence Mexican public relations roles and increase the development of public relations managers, in addition to technicians, in the country (Johnson 2005a). NAFTA, however, has increased the Mexican economy's dependence on the US, and Mexican public relations professionals must respond to economic fluctuations caused by the trade agreement (Molleda and Moreno 2006). In addition to NAFTA's implications, a study noted that Mexico's transition to democracy is rather unstable, with these resulting implications for public relations practice:

1) political groups are increasing service demands, 2) new positioning of "social communicators" in government as openness and transparency facilitators, 3) changing legal framework that allows the work of civic organizations and access to public information, 4) greater demand for lobbying services, 5) low profile of organizations in the political arena to avoid scandals, and 6) avoidance of politicized social movements as linkages to corporate social responsibility programs.

(Molleda and Moreno 2006, p. 108)

Mexican public relations efforts, however, still face challenges owing to unequal wealth distribution and distrust of media, politicians, and some businesses. As such, public relations practitioners working in Mexico must prioritize ethical practices, particularly in carrying out government and media relations. Further, economic inequality means that poverty and high illiteracy rates call for reliance on broadcast media and community relations programs to communicate with publics (Molleda and Moreno 2006). Private organizations are in partnership with non-profit organizations to help public relations serve a social function in assisting these publics.

Relationships between practitioners and the media are also changing. There is less government intervention in media, and the system is becoming more powerful and independent (Molleda and Moreno 2006). Mexican practitioners are following higher ethical and professional standards, but professionals in the Mexican Caribbean still complain about corruption and unprofessionalism (Molleda and Moreno 2006). Although personal relationships with media professionals are still important in Mexico, the pace of business means that the amount of personal contact required has declined. In the US, Mexico and other Latin American countries, business is being conducted at an accelerated pace. As a result, media people in Mexico now ask for news releases to be e-mailed to them. Interviews are being done over the phone because reporters want fast answers (Garrett 2005). Mexican public relations professionals also continue to rely on newspapers as an outlet, because there are a lot of them published in Mexico City and elsewhere.

Outside media relations, there are other developments in Mexican public relations. Companies are increasingly responding to stakeholders, for example. Chiquita Brands International, the once notorious United Fruit Company, now lets the Rain Forest Alliance certify its farms' environmental practices. As in other Latin American regions, public relations in Mexico continues to move beyond publicity and media relations functions (Garrett 2005). Research delineates the shift from government to industry representation, the move from press agentry and public information models to more research and counsel, centralization trends, and the evolving roles of practitioners from technicians to managers (Johnson 2005b).

Colombia

Colombia is a good example of how some Latin American countries are trying to balance public relations with socio-economic and political environments in transition. Colombia faces a non-official civil war against guerrillas, paramilitaries and drug traffickers (Molleda and Suárez 2005). Practitioners must keep a low profile because of security concerns, compete with other professions seeking public relations work, and encounter a lack of trust in institutions owing to the country's delicate political situation (Molleda and Suárez 2005). Public relations in Colombia really began in the 1990s under the Gaviria administration, which sought to modernize the state and privatize industry. Transnational corporations have helped develop public relations in the country. Before the economic downturn in 1999, public relations grew significantly between 1996 and 1998. Following the economic downturn, competition for business among agencies has become fierce, as there tends to be more supply than demand for public relations services.

Practitioners belonging to the Colombian Center of Public Relations and Organizational Communication (CECORP) offered a number of insights about the challenges facing the Colombian public relations practice. First, high levels of poverty and illiteracy affect the types of messages publics may receive. To compound the problem, technology and resources for communication are often scarce, though public relations resources may increase in light of funds administered to NGOs through the "Plan Colombia" economic aid program. Another problem the Colombian public relations profession encounters is a lack of trust in organizations and apathy toward civil engagement following the failures of previous government administrations. Professionals also note that government relations continue to be influenced by the personalities of administrators rather than by institutions, programs, or issues. Bids for projects may be tainted by corruption. Greater community engagement is needed, as is a reduction in violence and an increase in public safety, in order for the profession to become stabilized. As a result of all of these daunting challenges, public relations professionals in Colombia must participate in nation-building, encourage peace and organizational change, and develop campaigns to increase trust in organizations (Molleda and Suárez 2005). These practitioners face a tall order in implementing public relations progress.

In a study conducted among public relations professionals working in Colombia and Venezuela for a Latin American branch of a transnational corporation, professionals noted that they must perform a careful balancing act (Molleda and Suárez 2005). Venezuela, for example, seeks the globalization of its markets amidst high government intervention. Professionals in these two countries must adapt their organizations' cultures to their country's particular socio-economic and political environment. They must simultaneously act as change agents seeking to reduce social conflicts and forward democracy. As a result, public relations professionals in these arrangements often try to create more ethical, transparent and participative models of public relations practice. They are aware of the need for alliance-building with various public, private and non-profit sectors to ease poverty and social inequalities. Practitioners in these environments must take care to avoid corruption, bribes, nepotism and propaganda. Doing so helps boost legitimacy of their organizations within the countries and helps achieve good relationships with publics. Although public relations professionals often choose to keep a low profile in these countries and seek to dissociate themselves from politically discredited practices, they also feel a need to work outside the margins of local and national politics to help move toward more participative and ethical democratic systems in the respective countries.

Central America

Although many public relations firms and multinational companies target Brazil, Argentina, Mexico and Venezuela, it is important to include Central America as a region with a rapidly growing market. Burson-Marsteller has a Guatemalan affiliate, Ketchum has affiliates in Costa Rica and Panama, Porter-Novelli has affiliates in Costa Rica and El Salvador, and Fleishman-Hillard in Costa Rica and Guatemala. Katz (1998) notes that public relations opportunities in Costa Rica are probably the most advanced, with Panama and Guatemala gaining ground. In fact, Costa Rica has ten or twelve public relations firms and several universities that offer public relations degrees. Nevertheless, public relations may still be misunderstood in Central America. Katz points out that the first "public relations" executives popped up in local governments and were sometimes more concerned with misleading the public than with building relationships with citizens. As a result, journalists and governments may have an uneasy relationship with public relations practitioners. Further, advertising firms still dominate public relations firms in the region. Businesses may need to be educated as to the differences between the two practices. Even with these challenges, Central America offers a wide variety of industries as potential clients, with many foreign-owned industries such as airlines, high-tech, telecommunications and healthcare firms entering the region.

Questions for discussion

1. Do problems of inequality, unemployment and poverty in Latin America need to be addressed before public relations can flourish? Can public relations help with any of these problems?
2. Think of your home country. Are social components of cultural activities and social activities important to public relations as they are in Latin America?

3. Public relations as a profession in Latin America is still searching for legitimacy. What measures should Latin American practitioners take to make public relations a legitimate practice?
4. Among the specific areas discussed (Brazil, Mexico, Colombia and Central America), which country do you think is most developed in public relations? Which country is least developed? What can each country learn from the others?

Important issues in Latin American public relations

Now that we have briefly explored public relations practices in several Latin American countries, we turn to examining issues that are important to the region as a whole. Knowledge of this range of issues should help students get a better grasp of the overall public relations practice in the region. Indeed, public relations firms and practitioners have a number of challenges to consider when embracing this vibrant market.

Corporate social responsibility

Similar to other regions discussed in this textbook, Latin American citizens increasingly expect corporations to exercise social responsibility. In Brazil, for example, a recent study revealed that a third of Brazilian consumers expect companies to help improve society, though product pricing still remains important (Economic Intelligence Unit Ltd 2002). Unilever Corporation, for example, launched the Unilever Institute in São Paulo to boost perceptions of its social responsibility in the country. Unilever will invest US$1 million to support public and private initiatives (Economic Intelligence Unit Ltd 2002).

Companies based in Latin America are also increasingly realizing the importance of cleaner production techniques. Implementing cleaner practices boosts perceptions of corporate social responsibility as well as enhancing business efficiency. Chile, for example, is becoming a leader in the initiative that believes cleaner production can also boost export competitiveness (Metcalfe 2001). Similarly, industry-signed pacts in Colombia encourage economic competition by regularly publishing individual business improvements in environmental operating practices. Metcalfe (2001) reports that the Internet is another source to help Latin American countries boost clean production, but language barriers sometimes keep this resource from serving some of the most traditional, often highest-polluting, industries.

If locally based companies are beginning to address corporate social responsibility concerns, foreign investors and multinational corporations often face additional expectations from the region's citizens. In Latin America, even foreign investors with strong corporate reputations often face an initial degree of distrust from local consumers (Luer and Tilson 1996). Many multinational companies have long attempted to demonstrate a commitment to the countries in which they invest. In 1975, the Xerox Corporation tried to demonstrate its understanding of social concerns by supporting educational programs in Latin America (PRSA). It made a US$1 million grant to create a Latin American version of "Sesame Street", for example. Xerox felt that the children's television series could garner attention of parents, educators, opinion leaders and government leaders. It launched a multimedia campaign to help support awareness of the series in Latin American countries.

Similarly, Texaco Latin America/West Africa began a business and government relations program in Argentina and Uruguay to establish working relationships. These countries were reluctant to open their markets to the foreign corporation at first. Texaco, working with Bruce Rubin Associates, sponsored a visit by Miami's New World Symphony to the two countries. The New World Symphony is a training orchestra comprising young people. Concerts, along with media tours, receptions, dinners, meetings and the like, were designed to create relationships between Texaco executives and Argentinian and Uruguayan business and government representatives (PRSA). The orchestra visit and related activities resulted in positive news coverage, and positioned Texaco as "an important partner of the Argentinean and Uruguayan people" (PRSA 1990, p. 2). Texaco was able to open dialogs with Uruguay and Argentina that reaffirmed its planned investment.

Tilson (2004) warns that multinational companies need to make an extra CSR effort because improving telecommunication infrastructures, the development of business, and the development of public relations may be exacerbating unemployment, underemployment and poverty in Latin America. As Latin American economies become privatized, as in the case of Peru and Ecuador, the interests of élite and foreign investors may be favored over those of the citizens (Tilson 2004). Peru may have privatized its telecommunications, mining operations, electricity and oil industries, for example, but 40 percent of Peruvians lived in poverty as of 1994. Similarly, Ecuador is pursuing privatization and free-market reforms but ranks among the worst in terms of income distribution, with 35 percent of its citizens living in poverty. It is up to corporations operating in these environments to demonstrate their commitment to national success beyond economic gains, as pointed out earlier in Chapter 6 with the Shell Oil example.

Sidebar: Botnia in Uruguay – lessons in responding to cultural differences

Botnia is a Finland-based pulp producer and the largest foreign investor in Uruguay. In November 2007, after years of protests, diplomatic and governmental tensions, and public scrutiny, Botnia opened a controversial pulp mill in the country. The company's plant is predicted to create 8,000 jobs in southwest Uruguay and boost the country's gross national product by 1.6 percent. Even in light of these admirable gains for the Uruguayan economy, the controversy over the pulp plant shows no sign of stopping. Why does Botnia continue to face such difficulty as it expands its business into Latin American markets?

According to Ethical Corporation (2006), the company made three critical public relations misjudgments. All involve misunderstanding the significance of culture in successfully doing business in new areas. First, although Botnia tried to begin dialogues with non-profit environmental groups in the region, its efforts were not met with success. According to Annikki Rintala, Vice-President for Communications for Botnia: "We discuss with all the environmental groups who are interested in our operations. It is very much part of the culture here in Europe." Botnia sent letters to Uruguayan non-governmental groups at the outset of the project, yet the response was not positive. In fact, more than sixty environmental groups sent an open letter to the country's newspapers opposing the proposed mills. Next, Botnia appears to have overestimated citizens' level of trust in the private sector. Like other South American countries, Uruguay is recovering from a recession believed to be largely caused by foreign investors. Although Botnia commissioned studies to assess environmental impact, and relied on both independent Uruguayan experts as well as its own representatives, citizens were not reassured. That Botnia had used its own representatives in the study, while typical in the European region, was not acceptable in Latin American business operations. Finally, Botnia seems to have underestimated the political climate between Uruguay and Argentina. As the plant will sit across the border from Argentina, that country's residents, even including its president, Nestor Kirchner, have been protesting against the mill and forming blockades into Uruguay, stalling tourist revenue. The spat between the countries over the mill eventually reached the International Court of Justice in The Hague. The dispute may even harm relationships within Mercosur, the trade bloc of which both Argentina and Uruguay are members.

On paper, Botnia's plans to open the plant were legally, technically and financially sound. It embraced an open communication style with government, with media and with citizens. It held public meetings with citizens in both countries. It openly provided information to governmental bodies. Its Vice-President of Communications maintains: "From the beginning, we decided to create an open communication atmosphere in Uruguay and surrounding areas." Nevertheless, environmentalists still protest, tensions remain high between Uruguay and Argentina, and some foreign investors are cautious. The Botnia case emphasizes that, even when corporations plan appropriate communication campaigns and consider cultural norms, difficulties may still arise. In the coming years, it will be interesting to see how Botnia continues to manage the challenge of conducting public relations in a new region with different expectations.

Compiled from Ethical Corporation; see www.ethicalcorp.com for more information about this case study.

Addressing cultural differences and sensitivities

If practitioners need to consider responsibly Latin America's future and the consequences of US involvement to address CSR concerns, they also need to be culturally sensitivite to boost campaign success (Luer and Tilson 1996). Practitioners must keep in mind that strategies and tactics must be adapted to cultural, political and economic differences (Kotcher 1998a). Personal contact and building relationships with media and target audiences is very important. Knowing local customs is also imperative; for example, putting out a Spanish-language news release in Brazil would be a major blunder in this Portuguese-speaking nation. The region is also vast, requiring public relations professionals to integrate and coordinate campaigns across time zones. In order to coordinate campaigns across the region, partnerships between public relations agencies, exemplified by the WORLDCOM group, for example, help companies facilitate broad campaigns but implement tactics with a local focus.

There are other cultural considerations for public relations success. First, successful public relations in Latin America often requires a physical presence there. Along with language, cultural and social relationships, being there is very important. Regionally based public relations firms must be the "eyes and ears" for clients hundreds of miles away in home countries (Kotcher 1998a). Kotcher (1998a) also emphasizes the need for connected, coordinated communication among public relations agencies. Communication programs must contain regional flexibility. An example is seen in the launch of the Delta Air Lines service to seven new Latin American destinations. Ketchum public relations worked in its US and Latin American offices to generate local and regional media coverage. CNN en Español brought the story regionally, with many regional daily newspapers covering the story as well.

Unfortunately, Latin America's cultural environment is still often overlooked even as the region enjoys significant growth. Oliva (2007) points out that, in Latin America, how something is done may be just as important as – and sometimes more important than – what has to be done. He reminds students and practitioners that Latin American countries are proud of their cultural and heritage differences, warning, for example, that Spanish in Mexico is spoken differently than in Venezuela. Oliva (2007) offers three simple steps that organizations can follow when organizing their communication needs: (1) identifying strategic initiatives, (2) assessing regional resources, and (3) defining a path for local participation and contribution. Finally, Oliva (2007) notes that Latin America may work at a different pace from that which US practitioners may be used to. He recommends not rushing or imposing time standards and working to give local talent the opportunity to participate in regional activities and initiatives.

Several companies exemplify these attempts to be culturally sensitive while maximizing business success. JC Penney balances local tastes with American desire for multinational business success. JC Penney stresses local characteristics and incomes in its stores along the US–Mexico border and plans to open more stores in Mexico (Luer and Tilson 1996). As it does so, however, it must be careful not to erode Mexican identities and traditions. In another example, for the Latin American launch of Atkins Nutritionals, the creators of the wildly popular "Atkins Diet" and related products in the US relied on a public relations agency to earn advocates for the diet through education (Creamer and Wentz 2004). It sought to win over Latin American doctors and nutritionists in a region still dominated by staples such as rice and tortillas. Creamer and Wentz (2004) recommend this strategy to companies seeking a Latin American launch of products. Sometimes targeting influencers first and then seeking brand awareness among publics makes the most sense.

Addressing cultural preferences is becoming more difficult because Latin American public relations is really changing. It can be difficult to manage public relations on a country-by-country basis because of the increasing flow of news and information across national borders (Garrett 2005). People watching CNN en Español in Mexico City, Santiago, Buenos Aires and Los Angeles frequently see the same story. Pan-regional Latin American magazines may also circulate the same stories. Confusingly, similar products may be offered in different countries, but the brands may stand for different things in each (Garrett 2005). As a result, some multinational companies are now trying to coordinate the flow of information and manage public relations on a pan-regional basis, but they still must understand local markets and local media. As public relations executive Jeffrey Sharlach explains: "The challenge is to balance the issues in the local markets and cultures with the global messaging and the global brand reputation" (Garrett 2005, p. 38).

In essence, then, reaching people of diverse cultures requires deep understanding (Figueredo 2005). Strategies should highlight cultural characteristics and show a commitment to cultural sensitivity in a community. A large pipeline project in Peru, for instance, needs to address the concerns of indigenous people as well as of interest groups.

Figueredo (2005) notes that the world's top consumer brands include strong community-relations efforts to reach consumers, including Coke, Pepsi, McDonald's, P&G and HP. Community-based public relations strategies conducted in the local language and working with grassroots groups, in-store promotions and websites can be very effective. In addition to these observations, Figueredo (2005) offers five suggestions that will help public relations professionals target multicultural consumers:

1.   Make sure the team understands the customs and values of the target group.
2.   Make sure messages are culturally relevant.
3.   Multicultural consumers can be very loyal if targeted correctly.
4.   In language communication campaigns build loyalty across targeted publics.
5.   Community representative spokespeople are effective in establishing connections.

These suggestions are further complicated when companies seek to implement campaigns on a global scale. When clients seek to originate a global campaign, particularly in Latin America, public relations staff needs to understand the local business and its issues as well as possess a global perspective. As Lou Huffman, CEO of the Huffman Agency, points out, a lot of "American-itis" can negatively influence campaign execution: "So many of the decision makers [in public relations] are American and you see a lot of them actually have in their titles 'global' or 'international' public relations, but they don't really have the knowledge base and see things strictly as an American – that's something we are consistently dealing with" (Hunt 2004, p. 27).

Media relations

A discussion of cultural sensitivity easily connects to the importance of understanding how to conduct successful media relations in Latin America. Practitioners should keep in mind a number of tips when conducting media relations in the region. The media in Latin America are changing from a pay-for-coverage system to one committed to journalistic ethics, objectivity and responsibility. In terms of understanding media relations protocols, Latin American journalists are no longer paid in exchange for coverage and avoid going off the record.

In addition to these rules of thumb, keeping both cultural and language differences in mind is crucial for successful media relations. For example, Maza (2004) points out that a public relations person should not tell Latin American media that he has a solution for impotence problems, as this statement may be off-putting to Latin American masculinity. In addition, being flexible when setting up interview times is a good idea, as reporters may have a more fluid relationship with time. A 10 a.m. interview may end up being conducted at 10.30 a.m. or later. Having samples of products if you are working with consumer media is also smart because reporters may expect to receive a sample of the promoted product. Further, do not assume reporters will have background information about your company. Reporters should be given CDs of corporate information rather than assuming that they will visit your corporate website before an interview. Knowing specific information about particular Latin American countries is beneficial, of course, rather than gathering data about the region as a whole. Being aware of the specific political and social issues of a country is especially important. Not surprisingly, knowing some Spanish phrases is useful, especially if no one on the public relations team speaks Spanish.

Diplomacy and government relations

Particularly in a region with historically strong governmental control over public relations activities and success, conducting sound diplomacy and government relations initiatives is important.

Many foreign governments seek to strengthen diplomatic relationships with a variety of countries in Latin America to boost positive perceptions of their government's policies and leaders. Karen Hughes, the Bush administration's chief image strategist, for example, is working to boost the Latin American region's view of Washington and the United States. Hughes points out that, while 71 percent of Latin American élites have a positive view of the United States, many believe that Washington is ignoring the region. Indeed, another regional poll showed that three out of every five Latin Americans distrust the United States. Critics also charge that US diplomats do not understand the realities of the region. Hughes works to reverse these perceptions by underscoring the messages that the US and Latin American countries are friends and neighbors that can work together to help their citizens. Says Hughes: "We recognize that we have problems in our own country and in many countries throughout Latin America that are similar" (Bachelet 2006, p. 1).

Nevertheless, as many countries in the region have started to pull away from US free-market policies, Hughes has a tough job. She has implemented a variety of strategies and tactics to address the image of the US among Latin Americans. She increased the region's student exchange programs, allowed US ambassadors to speak out more, deployed new public relations specialists, and revised aid programs to the region's countries (Bachelet 2006). Regarding aid, for example, Hughes notes that aid programs need a "more visible and higher profile" (Bachelet 2006). Hughes has also organized more State Department public diplomacy officials to manage public relations in countries such as Ecuador, Nicaragua, Venezuela and Bolivia. Further, diplomats in various Latin American countries now do not have to ask permission from the US government to speak to the media. Hughes's rapid-response unit provides guidelines from the State Department designed to help US diplomats respond quickly to international news events. As she notes about this initiative: "I think it's important that they understand what the people of Latin America are waking up and hearing and reading about. What that does is tries to get the United States government, literally, on the same page" (Bachelet 2006, p. 3).

Of course, government and diplomacy efforts are not only conducted by countries seeking closer ties with Latin American governments. A variety of Latin American governments also work to strengthen their ties to the US and other countries. To help ensure that their countries participate in privatization and economic development efforts in beneficial ways, for example, many Latin American countries rely upon their embassies to represent their countries' interests and needs. Zaharna and Villalobos (2000) note that, while Latin American countries may have very different public relations goals, many successfully use their embassies to forward their countries' strategic promotional goals. For example, the Mexican embassy helped to spread awareness of the country as an emerging democracy and tourist destination. Colombia's embassy has been working on improving that country's image as ruled by drug tsars. Argentina's embassy uses the appeal of its national exports, beef and the tango, to cultivate a positive image in the US. Of course, government relations in Latin American countries are not limited to diplomatic activities. Venezuela's efforts include an advertising campaign in *The Economist*, *The New Yorker* and *Roll Call* that features the country's commitment to its citizens. One ad features the message, for example, "In the past, Venezuela's oil wealth benefited a few. Today, it benefits a *million*," encouraging readers to visit the campaign's website to learn more (Miller 2004). The Colombian Coffee Growers Association and Colombian flower growers hired a public relations firm to lobby for higher coffee prices, promote a better Colombian image, and ease export regulations on flowers (Strenski 1996). In essence, diplomats and government relations representatives from these and other Latin American countries work to gain the attention of American policy-makers, media and public.

Alternatively, sometimes government relations between two countries can sour and result in public relations campaigns that may boost tensions. For example, the Mexican government, angered by a US proposal to build a wall along the US–Mexican border to keep out migrants, has begun a radio campaign urging Mexican workers to denounce human rights violations in the US (Stevenson 2005). Meanwhile, it has also hired an American public relations agency, Allyn & Company, to improve the country's image among Americans. The firm's president, Rob Allyn, underscores the importance of moderating views about migration among the two countries: "If people in the US and Canada had an accurate view of the success of democracy, political stability and economic prosperity in Mexico, it would improve their views on specific bilateral issues like immigration and border security" (Stevenson 2005, p. 1). Nevertheless, the Mexican government has increased its defense of migrants in its campaigns and has recruited US churches, communities and businesses to oppose the wall proposal. The immigration issue and border concerns may call for more attention from public relations professionals, as many Mexicans are saddened and insulted by the US response. Some call for their government to take stronger action to fight against the US border proposals: "Our president should oppose that wall and make them stop it, at all costs. More than just insulting, it's terrible" (Stevenson 2005, p. 1). The conflict between Mexico and the United States over immigration thus highlights the challenges that can be involved in contemporary international government relations.

Tourism

Latin American efforts in boosting tourism of the region echo some of the diplomatic strategies discussed above. Tourism is big business in countries such as Mexico and now Uruguay, Bolivia, Chile and Ecuador are also increasing their efforts. Countries such as Ecuador, Colombia and Brazil work with public relations agencies to create public relations campaigns to boost tourism. Chile promotes itself as an upscale European-style destination renowned for wine, skiing and more (Strenski 1996). Already, demand for seats on flights to the region's cities is up 17 percent a year for Rio de Janeiro in Brazil and up 15 percent in Chile. Public relations professionals in other countries, such as the UK, argue that more tourists would visit Latin American countries if these countries' tourist boards established a more consistent presence in the targeted country. Some argue that tourist boards should also hire more experienced staff to boost tourism in the region: "Tourist boards sometimes seem to be a dumping ground for people's relatives, who haven't got a clue [and who tend to ignore international markets]. I have sat in a hotel in Rio and seen a TV advert for Brazil – but that ad isn't on in the UK" (Travel Weekly 2006, p. 2).

Employment and evaluation

Just as other regions confront particular topics in the public relations profession, Latin America works to address particular concerns. For example, women public relations executives in Latin America also struggle with issues of promotion as do women executives in other countries. One study by Mercer Human Resources Consulting in 2006 revealed that Latin America is the least-advanced region in the world when it comes to having women in powerful corporate positions (Rueda 2007). Still, more are becoming heads of companies and breaking new ground in attaining senior-level positions. Experts recommend companies work to ensure more fairness in companywide positions by dealing with work, family and educational challenges to get women *and* men in senior-level positions. One female Australian executive's comments about the challenges in hiring that face

Latin America describe the issue well: "My most important achievement has been to maintain a balance between my life and my work on par as I progress with new challenges at work. The company allows me to be flexible and work at distance through technology and remote connectivity" (Rueda 2007, p. 21).

Public relations evaluation methods and procedures are of concern in the region as they are elsewhere. Strenski (1996) points out that measuring the results of a campaign is difficult in a region where it is sometimes challenging even to reach the intended target audience. Nevertheless, evaluation methods are growing more sophisticated. The Jeffrey Group's system called PubTracker, for example, monitors media in sophisticated ways. Rather than tracking the mentions of the word "Kodak" and reporting that the company name appeared 925 times in Mexico during the month of November, its system allows clients to know "how many times certain messages appeared, and whether each mention was about digital cameras, sending photographs, and so on" (Garrett 2005, p. 39). One Latin American public relations practitioner, Jeff Hunt, warns that concerns about evaluating the effects of public relations are increasing worldwide: "There's a lot of pressure on us to quantify value" (Hunt 2004, p. 26). Public relations CEOs around the world continue to note that there can be an inherently unquantifiable quality in public relations work; yet the industry must work to prove it can move business results significantly (Hunt 2004).

Questions for discussion

1. What benefits do foreign companies have when practicing CSR in Latin America? Do you think all companies should be socially responsible?
2. If your company were expanding to Latin America, what measures would you take to ensure respect for cultural sensitivities?
3. What issues should one consider when implementing a diplomacy or government relations campaign in Latin America?

Conclusions and implications

As you can see, public relations in Latin America is exciting, challenging and growing. Several years ago, some scholars viewed the region as a "perpetual land of the future", meaning that public relations in Latin America had promise but faced seemingly insurmountable challenges (Tilson and Alozie 2004). Latin America's political instability, social problems and economic inequality seemed to make pan-region professional public relations development questionable. Although there were strong pockets of practice in certain countries like Brazil, some worried that other countries did not perhaps have the infrastructure and professionals needed to implement sound public relations practices.

This chapter has shown that Latin America's public relations future may indeed be here. We have examined how several countries have been developing the profession and looked at some of the common challenges across the region. Brazil and Mexico provide a level of public relations development on par with other industrialized, privatized markets throughout the world. Strategies and tactics used in both countries are similar to what we have come to expect in fully realized, well-developed public relations campaigns. Meanwhile, countries such as Colombia continue to seek the practice's realization but face ongoing difficulties in providing the environment needed for public relations to flourish. Perhaps that, too, will develop in the coming years. Public relations practitioners in Colombia and other struggling countries should be commended for trying to develop public relations in ways that honor their cultures, address citizens' concerns, and work for business and social integration.

In this way, the Latin American School of Public Relations philosophy is truly an apt description and prescription for the discipline in this region. We have looked at how this philosophy acts as a guiding force for many practitioners and serves as a rich source of research and scholarship that can contribute to the study of international public relations. If practitioners worldwide follow the Latin American School of Public Relations tenets in their practice, the profession as a whole should benefit. The focus on increasing ethical standards, serving as change agents in communities, and working for social goals along with business objectives is a worthy guide to follow in cultivating sound international practice.

Finally, examining topics such as media relations, government relations and corporate social responsibility in Latin American public relations provides the student with a sense of commonality and connectedness in the practice from one culture to the next. Seeing how practitioners around the world are concerned with similar issues means that international public relations is developing a set of standards and common "best practices" that helps to define the profession and correct global misperceptions. In Latin America and elsewhere, public relations is not just media relations, publicity and image-building. Instead, the examples detailed in this chapter highlight the work practitioners do to represent the interests of both their clients and their communities. This overview, then, should point to a bright future for international public relations.

Featured biography: Joe Carleo

Joseph A. Carleo, APR, is the founder and owner of an international boutique public relations agency, Advanced Language and Media Services, in suburban Charlotte, North Carolina. Carleo's informal education in international public relations began at a very early age with his family, where he constantly heard other languages besides English. Carleo speaks English, Spanish and French fluently. He received formal education at State University of New York/New Paltz and has over twenty years' experience as a public relations practitioner and broadcaster. Carleo is proud that he was able to recognize in the early 1980s that public relations would be his major career focus, though international public relations was very different then. Communications channels were fairly limited, and certainly there was no e-mail or Web access. US television included only the "big three" networks and clearly none of the new media communications opportunities that we can use today. Carleo remembers that, in the early days, business executives did not consider issues of language and diversity to be important. There was little concern about or interest in non-English-speaking audiences and organizations. Fortunately, today that outlook has changed completely. "Now, business leaders and communicators are asking me about effective ways to help them communicate with international audiences better," he continues.

Another professional achievement of which Carleo is proud is his accreditation in public relations (APR) received from the Public Relations Society of America (PRSA). Carleo says accreditation recognizes a practitioner's dedication to the public relations discipline and his or her goal of higher professionalism and knowledge. He is also proud of the opportunity to lead the PRSA South East District as its Diversity Chair for two years and as a national leader of the Diversity Committee. The PRSA South East District comprises eleven chapters in five states striving to attract more diverse practitioners who better reflect the US demographics today. Carleo has other experience working with diverse audiences. For example, he has worked successfully with Spanish-speaking audiences and received a Telly® Award as the producer of *Charlotte Hoy* (*Charlotte Today*), a Spanish program recently aired on a regional public television outlet. He also worked with one of the most famous professional baseball players in an outreach effort with Latino children. Carleo's firm helped this internationally known star by translating two inspirational books in Spanish designed to inspire young Latinos to make great life choices.

His work with Latinos has helped him develop a deep understanding of the importance of carefully reaching this audience in today's global marketplace. "Latinos are the fastest-growing US demographic group with huge purchasing power that will be around $1 trillion in 2010 and also they'll have greater political power in the future," Carleo maintains. He suggests that, when targeting Latinos, international public relations practitioners should do in-depth research about their family values, purchasing habits, attitudes and other areas important to the campaign. He recommends that public relations professionals working with Latino audiences should know the Spanish language and culture well. To succeed with Latino and other cultural groups, it is necessary to avoid communicating with "cultural blinders". Carleo suggests that practitioners ask themselves whether the "message offends Latinos or other internationals (even inadvertently)". He recommends doing focus groups with them before spending millions on a potentially wrong strategy or tactic. He says to make certain the message is delivered in a credible way that changes public opinion and gains public trust for the client or organization, and he notes that sometimes these practices are not in place:

> I sometimes receive advertising spots or public service announcements where the US ad agency is looking for a TV re-voice project in Spanish. The sad part is that the on-screen talent is non-Latino – so the audience is listening in Spanish and probably looking at Anglos. That is a real communications disconnect and makes the client look bad to Latinos.

When working with Latinos and other international groups, public relations practitioners should be able to communicate and service their clients effectively in today's global world, and globalization provides many opportunities and potential pitfalls. Carleo points out that, "on the upside, globalization often brings lower product prices to US consumers and sometimes allows more US product sales in other countries. On the downside, globalization brings such problems as outsourcing US labor, worker abuse outside America or possible product safety issues." There are other factors besides the product price that have to be considered in discussing the pros and cons of globalization. Carleo says that "products may be low priced, but if there is a recall because of safety concerns, there are at least two potentially negative results. The first result would be the very likely multi-million dollar cost of the recall, and the second is a badly tarnished image of the company – and the second is often far more damaging than the recall cost," he adds. A case in point is the toy recalls from China because of lead paint. That is why public relations practitioners should understand that working in international public relations there is a great opportunity and also the responsibility to be that "guiding light" – giving solid advice to a client or boss. Besides providing highly professional services to clients, public relations practitioners should increasingly encourage corporate citizenship to gain and maintain public trust. "Before the international consumer will buy your widget or trust your firm," he says, "your company must first earn respect in the marketplace, especially the increasingly international one," he continues.

Carleo cites four important areas on which students interested in international public relations should focus. "First you should be committed to life-long learning – whether it is a graduate degree or APR accreditation (or both!) and demonstrate your knowledge to your boss or clients." It is also important to give trustworthy and ethical advice based on research and a professional communication plan that includes evaluation. Knowledge of another language besides English and familiarity with different cultures is a very significant part of international public relations, too. The last area is to gain international experience while you complete your degree at a college or university. Many schools offer a semester or year of international study, and Carleo recommends that students take advantage of this great opportunity.

Recommended websites

CONFIARP http://www.confiarp.org.ve/

Instituto Universitario de Relaciones Públicas (IUDERP) http://www.iuderp.edu.ve/

Burson-Marsteller http://www.burson-marsteller.com

CECORP http://www.cecorp.org/main.htm

Ethical Corporation http://www.ethicalcorp.com/

Brazil Public Relations Consultants Association http://www.bprca.be/

References

Bachelet, P., 2006. Bush aide seeks better US. image in Latin America: Karen Hughes, President Bush's international image guru, is trying to improve the way Latin Americans view the United States. *Miami Herald*, April 18.

Creamer, M. and Wentz, L., 2004. Atkins PR targets Latin America docs. *Advertising Age*, 75 (34), p. 13.

Economist Intelligence Unit Ltd, 2002. Marketing watch. *Business Latin America*, June 24, p. 7.

Epley, J. S., 2003. *Perspectives from 17 Countries on International Public Relations*. WORLDCOM Public Relations Group.

Ethical Corporation, 2006. Latin America: Botnia in Uruguay: the lessons of culture class, [online]. Available at: www.ethicalcorp.com [accessed February 20, 2008].

Figueredo, F., 2005. Opening the doors: reaching multicultural consumers through relevant communications campaigns. *Public Relations Strategist*, fall.

Freitag, A., 2004. Peru's Fujimori: The campaign to sell the administration's neoliberal policies. In D. Tilson and E. Alozie, eds, *Toward the Common Good: Perspectives in International Public Relations*. Boston, Mass.: Pearson.

Gannon, M., 2001. *Working across Cultures: Applications and Exercises*. Thousand Oaks, Calif.: Sage.

Garrett, K. A., 2005. A new PR vision: the Jeffrey Group focuses on local needs, brand messaging. *Business Mexico*, March, pp. 36–40.

Hunt, J., 2004. Agencies take on the world. *Media Asia*, September 10, pp. 26–8.

Johnson, M., 2005a. Mexican public relations in the United States: international public relations in the pre- and post-NAFTA periods. International Communication Association Annual Meeting, New York, 1–31.

Johnson, M., 2005b. Five decades of Mexican public relations in the United States: from propaganda to strategic counsel. *Public Relations Review, 31*, 11–20.

Katz, M. E., 1998. A PR market grows in Central America. *Public Relations Tactics*, August.

Kenny, E., 1999. Public relations agency predicts continued expansion in Latin America. *Miami Herald*, March 22.

Kotcher, R. L., 1998a. The changing role of PR in Latin America. *Public Relations Tactics*, 5 (3), p. 26.

Kotcher, R. L. 1998b. Public relations south of the border. *Public Relations Strategist*, 4 (1), pp. 26–7.

Kunsch, M., 2007. Professional and academic institutionalization of public relations in Brazil and Latin America. International Communication Association Annual Meeting, New York, 1–31.

Lemmon, W. S., 1958. Our public relations responsibilities in Latin America. *Public Relations Journal*, June, pp. 3–5.

Lieras, M., 2007. Latin America's electoral turn: left, right, and wrong. *Constellations*, 14 (3), pp. 398–408.

Luer, C. and Tilson, D., 1996. Latin American PR in the age of telecommunications, JC Penney and CNN. *Public Relations Quarterly*, summer, pp. 25–7.

Lynch, N., 2007. What the "left" means in Latin America now. *Constellations*, 14 (3), pp. 373–83.

Maza, J., 2004. Latin American and Hispanic media training: more than just "media training in Spanish". *Public Relations Tactics*, December.

Metcalfe, R., 2001. Latin America cleaning up its act: bottom-line arguments are selling industry on environmentally sound production. *Business Latin America*, November 22, p. 2.

Miller, J. J., 2004. Friends of Hugo: Venezuela's Castroite boss has all the usual US supporters. *National Review*, December 27, pp. 36–7.

Molleda, J. C., 2000. International paradigms: the Latin American school of public relations. *Journalism Studies*, 2 (4), pp. 513–30.

Molleda, J. C. and Athaydes, A., 2003. Public relations licensing in Brazil: evolution and the views of professionals. *Public Relations Review*, 29, pp. 271–9.

Molleda, J. C. and Ferguson, M. A., 2004. Public relations roles in Brazil: hierarchy eclipses gender differences. *Journal of Public Relations Research*, 16 (4), pp. 327–51.

Molleda, J. C. and Moreno, A., 2006. Transitional socioeconomic and political environments of public relations in Mexico. *Public Relations Review*, 32, pp. 104–9.

Molleda, J. C. and Suárez, A. M., 2005. Challenges in Colombia for public relations professionals: a qualitative assessment of the economic and political environments. *Public Relations Review*, 31, pp. 21–9.

Newsom, D., 2004. Singapore poised for prominence in public relations among emerging democracies. In. D. Tilson and E. Alozie, eds, *Toward the Common Good: Perspectives in International Public Relations*. Boston, Mass.: Pearson.

Oliva, M. A., 2007. Capitalize on local flair: implement global corporate guidelines that make sense for a Latin American workforce. *Communication World*, March–April, pp. 18–19.

Public Relations Society of America, 1975. [Campaign profile], Xerox Corporation, [online]. Available at: www.prsa.org [accessed January 23, 2008].

Public Relations Society of America, 1990. [Campaign profile], The Texaco New World Symphony Tour of Latin America, [online]. Available at: www.prsa.org [accessed January 23, 2008].

Public Relations Society of America, 1999. Lucent branding success in Latin America: an integrated approach, [online]. Available at: www.prsa.org [accessed January 23, 2008].

Public Relations Society of America, 2007. PRSA celebrates lifetime achievements of global PR leaders: Nigeria's Mike Okereke and Mexico's Manuel Alonso M. receive 2006 Atlas Award. *Public Relations Tactics*.

Reed, J. M., 1968. Latin America: a status report. *Public Relations Quarterly*, spring, pp. 31–3.

Rueda, M., 2007. Breaking glass: women executives in Latin America are moving ahead, and in positions traditionally held by men. *Latin Trade*, August, pp. 20–2.

Shaker, F., 1970. The multinational corporation: the new imperialism? *Colombia Journal of World Business*, November–December, pp. 80–4.

Sharpe, M. and Simões, R., 1996. Public relations performance in South and Central America. In H. Culbertson and N. Chen (eds), *International Public Relations*. Mahwah, NJ: Lawrence Erlbaum, pp. 273–97.

Simões, R., 1992. Public relations as a political function. *Public Relations Review*, 18, 189–200.

Stevenson, M., 2005. Mexico retaliates for border wall plan. The Associated Press, [online]. Available at: www.breitbart.com [accessed February 19, 2008].

Strenski, J. B., 1996. The evolving practice of public relations in North and South America. *Public Relations Quarterly*, spring. pp. 27–8.

Tilson, D., 1996. The commodification of Latin America: a confluence of telecommunications, media and promotion. *World Communication*, 25, pp. 133–42.

Tilson, D., 2004. Privatization and government campaigning in Ecuador: caudillos, corruption, and chaos. In. D. Tilson and E. Alozie, eds, *Toward the Common Good: Perspectives in International Public Relations*. Boston, Mass.: Pearson.

Tilson, D. and Alozie, E. eds, 2004. *Toward the Common Good: Perspectives in International Public Relations*. Boston, Mass.: Pearson.

Travel Weekly, 2006. Time to awaken the sleeping giant. *Travel Weekly*, August 4.

Vale, N. P., 1978. Brazil, the economic giant of Latin America. *Public Relations Quarterly*, summer, pp. 12–14.

Zaharna, R. S. and Villalobos, J. C., 2000. A public relations tour of Embassy Row: the Latin diplomatic experience. *Public Relations Quarterly*, winter, pp. 33–7.

Chapter 12

Central and Eastern Europe

Contributed by: Ryszard Ławniczak and Gyorgy Szondi

Summary

This chapter addresses so-called transitional countries – countries of Central and Eastern Europe (CEE). Although CEE states exhibit different levels of economic and political development, there are many similarities among them based on history, culture and language. The region is characterized by common processes and trends such as democratization and development of a free-market economy. The chapter also discusses the development of pub-lic relations and its characteristics in CEE, and offers some practical tips for successfully communicating in the region. Poland, Hungary and Russia are studied in greater detail. The chapter presents a general overview of the countries, their cultural profiles, significant histor-ical, political, economic and social factors that influenced the development of public relations, as well as the current state of the profession.

Chapter goals

- Present the main characteristics of the region to help in understanding public relations prac-tice in CEE countries and appreciate national differences.
- Describe the cultural and historical dynamics that influence development of public relations in Poland, Hungary and Russia.
- Discuss the current state of and future trends for public relations in the region.

Emerging transition

In the eyes of many Western Europeans and US Americans, for decades Eastern Europe was a gray and homogenous area behind the Iron Curtain. Central and Eastern Europe (CEE) is more of a political and cultural concept than a geographical one. What all CEE countries have in common is the legacy of the former "communist system", as described in the US, or "real socialism" – as these countries used to refer to themselves. Today, these countries are called *transition countries* because of the political, economic and social transitions from a single-party political system toward a pluralistic society, and from a centrally planned economy toward a market economy. Countries of the region are at different stages of their transition, as some of them are already EU and NATO members while others are still struggling with the establishment of democracy and a market economy. Slovenia, Hungary, Lithuania, Slovakia, Poland, the Czech Republic, Estonia and Latvia became EU members in 2004, followed by Bulgaria and Romania in 2007. The Czech Republic, Hungary and Poland joined NATO in 1999, followed by Estonia, Latvia, Lithuania, Slovakia, Slovenia, Romania and Bulgaria in 2004. Albania, Belarus, Bosnia and Herzegovina, Croatia, Macedonia, Moldova, Montenegro, the Russian Federation, Serbia and Ukraine are still at earlier stages of their transition.

Although the transition started with the fall of the Berlin Wall in November 1989, the first cracks in communism date back to the 1980s when the Polish Solidarity Movement – the first independent trade union within the communist bloc – was recognized by the Polish communist government.

CEE boasts a great variety of peoples and languages; however, linguistically Slavic countries – such as Poland, Russia, Bulgaria, Slovakia, the Czech Republic, Slovenia and Ukraine – dominate the region with similar languages and religions. Slavic people can understand each other to varying degrees, and most of them are Roman Catholic except Russia, Ukraine and Bulgaria where the Orthodox Church dominates the religious scene. Russians, Ukrainians and Bulgarians use the Cyrillic alphabet, which is rather different from the Latin alphabet used by the other countries. The majority of CEE countries are Christian; however, Islam is practiced in former Yugoslav republics such as Montenegro, Bosnia and Herzegovina, as well as in Albania. Besides the Slavic languages, another language group is present in Eastern Europe: the Finno-Ugric language family, which is completely different from the Indo-European language family. Hungarian and Estonian belong to this group of languages, as does Finnish; these nations consider it offensive if they are mistaken for Slavic nations or languages. As for the political landscape, competitive democracies – underpinned by widespread political rights to participate in multiparty elections and an extensive range of civil liberties – have taken root in many but not all Central and Eastern European countries.

The transition countries of Central and Eastern Europe represent different levels of economic development. Table 12.1 summarizes key data from those countries that are members of the EU. The table includes Russia as well, as this chapter focuses on three CEE countries: Poland, Hungary and Russia.

So far, only Slovenia has been able to fulfil the so-called convergence criteria and joined the euro system in January 2007. The other new EU member states are planning to adopt the common European currency later, most probably between 2010 and 2012. EU membership means the following in economic terms for the CEE countries: opening of new markets for their products, services and labor force; inflow of capital from different EU funds; increased inflow of foreign investment. Altogether it should contribute to faster GNP growth and to prosperity. On the other hand,

TABLE 12.1 May 2007 World Audit

Country	Population (million)	GDP Per Capita (USD)	Press Freedom Rank	Corruption Rank
Bulgaria	7.3	10,700	45	47
Czech Republic	10.2	21,900	16	36
Estonia	1.3	20,300	11	21
Hungary	10.0	17,600	23	32
Latvia	2.3	16,000	18	39
Lithuania	3.6	15,300	16	36
Poland	38.5	14,300	29	51
Romania	22.3	9,100	56	71
Russia	141.4	12,200	123	105
Slovakia	5.4	18,200	20	39
Slovenia	2.0	23,400	23	23

Source: http://www.worldaudit.org

EU membership is imposing on them new, higher standards of democratization, privatization and liberalization of economic and political spheres.

Cultural profile

Despite decades of separation, Eastern Europeans do not differ significantly from Western Europeans. After CEE independence, many US and other Western companies came into the region, bringing with them new corporate cultures and management processes that have had an impact on the corporate cultures of many Eastern European companies. Hofstede conducted some research in Eastern Europe, but his findings are not always verified by local researchers. One example is Hungary, where several Hungarian researchers contradicted Hofstede's findings regarding individuality and power distance. Table 12.2 summarizes Hofstede's dimensions in some Eastern European countries.

Countries that ranked high on *uncertainty avoidance* (Poland, Russia) tend to have more written and formalised rules and many precise laws to avoid ambiguity. Citizens tend to be negative toward politicians, civil servants or the legal system, and the country is characterized by low participation in voluntary associations and movements. Xenophobia and ethnic prejudice are more likely to prevail in these countries, and religion and the church play important roles. In low uncertainty avoidance countries (Czech Republic, Estonia) people are more likely to take risks as uncertainty is a normal feature of life. Citizens tend to accept new products and technologies faster than in high uncertainty avoidance countries. A good example of this is Estonia, which has become an innovative and "high-tech" country: Internet use is the highest in Eastern Europe, and it is the home of Skype and e-government. Citizens of low uncertainty avoidance cultures are also more tolerant toward extreme ideas, foreigners and different belief systems.

TABLE 12.2 Power distance, degree of individualism, masculinity, uncertainty avoidance and long- versus short-term orientation scores among Central and Eastern European countries

Country	PD (Higher score = high Power Distance)	IDV (Higher score = high Individualism)	MAS (Higher score = high Masculinity)	UAI (Higher score = high Uncertainty Avoidance)	LTO (Higher score = strong Long-term Orientation)
Slovakia	104	52	110	51	38
Russia	93	39	36	95	*
Romania	90	30	42	90	*
Slovenia	71	27	19	88	*
Bulgaria	70	30	40	85	*
Poland	68	60	64	93	32
Czech Rep.	57	58	57	74	13
Hungary	46	80	88	82	50
Estonia	40	60	30	60	*

* Scores unavailable for some CEE countries
Compiled from Hofstede and Hofstede 2005

In high *power distance* countries (Slovakia, Russia, Romania) inequalities among people are expected; privileges and status symbols are important. Centralization and hierarchy are important in the workplace, where subordinates are expected to be told what to do. The society is characterized by large income differentials and by a small middle class. Hofstede also found correlation between power distance and corruption: corruption is widespread; officials, police and others in "power" are likely to accept side payments in large power distance countries. In low power distance countries (Estonia, Czech Republic) inequalities among people are minimized; in the workplace there are fewer supervisory personnel and decentralization of roles is common. *Power distance* has important implications for public relations as high power distance could present difficulties to public relations practitioners in becoming part of dominant coalitions (Sriramesh 1996).

According to Hofstede, Hungary is the most *individualistic* Eastern European society; however, Hungarian researchers' findings contradict this, placing Hungary more toward the collectivist societies and similar to the majority of countries in the region. Countries in transition, however, may change in this respect as they move toward individualism. Strong collectivist societies (Romania, Slovenia, Bulgaria) are characterized by high-context communication. Media is the primary source of information in individualistic societies (Estonia and Poland) where people tend to be more extrovert, and hiring and promotion decisions are based on skills and rules only. In a collective society, collective interests prevail over individual interests, and opinions are predetermined by group membership. Social network tends to be the primary source of information.

In *masculine* societies such as Slovakia, Hungary or Poland, challenge, competition, recognition and advancement are important, and so is doing things well and efficiently. *Feminine* countries such as Russia, Estonia or Slovenia are more service-oriented, where relationships and quality of life are valued. This has implications for the public relations industry as in masculine societies public relations is associated with females, and significantly more female practitioners work in public relations, while in a feminine society both genders are represented, and there is a higher share of working women in professional jobs. According to the worldwide International Standard Classification of Occupations, the proportion of women among administrative and managerial workers is highest in Poland (66 percent), followed by Slovenia (60 percent), and Hungary is fifth (58 percent).

A recent study of Consumption in a Wireless World (nVision 2007) compared advertising/marketing public relations against word of mouth when making a mobile phone purchase in Europe. Word of mouth played the greater role in Eastern Europe: as a source of influence it was six times more important than advertising/public relations marketing, which means that in these countries individual networks are very much based on personal sources and contacts rather than on advertising. Personal contacts and influences remain an important feature of Eastern European public relations.

In some CEE countries corruption is a widespread phenomenon (see Table 12.1). Under communism, governments and governmental organizations were discredited and distrusted as many officials and the political élite abused their positions. Communism left a very strong legacy in the political culture of CEE; and an apathetic society, in which people did not trust their new governments or each other, replaced the state instead of a trusting civil society (Badescu and Uslaner 2003). Old communist leaders and political activists became owners of new businesses after the fall of the Berlin Wall in a quick privatization process. The legacy of government propaganda, coupled with the low level of trust in governments, businesses and the media, has significant bearing on the perception of public relations and practitioners in the region. According to the Trust Index of GfK Custom Research Worldwide, only 14 percent of Central and Eastern Europeans trust their politicians, and 37 percent found managers trustworthy. In CEE the most trusted profession was teaching (84 percent), followed by doctors (77 percent) and the Army (65 percent).

Internet use in Eastern Europe is still below the EU average, but these countries are quickly catching up: CEE countries are projected to experience a significant boom in Internet usage, and the online environment is expanding quickly and cannot be ignored by any public relations practitioner. Media multitasking – listening to radio or watching television and using the Internet at the same time – is on the increase and presents serious challenges for the media sector as consumers' attention is becoming more and more fragmented, as is the media environment. In nVisions's survey, Hungarians led at watching television and using the Internet simultaneously (among EU countries). Seventy-five percent of Central Europeans have mobile phones. Fifty-four percent of the Central Eastern European élite do not understand sufficient English to watch an English-language channel, which further demonstrates the necessity to localize messages.

As a result of communist legacies, Eastern Europe is characterized by weak civil societies. Citizens throughout the region (Howard 2003):

1. maintain strong feelings of distrust of voluntary organizations;
2. continue to make use of private friendship networks, which serve as a disincentive to joining voluntary organizations;
3. feel rather disappointed with the new political and economic system, thus discouraging them even more from participating in public activities.

Special characteristics of public relations in the region

The effects and influence of public relations on society at large can be manifold, and Eastern Europe provides several examples. Public relations can help to (Szondi 2006):

- maintain the *status quo*;
- integrate a society (after the disintegration of the Soviet Union many Russians remained in the Baltic States, and public relations has been used to integrate Estonians and Russians);
- transform a society or economy;
- disintegrate countries, régimes (e.g. Yugoslavia, or Hill & Knowlton's infamous case about using alleged Iraqi atrocities to mobilize public opinion for a war against Iraq in 1991);
- build nations.

Many CEE countries engaged in nation- and state-building as part of the transformation following the collapse of state socialism. Slovenia, Slovakia, Estonia and Latvia had to create political and other institutions, and public relations played a crucial role (Hiebert 1992a).

There have been no precedents in the last two centuries for such a comprehensive transition from one political and economic system to another as the countries of Central and Eastern Europe have been undergoing for the past two decades. This process is difficult and, for some social groups, has proved to be long and painful. A key factor in its success is the degree to which social awareness can be changed. This would include the immediate elimination of negative habits related to "socialist" thinking and attitudes toward work, along with the removal of remaining fears and prejudices toward capitalism. Public relations strategies have proved useful in helping achieve such desirable transformations in social consciousness in the shortest time possible and ensuring more or less smooth transition from one socio-political and economic system to another.

The public relations industry faced a unique challenge – a chance to become involved in campaigns aiming at promotion of a positive image not only of a company, an institution, a politician or an organization, but also of a whole socio-economic and political system: market economy/capitalism (see Figure 12.1). However, the nature and range of public relations practices in developed market economies, such as those of the United States and the countries of the European Union, differ markedly from what can be labeled as "transitional public relations" – that is, public relations performed in the transition economies of Central and Eastern European countries and independent states of the former Soviet Union (Ławniczak 2001, 2003). There are three main features that distinguish those types of public relations:

- one is the burden represented by the legacy of the former system retained in the minds of the people and in the basic economic conditions in which transition economies operate;
- another is made up of the additional "transitional" role (such as managerial, technical, reflective and educational) (Van Ruler 2000) that public relations assumes in transition economies and is not observed in developed market economies (Ławniczak 2001);
- the third is the necessity to give careful attention to the "breaking up" and "coming together" (Culbertson 2004) trends as a result of a collapse of the Soviet Union, Yugoslavia and Czechoslovakia, where in effect new and competing independent states appeared on the political map of Europe.

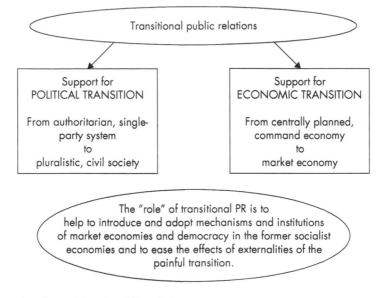

FIGURE 12.1 The role of transitional public relations
Source: Author's work

After two decades of transition, the legacy of "socialist democracy" and central planning is mani-fested in many areas of social life – including the practice of public relations – in almost all the transition countries of CEE and the former Soviet Union. It still can be seen, among other things, in the following areas:

1. the common perception of public relations as suspicious propaganda; this view stems from the historic role that censorship used to play in the mass media, the subjugation of all such media to a single doctrine (Hiebert 1992b), and the resulting stereotypical conviction that "the press lies";
2. the failure to understand the point of marketing and promoting products and businesses and building the images of companies and their executives; this problem originates from the fact that, at a time of severe shortages, all goods manufactured in the socialist economy were readily sold;
3. the belief that companies, their owners and/or their successes are better left unpromoted as high profiles may bring on additional tax sanctions; this view stems from the fact that, for ideological reasons, all privately owned operations were considered suspicious and subject to ad hoc taxation. (Ławniczak 2003);
4. the fears for the "negative externalities" (Grunig and Grunig 2005) of the privatization process and resistance to it.

Additionally, the above-mentioned "breaking up" and "coming together" trends have created the following functions of international public relations in transitional countries (Szondi 2006):

■ To distance the country(ies) from the old (economic and/or political) system that existed before transition. In the case of CEE countries, the aim was to distance themselves from the images of communism and the negative connotations evoked by "Eastern Europe", which often meant backwardness, despair, something poor or inferior.

- To change negative or false stereotypes or reinforce some positive stereotypes associated with the country in transition and its people.
- To position the country as a reliable and eligible member of the new system the transition is aiming for, or that of an international community.
- Countries in transition rely on the moral, financial and political support of more developed regions or nations, called "center nations", such as the Western European countries. The less developed or transitional countries are often situated on the "periphery". In their orientation the transitional countries are moving from the periphery toward the center position and the function of international public relations is to support and justify this "move" and demonstrate that these countries are worthy of the center nations' support.
- To position the country as the center of the region and the leader of transition. The periphery countries are competing with each other to become the center and/or the leader of the region/periphery. Competition for the financial, commercial, logistical, tourist or cultural center position (becoming a "hub") has been strong in Hungary, the Czech Republic and Poland.
- Public relations can also facilitate (re-)defining and (re-)constructing national identities as identity is also changing during transition. The countries and their peoples often face the questions "Who are we?" and "How do we want to be seen by others?"
- Reputation management can boost self-confidence and can be an expression of being proud of the achievements of transition. Transitional countries may have little confidence and often view themselves in a negative or pessimistic way, especially at the beginning of transition. Public relations can strengthen the "we" feeling and unite a country's people.

Central European countries saw another "big wave" of public relations activities when preparing for EU as well as NATO membership, which presented great challenges for public relations as it played a central role in the public communication campaigns to create awareness of membership benefits and opportunities as well as to increase participation in national referendums.

The public relations industry and market

After the accession to the European Union, the public relations sector in CEE has become one of the fastest-growing, though some markets are already showing signs of saturation. Almost two decades of experience, coupled with a growing number of well-qualified practitioners, has contributed to the growing professionalization and sophistication of the public relations industry in Central Europe. Some public relations agencies, such as Mmd (http://www.Mmdcee.com), have specialized exclusively in the Eastern European market, though other major international public relations consultancies have only recently moved into the region, such as Weber Shandwick or Pleon. The Eastern European networks of these agencies enable them to develop communication strategies for the CEE region as more and more clients demand a regional approach. It also calls for practitioners able to understand and appreciate the special features of the region, creating opportunities for international practitioners who can move easily around the region. Some major agencies even require their consultants to spend some time in another CEE country's office.

Because the majority of CEE countries are small, public relations specialization has been slow. Only a few agencies can afford to concentrate on only one area, such as financial relations or corporate social responsibility. Sector-specific specialization (health, energy, consumer relations) has been more common.

At the conclusion of this chapter you will find a list of the public relations associations of some CEE countries. These organizations have played an important part in the professionalization of public relations. However, cooperation among these organizations remains almost nonexistent and a missed opportunity.

Corporate social responsibility is one of the hottest issues in Central and Eastern Europe as CSR thinking and practice are slowly penetrating the region. However, CSR is still lagging behind Western European practices. A recent study of eight Central and Eastern European countries found that CSR is generally seen as an addition to core business activity and is often connected with philanthropy and sponsorship. Although more and more companies in the region are adopting CSR strategies and are involved in forms of stakeholder dialogue, the absence of a dynamic citizen movement limits the ability for stakeholder opinion to help shape strategy.

Unlike in Western Europe, in many CEE countries systematic government incentives and initiatives for social and environmental performance are generally absent. Owing to the socialist heritage, there is a general perception, however, both in the business community and in the public at large, that social responsibility and welfare are the primary roles of government.

Sidebar: Some practical tips for foreign practitioners trying to communicate with the Central and Eastern Europe market

1. Learn the geography. Do not confuse old countries with new ones, and do not mix languages.
2. Never use emigrants as translators. They have been out of their countries for decades, and the majority of them do not speak contemporary language, but the one spoken half a century ago.
3. Do not bribe. Although it might look like everybody is doing it, and that bribing might help you in the short run, in the long run you are destroying the public trust you are going to need in the future.
4. Take people seriously and not as some natives in Third World countries. Some of them are better-educated than you are.
5. Do not teach or preach. You are not going to impress anybody, but may alienate many.
6. Try to do business as usual. Your major partners are operating in EU markets and know what to expect.
7. Do not try to save too much money. It is true that you can get some services cheap – but expect the quality to be cheap as well. It is the same worldwide: You get what you pay for.
8. Do not create too many intermediaries. Some European companies establish CEE headquarters without any reason – their central HQ is close enough. Nobody wants to be considered part of CEE and distinct from the rest of Europe.
9. Do not try to impress with importing Westerners into the market itself. These times are gone. Use locals.

Source: Gruban (1995)

Poland

Situated in Central Europe, Poland since 1990 has shared its borders with Germany, the Czech Republic, Slovakia, Ukraine, Belarus, Lithuania and Russia's Baltic enclave. With an area of

312,683 square kilometers (129,725 square miles), it is the ninth largest country in Europe. At the end of 2006, Poland had a population of 38,632,000, ranking twenty-ninth in the world and eighth in Europe. Ethnically, Poland remains fairly homogenous, with ethnic minorities accounting for 2.6 to 3.9 percent of the population. Poland's prevailing religion is Roman Catholicism.

Some of the features that distinguish Poland from the region's other transition economies are: the size of its population and area, outstripped only by those of Russia and Ukraine; its long democratic traditions (the process of building democracy in Poland began as early as 1956 with the opposition to the government, backed by Poland's strong Catholic Church); Poland's relatively strong private sector in agriculture, operating since World War II (the country's private farmers held approximately 85 percent of farmland); and a significant private business ownership in the trade, crafts and service sectors since 1956. In effect, Poland was first among the CEE countries that blazed trails toward a more liberal economy, democracy, and opening up to the West.

Five main factors can be identified as vital to the development and performance of public relations in Poland of today:

1. the distinctive features of Polish culture;
2. 120 years' loss of statehood (1791–1918);
3. the influence of the Catholic Church;
4. the legacy of the communist system;
5. the neo-liberal model of transition applied since 1989.

Culture

In analyzing the distinctive features of Polish culture, applying the dimensions of culture proposed by Hofstede, we may observe that Polish society appears to be reluctant to support the government and to trust in its capacity to make a meaningful difference by participating in democratic elections. The above is evidenced by voter apathy (the turnout in the presidential elections of 2000 was 61 percent but dropped to 46.29 percent in the Sejm elections of 2001) and people's waning interest in politics. Confidence in the transition process also seems to be declining. The euphoria of the 1990s, when any change was thought to be for the better, was soon followed by disillusionment and widespread inertia. Economic problems, unemployment, and a growing sense of insecurity provided fertile ground for another wave of populism and collectivism. This sort of culture puts traditional public relations in a bad light and creates other problems such as the growing distrust of information campaigns, widening income gaps between various levels of society, more extreme attitudes and, in effect, the perception of traditional public relations tools as governmental propaganda.

Statehood

Situated between two superpowers, Germany in the west and Russia in the east, Poland has historically served as a corridor for passing foreign armies. This is why, starting in the seventeenth century, Poland has remained under constant threat of losing its national identity and why so much emphasis has been placed on protecting it. This happened at the end of the eighteenth century when the neighboring countries of Russia, Prussia and Austria joined forces to take advantage of Poland's military and economic weakness. As a result, they imposed three consecutive partitions, in 1772, 1791 and 1795, effectively wiping Poland off the map of Europe. Significantly, in 1775, Poland was 2.5 times larger than it is today. Poland did not regain independence until the end of World War I. The influence of the partition is extremely important. During the period when the country was torn between Germany, Russia and Austria, Poland grew even more devoted to Catholicism and more distrustful of the state and state authorities. Just over 170 years ago, and to some extent during the five decades of communist Poland, the establishment came to be seen as an alien hostile power imposed on the Poles. Civil disobedience and actions aimed at inflicting damage on the state were seen as acts of patriotism and received public support.

The Church

The third most important factor shaping the background for understanding public relations development in Poland is the role and influence of the Catholic Church. Being a real Pole has for ages meant being Catholic. This association became even stronger under communism, when authorities attempted to secularize the country through force and after Karol Wojtyła became Pope John Paul II. The Polish brand of Catholicism is family-oriented and underlines the important role of women (the cult of the Virgin Mary of Częstochowa.).

Communist legacy

Another factor that strongly affected Poles' collective view of the world was the five decades of socialist Poland. The cultural legacy of that period is a widespread conviction that everyone is entitled to equal benefits, no matter how hard they have worked, what knowledge they possess or how professional they are. For this reason, key tasks of transitional public relations were and still are to promote entrepreneurship; secure public approval for the concept of private property; and dispel perceptions of entrepreneurs as speculators and exploiters, presenting them instead as persons who create jobs and contribute to the economic welfare of the country. On the other hand, one of the positive sides of the former socialist system that affects the development of public relations in Poland is the rather high level of education. Illiteracy was fundamentally eliminated in the 1950s, and many educated Poles are women, dominating today's Polish public relations industry.

Market models

The most recent influence comes from the new model of market economy/capitalism implemented in transitional Poland. One of the most difficult tasks faced by Poland and other formerly centrally planned economies was to select the best market economy model. Poland's final decision on this debate has been written into article 20 of the redrafted constitution of April 2, 1997, which stated: ". . . social market economy lies at the heart of the economic system of the Republic of Poland."

Other factors

There is little doubt that labor unions have played a central role in the Polish transition. It was the "Solidarity" trade union, or social movement, that brought down the socialist/communist régime. In 2007, in the face of high unemployment (about 15 percent but falling), the Solidarity labor union is no longer a major force in society. It was surpassed in importance by Ogólnopolskie Porozumienie Związków Zawodowych (OPZZ), a competing post-communist trade union. This seemingly paradoxical situation has resulted from a phenomenon referred to by some as the "Solidarity paradox". This phenomenon suggests that the communist system in Poland was abolished by the working class employed in large socialist manufacturing enterprises (such as shipyards and mines). It was exactly that section of society that, according to the communist doctrine, was the mainstay of the system. Meanwhile, however, large and inefficient industrial behemoths were the first to fall victim to the process of market reforms. Governments formed by the Solidarity party were, therefore, internally torn between their recognition of the need for structural reform and their awareness of the social consequences of such reforms. These developments have triggered a wave of criticism of the neo-liberal economic development model. In one critical statement by a journalist, a claim was made that the predominance of neo-liberal ideas in today's Poland "is not as much an effect of their suitability for the Polish economy but rather of the effectiveness of neo-liberal marketing" (Markowski 2002).

The media and public relations

Similar to other Central and Eastern European countries, in the 1990s, Poland saw sweeping changes that affected both the structures of media and the rules that governed their operations. Conditions were then created for the media to represent a wide range of views and compete against one another. The state was deprived of its exclusive control over the press, and a number of new private broadcasting companies emerged to compete with public radio and television. Radio and television programming and press offerings became noticeably richer and more diverse. Many of the changes were driven by foreign capital. Foreign companies took advantage of the situation and achieved high market penetration, especially in the press sector.

The media market has been shaped by a spontaneous and largely unsupervised transition process. Most Polish media have fallen into the hands of, and therefore also under the control of, foreign capital. Foreign companies have gained a stronghold over national opinion-forming press controlling Poland's largest dailies, such as *Dziennik*, *Fakt* (Springer Verlag), *Gazeta Wyborcza* (with the minority shares owned by the US corporation Cox Communications Enterprises, Inc., and dispersed ownership control), *Super Ekspress* (controlled by the Swedish group Bonnier) and *Rzeczpospolita* (owned by Presspublica and controlled by British media group Mecom). Magazines catering for women and teenagers are dominated by Gruener + Jahr and Bauer of Germany and Edipresse of Switzerland. The regional and local press, too, is under the control of Western corporations, especially Passauer Presse of Germany, Norwegian ORKLA and British Mecom. Although Western investors have unanimously denied representing the interests of their home countries, parent companies, or other political groups, a strong case can be made to prove that it is exactly what they do. Polish public opinion is increasingly more concerned about the fact that foreign domination of the media results in promoting conservative and neo-liberal economic views and foreign political and economic interests (*Życie Warszawy* May 6, 1994, *Rzeczpospolita* June 7, 2002).

Some of the trends seen in the Polish press sector, especially foreign domination of media, have justified governmental efforts to protect the electronic media in Poland. The government has placed stricter controls over the radio and television market by imposing a new system of licensing that includes harsher rules for foreign capital.

Thanks to Poland's existing media infrastructure, the virtual nonexistence of illiteracy (0.3 percent in the population aged 15+) and a relatively low poverty rate, the media are capable of disseminating messages to practically the entire population. Daily newspapers reach a relatively unchanging 60 percent of the population, local dailies being the most popular form of press in most provinces. Channel I, which is Poland's most popular radio station, covers the entire country. Channels I, II and III of Polish radio reach 40 percent of Poland's population. Public radio in Poland faces strong competition from private stations (most of which are regional in outreach and specialize in music and other forms of entertainment) and from private national stations, one of the strongest of which among Polish Catholics is the Catholic radio station Radio Maryja.

Telewizja Polska SA (Polish Television), owned exclusively by the state treasury, offers three national channels and one channel available abroad via satellite. Channel I of Polish Television is accessible to 98 percent of the population. Private television, meanwhile, has been steadily gaining market share. Many stations in Poland transmit their signals via satellite, which gives them a reach that transcends Poland's borders.

Today's market belongs to advertisers, for whom the media fight fiercely. Public relations professionals/agencies play an important role in providing the media with "information subsidies". According to a study commissioned by the Polish Public Relations Consultancies Association, more than half of public relations practitioners believed that companies are given media coverage in return for placing paid advertisements in a given issue. Over 25 percent of public relations professionals claimed that press coverage is obtained by bribing a journalist (*Gazeta Wyborcza* 2002).

All this shows that direct access to the media in today's transitional Poland differs widely between individual groups of society. Groups such as the government and its institutions (e.g. the Ministry of the Treasury and the Ministry of Finance, which publish official announcements in the press), corporations (because of their sizable advertising budgets), and the so-called think-tanks among activist groups (which have access to foreign funds and private sponsors) are in a much better position to gain access to the media than the thousands of minor activist groups that deal with issues such as environmental protection, social care and drug addiction.

Development and evolution of the public relations sector

With little more than a decade of history, Poland's public relations sector is relatively young. Its emergence and evolution were a response to transformations occurring in the transitional economy. By 2006 the approximate annual value of the public relations market estimated by British firm Hudson Sandler grew from about 80 to 120–130 million zloty (about US$40 million), and according to the same source will reach 200 million zloty (about US$70 million) by 2007 (Rydzak 2006). No wonder that since 2005 we have seen the return of global agencies such as Edelman, Fleishman Hillard, Rowlans, Hill & Knowlton, or Pleon, though Burson Marsteller closed its Warsaw office in 2001. Altogether, public relations services are offered by some 500 specialized agencies, but only about fifty of these are fully professional (Łaszyn 2001), offering a wide range of services. Other agencies, typically run by one or two owners, have been set up by journalists and public relations experts who have chosen to leave their jobs in corporate public relations departments or large public relations agencies.

The evolution of public relations in Poland followed two routes. The first route was the effect of the change of the political and socio-economic system. This created opportunities for establishing broader foreign contacts, allowing for foreign investment and privatization to enter the country.

In effect, numerous Western enterprises that recognized their need for public relations services moved into the local market. As to the second route, before establishing certain market instruments, mechanisms and institutions (such as the stock exchange) that were absent in the command economy, the Polish government engaged public relations agencies to carry out public information campaigns. An example is the use of such agencies during the levying of direct and indirect taxes on the introduction of the national privatization program in the 1990s.

From 1990 to 1994, only eleven newly established companies claimed to have made public relations their core business. Still, their actual focus was on advertising. Nevertheless, thanks mainly to big governmental contracts (the above-mentioned public information campaigns, for instance), the first five years of public relations evolution in Poland witnessed a rapid development of the market with annual growth proceeding at the rate of 12 percent (Czarnowski 1999). In 1995 the annual sales of the largest agency – SIGMA International (Poland) – reached US$8.3 million (Rzeczpospolita 1996). By comparison, the market's annual growth between 2000 and 2002 was below 5 percent (Łaszyn 2001). (See Table 12.3.)

The years between 1995 and 2000 saw further dramatic growth of public relations in Poland. During most of the period, the growth was mainly quantitative. It was not until the late 1990s that actual quality improvements were made, as the need for crisis communication (in the wake of the Russian crisis of 1998), internal public relations and investor relations were recognized and actions in these areas were undertaken.

From 2000, a growing number of agencies recognized the need for specialization. This formerly fragmented market was consolidated through mergers and acquisitions. Many agencies were pushed out of business, partly because the first stage of transformations had been completed by then, and the government no longer offered large contracts to big Western agencies.

After Poland joined the European Union, new opportunities and challenges for the public relations industry appeared. The first, most courageous Polish public relations agencies decided to open their branch offices in Brussels (e.g. First PR), and the market for public relations services began to grow. By 2007 the "golden age" for Polish public relations had begun. Two factors contributed to this development: first, the dynamic growth of GDP – over 5 percent in 2006 and 2007 – and, second, the stream of structural funds from the European Union, which should amount to €67 billion within seven years. It is estimated that 2–3 percent of that amount should be devoted to promotion of different types of EU-supported projects. It means that between 2007 and 2013 there will be €1.2 billion available for the promotion of those projects, from which even some hundreds of millions of euros may be at the disposal of public relations agencies (Krzewińska and Paczkowski 2007).

Research

Public relations research in Poland is a relatively recent development. Some of the first public relations studies were conducted in the early 1990s (Wojcik 2005). Authors focused on general rather than specific issues. The approach is understandable as the discipline was new in Polish business practice. The year 2001 marked the first time that an original Polish theoretical concept appeared in an English-language publication. The concept is "transitional public relations", that is, a form of international public relations specific to former post-socialist countries (Ławniczak 2001, 2005).

Systemic transition has forced the business community to revisit its standing in the new and unknown reality of the market economy. State-owned enterprises were forced to reform their

TABLE 12.3 Public relations evolution in Poland

1990–1993 Infancy	1994–1999 PR flourishes and slowly matures	2000–2004 PR becomes professional, specialised and international	2005– New stage of stabilization, maturity and unprecedented opportunity after EU accession
First PR agencies established, first large governmental information and educational campaigns	*Dominance of media relations; PR combined and confused with marketing*	*Economic stagnation, diminishing PR and marketing budgets, tight competition, specialisation and first international achievements*	*Since 2006 – "the golden age" of Polish PR. First cases of two-way symmetrical communication*
1990 Establishment of first two Polish PR agencies: First PR (March) and Alcat Communications (September). **1991** Burson Marsteller opens branch office in Warsaw. **1992** Publication of first two Polish textbooks in PR **1992** NGO's campaign "Myths in the economy". **1992–1993** Two large governmental tax information campaigns (budget of US$2.5 million).	**1994** Establishment of Polish Public Relations Society (PPRS) (August). **1995** First two doctoral dissertations in PR. **1995** First issue of Information Bulletin of the Polish Public Relations Society. **1995** International conference on "Public Relations as the new tool of systemic transformation" held in Poznań (co-organised by Deutsche PR Gesellschaft). **1995** Establishment of the first regional office of the Polish Public Relations Society in Poznań (October). **1996** Code of Ethics of PPRS. **1997** The first Polish internet PR page. – "www.piar.pl"	**2000** Doctoral studies at the Poznań University of Economics. **2001** Establishment of the Polish Public Relations Consultancies Association (PPRCA). **2001** Customer Relations Code of the PPRCA. **2001** First issue of a new version of the bulletin of the Polish Public Relations Society *Na linii* ("On the line"). **2001** Burson Marsteller withdraws from Poland (April). **2001** Biggest achievement of Polish PR: BCA wins three Golden Awards of IPRA and is nominated for a special UN award. **2001** 2nd edition of the Public Relations Project Contest. **2001** The first of the yearly conferences organised for theoreticians and practitioners of PR in Rzeszów. **2002** The new professional internet service for PR practitioners – "internetPR.pl" (May). **2003** the new internet service of PPRS – "prsp.org.pl". **2004** May 1st – EU membership.	**2006** The first Polish professional bimonthly "piar.pl". **2007** NSZZ "Solidarność" trade union's PR campaign – "Low wages the barrier for development of Poland" – one of the first examples of two-way symmetrical communication. **2007** Polish Public Relations Society (PPRS) established its seventh regional branch. **2007** Five Polish PR agencies classified by Holmes Report in the ranking of the largest PR world consultancies. The largest Polish "SIGMA", at the 159 position. **2007** Two Polish agencies awarded in the IPRA Golden World Award competition.

communications policies to get their foreign shareholders to support privatization and retrenching. Public relations became an important instrument for supporting the transition of large enterprises from a command to a market economy. Nevertheless, the main client for public relations services in Poland was not state-owned companies, but rather international corporations and companies whose majority shareholders were foreign enterprises. The second-largest group of public relations clients was a new generation of large Polish private businesses: privatized State Treasury companies ranked in the top ten of Poland's largest business organizations. The groups least aware of the need for public relations are small and medium-sized entrepreneurs and large state-held enterprises that have not yet undergone privatization.

For the reasons mentioned earlier, the key roles played by public relations in Poland differ somewhat from those adopted in Western Europe and the US. A critical responsibility of public relations in today's Poland is to communicate with internal publics. The privatization of former state enterprises, very often in the form of takeovers by Western companies, awakens a fear among workers of the effects of "rationalization", which for them means dismissal from their jobs. That is why management must communicate with the company employees to calm the atmosphere resulting from the "negative externalities" created by the privatization (Grunig and Grunig 2005).

Position of public relations in organizations

A study carried out in 2001 by the euroPR Agency (http://www.europr.com.pl, retrieved April 20, 2001) has helped define the place of public relations in Polish enterprises. Forty-four percent of the companies place the public relations function in their marketing departments, 22 percent in their sales departments, 15 percent in their management board offices and 10 percent in their advertising departments. Two 2006 studies confirm that little has changed in that respect and that "putting public relations into the same drawer with marketing is common" (Rydzak 2006).

The rapid growth of the public relations market seen in the 1990s has given rise to the demand for the establishment of an organization associating public relations practitioners and theoreticians. The first such institution, the Polish Public Relations Association (PPRS), was set up in 1994. The other public relations association operating in Poland is the Polish Public Relations Consultancies Association (PRCA), established in 2001 to represent professional public relations services. At the time of writing, these two are the only public relations associations operating in Poland. In view of the size of Poland's public relations market and its evolution, it is unlikely any other associations will be established in the near future.

Sidebar: Lech Wałęsa's rejection of public relations counsel's help

Ever since Poland held its first multiparty presidential, parliamentary and local elections in 1989, a new need has arisen for ways to communicate with the electorate. There was increasing demand for expertise in political marketing and public relations. The first instance in the newly formed democratic Poland, when public relations played a pivotal role, was the presidential election of 1995. Lech Wałęsa rejected an offer by communication specialists who wanted to hone his communication skills. Wałęsa told specialists in social engineering and public relations that they could learn from him on how to build images and that he was going to win the election. However, Wałęsa's opponent, left-wing candidate Aleksander Kwaśniewski, took the opposite strategy and entrusted himself to the care of Jaques Sequel, a French public relations and political marketing expert. Kwaśniewski's complete trust in his advisor led to an election victory and a loss for Wałęsa. The color blue, built up as the symbol during the campaign (eyes, shirt), has since become the favorite color among Polish politicians. The paradox in the second round of the election was that, just five years after Solidarity's thumping victory, Poles were witnessing a confrontation between Lech Wałęsa, a world-renowned symbol of victory over communism, and a post-communist candidate who was an atheist and commonly considered a career-maker. The breakthrough in the campaign came with Aleksander Kwaśniewski's appreciation of the power of public relations, and particularly with the televised debate, which experts believe was the direct blow that led to Lech Wałęsa's defeat.

The outcome of the 1995 presidential election was also of great importance for establishing public relations as a force in the Polish political scene of the early twenty-first century. Since the 2000 presidential election, image consultants have been engaged by nearly every candidate as none wants to repeat Lech Wałęsa's mistake.

Source: Ławniczak, Rydzak, and Trębecki (2003)

As of the first half of 2007, the following are "hot issues" in Polish public relations:

- the habit of politicians and corporate executives of relying on the services of real and false image creation experts;
- tighter competition, leading ultimately to price wars among public relations agencies and independent consultants;
- new areas of public relations activities such as: public relations ethics, corporate social responsibility and investor relations;
- "love/hate" relationships between journalists and public relations practitioners and cases of journalist corruption (Wielowiejska 2000);
- growing interest in strategic public relations and public diplomacy as a specialized field of research and practice;
- intense campaigns and competition promoting cities and regions, with Wrocław the leader in that field;
- a new additional chance for the Polish public relations industry, thanks to the Euro 2012 soccer championship that will be jointly organized by Poland and Ukraine.

Questions for discussion

1. Describe the main factors that influenced development of public relations in Poland, and explain how these factors continue to affect the field.
2. Present and support your opinion about future developments in Polish public relations. Talk about possible trends, areas of interest, and obstacles.

Hungary

Political and economic environment

Hungary, located in the heart of Europe, has a population of 10 million, of which 2 million live in Budapest, the capital. Four million Hungarians live in neighboring countries including Slovakia, Romania, Serbia and Ukraine. Hungarians are of Finno-Ugric origin and as a people have been living in the Danube Basin for more than a thousand years. The Hungarian state was established by King Stephen I, who adopted Christianity in the year 1000. In the centuries that followed, Hungary became a leading power in Central Europe until Hungarian lands were subjected to Mongol invasion and a Turk occupation in the sixteenth century. In the mid-nineteenth century, Hungary established a liberal constitutional monarchy under the Austrian Habsburgs, but two world wars and a communist dictatorship in the twentieth century forestalled true independence. In 1956, Soviet tanks crushed an uprising by Hungarians seeking to liberalize the political and economic system and to break away from Soviet influence. The revolution remains prominent in the country's consciousness.

The beginning of Hungary's transformation into a market economy dates to the late 1960s and 1970s when the so-called "New Economic Mechanism" attempted to combine features of central planning and those of the market mechanism. During the 1970s, consumerism, a limited private sector in the form of small businesses, as well as Forint (Hungarian currency) millionaires emerged in Hungary, which became "the happiest barrack in the block". In the 1980s, small-scale private entrepreneurship was legalized and encouraged. Hungary played a key role in the collapse of the socialist system when in May 1989 the country opened its borders with Austria and allowed thousands of East Germans to escape to the West. Despite protests from the East German government, Hungary refused to close the border. After East Germany sealed its own borders, East Germans took to the streets of Leipzig, Dresden and Berlin, and mass demonstrations led to the fall of the Berlin Wall in November.

With about US$18 billion in foreign direct investment (FDI) since 1989, Hungary has attracted over a third of all FDI in Central and Eastern Europe, including the former Soviet Union. Of this, about US$6 billion came from US companies. Foreign capital is attracted by skilled and relatively inexpensive labor, tax incentives, modern infrastructure, and a good telecommunications system.

Although Hungary enjoyed one of the most liberal and economically advanced economies of the former Eastern bloc, the country's net foreign debt rose significantly – from US$1 billion in 1973 to US$15 billion in 1993 – owing largely to consumer subsidies and unprofitable state enterprises. Since mid-2006 there has been a shift in economic policy, aimed at deficit reduction. The Hungarian government embarked on a four-year consolidation program following a peak in the deficit in 2006 at 9.2 percent of GDP. The government is aiming at slimming state administration by 20 percent, seriously reforming healthcare, and imposing other cost-cutting measures. Politically, Hungary is a deeply divided country, and the gap between the left and the right does not seem to decrease; the lack of consensus has proved damaging to the nation's interest.

Public relations

Public relations in Hungary dates to the 1960s when the country embarked on economic and political liberalization. The first book on public relations in Hungarian, *Public Relations a gyakorlatban*

(*Public Relations in Practice*) by József Lipót, was published in 1968. The book was unique in many senses, as it brilliantly adopted and applied public relations as a "capitalist tool" to the socialist economic conditions (one might think of today's China where the term "socialist public relations" better describes the practice). Lipót's pioneering book was not only the first book devoted to public relations in Hungary but also the first book on public relations published in Eastern Europe. Lipót started his career at the Hungarian Chamber of Commerce, which was probably the first organization that consciously made use of and promoted public relations in Hungary. Only a handful of companies established public relations departments and employed "public relations officers", using the English title during the 1970s. In the 1980s public relations appeared as a chapter in marketing, export marketing and advertising textbooks, following the marketing view of public relations.

By the mid-1980s public relations as an emerging profession gained momentum (Szondi 2004). Hungarian public relations practitioners had a pioneering role in establishing and spreading public relations practice in CEE. In 1988, IPRA's annual conference took place in Vienna, and the participants were also invited to Budapest where IPRA's first East–West Public Relations Conference was organized. The Hungarian Public Relations Association (HPRA) was established in December 1990 with forty members. In 1992 public relations was recognized as a profession by the Office of Central Statistics under the aegis of "Business Counselling". In the same year, the HPRA developed and accepted a standardized public relations terminology. The first public relations courses at undergraduate level were launched in 1992. Within the framework of IPRA's annual conference, held in Budapest in 1996, the first International Public Relations Film and Video Festival Prince Award was launched at the initiative of Hungarian public relations practitioners. The first public relations magazine, *PRHerald*, was launched in 1995, and it was the monthly professional journal until its bankruptcy in 2001. In 2004 the journal was relaunched in an online format (http://www.prherald.hu) and serves as the news portal of the communication profession (Szondi 2004).

The development of Hungarian public relations was influenced by US, British, German and Austrian scholars and practitioners. When Hungarian public relations was being formulated during the later 1980s, the founders of the Hungarian Public Relations Association turned to IPRA and the Public Relations Society of America for professional help and support for establishing the profession.

An estimated 5,000 people are working in public relations, but this number is based on a broad interpretation of the profession. There are around eighty public relations agencies in Hungary, but this number includes registered freelancers. Membership of the Hungarian Public Relations Association is slowly increasing; in 2007, 320 practitioners belonged to the organization. The management of the Association is determined to increase membership and raise the profile of the profession.

By the mid-2000s the public relations industry has consolidated and now shows signs of saturation. The public relations market has become price sensitive, often at the expense of professionalism. Contracts are often won by the cheapest offer rather than by the most professional one as smaller local agencies are willing to work for less.

A 2005 survey of the top 200 companies' top executives or managers, to whom the public relations manager or agency reports, found that three-quarters of those executives considered public relations an important activity (http://www.marketinginfo.hu, retrieved October 15, 2007). The most common aims of public relations were identified as follows:

- to enhance the image of the organization (85 percent);
- to improve the company's market position (59 percent);
- to support the "fight" against competitors (54 percent);
- to gain and strengthen the trust of investors (54 percent).

Forty percent of the organizations surveyed did not have an in-house public relations practitioner or department and did not employ an agency, either: public relations was "managed" under the auspices of other departments, such as marketing. Every second executive agreed that the company should increase its public relations budget to be more efficient, though two-thirds of the companies would not change their public relations budget the following year. A third of the companies would probably decrease their budget in the coming three years. In 2005 the companies surveyed spent an average of €100,000 on public relations.

Public relations has mixed perceptions in Hungary for several reasons. The term became widely known between 1998 and 2002 under the conservative government of FIDESZ (Federation of Young Democrats). It was the first government consciously to use public relations. Newspapers close to the government were using the term "public relations" in a positive context, though the journalists not in favor of the government had very negative attitudes toward public relations, associating it with manipulation, propaganda and fake activities (Szondi 2004). Today the situation is the same, but the Socialists are in the government and FIDESZ is in opposition. Another factor that influenced the perception of public relations was lobbying and its unregulated practice during the 1990s. To make lobbying activities more transparent and accountable, the so-called "Lobbying Act" was passed in 2006, which determines and defines the duties and obligations of lobbyists, who must be registered and produce quarterly reports that disclose their lobbying activities, methods, clients and fees.

Since 2004 the number of forums, conferences and workshops devoted to CSR has been on the increase, and the public relations profession has had an important role to play in communicating and spreading the practice. In 2006 the public relations association launched the "CSR Best Practice" initiative to award companies that best engage in CSR. A number of issues, however, hinder the spread of CSR in Hungary. The first is that in many Eastern European countries CSR is wrongly associated with sponsorship. Second, the Hungarian media have a negative, skeptical and cynical attitude toward CSR, which makes CSR communication a difficult task. The media interpret CSR either as greenwashing or as "hidden advertising" where the companies' sole aim is to increase sales.

Public relations education

At the academic level, the first – and so far the only – department of public relations was established at the College of Foreign Trade in 1994 (the college is now part of the Budapest Business School). This department has been the forerunner of public relations education in Hungary where students specialize in public relations during their final year of study; prior to that, they receive a strong business foundation together with proficiency in two foreign languages. In 2006 the department was renamed Media Studies and Social Communication, and a new public relations curriculum was introduced that includes a course on international public relations. Today there are eight universities or colleges that offer undergraduate public relations courses and/or degrees full-time, part-time or via distance learning. At the other universities, departments of communication or media studies host most public relations courses. There are no master's degree programs in public relations. However, in 2002 an MA in lobbying was launched. Aiming at both students and practitioners, an online public relations knowledge portal (http://www.practice.hu) was launched in 2005 that offers downloadable surveys, articles, studies, videos, educational and other materials in Hungarian and partly in English. This portal partly fills the void caused by the limited number of public relations books available in Hungarian.

Mass and social media

Each successive Hungarian government has applied financial and political pressure on the media to secure favorable coverage. This pressure, coupled with weak ethical norms among journalists, has prevented the development of objective, independent media. Political intervention has manifested itself in many ways: during the 1990s newspapers were published by state-owned publishing houses, state-owned banks or other companies associated with the state. Many titles changed ownership several times in the 1990s and 2000s. Today, however, foreign ownership dominates the Hungarian press. The German Axel Springer, the Swiss Ringier, Sanoma, and Westdeutsche Allgemeine Zeitung are among current owners of newspapers in Hungary.

Hungarian media are politicized, so media outlets and journalists have strong political links. This interlocking of media and politics is so strong in Hungary that politicians are the major celebrities and are extensively covered by the press. Media celebrities often become governmental spokespersons, and former governmental officials or journalists function as public relations advisors in contemporary Hungary. Another consequence is that every issue becomes politicized even if it has nothing to do with politics. Public relations practitioners often struggle with keeping politics and politicians from interfering in areas in which they are not competent. The low level of professionalism among journalists is another problem not only in Hungary but in other countries of the region, too.

Despite the fact that the Hungarian media market is relatively small to sustain a sufficient number of titles, newer and newer media products are appearing in the media market. In 2005, 901 dailies, weeklies and monthly newspapers and magazines were published in Hungary, including thirty-six daily newspapers. The free newspapers have had an impact on the market as well – especially *Metro*, with a daily circulation of 324,000, making it the highest-circulation daily.

As far as newspaper circulations are concerned, in the second quarter of 2007 the circulation of print newspapers decreased by 1 million compared with the previous quarter. The number of subscriptions is also down, especially in 2007 when the economic, health, education and public-sector reforms resulted in lower disposable incomes and increased costs of living. *Népszabdaság*, the most popular daily, with a left stance, distributed 128,523 copies on average, the conservative *Magyar Nemzet* 64,500 copies, followed by the left-wing *Népszava* at 24,500 copies in 2007. *Blikk*, the most popular tabloid, sold 230,000 copies, followed by *Színes Bulvar Lap* (*Color Tabloid Paper*) with 66,000. Most of Hungary's newspapers, weeklies and magazines have online editions, and a selection of radio stations can also be heard online. Websites offer additional services such as discussion forums or newspaper archives.

The tax on newspapers and magazines is 15 percent, making it one of the highest in the European Union, where newspapers and magazines are often tax free. Advertisements cover about 50 percent of publishers' income, and the other 50 percent comes from the price of the newspaper. Perhaps this also contributed to the joint efforts of the major newspaper publishers in 2005 when they launched a campaign against "unauthorized secondary use" of their articles by media-monitoring services. The publishers wanted these services to pay a copyright fee for quoting and using published articles in their reviews. Public relations agencies were also affected because they are among the users of media-monitoring services or do monitoring themselves. The public relations industry voiced its disagreement: why should a public relations agency pay fees for an article that was fully or partly based on a news release issued by the agency? On the other hand, clients of monitoring firms are big companies who advertise in those newspapers as well. As a result of the negotiations, monitoring and public relations agencies – or their clients – are to pay between 20 and 50 US cents per article to the publisher. The publishers also demanded that monitoring firms should disclose their clients' names to the publisher, a demand later dropped for public relations agencies thanks to the efforts of the Hungarian Public Relations Association.

Until 1997 the state-controlled Magyar Televízió (MTV – Hungarian Television) enjoyed a monopoly. The 1996 Media Law opened the way for creating a dual broadcasting system, modeled on Western European traditions. There are now three terrestrial television channels: MTV, the public service channel; TV2, whose majority owner is Scandinavian Broadcasting System (SBS); and RTL Klub, which is owned by a consortium of CLT, Bertelsmann, Pearson, and the Hungarian national telecom company Magyar Telekom. In June 2007, sixty-two additional Hungarian-language cable channels were competing for viewers' attention.

Until July 2007, Budapest Radio was an important tool of Hungary's public diplomacy efforts, broadcasting programs in English, German, French, Russian and Spanish abroad about Hungary and her culture. This foreign-language service was abolished in July 2007 owing to a lack of resources. The *Budapest Business Journal*, the *Budapest Times* and the *Budapest Sun* are the leading English-language newspapers.

The most visited Hungarian websites and portals are Origo, Startlap, iwiw and Index (news portal). Iwiw, the Hungarian facebook, was launched in 2005 when the number of websites based on personal relations (social media) was mushrooming. Blogs have not become popular in Hungary; only 5 percent of regular Internet users read them on a regular basis. Forty-nine percent of them use blogs as entertainment, 42 percent as an information source, and 15 percent to gain professional knowledge (http://www.nrc.hu). Several public relations blogs have been launched during the last few years; however, none of them has become popular.

Ninety-eight percent of Hungarian households have television. Digital television is in an early phase. Every third household has an Internet connection (70 percent of them are broadband connections), and 2.5 million Hungarians use the Internet, which is still below the EU average (47 percent); the majority of them live in Budapest and western Hungary. Seventy-nine percent of Hungarians have at least one mobile phone, but the total number of mobile subscribers is 10 million.

Questions for discussion

1. What difficulties exist for public relations in Hungary? How can they be overcome?
2. How, in your opinion, does the Hungarian public view public relations? Is it similar to or different from their perceptions of other related professions such as journalism, advertising or marketing? How does that perception compare to their perceptions of corporations and government agencies? How are all those perceptions related?
3. How does the Hungarian public relations university program described compare to programs in your country? What are strengths and weaknesses of each?

Russia

Political and economic environments

For many foreigners, the Russian Federation remains a mysterious and controversial country almost two decades after the disintegration of the Soviet Union, the former Cold War enemy of the West. With an area of 17,075,400 square kilometers, it is by far the largest country in the world and extends into much of northern Asia and Europe. The administrative subdivisions of present-day Russia are rather comprehensive: the country is divided into seven large federal districts – four in Europe and three in Asia. The analysis of Russian public relations in this chapter covers only the development of the four European federal districts: Central, with Moscow; Northwestern, with St Petersburg; Southern; and Volga Federal District.

Russia's population is around 143 million people; ethnic Russians account for 80 percent of the total. The main official language is Russian; however, thirty other languages are also official languages in various parts of the country. Russia is home for more than 160 ethnic groups and indigenous peoples. As many as 80 percent of the ethnic Russians are Orthodox, but Islam, Buddhism and Judaism are also present. Muslims are the largest religious minority at around 15 million.

The winds of change date back to the reform-minded Mikhail Gorbachev, who introduced the policies of *glasnost* (openness) and *perestroika* (restructuring) in 1985 to modernize Soviet communism by economic and political reforms. Hardline communists tried to remove him from power in 1991 in an unsuccessful military coup, which led to the collapse of the Soviet Union. Boris Yeltsin was elected president in June 1991, just a few months prior to the disintegration of the Soviet Union, which broke up into fifteen independent states. Despite the fact that the country embarked on radical, market-oriented reforms (so called "shock therapy") under the Yeltsin presidency, the era was characterized by the deterioration of living standards, growing poverty, controversial privatization of state properties, an explosion of corruption and organized crime. As a result of the privatization policy, the wealth of the Soviet Russian state (the largest state enterprises) ended up in the hands of a small group, the so-called *oligarchs*. They were well-connected entrepreneurs who grew rich via connections to the corrupt government while the majority of the population plunged into poverty. In 1999, Yeltsin appointed Vladimir Putin, then head of the Federal Security Service (FSB), as prime minister, and he was elected president in 2000, then re-elected in 2004 for a second term. After taking office, Putin moved to consolidate his power, weaken the influence of the oligarchs, and reduce the influence of the legislature, regional leaders, the business community and the news media, while strengthening the FSB. High oil prices and growing internal demand boosted Russian economic growth, so Putin's presidency was able to show improvements in the Russian standard of living. When trying to evaluate the role of each of the three Russian presidents – Gorbachev, Yeltsin and Putin – the US student may have some problems. On the one hand, the majority of US commentators, politicians and journalists hailed Yeltsin and his breakup of the Soviet Union as a "breakthrough" to democracy and free-market capitalism. As for Putin, they were and still are criticizing him as a dictator, suppressing democratic media and NGOs. On the other hand, the great majority of Russians cannot forget that, as a result of Yeltsin's "shock therapy", about 80 percent of Russian people were plunged into poverty (Cohen 2000). In March 2008, Dmitry Medvedev was elected to succeed Putin amidst accusations of an unfair and repressive campaign as well as voting irregularities. Medvedev was Putin's choice, and the new president has vowed to continue his predecessor's policies.

The Economist rates Russia as a "hybrid régime", the building blocks of which are: bureaucratic –authoritarian political régime, state capitalism, selective social paternalism, and a foreign policy aimed at restoring Russia's role as a world power (Shevtsova 2006).

Many Western commentators argue that the economic and political power of today's Russia is concentrated in the hands of a small group of so-called *siloviki*, or "power guys", who are members of the Federal Security Service, the KGB's successor. This group controls the Kremlin, the government, the media and large parts of the economy, and are determined to restore Russian greatness and influence in the world (The making of a neo-KGB state 2007, August 23). This group of people seems to be united against the West and anyone who plays into the hands of the West, such as free-thinking journalists, NGOs or liberal politicians. Russian commentators, however, disagree with this viewpoint, arguing that Putin prevented the *siloviki* from gaining a monopoly on power, trying to preserve a measure of pluralism within the ruling élite (Shevtsova 2006). With regard to Russia's relations with the West, it is characterized as both partnership and rivalry. Russia is cooperating with the West on a range of international issues while it combats Western influence in Russia as well as in its former sphere of influence. Putin was a popular president: overall, three in four Russians (75 percent) expressed confidence in Putin to do the right thing in world affairs, according to a Pew Global Attitudes Survey conducted in April 2006 (http://www.pewglobal.org/ reports/display.php?ReportID=250). Sixty percent of Russians said they would prefer that Russia were led by a leader with a "strong hand", while 30 percent preferred democratically elected leaders to govern the country.

Russia's economy is the world's eighth largest, and GDP growth has averaged almost 7 percent a year during the last decade. Its economy is dependent on high prices for oil, gas and other commodities, but the country is less competitive in manufacturing, services and high-tech industries. Owing to high international oil prices, export revenue has soared since 2000. "Russia First", Putin's foreign and economic policy concept, has emphasized securing Russian economic interests and rebuilding Russia's economy as an important component of foreign policy. The Russian president injected greater coordination between governmental organizations, business interests and intelligence services, and exploited the country's energy concerns. The policy is also interpreted as a reaction to disenchantment with the failures of Westernization, the shortcomings of liberalism and alleged US aims to weaken Russia (Bugajski 2003). Despite this "Russia First" effect, the country remains an attractive market for investment. Economic development remains uneven throughout the country. Moscow and the major cities are central to economic development. In 2007, Moscow was named the world's most expensive city for expatriate staff to live (followed by London and Tokyo) for the second year in a row, while many people in the countryside live on just a few hundred dollars a month.

Russian media

Under communism, the state had total control and monopoly over Soviet media, which was an important propaganda tool. Gorbachev's *glasnost* and *perestroika* policy paved the way for newly independent and pluralistic media, resulting in private press ownership, independence of editors and journalists from owners, and the abolition of censorship. The early years of the 1990s were described as the "golden age of the free press", which was over by the mid-1990s when the system of state subsidies that existed under communism had vanished, leaving publications to struggle for their survival. Print media became the first victims of media commercialism, with media ownership concentrated in the hands of media barons (Zassoursky 2002).

The lack of funds and resources made the media vulnerable and dependent on outside funding such as the state and business organizations during the 1990s. The development of free media in Russia has been hampered by state interference, shortage of funds, the development of media corporations by Russian media tycoons, the lack of public broadcasting and the lack of public interest in the media (Zassoursky 2002). So one may say that only a very few media outlets are independent in Russia, and they are often under threat. Today the Russian state media are centrally funded and run by the government, which tightly controls the media through the Ministry of Press, Broadcasting and Mass Communication. Media owners, on the other hand, promote their commercial interests at the expense of professional standards and objectivity. Russian media are caught between state control and the commercial interests of the owners and advertisers. The first national channel – Public Russian Television (ORT) – is the biggest television channel in the country, with penetration of 98 percent of the Russian territory. ORT is both a state (51 percent of its shares belong to the state) and a private (49 percent) channel. National channels that broadcast from Moscow tend to have access to all Russian regions, but they do not cover local issues and problems, which is one of their weaknesses.

According to the Committee to Protect Journalists (http://www.cpj.org), based in New York, Russia is the third-deadliest country in the world for journalists, following Iraq and Algeria. One of the victims was Anna Politovskaya, whose assassination received worldwide coverage in 2006.

The two national television channels are the most accessible media for the Russian population, thus a control over them means significant influence on public opinion, which can also decide the outcome of elections. The situation is no better outside Moscow or St Petersburg. Regional media are controlled by local and regional governments and élites who often interfere directly to stop opposition publications, radio stations and television channels. State media have low credibility as they react very slowly to Russian and international events. Many journalists have long relied on the authorities for instructions and recommendations on what and how to report.

As far as the typology of television is concerned, cable television is aimed only at local and community audiences. Differentiation and diversification of Russian television is yet to come. Internet and satellite-transmitted radio signals contribute to the rapid development of local radio broadcasting. Local radio stations are springing up all over the country and in major cities, replacing national radio broadcasters, whose number is decreasing.

The print media market has changed in many ways since the collapse of the Soviet Union. Many national newspapers published in Moscow during the communist era have lost their national audience. Circulation of Moscow daily newspapers dropped from more than 100 million to 6 million. The circulation of *Komsomolskaya Pravda* and *Izvestya* has dropped significantly, with regional and local newspapers replacing them. Lower circulation is due to the high cost of newspapers and the lack of trust in the press by the public. Regional papers, however, pay less attention to national and international issues and, therefore, television's role becomes even larger in covering these types of events and issues. The lack of access to national and regional information results in the information fragmentation of the country and to further regionalization. Financial newspapers are developing rapidly and so are newspapers distributed free of charge, such as *Metro*. Some newspapers, such as the *Moskovskii Komsomolets*, combine the features of quality papers and tabloids to serve different levels of readers at the same time. The *Moscow Times* has become the most successful foreign-language newspaper in Russia.

Paying journalists and editors to publish material favorable to an organization (called *zaka-zukha* in Russian) is widespread in the Russian public relations industry. A study conducted by a Moscow-based public relations agency found that thirteen out of twenty-one Russian national news-papers and magazines were willing to publish a fake press release for a payment of a sum between $200 and $2,000 without even checking whether the content was accurate or not (Sutherland 2001). According to Alistair McLeish, Mmd's managing director who works in Russia, a half-page editorial in Russia's leading paper cost about US$7,500 plus some US$500 for a journalist in 2006. The local offices of international public relations agencies, which bring along a more professional and ethical practice, may change the landscape; however, this will be a long and slow process.

According to Pasti (2005), two types of professional role have emerged within contemporary Russian journalism. The older generation continues to view journalism as an important societal task in close collaboration with those in power. The new generation of journalist, however, views journalism's role as providing entertainment in support of a sensationalist media agenda. The members of this generation combine their journalism job with freelancing for commercial organizations (serving two masters). "They perceive journalism as a type of PR, working for the interests of influential groups and persons in politics and business" (Pasti 2005, p. 108).

Zassoursky (2002), a professor of journalism at Moscow University, sees great potential in the Internet, which creates new public space that can be used as a public sphere: "The internet counter-balances the development of a surrogate public sphere by presenting the global public space, opening the access for participation to individual citizens, civic groups thus promoting diversity and pluralism." Social media are yet to develop in Russia, and public relations has not utilized it to its full potential. An example of this is blogging, which is being simply monitored by public relations practitioners who do not utilize blogs as a proactive communication tool yet. In March 2007 there were around 28 million Internet users in Russia, which means a 19.5 percent penetration rate (only a 2 percent penetration rate in 2000). The Russian Internet and broadband markets are growing fast, together with the market for mobile phones.

Public relations in Russia

The first thing to note about Russian public relations is that it cannot be considered homogenous, as the country incorporates eighty-nine different regions, with almost a hundred different nationalities and eleven time zones, covering 17 million square kilometers. Although public relations in Russia has been influenced by US public relations scholarship and education, it is probably best not to try to describe it through the lens of US or Western public relations theory and development but rather to understand it as a unique phenomenon.

The country's bureaucratic economic and political environments, the legacy of decades of ideological and governmental propaganda, and official secrecy have significant bearings on the development of Russian public relations.

Public relations is still in its infancy in Russia; however, some periods can be clearly distinguished. Public relations emerged when the policies of *glasnost* and *perestroika* enabled freedom of speech and created fertile ground for public relations toward the end of the 1980s. Former journalists became the first public relations practitioners to work in public relations (Goregin 1996) and were able to turn media interest to the advantage of their organizations. The first local consultancies specialized in election campaigns and political public relations. The media's interest turned to business only later. Public institutions and government agencies started to employ press secretaries in 1992, and international public relations agencies were establishing their local offices around the same time. The Russian Public Relations Association (RASO) was founded in 1991. Sam Black, one of the founders of British public relations, conducted the first international seminar on public relations in 1992.

Following the fall of the Soviet Union, and with the arrival of Western and US economic advisors and multinational corporations, more and more Western public relations agencies and experts have established operations in Russia. In 1993, Burson Marsteller became prime communication advisor for the Russian Ministry of Privatization. As in other countries of Eastern Europe, public relations strategies and instruments have been applied in support of government privatization programs. For example, campaigns have been designed to increase awareness and understanding among citizens of such market categories and instruments as shares, bonds, the stock exchange or the rights of stockholders. One of the most important results was that there was no organized backlash to the privatization program (McElreath *et al.* 2001).

The second factor contributing to the growth of Russian public relations during the early 1990s was the political scene, with more than fifty political parties competing for citizens' votes. It was during this period that political consultants started to call themselves public relations specialists. In the pre-election battles, manipulative methods of misinformation were often used, described later as "Black PR".

The mid-1990s signaled a new era for public relations with some qualitative changes in the practice. Public relations agencies were mushrooming, and their role increased; however, this was more in the political arena than in economic life. In 1997 political consulting constituted 60 percent of Russian public relations services, with 40 percent left for the business public relations (Krylov 2003, p. 102). Russian public relations practitioners also started to develop professional relations with Western and US professional bodies. In 1997 the Russian Public Relations Association became a member of the European Public Relations Confederation (CERP). In 1999 the Russian Public Relations Consultancies' Association (AKOS) was established. This association is taking a leading role in developing unified professional standards, and in 2007 it was planning to conduct certification of both public relations specialists and agencies. This is made necessary by the diluting of the profession, as people lacking education or experience are trying to exploit the fact that there are no unified standards or established professionalism criteria.

The quality of information about the public relations profession has improved as several online journals (http://www.rupr.ru, http://www.pronline.ru) and portals are now devoted to Russian public relations, such as the portal of the Russian Public Relation Association (http://www.raso.ru) or the professional public relations portal (http://www.sovetnik.ru). The majority of the websites are concerned with providing practical advice on writing news releases, dealing with the media, organizing events or campaigns, but largely remain tactical in scope rather than strategic. Public relations is often presented on these sites as a quick fix, a practice the "secrets" of which can easily be learned.

Not only in Russia but also in Ukraine and Poland, the notion of "Black PR" entered the vocabulary of public relations in the 1990s, contributing to an overall negative image of the profession. In Russia the term refers to political campaigns during elections with the aim of creating negative images of the opposition or political rivals. Books and websites are devoted to the theory and practice of "Black PR". They detail strategies and tactics about fooling people, creating bad images of political rivals, lying about other candidates' plans and strategies or reacting to rivals' actions (e.g.

Ponidelko and Lukashev 2001). The notion of "black public relations" is often dismissed as manip-ulative propaganda or unethical practice; some US scholars even claim it does not exist at all. It also demonstrates that political use of public relations is dominant and widespread.

The dynamic economic development of Russia's economy in the last few years has created further demand for professional public relations: the Russian public relations industry grows at an annual rate of 30–40 percent. This demand comes from Russian as well as international com-panies investing in the country. The favorable market conditions and rising budgets have encouraged large international firms to expand their activities into the Russian market, such as Ogilvy, Pleon or Fleishman–Hillard, which have recently established local partners. Mmd's Moscow office has been very active since 2004, and Ketchum recently signed contracts not only with the Russian government but with Gazprom, too. Andrew Sveshnikoff, a Russian public relations consultant, estimated the Russian public relations industry to be worth around US$100 million in 2005 (http://www.webershandwick.co.uk/outcomes/issue7/topstory.html), and according to Gyroscope the total expenditure on public relations in Russia was US$300 million annually during the early 2000s (Gyroscope 2004). In 2004 around 160 agencies described themselves as public relations agencies, but public relations is likely to be broadly interpreted as it includes marketing and other communication agencies as well. Similarly to other Eastern European countries, Russian public relations is concentrated in the capital, Moscow, and other major cities such as St Petersburg. Political public relations, media relations, events management and marketing public relations domin-ate practice in Russia, while CSR, financial relations, strategic communication, risk communication or international public relations are developing slowly.

Public relations has been used not only domestically but externally as well to improve the image of Russia abroad (Szondi in press). Putin used an international public relations agency in prepara-tion for presidential elections in 2000, when an international media and advocacy campaign was developed to explain policies on the war in Chechnya and his approaches to economic and social reforms to Western opinion leaders. In 2006 the Kremlin decided to engage in an international media campaign in the UK, the US and China to "correct the negative and outdated stereotypes about Russia" and to give the country's image a makeover. The Russian government used public relations not only to improve Russia's image abroad (see case study below) but also to create a reputation for President Putin as a strong leader. Pictures of a bare-chested Putin during a fishing holiday were published on the front cover of leading magazines in August 2007.

Public relations education

Public relations education can have great potential in spreading more ethical practice. Around ninety higher educational institutions offer public relations courses or degree programs. Although public relations was accredited by the Federal Russian Committee of Higher Education in 1995, and in 2000 the Committee also accepted the requirements for public relations students (Krylov 2003, p. 106), only a few universities meet a certain level of Western standards. The first full-time courses in public relations were offered at the prestigious Institute of Foreign Relations of Moscow State University at the beginning of the 1990s. However, Electrotechnical University (LETI) in St Petersburg introduced the first university-based degree program. By now, public relations has become a pop-ular and fashionable degree program in Russia. Some universities use public relations programs as an income generator despite the fact that many departments are understaffed and public relations lecturers lack professional experience.

Sidebar: Ketchum and Russian Federation G8 organizing committee. Opening its doors to the world: Russia's presidency of the 2006 summit

Russia's hosting of the G8 summit in 2006 presented Ketchum with the task of trying to change the perceptions of journalists and commentators, as well as think-tanks and academics from all over the world. Ketchum's teams in the US, Canada, the UK, Belgium, Germany and France united to tackle the challenge of lessening Russia's negative press, estimated at more than 55 percent of international media coverage, and raising the positive coverage from just 7 percent.

The international team did broad research to learn how Russia is seen abroad and about the political challenges facing its G8 presidency. It determined that several élite media outlets could shape the way the rest of the coverage went for Russia's summit presidency. One judge called this campaign an "ambitious global program with an extraordinarily challenging client".

To take on that client, Ketchum's execution focused on the correlation between media relations and influencer outreach. The team used credible third-party sources and direct interviews with the Kremlin to win key media placements, such as the influential piece in the *Financial Times* that announced Russia's "re-emergence as a world force".

Ketchum team members attended the St Petersburg International Economic Forum to engage leading international businesses and secure their support. Prior to the summit, the team conducted briefings with influencers and Russian ambassadors in G8 capitals, laying the groundwork for open communications.

The firm's digital media development group, eKetchum, updated the official G8 website to incorporate realtime news delivery and conducted search-engine optimization for the website to increase its online visibility.

In the end, the public relations team achieved its goals by more than doubling positive media coverage and decreasing negative press by more than half. Ketchum made the once-opaque dealings of the Kremlin open to the world and shifted global views of Russia to recognize its more democratic and Western-friendly nature. Global Campaign of the Year 2007.

Source: http://www.prweek.com

Questions for discussion

- Do you think US American public relations should serve as a benchmark when describing and understanding PR in other parts of the world? Defend your position.
- What is the specific role of transitional public relations, and to what extent is it applicable to CEE countries including Russia?
- Is democracy a precondition for public relations? Explain your answer.
- How could you explain the strong influence of US public relations on the Russian public relations market?

Featured biography: Joanna Piskunowicz

Joanna Piskunowicz is completing her master's degree with the Department of Economic Journalism and Public Relations at the Poznan University of Economics in Poland. At 25, she is ready to start an international career: she has lived abroad, travelled to almost all European countries and worked with professionals.

During her first years at the university, she sought opportunities to use her natural interest and capability in communication, becoming a student-activist. Involvement in an international students' organization, AEGEE (the European Students' Forum), allowed her to discover the international and multicultural aspects of communication and public relations. With AEGEE, she organizes local activities, visits events abroad and serves as the association's president. Additionally, she helped develop the Public Relations Students Scientific Circle, joining a campaign promoting the university and the PR Department among Poznan high-school students. She encourages fellow students to adopt an active approach. "Studies are about so much more than studying," she says.

Being a student of the internationally oriented Poznan University of Economics has permitted Joanna to gain experience abroad. Through an ERASMUS scholarship, she studied one semester with Ecole Supérieure des Sciences Commerciales d'Angers in western France, an experience that helped shape her final thesis. In spring 2004, France and the US were debating the Iraq issue. Joanna was inspired. "Creating and sustaining a positive and recognisable image of a country is a long-term process where a dialogue with various publics is a must, not a preference," she observes. "This is what true public relations is about for me." She decided to write her master's thesis on the French and US application of public relations tools in rebuilding mutual perception of each country's images and economic relations after the disagreement over the war in Iraq.

Joanna was deeply involved in preparations for the 4th Transitional Public Relations Conference, organised by the PR Department's students and faculty. She became the person in charge of communication with all invited speakers coming to the event from all over the world. "I had a chance to exchange regular e-mails and personally welcome to Poznan such prominent experts of international public relations as professors James and Larisa Grunig, Michael Kunczik and Alan Freitag," Joanna says. "It was a remarkable experience to share my passion for public relations with them."

As a youth trainer, speaker, participant or organizer, she attended conferences and seminars in Germany, France, the Czech Republic, Serbia, the Netherlands, Ukraine, Spain, Estonia, Latvia, Greece, Italy, Finland, Malta, Turkey, Bulgaria and, of course, Poland.

In November 2005 she became a candidate for the European board of AEGEE. She needed to give a convincing speech, proving her competence and motivation in just five minutes in front of 700 delegates representing 15,000 members at the General Assembly in Izmir, Turkey. Joanna won their votes, explaining her experience and goals but also conveying an image of a consummate and driven professional. She became a member of the European board and eventually vice-president of the association. Joanna moved to AEGEE headquarters in Brussels. During her board term in the very heart of the EU, she has been involved in high-level EU politics and has represented youth interests. Joanna says: "Talking face-to-face with an EU Commissioner required considerable confidence, especially arguing about an unfavourable policy and trying to change his mind."

One year later she became project manager of the pan-European AEGEE initiative, "Education Unlimited!", on alternative forms of education and youth participation. For ten months, she led an international team of fifteen young Europeans, building and maintaining relations with the stakeholders and coordinating activities and events all over Europe.

With international practice on one hand, and good PR studies on the other, Joanna is a promising employee. She is ready to grasp upcoming professional possibilities. "Different situations I have been part of have trained me to be flexible and open," Joanna remarks. "For example, living abroad became a tempting opportunity. I want to have an international career, and I know I'm prepared for it."

Recently, she accepted an internship in the PR department of the Polish Information and Investment Agency in Warsaw. This agency (PAIiIZ) encourages foreign corporations to invest in Poland. She impressed her colleagues there, and at the end of the internship she received a job offer from the Head of the Promotion Department at PAIiZ. Joanna was planning to take up this offer when she graduates from the university.

In the long-term, she would like to work for an international organization where she could make good use of her economics education, international practice in public relations and NGO experience. "I imagine myself working, for example, for the World Bank. I think I could serve its mission well."

Recommended websites

Country	PR Association	Website	Established
Slovakia	Public Relations Association of the Slovak Republic	http://www.aprsr.sk	1999
Hungary	Hungarian Public Relations Association	http://www.mprsz.hu	1990
Poland	Polish Association of Public Relations	http://www.pspr.org.pl	1994
Estonia	Estonian Public Relations Association	http://www.epra.ee	1996
Slovenia	Public Relations Society of Slovenia	http://www.piar.si	1990
Russia	Russian Public Relations Association	http://www.raso.ru/	1991
Romania	Romanian Public Relations Association	http://www.arrp.ro	1995
Bulgaria	Bulgarian Public Relations Society	http://www.bdvo.org/index.phtml	1996
Croatia	Croatian Public Relations Association	http://www.huoj.hr	1994
Ukraine	Ukrainian Association of Public Relations	http://www.uapr.com.ua	2005

References

Badescu, G., and Uslaner, E., eds, 2003. *Social Trust and the Transition to Democracy.* London: Routledge.

Bugajski, J., 2003. Russia's new Europe. *The National Interest,* winter. p. 2.

Cohen, S., 2000. *Failed Crusade: America and the Tragedy of Post-Communist Russia.* New York: W. W. Norton.

Culbertson, H. M., 2004. Around Europe: an introduction. In D. J. Tilson and E. C. Alozie, eds, *Toward the Common Good: Perspectives in International Public Relations.* Boston, Mass./New York: Pearson.

Czarnowski, P. (1999). Polskie public relations – jakie jest, kazdy widzi. Paper presented at the meeting of the Polish Association of Public Relations in Warsaw, July.

Elreath, M., Chen, N., Azarova, L. and Shadrova, V., 2001. The development of public relations in China, Russia, and the United States. In R. L. Heath, ed., *Handbook of Public Relations.* Thousand Oaks, Calif./London/New Delhi: Sage.

Goregin, A., 1996. Evolution of modern Russian communication – public relations in Russia. *Communication World,* June–July.

Gruban, B., 1995. Performing public relations in Central and Eastern Europe. *Public Relations Quarterly,* 40, pp. 20–4.

Grunig,J. and Grunig, L., 2005. The role of public relations in transitional societies. In R. Ławniczak, ed., *Introducing Market Economy Institutions and Instruments: The Role of Public Relations in Transition Economies.* Poznan: Piar.pl

Gyroscope, 2004. The public relations landscape in Russia, [online]. Available at: <http://www.gyroscopeconsultancy. com/docs/ThePRLandscapeinRussia.pdf> [accessed September 16, 2007].

Hiebert, R. E., 1992a. Global public relations in a post-communist world: a new model. *Public Relations Review,* 18 (2), pp. 117–26.

Hiebert, R. E., 1992b. Public relations and mass communication in Eastern Europe. *Public Relations Review,* 18 (2), pp. 177–87.

Hofstede, G. H. and Hofstede, G. J., 2005. *Cultures and Organizations of the Mind.* 2nd edn. New York: McGraw-Hill.

Howard, M., 2003. *The Weakness of Civil Society in Post-Communist Europe.* Cambridge: Cambridge University Press.

Krylov, A., 2003. Diffusion und qualitaet von public relations in Russland: analytische darstellung (Diffusion and quality of public relations in Russia: analytical approach). In A. Krylov, ed., *Public Relations im Osteuropäischen Raum: Dialog und Erfahrung auf der Basis Gesellschaftlich-ökonomischer Transformation.* Frankfurt: Verlag Peter Lang.

Krzewińska, S. and Paczkowski, P., 2007. Prasa o public relations (Press about public relations). PRESS-SERVICE Monitoring Media Raport PR 05 (1).

Łaszyn, A., 2001. Poland's pr slowdown. *FRONTLINE.* IPRA. October, pp. 16–17.

Ławniczak, R., 2001. Transition public relations: an instrument for systemic transformation in Central and Eastern Europe. In R. Ławniczak, ed., *Public Relations Contribution to Transition in Central and Eastern Europe.* Poznań: Printer.

Ławniczak, R., 2003. The transitional approach to public relations. In B. Van Ruler and D. Verčič, eds, *Public Relations and Communication Management in Europe.* Berlin: Mouton de Gruyter.

Ławniczak, R. ed., 2005. *Introducing Market Economy Institutions and Instruments: The Role of Public Relations in Transition Economies.* Poznan: Piar.pl

Ławniczak, R., Rydzak, W. and Trębecki, J., 2003. Public relations in an economy and society in transition: the case of Poland. In D. Verčič and K. Sriramesh, eds, *The Handbook of Global Public Relations.* Mahwah, NJ: Lawrence Erlbaum.

McElreath, M., Chen, N., Azarova, L. and Shadrova, V., 2001. The development of public relations in China, Russia, and the United States. In R. L. Heath, ed., *Handbook of Public Relations.* London: Sage.

The making of a neo-KGB state, 2007. *The Economist,* August 23, pp. 25–8.

Markowski, K., 2002. Ekonomicznie poprawni. *Trybuna (Aneks.).* May 31, pp. A–Γ.

nVision, 2007. Media consumption in a wireless world: how the new "convergence culture" is changing television, radio and newspapers as we know them. www.nvisioneurope.com.

Pasti, S., 2005. Two generations of contemporary Russian journalists. *European Journal of Communication,* 20(1), pp. 89–115.

Ponidelko, A. V. and Lukashev, A. V., 2001. *"Chernij PR" kak sposob obladeniya vlastju ili bomba imidzmeykhera ["Black PR" as a Means of Power Acquisition or an Image Maker's Bomb].* St Petersburg: Izdateljskyy dom Biznis-pressa.

Rydzak, W., 2006. Czarny czy biały? Wizerunek public relations w Polsce (Black or white? The image of public relations in Poland). *Piar pl,* June–July.

Shevtsova, L., 2006. Russia's ersatz of democracy. *Current History,* October.

Sriramesh, K., 1996. Power distance and public relations: an ethnographic study of southern Indian organizations. In H. Culbertson and N. Chen, eds, *International Public Relations: A Comparative Analysis.* Mahwah, NJ: Lawrence Erlbaum.

Sutherland, A., 2001. PR thrives in harder times. *Frontline,* IPRA, 23, p. 52.

Szondi, G., 2004. Hungary. In B. Van Ruler and D. Verčič, eds, *Public Relations and Communication Management in Europe: A Nation-by-nation Introduction to Public Relations Theory and Practice.* Berlin/New York: Mouton De Gruyter.

Szondi, G., 2006. International context of public relations. In R. Tench and L. Yeomans, eds, *Exploring Public Relations.* London: FT/Prentice Hall.

Szondi, G., in press. Central European public diplomacy: a transitional perspective on national reputation management. In N. Snow and P. Taylor, eds, *The Routledge Handbook of Public Diplomacy.* New York: Routledge.

Van Ruler, B., 2000. Future research and practice of public relations: a European approach. In D. Verčič, J. White, and D. Moss, eds, *Proceedings of the 7th International Public Relations Research Symposium, Public Relations,*

Public Affairs and Corporate Communications in the New Millennium: The Future, Ljubljana: Pristop Communications, pp. 157–63.

Wedel, J., 1998. *Collision and Collusion: The Strange Case of Western Aid to Eastern Europe, 1989–1998.* New York: St Martin's.

Wielowiejska, D., 2000. Korupcja mediów (Corrupt Media). *Gazeta Wyborcza,* March 31, p. 1.

Wojcik, K.(2005). *Public Relations. Wiarygodny dialog z otoczeniem.* Warsaw: Placet.

Zassoursky, Y., 2002. Media and the public interest: balancing between the state, business and the public sphere. In K. Nordenstreng, E. Vartanova, and Y. Zassoursky, eds, *Russian Media Challenge.* Helsinki: Helsinki Kikimora Publication.

Chapter 13

Western Europe and "legacy" countries

Summary

Geographically, Western Europe constitutes only a small percentage of the world's land mass – examine a globe and compare Western Europe with, for example, Asia or Latin America. In terms of population, high density elevates Western Europe's global footprint, especially in countries such as Germany, Great Britain, Belgium and the Netherlands, each of which exceeds 225 people per square kilometer (compared to India at 336, the Republic of China at 137 or the United States at 37). Further, the political process that has led to the continuing development of the European Union marks the region as a powerful global economic and political force as well as an ideal environment for democratic structures that nurture and require the activities we define as contemporary pro-fessional public relations. This chapter examines the overarching trends and characteristics that define public relations practice in this import-ant region. We have chosen to include also a brief look at Australia in this chapter, labeling it along with New Zealand and Canada as "legacy countries" because of the extensive influence each derives from its Western European heritage. Of course, each of the three legacy countries boasts a proud indigenous heritage as well, but clearly the European her-itage has had the greater influence on public relations practice, though there is, thankfully, increasing recognition of the value indigenous cultures bring to human communication and the need to consider those cultures in the planning, design and conduct of communication efforts.

Chapter goals

- Understand the challenge of addressing multilevel cultural patterns in a region that might otherwise be assumed to represent homogeneity.
- Identify the subtle but important differences that distinguish Western European public relations practice from our baseline models in the United States.
- Complete our survey of the regions and nations in which public relations is practiced and appreciate fully the unique characteristics of that practice as well as the factors that influence it in each case.

Overview

The last region we shall consider might mistakenly be assumed to resemble closely the United States in its public relations practice. Granted, distinctions from that baseline we chose may be more subtle, but there certainly are differences in culture that affect professional communication practice. Also, in each other region we have examined, there are pronounced differences from one country to another within the region, and we do not diminish those differences. Grunig and Grunig (2004) accurately caution against homogenizing this or any region and suggest nation states are too large to serve as units of analysis. We agree and hope that by now you accept as merely expedient this approach to understanding the complexities of international practice. We shall continue our pattern of first painting a broad image of the region in terms of its communication-relevant characteristics, then look closer at three countries: Germany, Great Britain and Australia. Of course, it would be instructive to offer more thorough descriptions of practice in any number of other countries in the category such as Spain, France, Italy, Portugal, Sweden, New Zealand, Canada, and so on, but the aim is to equip students with the framework, skills and incentive to pursue just those avenues, and we look forward to seeing the results of your efforts! There is, in fact, a large and growing body of knowledge on nations in this region, so the student, scholar or practitioner wishing to delve more deeply will find doing so fairly easy.

In a broad sense, the development of public relations in Europe paralleled development in the United States from the nineteenth century. In fact, an argument could be made that there is a direct European influence on US public relations through US pioneer Edward Bernays. Bernays, a nephew of Austrian Sigmund Freud, freely acknowledged Freud's influence on his approach to persuasion and that he incorporated Freud's theories of mass psychology into his much trumpeted communication campaigns. Also, German philosopher Jürgen Habermas contributed terms and concepts to contemporary US public relations theory through his writings on, for example, his Communicative Action Theory (Nessmann 1995).

One common theme throughout Western Europe is not only the lack of a common definition for the term *public relations*, but often the deliberate reluctance to use the term at all. It seems there is a festering debate as to whether the practice referred to elsewhere as public relations should concern itself with communication or with relationships, though some researchers and practitioners in Western Europe argue that the terms are interchangeable. So, from the start, the standard US-centered descriptors of evolutionary models and the roles and functions framework begin to lose their relevance. Van Ruler and Verčič (2004, p. 6) offer a different functional model for Europe that reflects subtle but important differences from the US paradigm. Based on their extensive Delphi study, they deduced the following four functions for public relations:

Reflective: This, they said, involves the process of monitoring evolving societal values and standards, then apprizing organizational leadership of the potential impact of those changes on the organization. In turn, these communication managers assist leadership in shaping the organization in anticipation of and response to those changes. This function relates most closely to what US scholars and practitioners describe as "horizon scanning" – part of the issues management function.

Managerial: This function they described as being directly related to relationship development and management. It is concerned with creating and overseeing strategic communication approaches to building trust and understanding with internal and external publics.

Operational: This function basically mirrors the technician role in the US-style setting, but goes a bit beyond that, according to Van Ruler and Verčič. Rather than being limited to carrying out tactical functions, the *operational* practitioner in the European setting puts in place the means by which those functions can be conducted. Although this function involves carrying out strategic plans developed by the *managerial* practitioner, the *operational* practitioner shoulders ongoing responsibilities for formulating and lubricating the channels of communication required to execute communication plans.

Educational: This is a function largely absent from traditional US-centered models. The *educational* responsibilities for European practitioners include aiding organizational members in ongoing efforts to improve their communication skills. Granted, it is a common function of public relations managers in the US and elsewhere to conduct media training and perhaps public speaking training, but there is a distinct difference between those efforts and the communication education carried out in the European model, and it lies in the aim of that educational function. In the US model, the point is to improve the organization's ability to convey its messages to internal and external publics via interpersonal and mass-media conduits. In the European model, however, the point is to render organizational members increasingly capable of being responsive to societal demands.

Van Ruler and Verčič also lament that public relations is not fully appreciated by organizational and business leaders, and that the functional lines often blend with those of marketing and advertising in the minds of those unschooled in the discipline. Deepening that problem is the fact that public relations is far from widely accepted as a suitable academic discipline in Europe, seriously limiting its place in leading universities there. Consequently, serious teaching, research and theory development in Europe is spotty.

With that underpinning, we should more carefully define the region to which we refer. The chapter title uses the term *Western Europe*, but that is largely to distinguish the region from *Central and Eastern Europe*, addressed by Richard Ławniczak and Gyorgy Szondi in Chapter 12. This chapter actually addresses what could be defined as three separate regions: Northern Europe (Norway, Sweden, Finland, Denmark and Iceland); Southern Europe (Italy, Greece, Turkey, Cyprus, Malta, Spain and Portugal); and Western Europe (France, Germany, Switzerland, Belgium, the Netherlands, the United Kingdom, Ireland and others). Each deserves its own chapter, of course, but students and practitioners requiring that level of detail can easily conduct deeper research as needed. In this chapter, we shall refer to Western Europe as comprising all three subregions.

As we have consistently observed, history is an important and influential factor in many dimensions of national and regional culture, and the premise holds true in Europe as well. Aspects of religion, language, political ideology and social structures here can be traced and attributed to the influence of the Roman Empire 2,000 years ago. Upon that basis, over time, and especially in recent decades, with globalization, communication technology, spreading market economies and other trends described in Chapter 2, have emerged multiple centers of commerce and, as a result, multiple centers of public relations excellence throughout the region such as London, Brussels, Berlin, Paris, and so on. Culbertson (2004) notes three trends that characterize Europe since the dissolution of the Soviet Union. The first, he says, was the breaking apart of large segments of the region into new (or long-dormant) nations; this required nation-building. The second trend was the coming together of nations through new or expanding alliances; this required clarification of interdependencies among nations. The third trend, Culbertson says, is privatization and an increased focus on market structures. It is that second trend – changing and developing alliances – that most defines recent and ongoing historical developments in Western Europe. However, the context of nation-building and market transitions elsewhere in Europe, as described in Chapter 12, naturally has an impact on Western Europe.

These Western European governments all now subscribe to variations of representative democratic structures, though constitutional monarchies remain in place for some. The Heritage Foundation and the *Wall Street Journal* have developed an annual "Index of Economic Freedom" that rates and ranks countries according to ten factors including business freedom, trade freedom, property rights, freedom from corruption, and labor freedom – certainly factors that affect public relations practice (Heritage Foundation 2007). Of the top twenty "most economically free" nations, twelve are European. Australia, addressed later in this chapter, is ranked third behind Hong Kong and Singapore. The United States is fourth. The lowest-ranking for any Western European nation is France, listed forty-fifth among the 157 nations included in the index. Remember, this list measures freedom in terms of the degree of what the researchers term "government interference" with the economy – not human rights or personal freedom. Still, these are factors practitioners would need to consider when undertaking assignments in the region. Importantly, all Western European nations are ranked above the global average. It suggests that economic conditions are well suited to a flourishing public relations profession.

Further, the World Bank classifies nearly all countries addressed in this chapter as high income (World Bank 2007), and Germany, France, Great Britain, Italy and Spain are among the world's ten largest economies. The twenty-seven member states of the European Union can boast a population approaching 500 million (applicant countries would take the EU past that figure), and that considerably exceeds the United States. The EU generates a GDP exceeding US$11 trillion. All this from a land mass considerably smaller than the US. The open borders, widely common currency (the euro), and substantial commerce in the region promise to accelerate the process of cultural assimilation. Those factors matter. Rudd and Lawson (2007) report that, ten years ago, French graduate students replied to the question of their nationality by declaring they were French. More recently, though, they state that they are both European and French (pp. 185–6). This would seem to simplify the challenges of adapting communication approaches to accommodate multiple cultural settings, but Rudd and Lawson suggest the opposite. They say that a geocentric or regional approach might guide overall planning, but communication managers would still be dealing with individual counterparts who each bring unique cultural profiles. Consequently, planning must consider a two-layered approach in regard to cultural considerations.

One effect of these structural and economic factors in recent years has been the increased emphasis placed by corporations on lobbying government, with public relations playing an important role. As European governments continue to exert more influence on national economies, and as the European Union elevates its impact on trade and other issues, corporations recognize the importance of access to and influence upon legislators at all levels. What is not entirely clear yet is whether the direct role will be taken by professional lobbyists, as is prevalent in the United States, or whether legislators will insist upon direct contact with top organizational leaders (Haug and Koppang 1997).

Cultural profile

Depending upon the specific country examined, ranking on traditional cultural metric scales will vary widely (Hofstede and Hofstede 2005). Power distance rankings for Western European nations are well below the global average, with the exception of Switzerland (French) with a score of 70 and France at 68. Flemish Belgium scored 61, Spain 57 and Italy 50. Other Western European nations scored 40 or below, with nations from this region occupying ten of the lowest fifteen nations on the power distance scale; the other five in the lowest tier are Canada, Australia, Costa Rica, New Zealand and Israel. Given the method Hofstede and Hofstede used to gauge this metric, low scores for the region suggest employees are comfortable expressing disagreement with managers, and that decision-making in business settings is perceived to be more cooperative than autocratic. In a broader sense, the scores tell us that inequality, whether based on wealth, on status, on achievement or on another power base, is less of a factor in individual relationships in this region than it would be in, for example, many Arab, Asian or Latin American countries.

Sidebar: Weber Shandwick's campaign to save the North Sea

Weber Shandwick, one of the world's leading public relations firms, headquartered in New York but with offices throughout the globe, won the 2005 United Nations Grand Award for outstanding achievement in public relations for an environmental awareness campaign that addressed the North Sea's ongoing battle with the 20,000 tons of litter illegally dumped in its waters every year. The campaign was conducted by Weber Shandwick's Glasgow (Scotland) office on behalf of EU-funded not-for-profit organization Save the North Sea.

Weber Shandwick was tasked with raising awareness of the North Sea litter problem among fishermen, offshore workers, leisure-craft users, the shipping industry and the general public. The account team identified a series of stories with high news value, including the UK launch of "Fishing for Litter" – a scheme in which fisherman go out to catch rubbish as well as cod and haddock. The media campaign also focused on the findings of a study that revealed that 96 percent of dead North Sea fulmars (oceanic gull-like birds) had plastic in their stomachs.

Weber Shandwick worked closely with local, national and international media and news agencies to spread the message to a wide audience. The media relations-driven awareness campaign achieved worldwide press coverage potentially reaching 30 million readers and 10 million television viewers. Notable campaign coverage included BBC Radio Four and Five, the *Guardian*, the *Sun*, the New Zealand *Herald*, the *Hindu* and *New Scientist*.

"The positive publicity generated from the 'Fishing for Litter' media activities in the UK made it easier to encourage fishermen in other countries to participate in the activity," said Hanna Hedenius of Save the North Sea. "The media campaign helped to create and strengthen political contacts both nationally and internationally and the media coverage has helped to drive increased awareness of this EU project."

As with power distance, Western European nations group relatively close together on the scale of individualism versus collectivism. Recall that the US ranks first among all nations in valuing individualism, and nations in Western Europe as well as Australia, New Zealand and Canada follow closely behind, with nations in that category occupying eighteen of the top twenty ranked positions (only Hungary and South Africa break the monopoly). Only southern European nations (Spain, Greece, Portugal) appear roughly in the middle of all world nations ranked. The highly individualized societies in this region, then, would seek employment that preserves individual and family life, that allows more freedom in developing individual approaches to the job, and that offers a challenge along with a sense of accomplishment.

This cultural clustering disappears, however, when it comes to masculinity (assertiveness, achievement) versus femininity (nurturing, modesty). For example, although Austria, Ireland, Great Britain and Germany appear to value masculine cultural traits, Denmark, the Netherlands, Finland, Portugal and Sweden are at the opposite pole. Hofstede and Hofstede maintain that masculine societies draw greater distinctions between gender roles, while feminine societies generally view men's and women's roles as overlapping more. As one might expect, in feminine countries such as Sweden, women are quite prominent in the public relations profession – 75 percent of practitioners are women, according to Flodin (2003). At the other end of the spectrum, a European Union study (German gender pay gap 2002) a few years ago found the pay gap between genders to be greater in Germany (a high masculine culture) than in any other EU country.

Similarly, there is no common pattern among Western European and legacy nations in terms of uncertainty avoidance. The higher the intolerance for ambiguity, the higher the score on Hofstede and Hofstede's index. Countries scoring high, such as Greece, Portugal, France and Spain, would likely be characterized by more demonstrative displays of emotion, firm rules for what is appropriate behavior, and avoidance of undue risk. Countries low on this scale, such as Denmark, Sweden, Ireland and Great Britain, would more likely accept uncertainty as part of life, would conceal their emotions, and would view uncertainty with curiosity and interest.

The index depicting long-term versus short-term orientation is an eclectic mix as well, with northern European countries leaning toward a long-term orientation, though not nearly so much as Asian countries, and other European nations plus the European legacy nations leaning toward a short-term orientation. Long-term-oriented nations stress perseverance and sustained efforts for delayed results, and value thrift and conservation of resources. Short-term-oriented countries look for quick results, respect traditions, concern themselves more with social status, and focus more on spending than on saving.

Practitioners preparing for assignments in Western Europe can expect a degree of homogeneity along the high-context/low-context communication dimension, too, though moderate differences appear between northern and southern areas of the region. As you might expect, southern countries such as France, Spain and Portugal feature somewhat more pronounced high-context communication, and northern nations including Germany, Sweden and Norway are characterized by more direct, low-context speech patterns (Schmidt *et al.* 2007). The same authors identify a number of other patterns that distinguish communication within and among Western European nations and that certainly would affect practitioners working in this environment. For example, they report that the German business culture is a formal one, defined by a formal chain of command, attention to detail and punctuality. The French, on the other hand, place a premium on courtesy and quiet discussion, though a degree of argumentativeness is permissible. In France and Italy, they report, it would be inconsiderate to ask about one's profession, but discussion of sport, art or travel would be welcome. The first-name basis most US Americans might engage in early in a professional relationship would be unacceptable in Western European settings. Practitioners on assignment in Europe should also expect lengthy handshakes, even hugs and occasional kisses as part of greeting rituals in many countries; failing to engage in this manner could be interpreted as insensitivity or even engender mistrust. The customary US American "pushiness" would be wholly frowned upon in Western Europe; better to take time getting to know your counterparts before lunging into business matters.

Although some of these cultural measures are based on somewhat dated input, they cannot be dismissed. Hazelton and Kruckeberg (1996) observed some time ago that cultural assimilation among European nations would certainly progress, but they predicted distinctions would fade only gradually and that some distinctions would always exist. Also, remember that demographics are always changing, and Western Europe is no exception. On average, the Western European population is becoming older and more educated, and the growing Muslim population is certain to have an impact on culture, business practices and other facets of society.

The CERP

A fair indication of the sophisticated state of public relations in Europe is found in an examination of the Confédération Européenne des Relations Publiques (CERP) or in English the European Public Relations Confederation. This umbrella organization, with headquarters in Brussels, fosters contacts, exchanges and other links among all European professional public relations organizations. The CERP also supports research, teaching, and efforts to develop a unified system of professional ethics. It was founded in 1959 thanks to the leadership of Lucien Matrat, author of the 1965 Code of Athens, a landmark document that calls for high standards of ethical behavior and responsibility for CERP (and IPRA) members. The code also links ethical public relations practice with the highest principles of human rights. The code was expanded in the Code of Lisbon, adopted by CERP members in 1978. National counterparts to CERP include the Chartered Institute of Public Relations (UK), Deutschen Public Relations Gesellschaft e.V (Germany), the Danish Association of Public Relations Agencies, the Public Relations Institute of Ireland, the Federazione Relazioni Pubbliche Italiana (Italy), the Asociación de Empresas Consultoras en Relaciones Públicas y Comunicación (Spain) and others (see Recommended Websites at the end of the chapter).

Van Ruler *et al.* (2004) conducted a Delphi study among European practitioners representing twenty-five European countries and consequently described four paradoxes regarding practice there. The first is the "European Paradox" that finds a widely recognized need for unique European approaches and theories to guide European practice but a tendency to define practice here in terms based on US American scholarship and practice. This, the authors suggest, may stem from the lack of European-specific research or a lingering dependency on US public relations expertise. The second is the "Practice Paradox", which cites a lack of clarity regarding the nature of the profession. Practitioners report a deep desire to elevate the discipline to the status of a specialized management function, but find themselves mired in the expectations of their clients and superiors, whose expectations are largely in the technical or craft arena of public relations. The third is the "Conceptual Paradox" and refers to the term designating the profession. Study participants report fully understanding the nature of contemporary public relations, but in practice most organizations avoid the term, preferring instead to refer to "corporate communication" or simply "communication management". The fourth paradox is the "Theoretical Paradox" and has two dimensions. One is that study participants were nearly unanimous in their call for the accelerated generation of European-unique public relations theory, but they were unsure of what research needed to occur. The second facet is that, though the participants expressed lofty desires for new first-order theoretical directions, they acknowledged a greater need for practical skills and know-how.

Questions for discussion

1. Would you expect the regions of northern, eastern, western and southern Europe to grow more similar in their public relations practice or to retain strong vestiges of their individual cultural characteristics in the coming years? Why?
2. Do you expect developments in US practice to continue to influence European practice, or will the US become less of an influence? Explain your position.
3. What issues do you forecast will dominate European public discussions in the future? To what extent will social media affect those public discussions?

The United Kingdom

Its full name is the United Kingdom of Great Britain and Ireland, and it comprises four distinct parts: England, Wales, Scotland (these three occupy the island of Britain), and Northern Ireland (which, together with the Republic of Ireland, occupies the island of Eire). Each of the four has a distinct history, culture and even ancestral language. In social or business settings, it is wise to recognize these distinctions. Although the *CIA World Factbook* and most other sources addressing the geography of the UK place it in Western Europe, UK citizens do not customarily consider themselves Europeans. Illustrative of this dichotomy is the fact that the UK belongs to the European Union but has not adopted the euro as its currency. Less than a quarter of a million square kilometers in size (smaller than the US state of Oregon), its impact on world history has been astonishing. The UK was a leading nation in the development of parliamentary democracy, and it has made enormous contributions to science, art, literature and other areas. At its zenith in the nineteenth century, its empire included roughly a fourth of the earth's surface. The twentieth century, though, was difficult for the British as they suffered through two world wars. The UK nevertheless emerged from those challenges to become a vibrant, modern economic and political power. As in many leading economic nations, heavy industry continues to decline, replaced by ongoing growth in service industries such as banking and insurance.

Sidebar: Studying public relations in London

Many would maintain that London can claim title to being the center of gravity for international public relations. It is appropriate, in that sense, that the Prime Meridian dividing the Eastern and Western Hemispheres runs through Greenwich, just outside London. Because of London's increasingly important role in international pub-lic relations, the University of North Carolina at Charlotte conducts an annual four-week summer seminar in London for international public relations students. The eighteen to twenty students who participate each year have come from the US, Canada, Republic of China, South Korea, Turkey, Taiwan and elsewhere. The course is hosted by Regent's College in Regent's Park, London. Although the class meets four days each week, often those days find the students taking advantage of the many important public relations opportunities London offers. For example, students typically visit the world headquarters of HSBC Bank for discussions with communication and media relations managers, they visit the BBC to hear from public relations managers and World Service correspondents, and they enjoy briefings and discussions with key figures at leading public relations firms (Crispin Manners, featured in the biography at the end of this chapter, is a regular participant). A recurring event has been an afternoon of briefings and discussions on issues of public diplomacy with top officers at the US embassy. Class speakers include leading public relations practitioners and scholars addressing topics such as corporate social responsibility, an area in which the UK is setting the pace. Students also work on projects and conduct informal research unique to the London setting. Studying and experiencing public relations in London adds considerably to one's body of knowledge. Here is what past students have said: "I loved the program and recommend it to anyone, especially those with an interest in international public relations." "I want to go into international PR now more than ever." "By far my favorite class of my college career. . . . Gave me insight that I never would have gained otherwise."

Here's what Morrison and Conaway (2006) say about the British character:

> The English are somewhat closed to outside information on many issues. They will participate in debate but are not easily moved from their perspective. They are quite analytical and process information in an abstractive manner. They will appeal to laws or rules rather than looking at problems in a subjective manner. There is a conceptual sense of fairness – unwritten, as is the constitution – but no less vital. Company policy is followed regardless of who is doing the negotiating. (p. 538)

The authors then recommend that presenting objective facts rather than feelings is the proper approach to discussion and negotiation. As in the US, central tendencies in the UK favor individualistic leanings; achievement and individual initiative are valued. Unlike in much of Asia, the British are comfortable and confident in saying "no", but they will do so with the utmost politeness. Well above the median in uncertainty avoidance, the British prefer firmly established rules and procedures, and change is not automatically welcomed. They are highly sensitive to time constraints and deadlines, though they would customarily restrain from letting any anxiety (or most emotions, for that matter) appear obvious; they will also appreciate it if you refrain from emotional displays. Like US business managers, those in the UK tend to focus more on short-term gains than on long-term. Also as in the US, the British tendency is toward direct, low-context speech patterns. Nevertheless, and in a unique variation of this low-context pattern, the British have a tendency toward the understatement, subtlety, even a degree of imprecision, avoiding specific data in favor of more vague references such as "more or less".

The British respect authority and rank, so sending senior representatives will increase the likelihood of success in business matters. Good manners are prized. Gannon (2004) suggests the typical British house as a metaphor for British character and culture. He says: "[F]oundations are deep and strong; the floor plan does not vary and is unchanging over time . . . A house, like a way of life, should have strong foundations, be familiar, unchanging, and built in tried and tested ways" (p. 222). Gannon also says that the British expect business managers to conduct meetings and other proceedings efficiently and to maintain good relations with employees. Instructions are generally presented more as suggestions than as directions.

UK media enjoy considerable political and social freedom, though some restrictions apply to advertising and other content, with guidelines prepared and administered primarily by two government agencies: the Office of Communication and the Ministry of Culture, Media and Sport. The government-chartered British Broadcasting Corporation operates independently but is a public, non-commercial service; its charter requires it to maintain high content standards and to operate in the public interest. Newspapers – and there are a lot of them – are self-regulated but sensitive to citizen complaints lodged through a formal system. The Office of Communication licenses and regulates broadcast operations to ensure compliance with a detailed code regarding content, largely focused on advertising and protection of children from inappropriate content (McKenzie 2006).

There are ten national daily newspapers in the UK, with circulation led by the *Sun* at nearly 3.5 million a day; interestingly, the *Sun* is highly sensational and stresses entertainment news. The venerable *Times*, globally recognized for its serious coverage of national and global issues, is far behind at 720,000. Radio and television saturation in British homes is virtually 100 percent. Most national newspapers are associated fairly openly with particular political orientations. For example, *The Times* reflects the *status quo* of the government in power, the *Telegraph* leans to the right and the *Guardian* to the left. The *Independent*, despite its name, is more liberal and tends to advocate for the environment against war on principle. There is a stable of sensational tabloid-style newspapers including the *Daily Mirror* and the *Daily Express*, each with its own following (McKenzie 2006). The public relations practitioner, therefore, should be prepared for and expect openly biased coverage in both editorial and news content. This is far less true of radio and television coverage. On the other hand, practitioners will find coverage of news events and issues to be of considerable depth and breadth.

It was out of the crucible of the twentieth century that public relations emerged as a profession in the UK. For example, the high value placed on local government administration of services resulted in a coordinated communication campaign in the 1930s to resist a central government effort to diminish the local role. The campaign began to coalesce the dynamic forces that nurtured the nascent profession, and the need to rally public support and participation during the World War II further contributed to the refinement of the discipline. Following the war, the central government employed public relations tools in public diplomacy and to combat worker unrest in the face of economic difficulties and industrial mechanization. Business and commercial communication efforts were largely confined to advertising through most of the first half of the century, though a few public relations agencies appeared as early as the 1920s (L'Etang 1998).

Today, the guiding body for public relations in the UK is the Chartered Institute of Public Relations founded in 1948. The CIPR, with 9,000 members, is the largest association of this kind in Europe. It has played a leading role in public relations education and professional development, and administers a rigorous accreditation process for its members. It also publishes the trade magazine *Profile* and subscribes to an ethical code of conduct. For a thorough examination of the CIPR and especially its influence on public relations education, read Jacquie L'Etang's detailed and sometimes unflattering review based on CIPR archives (L'Etang 1999). Here's how CIPR describes its membership:

- CIPR membership has grown by more than 50% in the last ten years
- Approximately 60% of our members are female – this has grown from only 20% in 1987
- 45% of our members work in PR consultancy and 55% work in-house
- Two thirds of CIPR members are based outside London
- 40% of our members hold Managing Director/Head of Communications positions, 30% are PR Manager/Account Director level, 20% PR officer/Account Manager level and 10% PR Executive/Account Executive role

(Information about the CIPR 2008)

Germany

Germany's economy leads Europe, and its population of approximately 83 million is second in Europe only to Russia (about 142 million). The CIA World Factbook describes the nation as an affluent and technologically advanced nation, and says the Federal Republic of Germany (full name) appears to be emerging from a five-year period of economic stagnation that included relatively high unemployment. Germany saw healthier economic growth in 2006, accompanied by higher employment. Some of the economic sluggishness can be attributed to the continuing challenge of integrating the former East Germany into a united nation beginning in October 1990. Efforts such as industrial modernization and raising the retirement age are helping to boost productivity and reduce social security outlays. Despite the brief period of economic sluggishness, Germany remains a leader in many major industries: iron and steel, cement, coal, chemicals, machinery, vehicles, electronics, shipbuilding and textiles. German products have a reputation for high quality, driven in large part by German consumer expectations.

Culturally, Morrison and Conaway (2006) say that Germans avoid the unexpected and have traditionally been closed to outside information. They note, though – and Bentele and Wehmeier (2003) agree – that Germany is experiencing a generational dichotomy between the older, traditional generation that favors a sense of obligation and obedience as well as order, diligence and modesty, and a younger generation that prefers creativity, spontaneity and self-emancipation. The older sector values family, work and traditional gender roles (change in this respect is reflected in the election of Angela Merkel, the first female chancellor of Germany, in 2005), while the emerging sector focuses on freedom of lifestyle and self-expression. Regardless of the generation, Germans love nature and the outdoors, and they enjoy long vacations (generally six weeks per year plus holidays), often to participate in rigorous activity such as hiking, skiing and bicycling.

Practitioners on assignment in Germany are likely to find their German business contacts to be highly analytical and comfortable discussing issues at the conceptual level. They are selective in building relationships, but once established they are deep and enduring. They place a high value on abundant data and facts, and avoid emotional considerations. They can be stubborn once they have taken a position on an issue. Reaching a decision may take time, and every facet of the issue will be taken into account. Additionally, there will likely be a number of people within the organization who will need to reach consensus on the issue before that decision is rendered. Avoid discussion of personal matters during business activities, but do be direct and to the point in presenting your position or counsel. It would be risky to inject humor into business proceedings. Germans lean toward a near-term orientation and minimum risk. Perhaps more than anyone else, Germans appreciate and expect punctuality in both business and social settings. Probably needless to say, do not introduce the topics of World War II or anti-Semitism. As in most nations, there are some regional differences in culture, with southern (Bavarian) Germans tending more toward the informal and northern Germans retaining more rigid characteristics (Morrison and Conaway 2006).

Germany shares power distance and masculinity/femininity rankings with the UK, described earlier, but scores a good deal lower in individualism, aligning itself more with the Scandinavian countries in this category (Hofstede and Hofstede 2005). Germany ranks considerably higher in uncertainty avoidance than does the UK, suggesting that the central cultural tendency among Germans would be characterized by greater anxiety and stress, and that following strict rules would be expected in order to avoid social disruption. It also suggests that they would seek and value the opinions of the most respected experts.

Günter Bentele is certainly a leading scholar in German public relations, and his contributions to the literature provide a comprehensive analysis of the discipline's evolution and current status in his country. As this text has established and repeated, the public relations profession has been necessitated and shaped by a variety of social, political, economic and cultural forces, events and trends. In Germany, those factors in the past two centuries have sometimes been turbulent and have even exerted their influence in opposing directions. Consider, as Bentele and Wehmeier point out (2003), that the nation has experienced the German Alliance, the German Reich, the Weimar Republic, the Nazi period, the Second World War, the divided Germanies (East and West), and finally the reunification of East and West in 1990. Bentele and Wehmeier divide this historical tapestry into seven distinct periods described in condensed form in Table 13.1.

Of primary interest to current and aspiring practitioners would be developments since World War II. Following the media oppression and exploitation of the Nazi dictatorship, West Germany experienced a rebirth of the public relations profession as it built rapidly upon the strides that had been made up until 1933. The postwar period saw the establishment of the Deutsche Public Relations Gesellschaft (German Public Relations Association). Before the 1960s, however, public relations was thought of as "advertising for trust" according to Bentele, and stressed drawing media

TABLE 13.1 Bentele's German public relations periods

Pre-history	Official press
Period 1 (mid-19th century–1918)	Discipline development; first government press offices; war press releases; censorship; first public campaigns
Period 2 (1918–33)	Rapid growth of press offices; public relations extended to other sectors
Period 3 (1933–45)	Ideological party propaganda under Nazis; party control of media
Period 4 (1945–58)	Accelerated public relations development on US model; increased professional status, especially in business
Period 5 (1958–85)	Increased self-awareness of discipline; establishment of professional association; in East Germany, emergence of socialist public relations
Period 6 (1985–present)	Rapid increase in agencies; growth of formal education programs; application of scientific approach

Source: From Bentele and Wehmeier 2003, p. 200

attention to products and brands. In fact, in the first decades following the war, public relations practitioners endured terms such as *Sektglashalter* ("champagne-glass holder") and *Frühstücksdirektor* ("breakfast director", implying the practitioner's role was merely to be a companion for meals). In the 1970s, with increased social activism, there emerged increased recognition of the need for dialog, and public relations became increasingly defined in strategic communication contexts. The 1980s saw the growth of formal education programs in universities and *Fachhochschulen* (applied science or technical schools).

A term used today for public relations is *Öffentlichkeitsarbeit*. The direct English translation, if there were such an English word, would be "openliness work". The implication is a combination of communication and harmony between an organization and its constituencies. More than 20,000 people work in public relations in Germany now, though only about 10 percent belong to a professional association. Among all practitioners, 40 percent are in corporate settings, 20 percent in non-profits, 20 percent in government at various levels, and 20 percent work in agencies. It is estimated that 70–80 percent of practitioners have earned the equivalent of a university degree, though few have studied public relations; that is changing as more universities are offering courses in public relations principles, writing, campaigns, ethics, law and research. Bentele reports, too, that German public relations mirrors the pattern in other Western countries of the shift from a male-dominated profession to majority female. Another trend appears to be the elevated level of the public relations function within organizations; the vast majority of companies that maintain a public relations function do so at the executive level.

Bentele and Wehmeier (2003) say that the bulk of public relations professionals' time is spent in media relations. Independent media are free from government influence, but are charged with facilitating public opinion, monitoring government activities, and serving as a conduit between government and citizens. Until the 1980s, print media were private and broadcast media were public; now there is a dual broadcasting system of some private and some government radio and television stations and networks. Public broadcasting provides informational programming along with culture and sports. Private broadcasting, dependent upon advertising revenues, leans toward entertainment. Germans are heavy radio listeners – nearly 3.5 hours daily. Most Germans (80 percent) also spend around half an hour reading a daily newspaper.

Bentele and Wehmeier (2003) predict a continued trend in Germany toward specialization among the growing number of public relations agencies, for example in investor relations. He also forecasts rising appreciation of public relations capabilities by top organizational leaders. This, he says, will be driven by and will in turn drive the elevation of public relations as an academic discipline and as a process based on scientific approaches.

Questions for discussion

1. What cultural challenges would you predict for a British practitioner on assignment in Germany?
2. Would you consider it important for British media relations managers to maintain relationships with journalists and editors with the UK's tabloid newspapers? Why or why not?

3. What strategies would you recommend to encourage the establishment of more public relations programs at leading German universities? What do you think the barriers are that have slowed that effort?

Australia

Australian business professionals appreciate communication that is brief and to the point, according to Morrison and Conaway (2006), and hard-sell tactics and hyperbole will damage your message and your reputation. Direct honesty is the best approach. There is a distinct barrier between work and recreation, so avoid blending the two. Despite its large size (sixth-largest nation in the world), Australia is an isolated island nation, so its people have become accustomed to working with outsiders, including virtually, so they are quite approachable and comfortable in multinational working environments. They are open-minded, but at the same time rely heavily on policies and rules. They reason objectively and prefer facts but do not require exhaustive detail. Emotional appeals carry little weight. Australians appear high on the individualism scale, but they also reflect high egalitarianism and value outward manifestations of that quality – do not boast or imply that you are "better" than someone else. You will find citizens here modest and casual. Do not be afraid of a respectful argument – they appreciate candor and frankness.

With just two people per square kilometer, Australia is tied for first place in this regard, though 80 percent of its population lives in large cities within 85 kilometers of the coast (Gannon 2004). Nearly a quarter of its population was born in another country. Gannon says an apt metaphor depicting Australian culture is outdoor recreational pursuits, especially the barbecue. He says the backyard barbecue began as a casual backyard family event on a Sunday afternoon. Soon it grew to include several families. Now it has expanded to a beach event involving more friends and organized sports and games. This, Gannon says, accurately reflects Australia's progression from appendage of the British Empire to a far more inclusive and multicultural society. Still, it is a nation that scores quite high in individuality but low in power distance. Achievement is stressed less here than in other highly individual societies, though, and there is a distinct dislike of pomposity and arrogance, and that cautions against touting credentials or professional experience.

Singh and Smyth (2000) report that public relations has grown since the first professional association appeared at state level around 1950. Now there are 3,000 members of the national Public Relations Institute of Australia, an organization that helps coordinate professional development efforts by the academic and corporate sectors. Education programs are increasingly available through public and private colleges and universities. Singh and Smyth (2000) describe results of a 1999 survey of Australian practitioners, finding, for example, that the largest age bracket for public relations professionals was 25–30, suggesting that university programs are providing a well-qualified cadre of practitioners. More than 60 percent of all practitioners are women, and larger percentages of women appear in the younger age brackets. The vast majority of practitioners had tertiary education credentials, and about one in five had achieved PRIA accreditation. More than 70 percent report working in media relations. That was followed by internal communication, sponsorship/event management, community relations, government relations, and conference organization, in that order. Salaries followed the US pattern, with highest salaries found in corporate communication and lower salaries associated with non-profits and education. More than three-quarters of respondents reported working in a strategic mode, with research and planning part of the process. Most top public relations executives report directly to the CEO, reflecting Australia's organizational culture of participatory, democratic and accountable decision-making. There is also increasing emphasis on measuring results.

Sidebar: Mass shooting illustrates importance of issues management

On an April Sunday in 1996, a gunman walked into a café in Port Arthur, Tasmania, and indiscriminately shot and killed thirty-five people and injured thirteen more. Tasmania is an island state off Australia's southeastern coast. At once, the issue of gun control became sharply focused in Australia, with the flames of debate fueled by media coverage and efforts by various factions to sway public opinion by framing the event and the issue to suit particular points of view. Calls were raised for stricter gun laws at the national level – previously an issue left to individual states in Australia. There was widespread public support for moves in this direction, but opposition came from powerful and influential circles including state governments, some national government departments, the gun lobby, farmers and others. Mass media became an important conduit for groups seeking to make their point, and the media became willing participants in covering pseudo-events and publishing leaks that kept the drama on the public agenda – and boosted ratings and circulation.

Researcher Christopher Reynolds examined this event in the context of issues management, but the episode also illustrates elements of Australian cultural tendencies. A strong element of individualism probably bolsters the argument against stricter gun-control laws, but a strain of egalitarianism suggests, on the other hand, a desire for equal rights, including the right not to fear being the victim of a random, senseless act such as the shooting in Tasmania. Additionally, Australians love a good debate, and this event certainly provided one. It also illustrates the influence of expanding communication technology on public issues as well as an increasingly sophisticated public. In Australia, as in other nations, matters of weight such as public safety are no longer left solely to decisionmakers in the halls of power. Here was an issue that all the public could engage in, and politicians recognized the enormous power of public opinion. The media naturally reported the event, but they then kept the issue before the public by moving to address the issue underlying the event. The media gave voice to protagonists and antagonists, sometimes in provocative fashion. Factions on all sides of the issue capitalized on the opportunity to conduct aggressive communication campaigns in support of their position. Still, as Reynolds points out, the debate relied more on emotional appeals than on rational argument. Regardless, the debate eventually subsided or went dormant for now without any significant changes in Australia's gun laws. A similar pattern of issues management and campaigning through the media in Australia is described by Howell and Miller (2006) concerning health issues associated with asbestos.

Source: Reynolds (1997)

Australian public relations practitioners continue to face the same obstacles to professional excellence that plague their counterparts in the US and elsewhere. Probably chief among those obstacles is the difficulty in shifting from input- and output-based evaluative measures of success to measures of outcome. Xavier *et al.* (2005) analyzed more than a hundred award-winning entries in PRIA's Golden Target competition and surveyed PRIA's 2,800 members to assess attitudes toward and actual performance of evaluative techniques. Their results confirmed research conducted a decade earlier that found a genuine desire to improve measurement of campaign and program effectiveness, but little discernible progress doing so in actual practice. The emphasis appears to remain on measuring output rather than outcome.

Conclusion

We have not addressed Canada and New Zealand, and these two countries along with Australia share their British heritage, but a variety of factors have conspired to lend each a unique culture and subtle but important differences in their approaches to public relations. Each deserves in-depth study, and we encourage students and practitioners to pursue that, particularly in anticipation of assignments involving any of the three countries.

This ends our survey of the world's regions and the nature of public relations practice in each. We certainly do not consider these glimpses to have been exhaustive, but we do hope that they inspired the student and practitioner to delve more deeply into areas and countries that particularly interest them. We also hope that these regional chapters have provided a sense of direction for that exploration and a framework to guide it. What is left to accomplish is to consider emerging issues, trends and social forces that will continue to influence and be influenced by public relations practice. We do so in the next and final chapter.

Questions for discussion

1. Now that you have read about and studied all the global regions – at least to the extent that we have been able to address them in this text – what patterns do you see regarding the spread and adaptation of public relations practice?
2. Do you see the possibility of establishing universal standards of practice excellence? Of universal ethical standards? Why or why not?
3. We have talked about public relations *technicians* and *managers*, but do you see a role for another level – public relations *leaders*? What would distinguish that role from the first two?

Featured biography: Crispin Manners

Crispin Manners is Director of Service Innovation for Kaizo, a full-service public relations firm in London, a city at the vortex of international public relations activity. Kaizo is owned by the Argyll Consultancies PLC; and, as CEO from 1990 to 2007, Crispin built Argyll into one of the fastest-growing public relations firms in the UK. Committed to professional development, he is past chairman of the Public Relations Consultants Association, a Fellow of the Chartered Institute of Public Relations, and a Freeman of the Guild of PR Practitioners.

Manners stresses the need for practitioners to conduct activities based on unchanging fundamental principles. "PR functions best when organizations deal in truth and in countries where freedom of speech is a reality," he says. "The need to deal in truth is now sharply in focus because pervasive access to the Internet means that organizations have nowhere to hide." He finds London a wonderful place to practice. "For a long time, it was the natural first port of call for North American businesses wishing to enter Europe, though this has changed a little in recent years." He says sometimes practitioners come into the European market expecting a high degree of similarity from one country to the next. "Although we have a united Europe of more than half a billion people, in reality what exists is an incredibly fragmented situation that needs to be addressed through the PR strategy," he observes. "It is vitally important to recognize that there are also varying levels of maturity when it comes to PR across Europe. Some territories have well-entrenched rights to freedom of speech going back centuries, but in others freedom of the press is a relatively new phenomenon."

Manners's particular interest recently has been in Web 2.0. "In my opinion Web 2.0 places the PR person front and center in communications," he says.

It allows PR to operate at a scale hitherto limited to advertising and yet do so by direct engagement online. It is this ability to have a direct dialogue cost-effectively at a large scale that will shape practice over the next few years. It will mean practitioners need to change from a culture of "create and distribute" to one that stimulates individuals to interact, endorse and recommend.

He links Web 2.0 with word-of-mouth strategies, or WOM. "WOM is most accurately defined as the process of passing recommendations from one person to another," according to Manners. "PR has always been about creating recommendations – only usually we rely upon traditional influencers rather than individuals."

To gauge the effectiveness of WOM efforts, Manners employs the Net Promoter Score system, a metric developed by Bain & Company and Satmetrix that identifies the recommendability of a product, service or brand. Manners has adapted the NPS system to Kaizo's three-step consumer engagement methodology. "Net Promoter is an ideal tool for PR professionals because it focuses attention on the essential requirement to set expectations where they can be exceeded," Manners explains. "It also segments customers into three groups: those where expectations have been missed, met or exceeded. This allows PR professionals to create strategies tailored to the needs of these three groups." Manners acknowledges, though, that the Net Promoter Score system has been tested only in the UK and the United States; he cautions that cultural differences may affect system dynamics in other settings. Nevertheless, he sees no real limitations to internationalizing WOM strategies in general, though cultural differences must certainly be taken into account. "A one-size-suits-all approach to WOM in every territory will not work," he warns. "The strategies need to take account of local differences and the essential requirement for local content. To do this effectively requires PR management at a local level." That has been a strength for Kaizo, he notes.

It is particularly helpful to be able to call upon a partner office to deliver a short-term activity or to provide local market insight for a client's benefit. Although we live in a world where online information is available in an instant, there is no substitute for professional support on the ground if communications are to deliver sustained advantage.

Manners's twenty-five years' experience in public relations management and innovation have earned him recognition as a leading light of the profession. In 2007 his campaign for the Simple beauty brand won the inaugural Web 2.0 award from the PRCA. His communication planning tool, ValueFlow, won Kaizo the title of UK's Innovative Company of the Year in 2003. His success can be attributed to his ability to balance innovation and emerging trends with a solid underpinning of proven standards. "The incredible thing about public relations is that it is a constantly evolving discipline that is founded in immutable principles."

Recommended websites

Index of Economic Freedom   http://www.heritage.org/index/countries.cfm

The European Union   http://europa.eu/index_en.htm

BBC World Service   http://www.bbc.co.uk/worldservice/

Confédération Européenne des Relations Publiques   http://www.cerp.org/

Chartered Institute of Public Relations   http://www.cipr.co.uk/

Deutschen Public Relations Gesellschaft e.V (German Public Relations Association)   http://www.dprg.de/statische/ itemshowone.php4?id=140 (English version)

Danish Association of Public Relations Agencies   http://www.publicrelations.dk/index/index/?lang=5 (English version)

Public Relations Institute of Ireland   http://www.prii.ie/cgi-bin/default.asp

Federazione Relazioni Pubbliche Italiana (Italian Public Relations Federation)   http://www.ferpi.it/index.asp

Asociación de Empresas Consultoras en Relaciones Públicas y Comunicación (Spainish public relations association) http://www.adecec.com/index.html

Sveriges Informationsförenin-g (Swedish public relations association)   http://www.sverigesinformationsforening.se/ in-english.aspx (English version)

The Canadian Public Relations Association   http://www.cprs.ca/Welcome/e_Welcome.htm

The Public Relations Institute of Australia   http://www.pria.com.au/

References

Bentele, G. and Wehmeier, S., 2003. From literary bureaus to a modern profession: the development and current structure of public relations in Germany. In K. Sriramesh and D. Verčič, eds, *The Global Public Relations Handbook*. Mahwah, NJ: Lawrence Erlbaum, pp. 199–221.

Culbertson, H. M., 2004. Around Europe. In D. J. Tilson and E. C. Alozie, eds. *Toward the Common Good: Perspectives in International Public Relations*. Boston, Mass.: Pearson, pp. 127–32.

Flodin, B., 2003. Public relations in Sweden: a strong presence increasing in importance. In K. Sriramesh and D. Verčič, eds, *The Global Public Relations Handbook*. Mahwah, NJ: Lawrence Erlbaum, pp. 244–56.

Gannon, M. J., 2004. *Understanding Global Cultures: Metaphorical Journeys through 28 Nations, Clusters of Nations, and Continents*. Thousand Oaks, Calif.: Sage.

German gender pay gap is EU's largest, 2002, [online]. Available at http://www.eurofound.europa.eu/eiro/ 2002/11/inbrief/de0211201n.htm [accessed December 31, 2007].

Grunig, J. E. and Grunig, L. A., 2004. Foreword. In B. Van Ruler and D. Verčič, eds, *Public Relations and Communication Management in Europe*. New York: Mouton de Gruyter, pp. xi–xiii.

Haug, M. and Koppang, H., 1997. Lobbying and public relations in a European context. *Public Relations Review*, 23 (3), pp. 233–47.

Hazelton, V. and Kruckeberg, D., 1996. European public relations practice: an evolving paradigm. In H. M. Culbertson and N. Chen, eds, *International Public Relations: A Comparative Analysis*. Mahwah, NJ: Lawrence Erlbaum, pp. 367–77.

Heritage Foundation, 2007. Index of Economic Freedom, [online]. Available at http://www.heritage.org/index/ countries.cfm [accessed December 18, 2007].

Hofstede, G. and Hofstede, G. J., 2005. *Cultures and Organizations: Software of the Mind*. New York: McGraw-Hill.

Howell, G. and Miller, R., 2006. Spinning out the asbestos agenda: how big business uses public relations in Australia. *Public Relations Review*, 32, pp. 261–6.

Information about the CIPR, 2008, [online]. Available at http://www.cipr.co.uk/News/Newsrameset.htm [accessed January 21, 2008].

L'Etang, J., 1998. State propaganda and bureaucratic intelligence: the creation of public relations in 20th century Britain. *Public Relations Review*, 24 (4), pp. 413–41.

L'Etang, J., 1999. Public relations education in Britain: an historical review in the context of professionalisation. *Public Relations Review*, 25 (3), pp. 261–89.

McKenzie, R., 2006. *Comparing Media from around the World*. New York: Pearson Education.

Morrison, T. and Conaway, W. A., 2006. *Kiss, Bow, or Shake Hands*, 2nd edn. Avon, Mass: Adams Media.

Nessman, K., 1995. Public relations in Europe: a comparison with the United States. *Public Relations Review*, 21 (2), pp. 151–60.

Reynolds, C., 1997. Issue management and the Australian gun debate. *Public Relations Review*, 23 (4), pp. 343–60.

Rudd, J. E. and Lawson, D. R., 2007. *Communicating in Global Business Negotiations: A Geocentric Approach*. London: Sage.

Schmidt, W. V., Conaway, R. N., Easton, S. S. and Wardrope, W. J., 2007. *Communicating Globally: Intercultural Communication and International Business*. Los Angeles, Calif.: Sage.

Singh, R. and Smyth, R., 2000. Australian public relations: status at the turn of the 21st century. *Public Relations Review*, 26 (4), pp. 387–401.

Van Ruler, B. and Verčič, D., 2004. Overview of public relations and communication management in Europe. In B. Van Ruler and D. Verčič, eds, *Public Relations and Communication Management in Europe*. New York: Mouton de Gruyter, pp. 1–11.

Van Ruler, B., Verčič, D., Bütschi, G. and Flodin, B., 2004. A first look for parameters of public relations in Europe. *Journal of Public Relations Research*, 16 (1), pp. 35–63.

World Bank, 2007. Data & Statistics, [online]. Available at http://go.worldbank.org/K2CKM78CCO [accessed December 18, 2007].

Xavier, R., Johnston, K., Patel, A., Watson, T. and Simmons, P., 2005. Using evaluation techniques and performance claims to demonstrate public relations impact: an Australian perspective. *Public Relations Review*, 31, pp. 417–24.

Chapter 14

A look to the future

Emerging global trends likely to influence international public relations practice

Summary

In the 2006 PRSA State of the Profession Opinion Survey, US public relations professionals ranked the trends they believed would be most important in the coming years. Their responses suggest issues likely to influence the development of international public relations around the globe. Perhaps not surprisingly, the opportunities provided by new media ranked high on the list. New communication channels including social networking websites such as MySpace, and text messaging ranked highest among all trends affecting the profession. Professionals also ranked highly the continuing integration of marketing communications and globalization. They identified a number of important public relations challenges, too, including upholding credibility and demonstrating the value of public relations to management and society. Of course, practitioners have different concerns in different times. If you examine the chart that appeared in a June 1967 public relations journal, you will see some of the trends public relations professionals then predicted might occur. Although some of their concerns may seem amusing now, others are surprisingly accurate. This chapter addresses the emerging societal, media and professional trends influencing international public relations practice in today's world.

Sidebar: Predictions from the past

The following chart appeared in the June 1967 issue of *Public Relations Journal*, the monthly magazine published by PRSA until 1995. Under the headline "Be your own Nostradamus", a table listed thirty items that could occur between 1967 and 1987. According to the journal, "in terms of probability, everything with a 60 percent probability or above has an awfully good chance of happening. Here is the way the experts see the probabilities."

EVENT/PERCENT OF PROBABILITY

1. Effective worldwide anti-poverty program is carried out. 20%
2. Computer-programmed use of all agricultural land areas is introduced. 40%
3. Drugs to control personality are widely accepted and used. 60%
4. Annual wage of $6,000 is guaranteed to all breadwinners. 20%
5. Short-term weather forecasting is highly reliable. 60%
6. Effective worldwide fertility control is practiced. 60%
7. Wide practical uses are made of lasers in industry and medicine. 80%
8. Household robots are widely used and facsimile newspapers are printed in the home. 40%
9. Manned military space base exists. 80%
10. Racial barriers are effectively eliminated. 40%
11. The growth of new limbs and organs can be artificially induced. 20%
12. Expenditures for recreation and entertainment are double those of 1966. 60%
13. Free public education through college is available to all. 40%
14. Roadless vehicles open new areas for travel. 40%
15. Limited weather control is carried out globally. 20%
16. Private passenger vehicles are barred from most city cores. 60%
17. Annual investment in automated equipment is 10 times that of 1966. 80%
18. Economic production of fresh water from oceans is possible worldwide. 80%
19. Air and water pollution are under control. 40%
20. Three out of four people in the United States live in cities or towns. 80%
21. Manned lunar base exists. 60%
22. Defense budget is less than 10 percent of Gross National Product. 60%
23. Full-color 3-D TV is in use on a global basis. 60%
24. Human brains linked to computers extend man's intelligence. 20%
25. Most business is conducted by picture-phone. 20%
26. World agricultural production is 50 percent above that of 1966. 60%
27. Currency is virtually eliminated by credit cards. 60%
28. Average work week is shortened to 32 hours. 40%
29. Individual intelligence raised by drugs. 20%
30. Men land on Mars by 1986. 40%

© 2007 by Public Relations Society of America

Chapter goals

■ Acknowledge significant differences between past and present global trends, while also being sensitive to future, rising trends.

■ Comprehend specific public relations implications of growing multiculturalism, emerging democracy, globalization and the increasing expectation for corporate social responsibility.

■ Identify developing trends in new media and technology, and consider their impact on future public relations practice.

■ Recognize the opportunities presented by societal and media trends and understand their effect on the image of the public relations industry.

■ Explore the public relations profession's efforts to increase practitioner diversity, establish the value of public relations, and advance public relations education and professional standards.

Societal trends

It is clear that society has changed a lot since 1967. Today, businesses often need to "go global or go home" (Cook 2007). Globalization has helped public relations become a growth industry around the world, but the global marketplace is complex (McCleneghan 2005). The increasing spread of democracy and free enterprise makes for increased competition and communication. Meanwhile, barriers to business might be low, but cultural sensitivities are high: think of the controversial introduction of *Playboy* magazine in Indonesia and the angry reaction in the Muslim world to the Pope's anti-Islamic comments (Cook 2007). To succeed in today's world, companies and agencies must understand local behaviors and preferences (Cook 2007). In this section of the chapter, we shall explore the public relations implications of increasing multiculturalism, emerging democracy, and rising anger at the pervasiveness of Western lifestyles and values that globalization brings. Further, we shall look at how the increasing expectations for companies to be socially responsible and the need to manage crisis on a global scale deepen the challenges in executing successful international public relations.

Multiculturalism

Multiculturalism is an important trend with far-reaching implications for public relations. In the US, for example, minorities will comprise a third of the US population by 2016. One of the largest and growing minority groups in the US is Hispanics. According to the US Census Bureau, the Hispanic population is projected to reach 60 million by 2020. Asians comprise the second fastest growing US ethnic group. Meanwhile, US society is changing in other ways. Dominant baby-boomers are nearing 60, with Generation X poised to become more prominent and powerful (McCleneghan 2005).

Multiculturalism, however, is not limited to America. Non-native-born people make up 80 percent of Dubai's population. Immigration is changing the populations of European nations, with Africans emigrating to Italy and Spain and Russians settling into Western Europe (Cook 2007).

As a result of these types of population change, the world is witnessing a "cultural fusion" (Cook 2007). This cultural blend is apparent everywhere, even in food. Europeans now embrace the Doner sandwiches of transplanted Middle Eastern residents. Americans eat more salsa than ketchup. Starbucks, McDonald's and Pizza Hut join traditional restaurants the world over. What does cultural fusion mean for public relations? Multiculturalism presents several challenges. On the one hand, public relations must become more precise in its efforts to target audiences. On the other hand, public relations must keep a global perspective in mind when adapting to this new cultural environment. Examples of how public relations professionals have responded to these somewhat conflicting demands should highlight the complexity of managing this trend.

The growth of Hispanic audiences in the US provides one example of the opportunities and challenges in targeting public relations messages carefully. Hispanics represent currently almost US$1 trillion in buying power, and Spanish-language and Hispanic-toned media content is thriving (Solloway 2007). Spanish-speaking consumers can be reached on programs airing on Telemundo, ESPN Deportes, or MUN2. Content can be made available on the websites of newspapers in leading Hispanic markets including New York, Los Angeles, Chicago, Dallas and Miami (Solloway 2007). According to Manny Ruiz, chair of PRSA's Diversity Committee, indications that the Hispanic market will continue to spread present an opportunity for public relations. He notes that the fast-growing

Hispanic population in places such as Las Vegas, Utah and North Carolina is inevitably followed by radio and television stations that cater to these audiences. As he points out about using these channels, however, "People used to think that once Latinos learned English they would do everything in the English language and forget Spanish. That has been proven totally untrue" (in Cobb 2007a, p. 19).

In fact, a glance at demographics of Hispanic/Latino teens shows the diversity in languages, preferences and cultures that public relations professionals need to understand in order to reach these groups effectively. Within the US Hispanic teen population, half are bilingual and 26.7 percent prefer English as their primary language. For these teens, there is no such thing as speaking only Spanish or English, or consuming only Spanish or English media. They prefer media that embrace their complex and undefined bicultural identity – a mix of Latino, urban and US cultures (Reveron 2007). They see themselves as teenagers first and Hispanics second, living mostly in English and remaining connected in varying degrees to Latino culture and language (Reveron 2007).

Corporations and institutions are attempting to respond to these types of cultural and linguistic preference. Major league sports teams are working hard to reach Hispanic audiences, for example. To reach the more than 7.5 million Hispanics living in Los Angeles, the major league baseball team, the Dodgers, engages in grassroots public relations efforts and has partnered with Calvin Klein, Macy's and Coca-Cola. Major league soccer has strengthened ties with Latino fans since 1976. The Major League Soccer (MLS) league believes a third of its US soccer-base fans to be Latino and has tried to reach them through sponsorships with companies including Honda, Burger King and Panasonic. MLS also hired Colombian World Cup star Wilmer Cabrera as the "voice" of its Latino events including programs such as "Verano MLS" ("Summer MLS") (Ayala 2007).

Outside the sports arena, public relations staff for Hispanic consumer magazines such as *People en Espanol* are working hard to reach their target audience more effectively. In fact, *People en Espanol* reports positive circulation numbers when overall magazine newsstand numbers are in decline. *People's* partnership with the History Channel en Espanol, its efforts to cover breaking Hispanic news, and its switch from an all-Spanish website format to a bilingual one have helped to boost readership (de Lafuente 2007). These types of targeted approach used to reach Hispanic audiences represent one way to respond to the multicultural society trend.

Examining the public relations environment in Europe illustrates a different challenge in responding to multicultural realities. In Europe there are twenty-five countries, twenty-five different histories, twenty-five different cultures, and twenty-five different media landscapes (Macleod 2005). As a result, public relations practitioners must see beyond the more regional tactics employed by the Dodgers' public relations staff. Targeting on the basis of a common language is inadequate, and a more localized approach becomes necessary. To suit local tastes and preferences, one public relations scholar describes the public relations challenge in Europe this way: "As Heinz applies different recipes to its same name soups (depending on the country), so the public relations recipe needs to be altered" (Macleod 2005). That is, in the European market, reaching these varied audiences requires finding common ground and concerns but simultaneously considering the exponential impact of time, distance, culture and language when developing a campaign (Macleod 2005). To be successful, practitioners must develop a local angle, cultivate key relationships, foster contacts and build databases, translate/adapt to cultural tastes, and target (Macleod 2005).

Examining PR efforts in reaching European and Hispanic audiences highlights the notion that, despite an emergence of a global "cultural fusion", responding correctly to specific audiences requires great care and sensitivity. Reaching audiences *en masse* has become even more difficult. The European

Association of Communication Directors, for example, argues that some efforts to embrace holistically the world's cultures with public relations messages have missed the mark. August 2007's *Communication Director* includes commentary about Live Earth, a 24-hour, six-continent concert series, designed to take a multicultural approach in making people aware of climate change. After all, music is a powerful form of communication. Musicians may have more influence than politicians among young people. However, *Communication Director* warns that the Live Earth strategy might have been slightly misguided:

> Jet setting rock stars may send mixed messages about energy conservation. In 2006, Madonna's world tour produced an estimated 485 tons of carbon dioxide in four months ... one might also wonder how much energy and emissions might have been saved if millions of people would have stayed at home in front of the TV on 7/07/07 rather than taking a plane or a car to learn more about saving energy.
>
> (Zur Hausen 2007).

And, as even The Who's Roger Daltrey argued: "The last thing the planet needs is a rock concert" (in Zur Hausen 2007). It seems that, although music might be the global language, reaching the world's populations with a global message and approach is tricky. In contrast, other efforts in responding to the emergence of global fusion are met with more success, as seen in efforts to expose Indian consumers to wine (see the sidebar, "Finding India's nose for wine").

Sidebar: Finding India's nose for wine

Call it Grape Expectations. Puns aside, India's wine industry is growing significantly. Its expansion signals one way a consumer trend can take on a multicultural dimension. In fact, some call the development of interest in wine in India one of the fruits of globalization (Moreau 2007). In the past, many Indians either chose not to drink or tended to drink beer and liquor. With the circulation of Western media and lifestyles, though, wine is becoming increasingly popular among Indian consumers. As Abhay Kewadkar, winemaker for Banaglore-based United Breweries, observes about India's consumers: "They are exposed to this Western lifestyle. They want to be stylish. Wine fits that bill" (in Sengupta 2007a). Another observer adds: "As globalization has stoked India's economic boom, its growing middle class has become increasingly accustomed to the pleasures and conveniences of the West, including well-made wines" (Moreau 2007, p. 1). As a result, wine clubs are emerging, wine tours of young Indian vineyards are attracting visitors, and there is a wider availability of wine in supermarkets and upmarket restaurants. There is further evidence that the "cultural pendulum is starting to swing" (Moreau 2007). Actors in Bollywood films are now drinking wine, and Indian wine makers are planning major expansions financed by US venture capitalists. So far, the industry is targeting the Indian consumer with easy-to-drink, inexpensive options. As Moreau (2007) notes about reaching these new consumers effectively: "The goal is to lure – not intimidate – young Indian professionals" (p. 3). As India's taste for wine continues to develop, public relations professionals will need to find more ways to customize wine's characteristics to Indian preferences. Cheers!

In addition to bearing in mind these examples of precisely targeting various audiences in a multicultural world, there are a number of more general suggestions for the international public relations student eager to respond to the multiculturalism trend. Experienced international practitioners advise students, particularly those with a US background, to be less ethnocentric in evaluating the success of their approaches and to be open to new ideas and perspectives (Epley 2003). Further, executives observe that US Americans need to understand and respect cultural differences more fully and not only look at a country from its economic point of view, but also really listen, research target audiences and the main trends of a home country, be able to adapt to cultural and social differences, and avoid being judgmental of these differences.

Responding to the multicultural trend means recognizing also that knowing a language of a particular country is not enough. Ninety-two percent of the world's 5.9 million consumers do not speak or read English. English is just one of 7,600 languages worldwide (Poulin 1997). Similarly, even if a variety of countries speak a common language such as Spanish, practitioners should recognize that these countries will not be identical culturally. Indeed, if one learns one of these languages but not the culture, "One feels like a clumsy elephant in a dainty china shop – moving carefully and still sending china crashing to the floor" (Beeth 1997). Ihator (2000) warns that direct translation into other languages of English-produced documents may not produce the intended meaning. Native speakers will need to translate "killing two birds with one stone", which is "hitting two flies with one swat" in German and "catching two fish with one rod" in Korean. In other words, public relations people must spend the time learning and getting to know the subtleties, in addition to the language(s), of a given country.

As we have done repeatedly in this text, we return to public relations scholar Zaharna (2001), who provides a highly useful way for international public relations students to consider these language, cultural and national differences. Recall, she describes three primary ways of describing client–practitioner differences in international public relations: country, cultural and communication profiles (Zaharna 2001). Country profiles outline what may be *feasible* in a country (in terms of the country's political structure, economic structure, mass media, infrastructure, legal structure and social structure) but the cultural profile speaks to what might be *effective*. This profile includes knowing whether the country has a high- or low-context culture, their relationship to time, the preference for doing or being, and whether the culture is linear or non-linear. Finally, the communication profile speaks to how cultural differences affect specific individual public relations practice. There can be cross-cultural variations among the following components of public relations efforts: verbal communication, non-verbal communication, visual communication, rhetorical style and the general communication matrix. Identifying these profiles will help the practitioner identify and respond effectively to differences. An appreciation of these profiles can especially help students conduct effective public relations in emerging democracies around the world.

Public relations in emerging democracies

Addressing the multicultural trend is complex enough in open, democratic societies. This task becomes even more difficult in light of the second trend of more nations emerging as democracies. Many emerging democracies are moving from state-controlled media to a more open journalistic system, which, as we have learned from other chapters, has implications for public relations. Sometimes, as countries open up after war or in a quest to strengthen democracy, public relations challenges arise. In Bosnia, for example, alternative media channels appeared to be more trustworthy than either state media or local government officials. Government leaders and public relations practitioners needed to be aware of public perceptions toward each type of media. Because Bosnians trusted alternative channels more, messages needed to be shared accordingly. Government leaders and practitioners needed to meet with media across the political spectrum and help Bosnians have a variety of trustworthy sources from which to gather their information. Discovering these types of credible communication channel is imperative in rebuilding civil societies, and public relations practitioners and theorists must give significant attention to all available channels (Botan and Taylor 2005).

In addition, the media of some emerging democracies continue to follow a "cash for news coverage" arrangement as they convert to a more open media environment (Kruckeberg and Tsetsura 2003). In Poland, for example, public relations people often face media bribery in the workplace, in direct and indirect forms. This media bribery includes publishing publicity materials in exchange for advertising in the same media and putting financial pressure on media outlets to present information that comes from companies and public relations agencies. As a result, there is a dispersion of perceptions about the ethicality of public relations practices in Poland. In one survey, a majority of respondents (72 percent) strongly agreed that the media bribery practice is unacceptable. Almost half of public relations people reported that public relations is practiced in an ethical manner, but almost a quarter of public relations people, 40 percent of journalists, and almost half of marketing specialists disagreed (Kruckeberg and Tsetsura 2003). Public relations professionals in Poland and in other countries used to a cash-for-coverage system have a responsibility to show how media relations can work ethically. In general, public relations professionals in emerging democracies need to show what can and cannot be done if one wants to practice public relations ethically (Tsetsura 2005).

Need for US diplomacy

Just because globalization now represents a major economic force, and more democracies are emerging, does not mean that the world's populations are always pleased with the often attendant spread of Western values and lifestyles. If the spread of democracy is a trend that entails challenges for the public relations profession as discussed above, responding to the economic changes brought about by US-led globalization represents a third societal trend in public relations. According to McCleneghan (2005), global jealousies are fueling terrorism and anti-Western feelings, forming important and disturbing trends. For instance, among the US private sector there is growing concern about the ability of US American global companies to do business abroad. Business executives feel that the image of the US, which is seen as leading the spread of "Westernization", faces opposition throughout the world. To address this challenge, businesses are working to alleviate negative sentiment. One hundred and fifty top public relations professionals and US State Department leaders partnered to work together to foster more positive views of the US around the world (Private Sector Summit on Public Diplomacy 2007). The partners identified a number of important steps for improving US public diplomacy. They suggested that businesses make public diplomacy a core part of international corporate public action and work to promote understanding of US society, culture and values. They also stressed the importance of building relationships of trust and respect with local constituencies. Citibank, the largest financial institution in the United States, provides an example of operating globally in a socially responsible manner that supports public diplomacy. The company has a presence in a hundred countries, employs 350,000 people, and seeks to operate with local conventions and issues in mind. It keeps 95 percent of its employees local in the countries in which it does business. It also promotes positive views of the US through two programs. Citigroup has made $100 million in loans to thirty-nine countries and helped with getting global companies to work together on the 2004 tsunami relief effort. Citibank is working to support local community development, helping with community financial planning, and responding to NGOs as clients (Private Sector Summit on Public Diplomacy 2007).

Although examples from US public relations practice are included here, practitioners working in any region where anti-Western sentiment exists need to address carefully these feelings among local target populations.

CSR and managing crisis

The Wal-Mart Corporation is ranked second, after Ford, as the most distrusted brand in the US (O'Loughlin 2007). Why? Today, corporate social responsibility (CSR), or acting in a way that is acceptable to a given society, is increasingly important to consumers. Wal-Mart is not making a good CSR grade. It is portrayed in the media as a bad corporate citizen who hurts the environment and does not treat employees well (Kabel 2007). More and more, consumers care about corporate reputation, and Wal-Mart is not meeting expectations. Positive corporate reputations must be earned: "Consumers are aware of corporate behavior, and it impacts their impression of the company and its brands. The data tell us consumers care about the actions of corporate parents" (O'Loughlin 2007). Indeed, as the younger generation gains more prominence, CSR is likely to become even more important. Scholars warn that younger generations are more concerned about a corporation's values than about its prices (Kabel 2007).

In the US, neither Wal-Mart nor any other organization is legally required to implement CSR practices, but the situation may be different elsewhere in the world. It is generally agreed, for example, that CSR is most advanced and enforced in Europe (May 2004a). France requires companies to report on social and ethical performance. The British government's operating and financial review is looking to make environmental and social reporting a legal requirement for listed companies (May 2004a). Activists and NGOs are helping also to raise awareness about CSR issues, and CSR performance is monitored by consumers, regulators, investors and insurers.

Even if companies implement sound CSR practices, crises can still arise – and with today's global markets come globally scaled crises. This challenge is evident in numerous recent brand recalls resulting from global business partnerships. Product recalls are serious public relations issues. Fifty-five percent of people said they would switch brands temporarily in the case of a safety and health recall, and 15 percent said they would never again purchase a recalled brand. Recalls today can become even more difficult to manage, because the more people learn about a recall, the more difficulty a company can have. Because abundant communication channels make it easy for consumers to hear about recalls, companies face a precarious situation (Newman 2007).

For example, China now produces much of the US's toys and other consumer goods. Its differing labor standards and practices can result occasionally in a crisis public relations situation for those companies relying on Chinese firms to manufacture their products. Witness the 2007 spate of US pet food recalls on brands produced in China. As more and more US dogs and cats were reported to be sick, many different pet foods brands tainted with a poisonous substance were found to be affected. As the petfood industry learned that their Chinese manufacturing procedures were causing the problem, they were faced with angry pet-owners, aggressive media, and factory management and inspection issues. US pet food companies were faced with a major crisis regarding how to handle the complicated issue. As days went by, more products sold by US pet companies had to be recalled. Duane Ekedahl, president of the Pet Food Institute (PFI), called the crisis the "perfect storm" because a co-manufacturer in China made hundreds of products for many US pet food companies. Further, the substance causing the toxic problem was initially misidentified. Finally, the rolling nature of more and more foods that had to be recalled created skeptical and fearful consumers and journalists. Unlike previous recalls involving spinach tainted with *E. coli* bacteria or Tylenol's poisoned capsules, pet food companies did not pull everything from the shelves, as some brands were affected and some were not. Although 99 percent of the pet food products on the shelves were safe, it became very difficult for pet food companies to reassure consumers (Bush 2007). With consumers growing more confused and anxious every day, the pet food companies had to ensure delivery of an accurate and comforting message. Today, the pet food industry continues to work on sharing the facts about the recall and how the industry is working on the problem. The pet food crisis example shows the unique challenges global business partnerships can create for public relations. Take a look at the crisis timeline below to learn more about how public relations professionals attempted to manage the crisis. Similarly, the brief case study of Mattel's toy recall (see pp. 142–3), highlights the difficulty in managing a globally scaled crisis.

Sidebar: Timeline of industry's response to 2007 petfood recall

March 16: Initial recall announced by Menu Foods of certain canned "in gravy" products; PFI notifies members and develops key talking points, putting scope of recall into perspective.

March 17: PFI issues release on recall.

March 21: Public relations working group formed by PFI to develop materials and manage public communications on recall.

March 23: New York Commissioner of Agriculture announces finding of aminopterin in petfood, which is later disproved. PFI issues release reassuring consumers.

March 27: PFI hires Levick Strategic Communications.

March 30: FDA announces finding of melamine in the petfood ingredient wheat gluten and in finished petfood products; confirms wheat gluten was imported from China. Numerous recalls follow.

April 6: PFI's initial survey finds consumers think petfoods are safe and will continue to buy their brands.

April 12: PFI places full-page ads in the *Washington Post* and *USA Today* in the form of an open letter to consumers. PFI announces formation of the National Pet Food Commission. Ekedahl testifies before Congress on the recall.

April 16: Recalls begin related to the second contaminated ingredient.

April 26: PFI issues letter to US Trade Representative and FDA commissioner urging them to determine how melamine found its way into simple ingredients for petfood.

Source: PR Week (May 17, 2007)

Of course, if companies and organizations act responsibly and exercise two-way communication, they can help to avoid the pitfalls of not being viewed as a good corporate citizen or of finding themselves in a crisis situation. They will also be better-prepared to communicate with non-governmental organizations (NGOs) and activists. According to a UN report, there are nearly 40,000 international NGOs (Cook 2007). NGOs are growing in power and have the tools to attack major corporations. Further, other types of activism are on the rise through technology. It is much easier for activist groups to spread anti-organizational messages quickly and pervasively as a result of the Web. As a result, Cook (2007) cautions international public relations practitioners that informing activist groups will not be enough; engaging with them will become crucial. Indeed, Dougall (2005) argues that the profession has been incorrect in viewing activists as hostile but external publics in an organization's environment. Rather, she says, activists are, first and foremost, "active organizational publics" (p. 4). This fresh perspective shows that the typical public relations advice of downplaying activist concerns is not always sound in today's world. Organizations pursuing a "neutral comment" strategy in the media in light of activist claims spur more activist efforts and result in more media attention to which the accused companies must respond. In essence, then, organizations are typically better off in today's communication environment if they treat activist concerns seriously. The more activists and NGOs are thought of as legitimate publics, the more productive conversations between activists and organizations may become.

Questions for discussion

1. How have societal trends changed and progressed in your lifetime? Do you find these changes to be significant or irrelevant to the public relations industry? Explain.
2. Provide examples of multiculturalism present in your everyday life. Are these examples of "cultural fusion" successful in reaching their target audiences and maintaining a global perspective?
3. In what ways have you noticed the spread of Western values and lifestyles around the world, if at all?
4. Cite personal examples of companies effectively engaging in corporate social responsibility (CSR). Do you feel companies should be required to implement CSR practices? Why?

Trends in new media: Web 2.0 and the digital revolution

In the previous section, we examined briefly how important new media can be in resolving crises and in forwarding activist challenges. The importance of new media to international public relations does not stop there. After all, the world is becoming increasingly digitized (Cook 2007). Consider a few examples. There are 2.6 billion cellphone users today. In Asia, Muslims use cellphones to indicate the direction of Mecca and to receive prayer alerts five times a day. Hindi worshippers send text messages to the temple of the Hindi god Ganesh. Other digital technologies are increasing in popularity. Fifty million personal digital assistants (PDAs) are in use. Apple has sold 67 million iPods. In three years, 100 million people are predicted to watch television on their handsets (Cook 2007). Interesting statistics, but what do they mean for future public relations practice?

Public relations scholar Ray Hiebert (2005) suggests that these technologies represent an innovation in public communication. He thinks that people are more interested in participating in public communication because of the computer, the Internet, the Worldwide Web and wireless digital communication. As Hiebert notes, one key component of the new technology revolution in public relations is this increased Internet and Web use. The Internet and the Web offer varied types and amounts of information for consumers, especially as compared to more traditional public relations outlets such as newspapers, radio and television. The Internet has also become a social environment where news and information are traded regularly, peer-to-peer, with no news media involvement (WestGlen n.d.). Social media sites such as YouTube and MySpace provide powerful targeted channels for reaching consumers. Other online tactics such as webcasting, webinars, podcasting, iTunes and more serve as powerful methods to reach key audiences (WestGlen n.d.).

Although engaging the brave new world of new media in public relations can be daunting, most public relations professionals are embracing these opportunities: "Rather than lamenting the decline of traditional media's influence, the public relations industry is embracing the new platforms and communities that test their creativity" (Hood 2007).

What should public relations professionals know in order to capitalize on new media trends? First, different audiences use new media, not just young adults or teens. In fact, a 2006 study of media usage in the US offered some interesting findings (Looker *et al.* 2007). Blogs were relied on by only 13 percent of the respondents. Consumers still rely on traditional media, including newspapers and local television. Both men and women find local media to be the most credible, followed by traditional newspapers and broadcast news. Men and women use these traditional media outlets equally. Young adults rely more on new media, but they also continue to rely on traditional media. A 2007 report from the Joan Shorenstein Center on the Press, Politics and Public Policy reported, though, that young Americans are increasingly estranged from the daily newspaper and rely more heavily on television than on the Internet for their news. In the past, there were only small differences in news habits and daily information levels of younger and older Americans. Today, however, younger Americans do not make the news a routine part of their day, unlike older Americans. So it is important for budding professionals to consider a variety of media channels when planning message strategy. Nevertheless, it is impossible to ignore the growing opportunities presented by new media – especially blogs, social networking sites, podcasts, videocasts and mobile media (Looker *et al.* 2007).

One way to capitalize on new technology opportunities is by tweaking traditional public relations techniques. Word-of-mouth communication (WOM), with one person sharing information with another, is increasingly important, with consumers looking for a "personalized touch" when gathering information. Word-of-mouth marketing is very influential with consumers, with 50 percent of executives reporting that they are highly likely to buy a product or service based on word of mouth and 49 percent passing on that information to others (PR Newswire 2007). Some executives report that WOM has more influence than advertising, direct mail, or press coverage on purchasing decisions (PR Newswire 2007). Professionals can even use the Internet to increase the power of these WOM techniques. Procter & Gamble, for example, tapped into the influential women's social email network by aligning itself with a charitable organization and forwarding the Tide Coldwater Challenge through e-mail. The challenge donated money collected to the National Fuels

Fund Network to assist families with their utility bills, touted the energy-saving benefits consumers would receive by washing their clothes in cold water, and the resulting environmental benefits of consuming less energy (Krueger 2007). Companies have also been using viral marketing for the last few years, by which citizen marketers distribute messages for their employers (Johnson 2007). This technique has also been adapted to the online environment. During the 2004 presidential election, supporters of George W. Bush used the Internet to spread malicious rumors about John Kerry's wife Teresa, helping to influence Kerry's campaign negatively (Stokes 2005).

Particularly exciting are the opportunities presented by social media. Social media, or blogs, video-sharing sites, and social networking sites allow consumers to filter messages from companies but also create, shape and spread their own messages (Johnson 2007). The popularity of sites such as YouTube.com indicates the potential of this message channel for public relations. For example, anti-Wal-Mart documentary film producer Robert Greenwald and friends produced a series of "parody ads" along with the movie trailer and posted them on YouTube.com. The spots were downloaded 100,000 times ("When Viral Marketing Attacks" 2005). Similarly, Facebook's social networking site has expanded beyond its initial college student demographic to embrace other publics. Companies such as Wal-Mart, Target and Reebok now conduct branding campaigns on the site to appeal to various groups of consumers. Reebok's "Run Easy" campaign drew 14,000 users. Wal-Mart's "Roommate Style Match" allowed college students to browse dorm-ready furnishing and appliances and keep track of them on a personalized checklist. Target's similar initiative attracted 6,185 members (Newman 2007).

In addition to embracing these channels, Amis (2007) suggests that videocasting, also called video podcasting, and blogging will become increasingly important for public relations professionals. Further, some firms are now using multimedia news releases (MNR) to capitalize on this migration toward the Web. For example, a company working on treatments for heart disease could produce an MNR to explain treatment options, provide a video FAQ with doctors, and create educational segments about the causes and treatments of heart disease (Yehuda 2007). When considering that 70 percent of US adults use the Internet, with 66 percent preferring to access news and information online, the Web does indeed seem to be the next frontier for public relations professionals (Yehuda 2007).

The Web 2.0 revolution also increases opportunities for integrated marketing communication. Some public relations and marketing campaigns blend Web, television and sponsorship techniques to disseminate messages. This trend is also projected to continue. One recent example of this blending of communication channels is seen in Unilever Pond's sponsorship of the USA Network's series "The Starter Wife". Echoing the story of a woman who makes changes in her life following a divorce, Pond's was the presenting sponsor of the series, got its products and brands featured in the programs, and sponsored "Pond's 40 and Fabulous" contest (Burg 2007). It also used a "watch and win" promotion where viewers could learn more about the prizes on the usanetworks.com website.

Of course, new media also carry implications for crisis public relations. In 1982, before the age of the Internet, e-mail, blogs and video-sharing, Johnson & Johnson led the way in crisis communication through its use of nationwide video news conferences. In the wake of its poisoned capsule crisis, Johnson & Johnson employed the video conference to address the questions and concerns of its varied stakeholders. Today, practitioners have many more channels to disseminate their messages, but the need to show leadership, decisiveness and the willingness to do the right thing quickly is still critical in dealing with crisis public relations (Cobb 2007a). For example, in the March 2004 train bombing in Madrid, terrorists used mobile phones to detonate the bombs, but those same phones were used for text messages and e-mails that raced around Spain, urging support for the popular ruling socialist party to help alleviate the crisis (Hiebert 2005). Cellphones may have tipped the scales in that election (Hiebert 2005). In this way, the Internet and cellphones can be used to help rally mass support in times of crisis.

These technologies can also be a conduit of information for the media during a crisis, often called "I-witness" news. During the Virginia Tech campus shooting tragedy, Virginia Tech graduate student Jamal Albarghouti used his cellphone to capture video of police charging into Norris Hall, with the sound of gunfire in the background. The video was posted on CNN.com and was viewed 900,000 times (Stewart 2007). The ability of citizens to influence news coverage in this manner presents both challenges and opportunities for public relations professionals. On the one hand, immediate access to images and the possibility for quick distribution give savvy public relations practitioners a way to gain media control of a crisis. On the other hand, "I-witness" news might portray the wrong information or be impossible to manage from a public relations standpoint. When thinking about the number of people who possess camera-equipped cellphones, it is not difficult to understand how crises may be magnified by unrestricted sharing of images and information.

The increasing difficulty in managing crises in light of new media extends to employee public relations. When Shahram Ahari's videotaped criticism of his employer, Eli Lily & Co., landed on YouTube.com, Lily had to decide how to deal with this type of Web-based criticism. As executive Sarah Robbins points out about the difficulty of handling these types of situation: "Companies used to have much more control over the information they put out. Now, the informal media have much more direct contact with the public" (Smith 2007).

In other words, companies entering the brave new world of multichannel, Web-engaged forms of public relations should proceed with caution. For example, Anheuser-Bush budgeted roughly $30 million for Bud.tv, which launched during the 2007 US Super Bowl. Bud.tv was designed to be an entertainment hub for the Budweiser beer brand, featuring television programs and forms of product-placement advertising. But, because Bud.tv content could not be linked to YouTube, Digg or MySpace, the social networking sites used most by the company's target male demographic, Bud's efforts at combining product placement with social marketing fell flat and failed (Brand Week 2007).

Practitioner Jeffrey Geibel also warns that digital public relations requires professionals to rethink and restructure conventional techniques. He says the "Google zone", for example, changes everything. Because of that search engine, a news release may go to unintended audiences, be available for a long time, and embarrass the sender organization for years. Geibel suggests that, more than ever, the communicator must weigh not only the timeliness of the content and its method of dissemination, but also its complete accuracy. The "Google zone" may be both positive and negative for public relations. Anyone with an Internet connection can find and download anything at any time, but now everything produced by an organization has an "afterlife". Whether on Google, on a newsmedia website, or on a blog, anything that a company can do, good or bad, can live online forever in a virtual library that can be accessed by anyone at any time (Vaughn and Cody 2007).

Societal and media trends and the image of the public relations profession

The revolution in new media and the varied societal influences discussed earlier provide undeniably exciting opportunities for the public relations profession. These trends may also offer ways to help improve the profession's ongoing image problem. This section will look at current trends affecting the image of public relations. Unfortunately, public relations is still frequently misunderstood. It continues to be characterized as having slick, unethical practitioners who trick the public into supporting a client or issue. For example, more than 80 percent of people believe environmental public relations pros mislead the public, according to the Canadian Public Relations Conference (McCauley 2007). To help correct this misperception, professionals attending the conference were encouraged to distance themselves from questionable practices. Speakers noted: "We need to encourage clients to act decisively and honorably on environmental issues. We can't keep helping them try to spin their way out of responsible action" (McCauley 2007).

Ethics

So, in 2007 and beyond, public relations must continually address the ethics and image questions facing the profession. Some current practices raise red flags. Indeed, in the US, almost 17 percent of senior marketers say their organizations have bought advertising in return for a news story (Business Wire 2007). The willingness to pay in return for a news story creates an ethical issue, because media are assumed to be an unbiased source of information for consumers. These types of unethical practice must end for public relations to become a more trusted and respected profession. The need for ethical behavior will continue to be a strong trend in the discipline. As Gail Rymer, director of communications for Lockheed Martin, notes about ethics:

> Ethics is probably the No.1 priority. From a communications perspective, public relations needs to be leaders in that because we are the people out front dealing with the media, with consumers, with the public. If we do business ethically, everything else will follow.
>
> (Stateman 2007)

Indeed, the ability for people to gain information about organizations quickly and thoroughly online has resulted in increased demand for honesty, authenticity and transparency in public relations. Today, companies and CEOs are often suspect, with consumers wanting more accountability and higher standards of ethical conduct. James Lukaszewski, APR (2007), predicts that, as consumers demand to know the sources of information, communicators will have to become identified and attributed, which could increase the credibility and responsibility of information. Public relations executive Andrew Heyward cautions that "hype and spin are going to be less effective over time in a wired world because as consumers have access to information and they have access to as many sources as we do they become as powerful as they have, it's going to be much harder to sell something if it's not an actual authentic message" (Russell 2007). As a result, authentic messages in today's media environment are a must. Jon Stewart of "The Daily Show" and Stephen Colbert of "The Colbert Report" are popular because they are seen by the public as more authentic than the people they are parodying (Russell 2007).

Employees are also seeking greater transparency and openness about corporate policy from their employers. In the face of rising criticism about CEO and top executive pay, US corporation Aflac Insurance, best-known for its quacking duck commercials, voluntarily offered its shareholders a "say on pay" (Sloan 2007). Although shareholders at other US publicly held companies such as Verizon, Blockbuster and Merck approved similar measures, corporate management did not. With the US Congress considering proposals to mandate non-binding advisory shareholder say on executive pay, Aflac appears to be ahead of the curve. By letting shareholders have a say on corporate pay structures, Aflac's effort to "duck" confrontation with shareholders succeeded. A social-research analyst for an asset management firm commented about Aflac's transparency initiatives: "They were very open – it was very refreshing" (Sloan 2007). In responding to the authenticity and transparency trend, then, the lesson seems to be that efforts to be more open with share-holders, consumers and stakeholders will be received positively.

On the other hand, new media create the temptation for public relations professionals to try to skirt the demand for greater transparency and authenticity. Numerous fake blogs and websites, and the cloaking of online identities, are a focus of public debate (Business Wire 2007). Some public relations professionals are very concerned by the dishonest corporate blog trend. Tonya Garcia of *PR Week*, for example, argues that practices such as corporations creating websites that appear to be totally consumer-generated are dishonest. She agrees that consumers are looking for more transparency from companies:

> Does it really need to be said that obscuring the truth from consumers is wrong? Apparently, it does. Being vague about what entity is behind a movement is as bad as an overt lie. I'm certain these organizations will one day get caught pulling one of these scams. The conse-quences will be far worse than if they had been truthful from the beginning.
>
> (Garcia 2007)

The profession is, however, working on ways to embrace the power of blogs and websites with-out crossing an ethical line. The Word of Mouth Marketing Association, for example, has created a code of ethics to address such practices.

The fifth annual PRWeek/Manning Selvage & Lee survey (2007) underscores the need for public relations professionals to respond to the increased attention to ethical, transparent and authentic public relations behavior in new media and elsewhere. Fifty-five percent of respondents were troubled by Wal-Mart's non-disclosure of its authorship of a blog purported to be written by supporters of the company. It hired Edelman public relations to help organize a group called Working Families for Wal-Mart. As part of the Working Families group, Edelman then paid a woman to travel across America in a recreational vehicle and keep a blog about her visits to Wal-Mart employees who positively described their work with the company. When *Business Week* reported that the trip had been financed by Wal-Mart and implemented by Edelman, criticism about the companies swirled (Goldberg 2007).

Protecting organizational reputation

Companies must guard against the temptation to be less than honest in the online sphere, but they must also be wary of becoming victims of Web-based corporate sabotage. Coca-Cola, for example, is dealing with the problems of Internet smear campaigns on an international scale. Coke's Argentinian subsidiary filed a criminal complaint against a unit of French food and drink maker DANONE and public relations firm Euro RSCG, accusing the two of circulating a two-year Internet smear campaign against Coke's Dasani water brand (Weber 2007). The suit charges that firms made false statements against Dasani, calling the product into question, misleading consumers and hurting the reputation and sales of Dasani and parent Coca-Cola in Argentina and other Latin American countries (Weber 2007). The rumors called the brand "bottled tap water" and "cancer water" on the Internet, causing stores in Argentina and elsewhere to refuse to sell the product. Although Coke says Dasani water is "from a municipal source" that is "subjected to multi-barrier filtration", activists staged a tap-water challenge to passersby outside Coke's annual meeting in 2006, trying to demonstrate that Dasani tastes no better than tap water but is more expensive (Weber 2007). Clearly, these types of smear campaign create difficulties for companies, as word can now spread from person to person and from country to country with the click of a mouse. Indeed, university students in North Carolina in the United States circulated rumors of Dasani's poor quality following the Internet-based smear campaign.

New media and global connectedness, then, forces companies to counteract negative perceptions on a global scale. If not handled carefully and proactively, these negative perceptions can escalate into broader, more problematic charges against companies and organizations. The developing world's anger at multinational drug companies, for example, has now boiled over into criminal charges against some companies. News coverage of these charges, of course, can affect the companies' reputation around the globe. Pharmaceutical giant Pfizer is faced with criminal charges in Nigeria, where officials charged that the company played a role in the death of children who received an unapproved drug during a meningitis epidemic (Stephens 2007). The charges against Pfizer include counts of criminal conspiracy and voluntarily causing grievous harm during a 1996 clinical drug trial. These charges represent more public relations problems for Pfizer as a result of the clinical trial. Although Pfizer maintains it did nothing wrong in the clinical trial and emphasized that children with meningitis have a high fatality rate, they now must manage their reputation in the court of public opinion as well as in a court of law. The suspicions many around the world feel toward the drug companies make such management exceedingly difficult. Within the context of global access to news about the Nigerian criminal charges, movies such as *The Constant Gardener* about pharmaceutical companies' ethically questionable practices in developing countries, and consumers' rising anger at the cost of prescription drugs, Pfizer faces an increasingly difficult international public relations challenge.

Trends within the profession and the need for public relations leadership

We have explored a number of trends likely to influence international public relations in the coming years. What is left to explore is how the profession is working to respond to these trends and meet the myriad challenges they present. Within the profession, there are a number of areas that are of particular interest in light of the societal and media trends discussed previously. This section will explore the profession's efforts to increase the diversity of practitioners, demonstrate the value of public relations to management, and improve public relations education and professional standards.

Diversity in the profession

With an increasingly multicultural society, public relations needs to reflect better the diverse society it represents (Cody and Vaughn 2007). One main concern in this area involves addressing the field's gender imbalance issues. According to a 2006 Commission of Public Relations Education report, females now constitute two-thirds of all practitioners. Although this number is a source of pride for women previously facing discrimination in a male-dominated workplace, the high number of women in the profession is also a source of concern. Public relations professionals need to represent the varied needs and interests of their clients, and ensuring a diversified workforce helps them reach this goal. One way to get more men interested in public relations starts in university (Guiniven 2007). Historically, the Women In Communication association has made great strides in recruiting young women to the profession, but adding a men's group of this sort might help reverse the feminine trend (Guiniven 2007). Indeed, if an occupation is labeled a women's profession, salaries tend to drop. Recruiting more men to the profession would address this issue while maintaining the gains women have made in the public relations workplace. Addressing the gender imbalance is only one way to increase the types of people who practice public relations. The profession would benefit from adding persons of a variety of races, ethnicities and cultural backgrounds to its ranks. Public relations should also call upon professionals of non-traditional background (nurses, lawyers, journalists, academics and others) to add to the expertise of the public relations team (Cody and Vaughn 2007).

Demonstrating the value of public relations to management

Meeting the challenge of increasing diversity may also help the profession continue to demonstrate its value to corporate management. The final report of the 2007 Study of the Priorities for Public Relations Research indicated that demonstrating the value of public relations to management is an ongoing concern. Professionals continue to work on making public relations a fundamental management function through contributing to strategic decision-making, strategy development and realization, and organizational functioning. The study also noted the need to demonstrate the value public relations creates for organizations through building social capital, managing key relationships, and realizing organizational advantage. Overall, public relations needs to continue to work on the perception that it is a separate part of the organization that serves only a technical function. The belief that public relations is an "add on" organizational function responsible for distributing news releases and announcing promotions persists. Rectifying this misperception is difficult, but James Lukaszewski (2007) suggests that one way to gain a seat at the management table is to develop a management mindset in which communications "is but one component". The more public relations professionals can speak the language of the management team, the more they will be able to demonstrate their value in credible ways.

Addressing this challenge is increasingly important because some observers warn that public relations is becoming increasingly considered a commodity (Cody and Vaughn 2007). Corporations looking to hire public relations firms often use procurement officers within the company. These procurement officers are trained often to look for public relations services that can be "ordered in volume and chopped in price". Cody and Vaughn argue that too many public relations firms have played along with these practices. They argue that public relations firms need to enlighten these procurement officers, in addition to the broader corporate management team, to the valuable role public relations plays. Norman Mineta, vice-chairman of Hill & Knowlton, suggests that public relations professionals engage procurement officers early in the agency selection process to remedy the commodity perception danger (Lucaszewski 2007).

Another answer to the management perception dilemma may lie in further evaluating and quantifying the unique benefits of public relations. One study researched Australian practitioners' evaluation practices and attitudes (Xavier *et al.* 2005). Data suggest that, despite the attention paid to evaluation by the academy and industry, practitioners still focus on measuring outputs, not outcomes, to demonstrate performance. This means that public relations professionals still count the number of news releases distributed in a given month, for example, rather than determining how many media placements and media relationships resulted from disseminating these news releases. Practitioners also continue to rely too heavily on media-based evaluation methods. Measuring the impact of media relations needs to move beyond clip services and counting the number of placements, instead measuring what publics *did* in light of the coverage. Still, practitioners seem to recognize the importance of evaluation and measurement in helping to demonstrate the importance of public relations management. The final report of the 2007 Study of the Priorities for Public Relations Research showed an interest in improving the measurement and evaluation of public relations both offline and online.

Another way to demonstrate the value of public relations to management lies in increasing professionalism and improving educational standards. This trend is expected to continue. The final report of the 2007 Study of the Priorities for Public Relations Research showed that professionals sought more research into standards of performance among public relations practitioners and wanted to explore further the possible need for licensing. Although this trend is positive, one area that continually surfaces as a negative trend listed by seasoned professionals is the lack of adequate skills and training among entry-level workers. Guiniven (2007), for example, notes that "practically everyone agrees that the writing skills of younger people, including college graduates, are generally poor" (p. 6). Indeed, Cody and Vaughn (2007) argue that across the board horrific writing on the part of junior public relations executives is one of the "dirty little secrets" of public relations (p. 1). In addition to addressing writing skills, executives advise new practitioners to broaden their skills set beyond the communication realm. Norman Mineta suggests that practitioners develop expertise in an industry or economic sector before joining public relations agencies or departments (Lucaszewski 2007).

Other public relations executives recommend broadening young practitioners' knowledge in other ways. They argue that today's students do not know enough about the world around them, except for entertainment, celebrities and general pop culture. Thomas Harris, APR, gives an example: "My son hired a young woman who had a master's degree, very bright. He happened to mention the name Karl Rove, and she said, 'Who's that?' " A colleague, Richard Weiner, APR, agreed, saying: "The majority of young people know Paris Hilton but not Karl Rove; they know Lindsay Lohan but have never heard of the Vietnam War. I found it shocking when I was speaking with a young person one time, and she said, 'What's the Vietnam War?' And this was a university graduate" (in Elsasser 2006, p. 1). These examples provide a compelling reason for the need to know more about the world than just the latest in celebrity gossip. To earn the respect of future colleagues, it is imperative that students develop an interest in understanding today's international news, politics and concerns.

Executives from a variety of countries also provide advice for new international public relations practitioners (Epley 2003). They suggest young public relations people travel as much as possible, learn to look behind the cultures they are doing business with, be willing to learn and read widely, and never assume that they have the same values and culture as the people with whom they are communicating. They also suggest recognizing that each country has its own way of doing business and relating to other people. Similarly, students need to realize that developing a global attitude is imperative, meaning that they should understand their own cultural values and assumptions about other cultures (George 2003). Finally, students should develop competence in language, business protocol, social relationships, and respect for other cultures (Epley 2003). They should be guided to understand the non-verbal cues and the cultural context in which communication unfolds. A US American not knowing that the US "OK" sign, with thumb and forefinger making an "O", means "You're a zero" in other cultures makes for an uncomfortable public relations encounter with a potential client.

In summary, public relations professionals have the opportunity to demonstrate leadership in light of the trends discussed throughout this chapter. Instead of fearing the loss of control the digital revolution may bring, public relations executives can harness the power of the myriad channels to craft better, more relevant messages (Cody and Vaughn 2007). Public relations professionals have the chance to lead change in educational standards to meet the demands of a more sophisticated, multicultural, information-seeking society. To correct the poor training many students receive in writing and grammar basics, for example, Cody and Vaughn (2007) argue that public relations could reach out to middle schools and design programs to improve basic spelling, grammar and writing. Public relations professionals also have the opportunity to improve the societal misperception about the industry. To counteract and correct this pejorative characterization, professionals must do a better job in educating society about the occupation. As has often been said, public relations must do more public relations for the profession. Cody and Vaughn (2007) point out that this type of "re" education may be necessary to recruit the best and brightest to work in public relations. Public relations also has another leadership opportunity in training professionals to speak out on the US and other countries' unfortunate global image, the role of public relations in a digital world, the need for licensing, and the risk of commoditization. Public relations professionals may have a lot of work to do in meeting the demands of various trends facing the profession and in demonstrating leadership, but it is an exciting time to work in the field. Today's trends become tomorrow's standards. New generations of practitioners might look back at this textbook, as we did in reading about 1967's trends at the beginning of the chapter, and smile to see how far the profession has come.

Questions for discussion

1. How have new technologies increased global participation in public communication? Provide examples, if possible.
2. What are the advantages and disadvantages of digital public relations?
3. Have you found new media to enhance or hinder the image of public relations? Explain.
4. Imagine yourself as a global public relations practitioner. What would you do to meet the challenges presented by the societal and media trends discussed in this chapter?

Featured biography: Iryna Bugayova

Iryna Bugayova is a graduate student at the University of North Carolina at Charlotte studying international public relations in the Department of Communication Studies. Iryna is from a small rural town in Eastern Ukraine where she grew up and received comprehensive education through her bachelor's degree in Modern Greek and English. She was raised in a Russian-Greek family and, thanks to her family heritage, she became interested in different languages and cultures, especially Modern Greek and English. Iryna remembers that her ambition was always to pursue higher education, and she worked hard to achieve this goal. As a result, Iryna's excellent grades in school, combined with her academic and research achievements, helped her gain entrance to the State University of Humanities in Mariupo, Ukraine, with a full scholarship to study Modern Greek and English language and literature.

Iryna says her decision to pursue a graduate degree in international public relations evolved from her life experiences. Initially, while studying at her home university, Iryna's interests revolved around a career in education focusing on teaching foreign languages. Over time, her professional goals broadened as she took an interest in courses such as political science, philosophy and cultural studies.

Another development in Iryna's educational experience influenced her interest in graduate education in international public relations: she became a finalist in the competitive Freedom Support Act Undergraduate (FSAU) Program. After many rounds of evaluation, Iryna was chosen to come to the US courtesy of the United States government to study at Lees-McRae College in North Carolina for one academic year. She points out that "winning this opportunity was a crucial moment in my life that has continued to influence me". It was her first cross-cultural international experience and allowed her to discover new insights into US people, culture, traditions and educational systems. Iryna says she was influenced also by new and interesting people who helped her explore who she was and wanted to be. Iryna says that before coming to the US she held a lot of stereotypes about the country and its people, partly created by Hollywood images. "During my stay," she observes, "I learned a lot and listened to local people, and it helped me understand who US Americans are and what they stand for in the world."

Upon returning to Ukraine from her first US visit, Iryna took advantage of her opportunity to study abroad to share her experience with others in an effort to enhance their knowledge of and appreciation for US culture. These experiences influenced her decision to pursue work as an Interpreter/Program Assistant for Civic Programs at the National Democratic Institute (NDI) for International Affairs in Kiev. Iryna says "for a person who came from a small farming town, this has been a big step". She notes that her job helped her develop her knowledge of current international issues, improved her written and spoken English, and built her wealth of experience to a level ready for graduate study. Working at NDI in the capital of Ukraine, Iryna had the opportunity to become more knowledgeable about Ukrainian public relations and its development and challenges. Iryna says her active participation in developing democracy in her native country has given her "new insights into the process of nation building and democratic development and the role of public relations in these processes". Iryna has been observing this process for years, but "the recent political events around the Orange Revolution and parliamentary elections led me and many other Ukrainians to begin to realize our power and the ability to change Ukraine for the better".

Iryna stresses that to understand the state of Ukrainian public relations it is important to look at recent political events. Public relations has played an extremely important role in the last presidential and recent parliamentary elections; in fact, the field has experienced fast development during this period and has gained much attention, both positive and negative. On the one hand, more public relations agencies emerged, and the existing ones advanced their service quality and improved their professional and ethical standards. Further, there is more interest from local and international companies to work with Ukrainian public relations firms. There are also positive changes in public relations education in Ukraine. The number of educational establishments, academic programs and professional seminars that offer training in public relations has increased over the last four or five years. On the other hand, there are still many issues, such as ethical standards, so-called "black PR", and the credibility of the media and their financial dependence on political and business groups, that challenge the work of public relations professionals and development of the field.

Recommended websites

For Immediate Release – The Hobson & Holtz Report Http://www.forimmediaterelease.biz

Foreword Thinking – The Business and Motivational Book Review Podcast Http://www.forewordthinking.com

Inside PR – Exploring the World of Public Relations   Http://www.insidepr.ca

On the Record Online   http://ontherecordpodcast.com/pr/otro/default.aspx

Twistimage Blog   http://www.twistimage.com/blog

References

Amis, R., 2007. All abroad? The videocasting juggernaut continues. *Public Relations Tactics*, 14 (6), p. 15.

Ayala, N., 2007. Sports toss more than soft pitches for Latinos, [online]. Available at: http://adweek.com/aw/magazine/article_display.jsp?vnu_content_id=1003596731 [accessed July 19, 2007].

Beeth, G., 1997. Multicultural managers wanted. *Management Review*, 86 (5), pp. 17–21.

Blended media strategies and audience development tactics, 2007. *WestGlen Communications* [Guide Book].

Botan, C. and Taylor, M., 2005. The role of trust in channels of strategic communication for building civil society. *Journal of Communication*, 55 (4), pp. 685–702.

Brand Week, 2007. News analysis: branded content seeks a second act, [online]. Available at: http://www.brandweek.com/bw/magazine/current/article_display.jsp?vnu_content_id=1003590828 [accessed June 5, 2007].

Burg, E., 2007. USA networks starts off "starter wife" with interactive lifestyle campaign. *Media Post Publications*, [online]. Available at: http://publications.mediapost.com/index.cfm?fuseaction=Articles.showArticleHomePage& [accessed May 29, 2007].

Bush, M., 2007. AT&T reacts swiftly to iPhone complaints. *PR Week*, July 16. Available online: http://www.prweekus.com/ATT-reacts-swiftly-to-iPhone-complaints/article/57349/.

Business Wire, 2007. 17 percent of senior marketers say their organizations have bought advertising in return for a news story, [online]. Available at: http://www.home.businesswire.com/portal/site/google/index.jsp?ndmViewId=news_view&news [accessed August 9, 2007].

Cobb, C., 2007a. Coming of age: the growth and influence of Hispanic media outlets today. *Public Relations Tactics*, 14 (6), p. 19.

Cobb, C., 2007b. The Taco Bell E. Coli outbreak: calming public fears during food-borne illness scares. *Public Relations Tactics*, 14 (2), pp. 11–12.

Cody, S. and Vaughn, R., 2007. Seven trends for 2007: what's around the bend? *Public Relations Strategist*, [online], winter, Available at: http://www.prsa.org (Public Relations Society of America) [accessed February 25, 2008].

Commission on Public Relations Education, 2006. The professional bond – public relations education and the practice, [online]. Available at: http://www.commpred.org/report/2006_Report_of_the_Commission_on_Public_Relations_Education.pdf [accessed July 10, 2007].

Cook, F., 2007. It's a small world after all: multiculturalism, authenticity, connectedness among trends to watch in next 50 years. *Public Relations Strategist*, [online], Winter. Available at: http://www.prsa.org (Public Relations Society of America) [accessed February 25, 2008].

De Lafuente, D., 2007. ABC fas-fax reports gains for Hispanic titles in first-half '07. MarketingyMedios.com, [internet]. Accessed through LexisNexis database [February 22, 2008].

Dougall, E., 2005. Taking organization–public relationships over time: a framework for longitudinal research. 8th International Public Relations Research Conference, March 10–13, Gainesville, Fla: The Institute for Public Relations Research and Education.

DummySpit, 2007. Final report of the study of the priorities for public relations research, [online]. (Updated July 30, 2007.) Available at: http://dummyspit.files.wordpress.com/2007/07/delphi-study-final-report.pdf [accessed August 5, 2007].

Elsasser, J., 2006. You need more than the facts these days to get people's attention: two renowned PR pros discuss commercialization, technology and globalization. *Public Relations Tactics*, 13 (12), pp. 24–5.

Epley, J., 2003. *Perspectives from 17 Countries on International Public Relations*. WORLDCOM Public Relations Group.

Garcia, T., 2007. The cycle. *PR Week*, [online]. Available at: http://thecycle.prweekblogs.com/2007/05/15/ethics-101/ [accessed May 29, 2007].

George, A. M., 2003. Teaching culture: the challenges and opportunities of international public relations. *Business Communication Quarterly*, 66 (2), pp. 97–113.

Goldberg, J., 2007. Selling Wal-Mart. *The New Yorker*, [internet]. April 2. Available at: http://www.newyorker.com/reporting/2007/04/02/070402fa_fact_goldberg/ [accessed April 4, 2007].

Goldman, A. and Reckard, E., 2007. Tactics differ for 2 firms in crises. *LA Times*. Retrieved October 13, 2007, from http://articles.latimes.com/2007/aug/18/business/fi-pr18.

Guiniven, J., 2007. A woman's profession? Addressing the gender imbalance. *Public Relations Tactics*, 14 (3), p. 6.

Hiebert, R., 2005. Commentary: new technologies, public relations, and democracy. *Public Relations Review*, 31 (2005), pp. 1–9.

Hood, J., 2007. Public relations 3.0? What the . . . , [online]. Available at: http:thecycle.prweekblogs.com/2007/04/25/public-relations-30-what-the/ [accessed May 29, 2007].

Ihator, A., 2000. Understanding the cultural patterns of the world – an imperative in implementing strategic international PR programs. *Public Relations Quarterly*, 45 (4), pp. 38–44.

Johnson, A., 2007. Social media blurs the lines in modern marketing. *The Arizona Republic*, July 17. Available online: http://www.azcentral.com/arizonarepublic/business/articles/0717bizaz-techmarketing0717.html

Kabel, M., 2007. Ad agency: Wal-Mart lacking respect, [online]. Available at: http://www.ap.org/ [accessed May 5, 2007].

Kruckeberg, D. and Tsetsura, K., 2003. International index of bribery for news coverage, US Institute for Public Relations Report, [online]. Available at: http://www.instituteforpr.com/international.phtml?article_id=bribery_index [accessed March 30, 2005].

Krueger, M., 2007. Tap women's social networks with email. *Media Post Publications*, [online]. Available at: http://publications.mediapost.com/index.cfm?fuseaction=Articles.showArticleHomePage& [accessed May 29, 2007].

Looker, A., Rockland, D. and Taylor, K., 2007. Media myths and realities: a study of 2006 media usage in America. *Public Relation Tactics*, 14 (6), p. 10.

Lukaszewski, J. E., APR, 2007. What's next? The relationship of public relations to management, journalism and society. *Public Relations Strategist*, winter, pp. 21–3.

McCauley, K., 2007. "Crushing" image problem threatens environmental PR. The Lexis Nexis Academic Database, [online]. Available at: https://connect2.uncc.edu/niverse/,DanaInfo=web.lexis-nexis.com+printdoc [accessed July 30, 2007].

McCleneghan, S., 2005. PR practitioners and "issues" in the early millennium. *Public Relations Quarterly*, 50 (2), pp. 17–22.

Macleod, S., 2005. *PR in Europe*. Gainesville, Fla: The Institute for Public Relations Research and Education.

May, B., 2004a. An American in Europe: why corporate responsibility is a must-have for US corporations operating in Europe, [online]. Weber Shandwick. Available at: http://www.webershndwick.co.uk/outcomes/issue9/article2.html [accessed July 24, 2007].

May, B., 2004b. Much more than a gimmick: why CSR matters, [online]. Weber Shandwick. Available at: http://www.webershandwick.co.uk/outcomes/issue5/story3_print.html [accessed July 24, 2007].

Mineta, N., 2007. Yes-people need not apply. *The Strategist*, winter, pp. 8–9.

Moreau, R., 2007. Grapes of their own; India's middle class embraces wine. *Newsweek, International edn*, [internet], April 30 [accessed through LexisNexis database February 22, 2008].

Newman, E., 2007. Research: study: product recalls scare some away, forever. *Brandweek*, [internet]. Available at: http://www.brandweek.com/bw/magazine/current/article_display.jsp?vnu_content_id=1003596642 [accessed July 19, 2007].

O'Loughlin, S., 2007. . . . But image woes continue. *Brandweek*, [internet], April 2. Available at: http://www.brandweek.com/bw/magazine/current/article_display.jsp?vnu_content_id=1003565838 [accessed April 4, 2007].

Page, R., 2007. General session summary: Andrew Heyward on the power of the remote and the rise of new media. *Public Relations Tactics*, 14 (1), pp. 18–27.

Poulin, E., 1997. Quoted in *Public Relations Reporter*, 40 (41), pp. 1–2.

PR Newswire, 2007. Word of mouth the #1 influence on business buying decisions, [online]. Available at: http://prnewswire.com/cgi-bin/stories.pl?ACCT=ind_focus.story&STORY=/ [accessed May 29, 2007].

Reveron, D., 2007. Bicultural can-do. *Marketing y Medios*, [internet]. Available at: http://www.marketingymedios.com/marketingymedios/magazine/article_display.jsp?vnu_content_id=1003596621 [accessed July 19, 2007].

Russell, P., 2007. General session summary: Andrew Heyward on the power of the remote and the rise of new media. *Public Relations Tactics*, 14 (1), pp. 18–27.

Sengupta, S., 2007a. India develops a nose for wine. *International Herald Tribune Online*, August 10. Available at: http://www.iht.com/articles/2007/08/10/news/india.php

Sengupta, S., 2007b. India finds a nose for wine; moneyed classes sipping as never before. *The International Herald Tribune*, August 11, pp. 5–6.

Sloan, A., 2007. Aflac looks smart on pay. *The Washington Post*, [online]. May 29, p. D-01. Available at: http://www.washingtonpost.com/wp-dyn/content/article/2007/05/28/AR2007052801055_pf [accessed June 5, 2007].

Smith, E., 2007. Companies struggle with unauthorized sites. IndyStar.com, [internet], June 28. Available at: http://indystar.gns.gannett.com/ [accessed February 22, 2008].

Solloway, S., 2007. A growing influential audience: Spanish-language broadcast outreach that works. *Public Relations Tactics*, 14 (6), p. 18.

State of the PR Profession Opinion Survey, 2006, 2007. Public Relations Society of America/Bacon's.

Stateman, A., 2007. The 2006 state of the profession opinion survey: exploring perceptions, issues, trends and challenges. *Public Relations Tactics*, 14 (3), p. 24.

Stephens, J., 2007. Pfizer faces criminal charges in Nigeria. *The Washington Post*, [online]. May 30. Available at: http://www.washingtonpost.com/wp-dyn/content/article/2007/05/29/AR2007052902107_pf [accessed June 5, 2007].

Stewart, J., 2007. Do-it-yourself video that makes the grade – and the newscast: the continuing trend of I-witness news. *Public Relations Tactics*, 14 (6), p. 17.

Stokes, A., 2005. Discrediting Teresa: wounded by whispers on the Web. In A. P. Williams and J. C. Tedesco, eds, *The Internet Election: Perspectives on the Web in Campaign 2004*. Boulder, Colo.: Rowman & Littlefield.

Tsetsura, K., 2005. *Bribery for News Coverage: Research in Poland*. Gainesville, Fla: The Institute for Public Relations Research and Education.

US Department of State and PR Coalition, 2007. *Private Sector Summit on Public Diplomacy*, Washington, DC, January 9–10. PR Coalition: Washington, DC.

Vaughn, R. and Cody, S., 2007. Seize the day: dynamics that will raise the profile of public relations in 2007. *Public Relations Tactics*, 14 (1), p. 10.

Weber, H. R., 2007. Coca-Cola: competitors smeared Dasani. *Houston Chronicle*, [online]. Available at: http://www.chron.com/disp/story.mpl/ap/fn/4964027.html [accessed July 19, 2007].

WestGlen, n.d. *Blended Media Strategies and Audience Development Tactics: How to Bring Your Message Directly to the Audiences You Need to Reach and Ensure the Success of Your Broadcast PR Campaign*. New York: WestGlen Communications.

When viral marketing attacks: taking a whack at Wal-Mart, 2005. *Brandweek*, [internet], October 24. Available at: http://web.lexis-nexis.com [accessed November 3, 2006].

Xavier, R. *et al.*, 2005. Using evaluation techniques and performance claims to demonstrate public relations impact: An Australian perspective. *Public Relations Review*, 31 (3), pp. 417–24.

Yehuda, B., 2007. Harnessing the power of emerging media: broadband connectivity is reshaping the world of broadcast marketing. *Public Relations Tactics*, 14 (6), p. 16.

Zaharna, R. S., 2001. "In-awareness" approach to international public relations. *Public Relations Review*, 27, pp. 135–48.

Zur Hausen, C., 2007. Live Earth – "the last thing the planet needs is a rock concert". *Newsletter for Corporate Communications and Public Relations*, [online]. Available at: http://www.communication-director.com/_files/newsletter/13.pdf [accessed July 20, 2007].

Index